Advances in Database Research

Advances in Database Research

Proceedings of the 4th Australian Database Conference

Brisbane 1–2 February 1993

Editors

M E Orlowska
Department of Computer Science
The University of Queensland
Australia

M Papazoglou
School of Information Systems
Queensland University of Technology
Australia

World Scientific
Singapore • New Jersey • London • Hong Kong

Published by

World Scientific Publishing Co Pte Ltd
5 Toh Tuck Link, Singapore 596224
USA office: 27 Warren Street, Suite 401-402, Hackensack, NJ 07601
UK office: 57 Shelton Street, Covent Garden, London WC2H 9HE

British Library Cataloguing-in-Publication Data
A catalogue record for this book is available from the British Library.

ADVANCES IN DATABASE RESEARCH
Proceedings of the 4th Australian Database Conference

ISBN-13 978-981-02-1331-2
ISBN-10 981-02-1331-X

Preface

The 4th Australian Database Conference (ADC'93) continues to provide a popular forum for the presentation and discussion of ideas on research, development and novel applications of database systems. The Australian Database Conference is this year organised jointly by the University of Queensland, Queensland University of Technology and Griffith University, and is sponsored by the Australian Computer Society, the CRC for Distributed Systems Technology, Simsion Bowles & Associates and Oracle (Australia) Pty Ltd.

Like its predecessors, the aim of ADC'93 is to bring together researchers, developers and users of database systems, especially from the Pacific region, to exchange ideas and knowledge and in general explore recent and future developments in this exciting field.

Topics covered at the conference include: database design, parallel and distributed databases, storage structures, integrity constraints, deductive databases and theoretical aspects of databases. This year we received 46 papers from 15 countries including among others, US, Canada, Japan, Singapore, India, France, Germany, Holland and Austria. The selection of the papers for presentation was admittedly a formidable task, as many quality papers had to be rejected due to the limited number of time slots available for presentation. Consequently only 25 papers have been selected for presentation and inclusion in the proceedings. The review of the papers was handled by the program committee members and each paper was reviewed by three reviewers solicited by the two Program Chairs. Additional reviews were carried out on papers which received conflicting reviews.

On behalf of the Program Committee, we would like to express our sincere gratitude to the authors, session chairpersons, and last but not least to the reviewers who provided us with timely and helpful evaluations. We are also deeply indebted to Prof. Rodney Topor, the Organising Committee Chair, who has helped us enormously throughout the difficult process of putting this conference together. Our gratitude also goes to the program committee members who have carried out the painstaking process of carefully evaluating the submitted papers. Finally, our sincere thanks go to Kathleen Williamson for her untiring help in handling the submitted papers and the referee reports.

Brisbane
February 1993

M. Orlowska & M. Papazoglou
Program Committee Co-Chairs
ADC'93

ADC'93

Fourth Australian Database Conference

Brisbane, Australia 1-2 February 1993

Program Committee Co-Chairs:

Maria E Orlowska, The University of Queensland
Michael Papazoglou, Queensland University of Technology

Organizing Committee Chair:

Rodney Topor, Griffith University

Program Committee:

Peter Bernus, Griffith University (Australia)
Tok Wang Ling, National University of Singapore (Singapore)
Timos Sellis, University of Athens (Greece)
Robert Colomb, University of Queensland (Australia)
Frederick Lochovsky, Hong Kong University of Science & Technology (Hong Kong)
John Smith, CSIRO Division of Information Technology (Australia)
Philip Dart, University of Melbourne (Australia)
Grace Loo, Victoria University (New Zealand)
Bala Srinivasan, Monash University (Australia)
Alan Fekete, The University of Sydney (Australia)
Katsumi Tanaka, Kobe University (Japan)
Vincent Lum, Chinese University of Hong Kong (Hong Kong)
Gopal Gupta, James Cook University (Australia)
Anthony Montgomery, Royal Melbourne Institute of Technology (Australia)
Yahiko Kambayashi, Kyoto University (Japan)
Ron Sacks-Davis, Royal Melbourne Institute of Technology & University of Melbourne (Australia)
John Zeleznikow, La Trobe University (Australia)
Günter Schlageter, Fern University (Germany)
Chi-Ping Tsang, University of Western Australia (Australia)
Ramamohanarao Kotagiri, University of Melbourne (Australia)

Table of Contents

Theoretical Issues

Application Development

Recent Advances in Transaction Management

Alan Fekete
Department of Computer Science,
University of Sydney, 2006, Australia

1 Introduction

Any database provides a variety of operations that users can perform on the stored information. For example, an SQL system provides queries that can update one relation, or retrieve information from several relations. Similarly, an objectbase may provide the ability to invoke one method of one object specified by OID. For many applications, this repertoire of provided operations is insufficient, and therefore almost all systems allow users to embed database operations in a more powerful programming language. Using the control structures of the programming language, one can write an application that updates several relations, or perhaps invokes a method only if some other method returns a particular result.

An execution of an application thus involves the performance of a sequence of operations each provided by the database. It is well-known that unexpected results can be produced if several applications act concurrently, with their constituent operations interleaved. For example, two applications could each add 10 to a field (by reading that field and later writing the increased value) but the final result might have the field only 10 higher than originally. This is called a "lost update". Also an audit application that determines the sum of a collection of values might return the wrong total when a concurrent application was adding to one value and subtraction an equal amount from another. Other problems can be caused by crashes that corrupt volatile storage, if updates are applied first to cached copies, and only propagated later to the stable database on disk.

The concept of a transaction has been widely accepted as a way to avoid these problems. In essence, making an application a transaction gives users the appearance of having an enriched repertoire of basic operations, since the application will *seem* to be a single operation, in that it will apparently execute as an instantaneous whole. No errors due to concurrent activity or badly timed crashes will be noticed, either by users or in the final state of the stored data.

Of course, the convenience for users of a transactional application does not come for free: the system must use locks, logs and other mechanisms to ensure this appearance. The main techniques were invented almost two decades ago, and then a substantial body of theory has arisen to verify their correctness. While many research papers have been written about transaction management, most systems have been based on three fundamental ideas: two-phase locking, write-ahead logging, and two-phase commit. This understanding is summarized in two essential books: the fundamental ideas are given by Bernstein, Hadzilacos and Goodman [3], and many crucial implementation details by Gray and Reuter [11].

Recently, there have been several exciting advances in the field, that promise to have an impact on practical implementations. These include important new algorithms, especially several proposed by a group of researchers led by Mohan at IBM Almaden Research Center. Also there have been some significant proposals for enriching the basic transaction model to provide the functionality needed in "advanced application domains" such as CAD and CASE. This paper provides an introduction to some of these ideas, with pointers to the literature where the details can be found.

2 Interfaces

Because of the complexity of transaction management, one usually considers the system as a combination of aspects, each of which is described separately. These aspects may actually be implemented by separate processes (even on different machines), or they may involve different procedures within one process. Many research papers describe solutions to a single aspect as if it ran in isolation. In order for one to use these papers in system-building, more attention must be paid to the interface between these aspects.

Understanding the interface between two parts of a system includes both syntactic and semantic aspects. We need to know what interactions (such as a message transfer, or a procedure call) allow information to pass between them, and we also need to know the circumstances under which an interaction may take place. We would like to abstract as much as possible, stating minimal conditions on one part that will allow the other to work correctly. By doing so we allow maximum flexibility to the system designer, who may replace one part by any other component that meets the same conditions, without fear that correctness of the whole system will suffer. For example, a distributed commit protocol using presumed abort two-phase commit might be replaced by one using non-blocking three-phase commit.

Let us give a few examples of the importance of precision in describing interfaces between components. Much recent work in multibase transaction management implicitly assumes an interface in which the global manager acts as an application in its interaction with each local database; that is, it submits a sequence of operation requests, and finally submits a request to commit. In contrast, other work assumes that the global manager acts as a user: it requests that the local database run a local subtransaction, and eventually receives the committed result. This latter style (called *inseparable*) makes many algorithms (which depend on delaying the local commit) unavailable to the global manager.

As another example, a distributed commit protocol interacts with resource managers by requesting a *vote* on whether to commit a transaction. Some resource manager algorithms have been proposed that release read-locks at the time of the vote (rather than waiting till learning of the commit decision), but such algorithms only give correct transaction management if the request for a vote is not issued till after the transaction has finished executing. Thus while early-release resource managers work with a normal commit protocol, and normal resource managers work with an eager-prepare commit protocol, we can't use both optimizations: early-release managers with an eager-prepare protocol gives incorrect behavior.

Another interface issue in commit protocols concerns the determination of the resource managers that participate. A major textbook ([5]) indicates that votes must be obtained from the sites where data was updated. Some commercial systems use this idea, and thus do not involve read-only sites in the first phase of the commit protocol. In particular, they do not run two-phase commit at all for read-only transactions. It is easy to construct executions where integrity constraints are violated for such a system, due to the loss of read-locks during a site failure. For correctness, the commit protocol must collect votes from all sites where any operation of the transaction happened.

To provide clarity of description, and a sound basis for reasoning, one needs to describe various concurrency control and recovery algorithms and interfaces in a formal model. Similar problems have long been faced in the design of communication networks, and a number of models have been proposed. These include ones based on finite-state machines [15], infinite-state machines [18, 12], temporal logic [19, 6], or process algebra [14, 4]. My own work has been done with I/O automata [18], but I feel that what is important is not the widespread use of any particular model, but rather the recognition of the value of forcing system builders and algorithm designers to state explicitly the assumptions each component makes about its environment.

3 Modular Atomicity

One important change in attitude to transaction management has come from the interest in heterogeneous multibases, extendible systems, and object-based systems. In each of these types of system, it is not true that all of the system is implemented in the same way. Instead, the data is partitioned, with different people being responsible for implementing each partition. In a multibase, the partition is between the separate local databases; in an object-based or extendible system each class or ADT may have its own code to manage it. Thus one needs to consider how different implementations of transaction management can coexist in a single system. This problem was addressed and solved in the 1984 thesis of Weihl at M.I.T.; the following discussion is a brief summary of the main ideas, whose details are in [28].

The starting point for any analysis of modular transaction management must be the data type of the information in one part of the database. This is called a *serial specification*, since it describes how the operations are understood by the user who wishes to see results as if in a serial system. The simplest data type is a *register*, with operations to read and write (this is assumed in much theoretical work). More realistic for a relational database is a *bag* type with operations to insert an entry, delete all entries satisfying some condition, and return all satisfying a condition. It has long been known that one cannot treat a bag as if it were a collection of registers, with an insertion locking the new entry and a query locking those entries it returns; when this is done the *phantom problem* occurs, and a query can return a collection of entries that include some but not all of those inserted by a concurrent transaction [9]. Subtle variations in specification can have significant effects on the concurrency control: a *set* is similar to a bag, but one may not insert a duplicate of an entry already present (this is essentially provided in many relational systems by declaring an attribute to be a primary key).

The key insight in Weihl's approach is that each independently implemented part of the database will respond to queries as if the transactions occurred in a particular *serialization order*. Correctness requires that there be a single order on transactions with which *every* part's serialization is consistent. In systems using two-phase locking, this order is given by the time of commit. In a complex system it is likely that two-phase locking will be used for most parts; only those *hot spots* where contention is great will require special high-concurrency algorithms. The results of [28] show that the system implementor can merely check that each part's implementation is *dynamic atomic*, that is, uses the commit time to determine the serialization order.

Concurrency control algorithms for the set and bag types are especially important in practice. Mohan and his colleagues have recently invented a high-concurrency algorithm called ARIES/IM that provides dynamic atomicity, using a B-tree index, usually present anyway for efficient retrieval [20]. This work is especially valuable because most earlier papers on concurrent search structures have discussed providing the appearance of atomicity for each individual operation such as an insertion, rather than for whole transactions. The ARIES/IM algorithm is based on a clear distinction between latches that are held on a part of the index for a short time (at most for the duration of an operation) and locks that are held on data records until transaction commit.

The discussion above assumes that each part of the database receives operations on its data, and is eventually informed of each transaction's fate (whether it committed or aborted). By giving a more complicated interface, more concurrency can be allowed. For example, the interface described above usually leaves each part of the database in ignorance about the serialization order between concurrent transactions, so responses must be consistent with all possible orders. Instead, each transaction might be assigned a value (called a timestamp) indicating its position in the serialization order. This allows the parts to check that their responses are consistent with exactly the serialization order being used. In some systems the timestamp is assigned when the transaction is created, so the serialization order is not the commit order. In other systems, the commit order is used[1], so the timestamp must be assigned only when the transaction finishes. Still other systems use commit time as serialization for general transactions, but allow read-only transactions to get their timestamp at creation, and then return values that are not current (this requires the system to keep multiple versions of the data, but reduces lock contention). Papers exploring these ideas include [26, 24, 22]

Another possibility for this interface is one where each part of the database can delay or reject the commit event for a transaction[2]. In this case, commit order is still used for serialization, but the order is not determined unilaterally by the transaction manager. This allows queries and updates to proceed without being delayed waiting for locks, and it is often felt that delaying a transaction only once, at the end, is more efficient than delaying repeatedly during execution. There has been a lot of interest, especially for object-oriented databases, in optimistic methods, where new versions are kept as local copies, and not stored in the database until commit, with the commit being rejected if the data has already been modified at that time [25, 13]. The *constrained-sharing locks* of [1] are similar, but involve delaying rather than refusing to commit.

4 Recovery

Traditional write-ahead logging keeps a field (the Log Sequence Number) in each page of the database, and records in this the location of the last log record recording a change to that page. This LSN is also used during restart processing to eliminate unnecessary undo and redo steps. It is well-known that this places a requirement on the concurrency control mechanism, which must ensure that at no time is any page affected by two active transactions (that is, the execution

[1] This means that two-phase locking may be used as the default technique in the system.

[2] The interchange of information involved does not cause delay if the system is distributed, as it can occur piggybacked on the messages needed for two-phase commit.

must be *strict* on pages). Unfortunately, this rules out many high-concurrency locking mechanisms, including the use of record-level locks. Another interaction between concurrency control and recovery occurs when operation logging (also called logical logging) is used in recovery; in this case lock modes must be chosen so operations are not allowed concurrently if they ***or their logical inverses*** interfere with each other.

Recently, Mohan and his colleagues have introduced a new paradigm for recovery. Called ARIES [21], this algorithm involves redoing missing operations of all transactions *including* those that aborted or were active at the time of the crash, and then undoing those that were performed by transactions that did not commit. Unlike other methods, ARIES works correctly even when concurrency control uses fine-granularity locks or other semantic locks. The paper on ARIES contains a wealth of details about implementing recovery, and in my opinion it has had more impact on transaction management than any other in the past five years. ARIES is also unusual among recovery algorithms because significant aspects have been formally proved correct [16].

Another interesting aspect of the interface between recovery and concurrency control has been shown by Weihl in [27]. If semantic locking is being used, the precise compatibility relationship between lock modes must alter, depending on whether or not the value read in an operation shows the effects of concurrent transactions' operations.

5 Advanced Transaction Models

The traditional transaction model has proved ideal for commercial applications. however, new application domains are revealing the need for more flexible concepts. Many suggestions have been made, though none has achieved general acceptance. In part, this must be due to a lack of semantic content: many models are defined only by locking rules (that is, by an implementation), without any matching description of what the user sees or what integrity is guaranteed. Thus there is an important research direction waiting here.

One of the earliest alternative models was nested transactions [23]. This is close to the traditional model, in that users expect transactions to seem to run instantaneously or not at all. It is richer since each application may be written in a concurrent rather than sequential language, and to facilitate this, concurrent activity without interference, and recovery from failure are available within each application. Nested transactions have been used as the model provided in two important research prototype systems: Argus [17] and Camelot [8]. The theory of concurrency control for nested transaction systems has been given by myself and others, using extensions of the ideas summarized above [10].

For applications like CAD, there is a need for a transaction model in which concurrent applications can cooperate, rather than being completely shielded from one another. One of the simplest ideas is Sagas, in which each application is divided into stages. Each application runs to completion or is completely undone, but interleaving is allowed so long as each stage appears indivisible. One implementation difficulty is that each stage needs a user-provided inverse.

A large number of transaction models are discussed in the excellent survey by Barghouti and Kaiser [2], and in the book edited by Elmagarmid [7].

References

[1] D. Agrawal and A. El Abbadi. Locks with constrained sharing. In *Proceedings of ACM Symposium on Principles of Database Systems*, pages 85–93, Nashville Tennesee, April 1990.

[2] N. Barghouti and G. Kaiser. Concurrency control in advanced database applications. *ACM Computing Surveys*, 23(3):269–318, September 1991.

[3] P. Bernstein, V. Hadzilacos, and N. Goodman. *Concurrency Control and Recovery in Database Systems.* Addison-Wesley, 1987.

[4] T. Bolognesi and E. Brinksma. Introduction to the iso specification language lotos. *Computer Networks and ISDN Systems*, 14:25–59, 1987.

[5] S. Ceri and G. Pelagatti. *Distributed Databases: Principles and Systems.* McGraw-Hill, 1984.

[6] K.M. Chandy and J. Misra. *Parallel Program Design: A Foundation.* Addison-Wesley, 1988.

[7] A. Elmagarmid. *Database Transaction Models.* Morgan Kaufmann, 1991.

[8] J. Eppinger, L. Mummert, and A. Spector. *Camelot and Avalon: A Distributed Transaction Facility.* Morgan Kaufmann, 1991.

[9] K.P. Eswaran, J.N. Gray, R.A. Lorie, and I.L. Traiger. The notions of consistency and predicate locks in a database system. *Communications of the ACM*, 19(11):624–633, November 1976.

[10] A. Fekete, N. Lynch, M. Merritt, and W. Weihl. Commutativity-based locking for nested transactions. *Journal of Computer and System Sciences*, 41(1):65–156, 1990.

[11] J. Gray and A. Reuter. *Transaction Processing: Techniques and Concepts.* Morgan Kaufmann, 1992.

[12] I. Hayes. *Specification Case Studies.* Prentice Hall International, 1987.

[13] M. Herlihy. Apologizing versus asking permission: Optimistic concurrency control for abstract data types. *ACM Transactions on Database Systems*, 15(1):96–124, March 1990.

[14] C.A.R. Hoare. *Communicating Sequential Processes.* Prentice Hall International, 1985.

[15] G. Holzmann. *Design and Validation of Computer Protocols.* Prentice Hall Software Series, 1991.

[16] D. Kuo. Model and verification of a data manager based on aries. In *Proceedings of the 4th International Conference on Database Theory*, pages 231–245, Berlin, Germany, October 1992.

[17] B. Liskov. Distributed computing in Argus. *Communications of ACM*, 31(3):300–312, March 1988.

[18] N. Lynch and M. Tuttle. An introduction to input/output automata. *CWI-Quarterly*, 2(3):219–246, 1989. Also in Technical Memo MIT/LCS/TM-373, Laboratory for Computer Science Massachusettes Institute of Technology, November 1988.

[19] Z. Manna and A. Pnueli. *The Temporal Logic of Reactive Systems.* Springer Verlag, 1991.

[20] C. Mohan and Levine F. Aries/im: An efficient and high-concurrency index management method using write-ahead logging. In *Proceedings of ACM Conference on Management of Data*, pages 371–380, June 1992.

[21] C. Mohan, D. Haderle, B. Lindsay, H. Pirahesh, and P. Schwarz. Aries: A transaction recovery method supporting fine-grained locking and partial rollbacks using write-ahead logging. *Transactions on Database Systems*, 17(1):94–162, 1992.

[22] C. Mohan, H. Pirahesh, and R. Lorie. Efficient and flexible methods for transient versioning of records to avoid locking by read-only transactions. In *Proceedings of ACM Conference on Management of Data*, pages 124–133, June 1992.

[23] J. E. B. Moss. *Nested Transactions: An Approach to Reliable Distributed Computing*. PhD thesis, Massachusetts Institute Technology, 1981. Technical Report MIT/LCS/TR-260, Laboratory for Computer Science, Massachusetts Institute Technology. Also, published by MIT Press, March 1985.

[24] C. Pu. Superdatabases for composition of heterogenous databases. In *Proceedings of IEEE Conference on Data Engineering*, pages 548–555, 1988.

[25] A. Thomasian and E. Rahm. A new distributed optimistic concurrency control algorithm and a comparison of its performance with two-phase locking. In *Proceedings of IEEE Conference on Distributed Computing Systems*, pages 294–301, June 1990.

[26] W. E. Weihl. Distributed version management for read-only actions. *IEEE Transactions on Software Engineering*, SE-13(1):55–64, January 1987.

[27] W. E. Weihl. The impact of recovery on concurrency control. In *Proceedings of the 8th ACM Symposium on Principles of Database Systems*, March 1989.

[28] W. E. Weihl. Local atomicity properties: modular concurrency control for abstract data types. *ACM Transactions on Programming Languages and Systems*, 11(2):249–282, April 1989.

Implementation of Very Generalised Data Structures

Graeme Simsion
Simsion Bowles & Associates
15 Collins Street Melbourne Vic 3000 Australia

The selection of the most appropriate level of generalisation for tables and columns is a critical decision in relational database design. It involves a tradeoff between semantic content (and associated enforcement of constraints) and flexibility. Very high levels of generalisation have been employed in some commercial database designs, with mixed success. In some cases, they have formed the basis of very flexible systems, which can provide a competitive advantage through better responsiveness to business and regulatory change. In others they have been the source of insurmountable implementation problems. This paper discusses the advantages and disadvantages of very generalised data structures, and highlights some practical implementation issues.

Indexing in an Extensible Database System

LUKAS RELLY
Department of Computer Science,
Swiss Federal Institute of Technology,
8092 Zürich, Switzerland.
relly@inf.ethz.ch
and
ALAN KENT
Department of Computer Science,
RMIT, GPO Box 2476V, Melbourne 3001, Australia.
ajk@citri.edu.au

ABSTRACT

Extensible database management systems are more flexible at supporting advanced applications as they allow parts of the database system to be tailored to the application. In this paper the indexing and data storage subsystem of an extensible database system being constructed within the Hypermedia Group at CITRI[†] is presented. Our approach has been to define a generic index interface for all types of indexes enabling indexes to be easily interchanged. Defining a generic interface also allows composite indexes to be constructed which build upon the work of other indexes.

1 Introduction

Database systems have greatly simplified the implementation of applications requiring storage of large volumes of data. This is because they provide stable, reliable storage of data; efficient ways of retrieving and manipulating subsets of data from large collections; reliable concurrent access to data; and access security. Relational database systems have proved popular as they store data in a form that is simple to understand. Many data processing applications have large volumes of similarly structured data suitable for relational systems, but as the needs of applications become more complex, relational style systems are less able to satisfactorily support applications.

Several data models have been proposed to overcome the restrictions of the relational model. These include object oriented data models and complex object (including nested relational) models[13]. Extensible database systems[1,2,6,13] attempt to overcome restrictions by allowing the application builder to alter some parts of the database system in order to more directly support the application. This extensibility is also useful from a research perspective—alternative strategies can be easily put in place in order to examine changes in performance.

[†]The Collaborative Information Technology Research Institute, jointly owned by RMIT and The University of Melbourne.

One project within the Hypermedia group at CITRI is to develop an extensible database system. The aim of this project is to incrementally develop a series of flexible subsystems, eventually integrating them into a complete extensible database system. Developing independent subsystems should increase the flexibility of the overall system. For example, a previous database system developed within the group, Atlas[9], was originally based solely on the use of signature file indexes. Simplifications in the design were made based on this knowledge. This made it difficult to later add new indexing schemes to the system. Obviously it is not possible to design all subsystems in complete isolation. Encouraging the isolation and minimizing interdependence however is a worthwhile goal.

In this paper, current work on the design of the indexing and data storage subsystem is presented. In Section 2 assumptions about the architecture of the database system the indexing code will reside in are described. A generic definition of an index is introduced in Section 3. Sections 4 and 5 demonstrate how different indexing schemes map to the generic interface. Section 6 describes how query processing can be performed when integrating the results of a number of independent indexes. The work presented in this paper is not complete. Many interesting issues have been raised which have not yet been satisfactorily resolved. Section 7 discusses a number of such problems and presents some tentative solutions. Finally, conclusions are given in Section 8.

2 Database System Architecture

In this section the environment in which the index and data file manager reside is described (see Figure 1) as well as terminology used in this paper.

A *record* is a package of data that the database system will ask the index and data file manager to store and retrieve. Collections of records are stored in *tables*. Tables can contain duplicate records. Associated with a record is a set of *index terms* which can be extracted from the record. Only single table access is considered—indexes spanning multiple tables (such as join indexes) are beyond the scope of this paper, although the methods presented here appear to also be applicable to multi-table indexes. An index term consists of an *index attribute* identification and a value.

Associated with index attributes are rules which define how to extract values from records. The simplest rule is to return the value of a record attribute. Other more complex rules can however be used. For example, a series of index terms can be formed from a single text field in a relational system (one index term per word). This is one reason why there can be multiple index terms associated with one attribute of one record. Index terms can also be formed from the concatenation of multiple record attributes, for example, when there is a composite key. Another example of index terms not being exactly the same as a record attribute value is where some function is applied to an attribute value before indexing. For example, the record attribute value may be converted to lower case allowing the index to support case insenstive searches. Rather than adding additional complexity to the indexing subsystem, rules for extracting index terms from records must be defined outside the

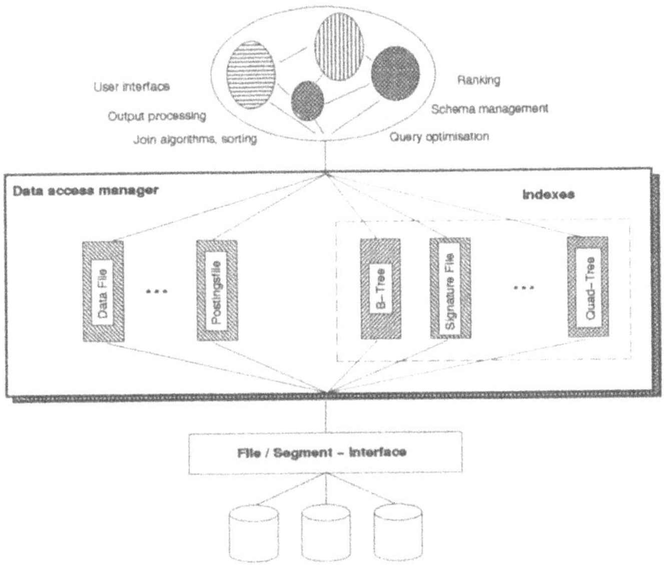

Figure 1: System Architecture

indexing subsystem.

A *query* specifies from which table records are to be retrieved and a set of query conditions connected by boolean operators that should hold on the index terms associated with the records. Query conditions must specify on which attribute the condition must hold. Note that user queries submitted to the database system may need to be converted into a simpler form before being passed to the indexing subsystem. Multiple index terms can be associated with an index attribute of a record in which case a query condition will hold for a record if any one of the index terms will satisfy the condition.

These definitions are sufficient to support the relation model, the nested relation model, and most complex object models. They may even be sufficient for object oriented data models, although there are special issues relating to efficient indexing of class hierarchies.

In many database systems, storage of records and indexes are considered to be independent. Indexes point to records in the data file. In this paper, record storage and indexing are considered together, as in some cases it is desirable to store records directly in an index file rather than maintaining a separate data file. An example scenario is where records are stored in a hash file using a numeric primary key with secondary indexes on other record attributes. Secondary indexes can point to the data record using the value of the primary key.

As can be seen in Figure 1, persistent data storage is accessed through an interface which is external to the indexing subsystem. Behind this interface could be a normal file system, a memory based disc (acting as a large write-through cache to disc), or a network interface to a remote data store. In a full database system with transaction support, a buffer manager would reside behind the interface. In order to simplify this paper, transaction management is not considered. This is not because transaction management is not important, but rather because it is does not change the approach described in this paper. If, for example, the ARIES[7] transaction manager was implemented then the implementation of the individual indexes would have to change (to perform such tasks as generating the write-ahead log), but the way in which the indexes interact would not change.

3 A Generic Index Interface

The philosophy used during the design of the indexing subsystem is that an index should try to reduce the set of records that will be returned as the result of a query, but may return additional non-matching records. It is left to the query evaluator in the database system to discard non-matching records. Thus an index can be considered to be a filter. In the worst case, where none of the available indexes are able to support a query specification, all records in a table will be returned. This definition allows a data file to be considered as an index—data files are indexes which never support query specifications. For this reason and others that will be described later, a data file will be considered to be a special type of index in the rest of this paper.

One of the aims of our indexing subsystem is to permit any combination of indexing modules to be put together to build a composite index on a table. Our approach is to define a generic interface to which all index implementations conform, and then to define general algorithms to support query evaluation for any interconnection of indexes. Defining a generic interface is also as desirable as it:

- Simplifies the replacement of one index with another index more suitable for a specific application,
- Simplifies integration of new indexing modules into the database system, and
- Allows the performance of different indexes to be compared within the same environment as they can be easily interchanged within the same database system.

The concept of composite indexes, indexes which are built using other indexes, is greatly simplified with the definition of a generic index interface. There are two catagories of composite indexes: those which act as wrappers around a fixed number of other indexes to provide additional power over the original indexes, and more general indexes which allow arbitrary numbers of indexes to be connected to form an index across multiple attributes. Composite indexes are described in more detail in Section 5.

Defining an interface suitable for all indexing schemes will only be acceptable if implementing an indexing technique using the generalized interface is not significantly more complicated than implementing the indexing technique in a dedicated database system, and if the performance of the indexing technique using the general index is not significantly worse than using the optimal interface. Each index has different properties which impose restrictions on what can be stored in the index and what queries can be supported. In defining a generic interface, the aim is not to support the complete functionality of all possible indexes. However, it is not acceptable to use the minimal common interface. Instead some middle ground must be found which is suitable for supporting most applications. This does not mean that specific features of one indexing technique cannot be benefited from. It means that if the additional features are used, it may no longer be possible to substitute a different index in its place. Parts of the database system outside the indexing subsystem will also need to be modified to access the feature.

We now present our proposed generic index definition. This definition is more powerful than can be supported by some indexes, and so indexes must define which properties they support. There is however a minimal set of properties which all indexes must support, including the ability to insert and delete entries and the ability to query the index. One example of an optional property is whether an index is a multi-valued index, such as a signature file[4,11], or a single valued index, such as a B-tree[3]. Due to these restrictions, some combinations of indexes are not legal. This is not a serious problem as such errors can be detected at index creation time.

In general, an index associates a set of index terms with an *entry*. Entries can be database pointers, record numbers, or file offsets. While all indexes must be able to store entries, the representations of entries supported by different indexes may be different. For example, some indexes can only support fixed length entries, others variable length with an upper bound of say a page size, while others still allow any entry than can fit in memory. Given a query condition, an index can be requested to return an *entry match set*, a set of entries for which the associated index terms match the query condition. The match set returned by a query is permitted to contain entries which do not match the query. This is permitted as the index may be able to only partially support the query condition. For example, the query may be a conjunction of query conditions and the index may only be able to support one of the query conditions. As the entries often do not contain the index terms associated with the entry at insertion, the index cannot perform any further filtering. An index can also return a special match set indicating that it was unable to support any of the query conditions.

Some indexes take advantage of additional invariant internal information about where entries are stored to improve query speed. Signature files for example associate entries with record numbers. If a set of record numbers can be provided by a higher level index at query time, this can improve query evaluation significantly by reducing the search space. Such indexes are normally referred to as multi-level indexes. To support this possibility, indexes can return a *locator* on insertion. In signature files, the record number would be the locator as no matter what other operations are

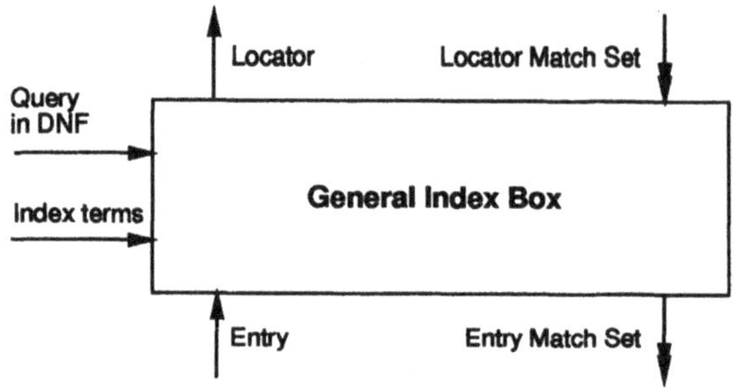

Figure 2: General Index interface

performed on the index, the record number associated with an entry on insertion will not change. Locators are an optional property as some indexes have no internal stable information they could return to improve queries. This is particularly true of dynamic indexes which move the contents of the index around as operations are performed on the index. Indexes may also accept a *locator match set* on query. This set provided at query time enables the index to reduce its query search space. For example, in a signature file index, if a set of record numbers was supplied, only the descriptors of the identified record numbers would need to be examined. It should also be noted that locators are not required to be unique. Two insertions into an index can return the same locator which implies that a locator may identify more than one entry. An example of this situation is where the locator generated by an index is the head page of an overflow chain in a hashing scheme. The entry may be moved within the overflow chain, but will never be moved to a different chain as its hash value will never change.

Figure 2 shows the inputs and outputs of indexes discussed so far. These inputs and outputs are necessary to building composite indexes from other indexes.

So far insertion and querying have been mentioned. There are two other common operators that are performed on an index: deletion and update. For the purposes of this paper, update is not supported. Instead, a deletion then insertion must take place. Update can be considered as an optimization to the procedure of delete then insert, and so should not introduce any significant problems. In a real system, supporting updates is very imporant and can bear a major influence on the way indexes are used together. For example, if there are many indexes pointing directly to a record in a data file, moving the record (due to a record update) will require all of the indexes to be updated even if no index terms were changed. A better approach may be to introduce a level of indirection so that only one pointer to the record is stored. In this case, the index manager should be intellegent enough to realise that the other indexes do not need to be updated. Deletion is very similar to insertion. In order to delete an entry from an index, the entry and the index terms associated with the entry must be supplied. The exact set of index terms supplied during insertion must be supplied again during deletion to ensure index integrity. Frequently deletion occurs as the result of a query. If an index was used to support the query, then much of the work to perform a deletion would have already taken place. This would indicate that it may be worthwhile having a special interface for deleting the last retrieved entry. It was decided not to do this however due to problems when evaluating complex conjunctions and disjunctions of query conditions. Rather, it is left to an index implementation to examine its own caches to determine if any optimizations can be made.

4 Basic Indexes

In this section we show how several indexes, such as B-trees, primary key hashing, and signature files, can be made to conform to the generic interface defined. This list is by no means comprehensive, but demonstrates that the interface is capable of at least supporting a reasonable range of indexing techniques.

B-tree. B-trees[3] can only associate a single index term with an entry, unless copies of the entry are made. On insertion, a B-tree would store the entry in the index using the index term to find the position in the B-tree to insert the entry. The only value that could be returned as a locator for a B-tree is the index term itself as index terms in the tree can move during tree balancing operations. B-trees are capable of several forms of query including range queries and exact match queries. Range queries result in a set of entries being returned while exact match queries result in a single value being returned.

Primary key hashing. In a typical primary key hashing scheme, the key of a record is hashed to form a bucket address in which the record is placed. A simple overflow scheme is used to handle situations when the space required to hold all the records which hash to a bucket exceeds the capacity of the bucket. Such an index can be made to supported fixed length or variable length records but can only index on a single attribute value. While normally used for primary key retrieval, the scheme does not actually require the key to be unique. The locator generated by a hash index might be the indexed value itself or the hashed form of the value which would be a smaller, fixed length value.

Signature Files. A superimposed signature file index[4,11] is built from descriptors that describe the contents of records or blocks of records. The descriptor is constructed by superimposing (OR-ing) term descriptors formed by hashing individual index terms. A common way of forming a term descriptor is to hash the term producing a bit pattern with exactly k out of b bits set, where k and b are parameters of the index. Querying involves hashing the query terms and searching through the descriptors for descriptors with all of the query bits set. Due to the way descriptors are formed, false matches can occur and so the records need to be retrieved and checked to ensure a correct match. Various techniques exist that make searching for matching descriptors fast. Signature files are different from most other indexes as they allow multiple values to be indexed on in one descriptor. Thus querying on conjunctive sets of query conditions can be supported efficiently.

There are two different ways in which descriptors can be stored on disc. The first approach where complete descriptors are stored one after another in an index file is called the *bit string* method. Queries are performed by sequentially reading all of the descriptors from the file, checking each one to see if it matches. Using this approach, a fixed length entry can be easily stored along with each descriptor. This information would typically be a pointer to a data file. The other approach for storing indexes is called *bit slicing*. In this approach the index file is clustered by bit number in the descriptors. That is, bit zero of all descriptors is stored first, followed by bit one and so on. Each grouping for a bit position is called a bit slice as with a single seek and read it is possible to get the value of a bit position for all descriptors stored in the index file. This 'slice' is a bit vector identifying which records have this particular bit set. When searching for a matching descriptor only certain bits need to be checked and so the bit slice approach is more efficient than the bit string approach for large files. The bit slice approach however can only identify matching records using a record number (the offset in the bit vector retrieved from disc). A separate pointer file must be used to map record numbers to offsets in a data file. The locator generated by an insertion to either type of index would be a record number which identifies the position of the descriptor in the index file.

Spatial Indexes. Spatial indexes, for example R-trees[5], grid files[8], and Quad trees[12], are typically used to support queries on regions or points. Query conditions are specified using geometric operations such as 'intersects with' or 'contained by' rather than more tradition query operators such as equality. Often, spatial indexes try to reduce the costs of expensive geometric operations by approximating complex geometric objects by simpler ones. The data space is divided into subspaces and the expensive operations are only performed on objects in the same subspace. Some of the methods are useful for clustering spatial data in the index allowing fast access to objects that are close to each other.

Data files. The current scheme also allows a data file to be considered as an index, although it can never use a query condition to generate a match set. What a data file can do however is insert an entry generating a locator, and on query when given a locator match set it can return the entries identified. While this stretches the definition of what people normally think of as an index, it is a useful extension as it allows a data file manager to be connected to other indexes in the same way as a multi-level index would be constructed. In this mode of operation, the data file is more a mapping function rather than an index.

5 Composite Indexes

One reason for having a common interface to all indexes is to be able to build more complex indexes out of simpler ones. This also allows one index to be replaced by

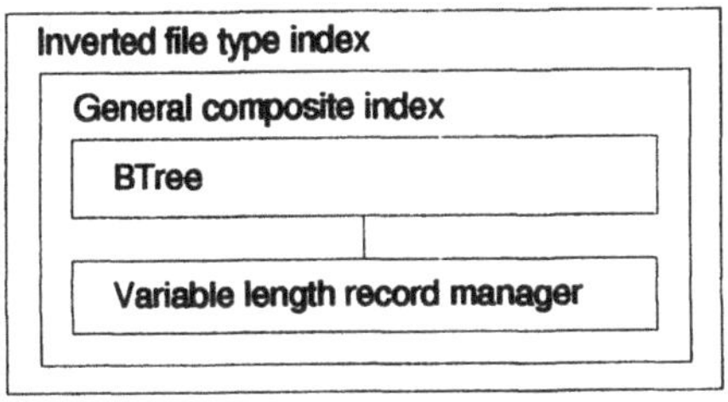

Figure 3: Inverted file index

another index with the same capabilities allowing the most appropriate index for an application to be used. For example, different strategies may be used for managing an overflow file depending on the average length of an overflow chain. Linear hashing schemes normally use a linked list of overflow pages. Recursive linear hashing[10] however uses further linear hashing files to manage the overflow chains, obtaining much better storage overheads.

5.1 *Fixed Structure Composite Indexes*

As a first example, we build an *inverted file* index assuming we have a vocabulary index which is capable of storing variable length entries with no restriction on length. The vocabulary index implements a one-to-one mapping between index terms and entries as distinct from an inverted file index which associates many entries with a single index term. It is the responsibility of the inverted file index to maintain the pointer lists, supplying the lists as entries to be stored by the vocabulary index. A typical vocabulary index would itself be a composite index of a primary key indexing technique (such as a B-tree) and a variable length record manager. The B-tree would hold a pointer into the variable length data file. Figure 3 shows how the indexes would be connected to build this form of index index.

The generic definition of an index requires that the index be able associate more than one index term with a single entry. Many indexes do not support this property. They must instead associate a copy of the entry with each of the index terms provided. Rather than require all indexes to support duplicate entries within the index, an iterator box can be defined. An iterator box on insertion (or deletion) iterates over the set of index terms and inserts (or deletes) one index term at a time. On query the iterator box is also responsible for correctly merging match sets and eliminating duplicate values. Iterator boxes do not generate locators or accept locator match sets as there is no single locator value that will match all of the index terms associated with the entry. Note that storing user records using an iterator box would be in general undesirable as multiple copies of the record would be stored in the index. Update consistency would actually not be a problem with user records as the iterator box would make the update appear like an atomic operation.

5.2 General Composite Index

The composite boxes mentioned so far are shells around a fixed number of other indexes. You simply 'plug' an index into the 'socket' inside the composite index. As long as the plug and socket are compatible (that is, the properties required by the socket are supported by the plug) everything will work correctly. A more powerful composite box is one that allows multiple indexes to be joined together in non-predefined ways.

Consider a general composite box which allows a set of indexes to be built into a tree, where the root of the tree is at the bottom level of the tree, and any index in the tree can have zero or more indexes above it. The following shows how the inputs and outputs of the composite box connect to inputs and outputs of component indexes, and how the indexes are internally interconnected to build up the index tree.

Firstly, the query and index terms of all operations are made available to all indexes within the tree. It is up to each index to determine which of the terms (using the attribute identification component of the index terms) it must use. Indexes are told which attribute(s) they are to index on when the indexes are created. On insertion, the entry supplied to the composite box will be inserted into the root index of the tree. The locator output of the composite box will be the locator generated by one of the leaf indexes of the index tree, or else not supported. Deletion of an entry follows the same process as insertion. On query, the entry match set returned by the composite box will be the entry match set returned by the root index. Any locator match sets supplied to the composite box are passed to the same leaf index that generated the locator.

Within the tree, indexes are connected so that the lower index's locator output is supplied as the entry for insertion into higher index(es). This implies that non-leaf nodes in the index tree must support locators. Insertion into the composite box therefore starts at the root of the tree, and progresses up the tree as locators are generated. Queries result in the opposite order of processing. The entry match sets generated by higher indexes are supplied to lower indexes as locator match sets, eventually resulting in the root index returning a single match set. The problem of merging entry match sets generated by multiple higher indexes is addressed later.

With general composite indexes, the whole indexing subsystem can become a single index. Operations sent to the indexing subsystem would simply be passed directly to the composite index. The composite index would normally be built from a data file manager as the root index node, with indexes one level above it. An extra level would only exist in the tree if a multi-level index was used. For example, the indexing scheme supported by Atlas is shown in Figure 4. In this figure, the bit string file holds data file offsets and the bit slice and linear hashing indexes both store record numbers which the bit string file can convert to data file pointers.

6 Query Processing

As mentioned previously, given a query specification, an index must identify at least all entries associated with index terms which satisfy the query. A single table may be indexed using multiple indexes. These indexes may be on different attributes or be

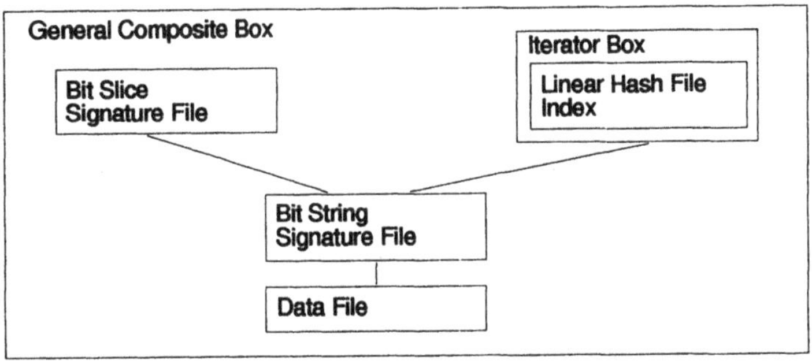

Figure 4: Equivalent composite box to indexing supported by Atlas

used to support different types of queries on the same attribute. Locator match sets also introduce an additional level of complexity to query evaluation. In this section the structure of query specifications will be described in detail, and a processing strategy for general composite indexes that we believe will give the best overall performance.

A query specification is built from a set of query conditions connected by boolean operators. In order to standardize the format of queries, query specifications must be supplied in disjunctive normal form (DNF). For example, $(a \vee b) \wedge c$ must be converted to $(a \wedge c) \vee (b \wedge c)$. All boolean NOT operations will be pushed down into the query conditions. For example, $\neg(a = 3)$ would be converted into $a \neq 3$. Thus queries will always consist of a set of conditions connected by OR operators above AND operators. DNF was selected as the standard form as it groups conjunctions of conditions rather than disjunctions. This helps reduce the size of match sets. If conjunctive normal form was used, larger intermediate match sets would be formed.

As mentioned previously, query conditions are composed of an attribute identification, an operator, and a constant (the constant can be a structured value). The set of operators is not predefined, but rather new operators can be introduced by new indexes. For example, a spatial index may introduce a containment operator where the constant specifies a region. From a high level query processing perspective, the operator is not important. It is however important to be able to determine whether an index will be able to support a query condition or not.

Given a complex query, a specific index may be able to support parts of the query, but not all parts. For example, consider the DNF query $(q_1 \wedge q_2) \vee (q_3)$ where q_1, q_2, and q_3 are query conditions. If only q_3 can be supported by an index, then there is no point in using the index as all records will have to be retrieved anyway in order to find other records that match $(q_1 \wedge q_2)$. If q_1 and q_3, but not q_2, were supported by indexes, it is worthwhile using the availble indexes to evaluate the query. In this case, if q_1 and q_3 were supported by different indexes then the match sets from the two indexes must be union-merged. If both q_1 and q_2 were indexed, then the match sets for these two conditions must be first intersect-merged before the union-merge takes place. As can be seen, there are many different possible senarios. A general query processing algorithm must be able to efficiently support all situations.

First let us consider the case of a single query condition, q_i. Given a composite index formed from a tree of connected indexes, the query term can be supplied to all index nodes in the tree. If an index can support the term, it should do so. If an index is a non-leaf node, then it may recieve a locator match set from a higher index. Locators in this match set must be mapped to entries held in the index even if the index cannot support the query condition q_i. If it can support the condition, then the index should further reduce the size of the entry match set generated by removing entries which do not satisfy the condition. Note that if more than one higher level index generates a match set, then the intersection of the two match sets must take place. It is intended that this intersection take place within the lower index where the match sets from higher indexes converge. The reason for this is that it has greater potential for optmization. The lower index knows what a locator is as it generated the locators. This makes it possible to use stategies based on the type of locator values. In fact, the intersection may automatically take place during the mapping from locators to entries (depending on the implementation of the index). If the intersection was performed outside the index, a general sort-merge approach would be required.

So far only a single query condition has been considered, although the condition may have been suported by more than one index. The case where the query is a conjunction of conditions, such as $(q_1 \wedge q_2)$ in the previous example, is in fact no more complex. The same intersection of match sets must occur.

A query optimization issue is raised here. If there are two indexes that support a condition, it may be that after using one index, the cost of using the second index is greater than the benefit gained by consulting the second index. There are several possible solutions including maintaining selectivity information of indexes, informing the second index of the size of the match set produced by the first index and thus giving the second index the option of not doing anything, or simply always using all available indexes on the assumption that while unecessary work may be occasionally done, overall performance should not degrade too much.

Considering a full disjunctive query introduces new problems. First, if any operand of a disjunctive query can not be supported by an index, there is no point in using an index for any other part of the query as a full data file scan will be required to check the non-indexed query conditions. When all conjunctive operands are at least partially supported, the first naive approach to evaluating a disjunctive query is to evaluate each conjunctive operand independently and then merge the results removing duplicates. This however can be very inefficient, especially when multi-level indexes are involved. The inefficiency is due to not eliminating duplicates at the earliest possible stage. If an index is presented with two disjunctive locator match sets, eliminating duplicates while processing the query will be more efficient than mapping the duplicate locators to the corresponding entry multiple times. If it is remembered that the data file is also treated as an index, then it is clear that duplicate pointers should be removed before retrieving data from the data file rather than eliminating duplicate records after they have been retrieved.

Eliminating duplicates is actually a greater problem than is apparant from the above discussion. The problem is related to the definition of a duplicate. From outside an index, a duplicate is when one entry is inserted but on query two entries come back. If however the same entry is stored twice in the index, then it should normally be retrieved twice. In fact, not all indexes support this, but it should be at least true of a data file. For example, a bit slice index file generates a match set of record numbers using bit vectors. No matter how many times a number is inserted as an entry, the corresponding bit can only be set once, and so on query the record number will only be returned once. The best approach to removing duplicates seems to be to remove them when an index processes locator match sets from higher level indexes. Any query conditions supported by the current index can be thought of as generating a new locator match set which is then intersected with the locator match sets from the higher indexes. Eliminating locator duplicates means that it is never necessary to eliminate duplicate entries in the output match set if there is a one to one mapping between locators and entries. More care must be taken if two distinct locators can result in the same entry matching.

The next approach therefore seems to be to get indexes to perform merging of all locator match sets as soon as they are available. There is only one problem with this approach. Care must be taken not to merge disjunctive match sets too eary. Consider for example if one branch of an index tree supported q_2 and q_3 from the previous example and another branch supported q_1. The match sets of q_2 and q_3 cannot be merged until after q_1 is intersected with the results of q_2 or else the index would be evaluating the query $(q_1 \wedge q_2) \vee (q_1 \wedge q_3)$. This is only a problem when multi-level indexes are involved.

7 Other Issues

Work on defining a general interface to indexes is by no means complete. There are many unresolved issues yet to be addressed. In this section a number of such issues are raised along with some tentative solutions.

Some indexes support variable length entries, but have an upper bound on the entry size (for example, page size may be a limit). Sometimes indexes are requested to store very large entries. Does this mean all indexes should be made to support records of unbounded length? We believe not. Building a special composite index which uses a separate variable length record manager to store long entries should be sufficient. Normal entries would be placed in the index. Longer entries would store a pointer to the entry in the separate overflow file. This approach to building new indexes can greatly reduce the amount of code to be written to implement a new indexing scheme.

Index creation has not been discussed in much detail in this paper. When an index is created, there are many index specific parameters. It is felt that there is no way to generalize such parameters. Problems also arrise when index parameters are changed or new indexes are added. For example, how can a new index be inserted into an existing general composite box as the result of an CREATE INDEX command from a user? Work to date has assumed that all indexes would be created when the table is created.

So far match sets are not ordered. Some indexes, such as B-trees, allow entries to be retrieved in a certain order. This can be very useful, for example, when joining two tables using a sort merge algorithm. A problem with ordered match sets is how would operations such as intersecting match sets maintain the ordering? If the lists were in sorted based on the entry values, this would not be a problem. However if the entries follow some unseen sorting criteria then performing intersection and union opertions on match sets may not be possible.

Text support has not been satisfactorily been addressed yet. One form of text support is to store word positions in an index to enable word proximity conditions (find two words at most n words apart). One approach is to make the index term hold both the word to index on and its position in the text. Special indexes would be needed however to correctly process queries. Another text related issue is what support is necessary for ranking. One approach would be simply to build indexes capable of performing ranking queries directly, although again the issue of ordering match sets must be resolved for a satisfactory solution.

Lazy evaluation of match sets may also be necessary. This is where matches are retrieved from disc only as they are required. If user records are stored in an index, it is important that the index manager does not attempt to immediately load all matching records into memory as may be the normal policy for pointer list match sets.

There are numerous other issues which are important for efficient processing. For example, efficient batch loading of entries exists for many indexing schemes. However it is not felt that these issues will pose any significant problem to the approaches proposed in this paper.

8 Conclusions

We have now spent some time defining a generic interface definition which can be mapped to existing indexing techniques without significant loss of efficiency with the aim of allowing indexes to be combined in new and interesting ways. While the basic concepts seem relatively straight forward, defining a general scheme which is able to efficiently support a diversity of indexing schemes has not been easy. Many issues have not been discussed in this paper due to space constraints, and many other issues are yet to be fully resolved.

One outstanding question is whether to allow user records to be stored directly in an index. The advantage is speed. Consider a vocabulary file to support ranking which holds words and word frequencies. The only form of query that will ever be made is on a word. Requiring records to be stored in a separate file can easily be twice as slow as storing the records directly in the index, as well as being less space efficient. Allowing records to be stored in indexes however introduces a number of problems, some of which have been mentioned in earlier sections.

In defining the generic interface, we have tried to cater for all of the different indexing schemes we could find in the literature. Paper solutions so far look promising. Our next step is to implement some of the modules in order to discover insuffiencies in the generic interface defined.

1. M. Carey, D. DeWitt, J. Richardson, and E. Shekita. Object and file management in the EXODUS extensible database system. In *Proceedings of the Twelfth International Conference on Very Large Databases*, pages 91–100, Kyoto, Japan, August 1986.
2. M. Carey and L. Haas. Extensible database management systems. *SIGMOD Record*, 19(4), December 1990.
3. D. Comer. The ubiquitous B-tree. *ACM Computing Surveys*, 11(2):121–137, 1979.
4. C. Faloutsos. Access methods for text. *ACM Computing Surveys*, 17(1):49–74, 1985.
5. A. Guttman. R-trees: A dynamic index structure for spatial searching. *Proc. ACM SIGMOD Int. Conf. on the Management of Data*, pages 47–57, 1984.
6. L. Haas, W. Chang, G. Lohman, J. McPherson, P. Wilms, G. Lapis, B. Lindsay, H. Pirahesh, M. Carey, and E. Shekita. Starburst mid-flight: As the dust clears. *IEEE Transactions on Knowledge and Data Engineering*, 2(1):143–160, March 1990.
7. C. Mohan, D. Haderle, B. Lindsay, H. Pirahesh, and P. Schwarz. ARIES: a transaction recovery method supporting fine-granularity locking and partial rollbacks using write-ahead logging. *ACM Transactions on Database Systems*, 17(1):94–162, 1992.
8. J. Nievergelt, H. Hinterberger, and K. Sevcik. The grid file: An adaptive symmetric multikey file structure. *ACM Transactions on Database Systems*, 9(1):38–71, 1984.
9. R. Sacks-Davis, A. Kent, K. Ramamohanarao, J. Thom, and J. Zobel. ATLAS: a nested relational database system for text applications. Technical Report 52, Collaborative Information Technology Research Institute (CITRI), July 1992.
10. R. Sacks-Davis and K. Ramamohanarao. Recursive linear hashing. *ACM Transactions on Database Systems*, 9(3):369–391, September 1984.
11. R. Sacks-Davis, K. Ramamohanarao, and A. Kent. Multi-key access methods based on superimposed coding techniques. *ACM Transactions on Database Systems*, 12(4):655–696, 1987.
12. H. Samet. The quadtree and related hierarchical data structures. *ACM Comp. Surveys*, 16(2):187–260, 1984.
13. H. Schek, H. Paul, M. Scholl, and G. Weikum. The DASDBS project: Objectives, experiences, and future prospects. *IEEE Transactions on Knowledge and Data Engineering*, 2(1):25–43, March 1990.

Storage Management for Files of Dynamic Records

JUSTIN ZOBEL
Department of Computer Science,
RMIT, GPO Box 2476V, Melbourne 3001, Australia.
jz@kbs.citri.edu.au

ALISTAIR MOFFAT
Department of Computer Science
The University of Melbourne, Parkville 3052, Australia.
alistair@cs.mu.oz.au

and

RON SACKS-DAVIS
Collaborative Information Technology Research Institute
723 Swanston St., Carlton 3053, Australia.
rsd@kbs.citri.edu.au

ABSTRACT

We propose a new scheme for managing files of variable-length dynamic records, based on storing the records in large, fixed-length blocks. We demonstrate the effectiveness of this scheme for text indexing, showing that it achieves space utilisation of over 95%. With an appropriate block size and caching strategy, our scheme requires on average around two disk accesses—one read and one write—for insertion of or change to a record.

1 Introduction

Many database applications require that files of variable-length dynamic records be managed. For example, inverted files are frequently used for indexing stored data. For non-key attributes, each distinct indexed value can occur many times, so that the entry for each distinct value—that is, the list of records containing that value—can be of any length, and, moreover, can change in length as records are inserted, deleted, or updated. Space efficient representations of these entries require that each be stored as a unit[1,2,3], hence the necessity that variable-length dynamic records be stored efficiently. This behaviour is also typical of other applications, for example, the disk buckets of a hashed file, and the nodes of a B-tree.

We propose a new method for managing dynamic records on disk, based on storing records in large, fixed-length blocks. This scheme was sketched briefly by us in a previous paper[3]; here we give both details of our proposal and experimental results in support of our performance claims. In our scheme, each block contains several records, a table describing those records, and, in general, some free space. The amount of free space is kept small by relocating records when blocks overflow. Disk access costs are kept low by the observation that, with current technology, it is not much more costly to retrieve a large block than a small block, and by storing the contents of each record contiguously.

We have tested our scheme, using as an example the management of indexes for full-text database systems. We generated inverted files for several test databases and simulated the performance of our scheme on these indexes, measuring space utilisation and the number of disk accesses required as each term was inserted into its inverted file entry. These simulations showed space utilisation of, in most cases, over 95%.

Our results compare well with those quoted for earlier schemes. Knuth's description of memory management schemes, including best fit methods and the buddy system, includes experiments that show space utilisation of less than 80%[4]. Biliris has described a page allocation scheme for large objects that achieves excellent within-page space utilisation, but relies on the buddy system to supply it with appropriate pages[5,6] and thus, if we include the cost of unused pages, does not achieve such good utilisation overall. Nor have other schemes for index management been as effective. The schemes surveyed by McDonell[7] appear to have space utilisation of up to 50%; the exact utilisation is unclear, as items such as pointers between list nodes are regarded as part of the data, whereas we would include these as overhead. The schemes described by Faloutsos and Jagadish do better; they do not give space utilisation for their experiments, but in their graphs the maximum utilisation is about 90%[8].

Our results can be applied to problems such as B-tree indexes. Utilisation in B-trees is usually quoted at 69%, and a recent B-tree scheme 'with good performance' only achieves space utilisation of 82%[9]. We are currently developing B-tree algorithms based on our space management scheme that we believe will have substantially higher utilisation ratios.

In Section 2 we review inverted file indexing. The indexes and test databases we used to test our scheme are described in Section 3. In Section 4 we describe the structures we propose for managing dynamic records on disk; maintenance of these structures is described in Section 5. Results of simulation of our scheme are given in Section 6.

2 Inverted file indexes

A general inverted file index for a text database consists of two main components: a set of *inverted file entries*, being lists of identifiers of the documents containing each indexed term; and a *search structure* for identifying the location of the inverted file entry for each term, containing a *vocabulary* of query terms, and an *index mapping* that maps ordinal term numbers onto disk addresses in the inverted index. This arrangement is illustrated in Figure 1. The index mapping can either be stored on disk as a separate file, or can be held in memory with the vocabulary. We assume that inverted file entries store ordinal document numbers rather than addresses, and so to map the resulting document identifiers to disk addresses there must also be a *document mapping.*

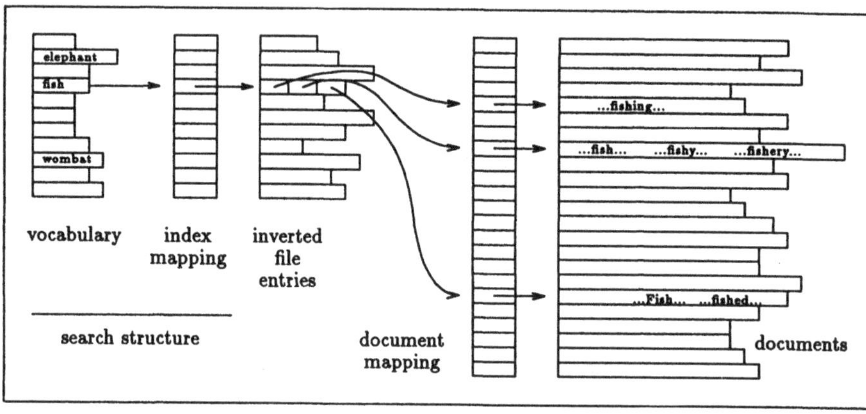

Figure 1: Inverted file index structure

We assume that the contents of each inverted file entry are stored contiguously, in contrast to other schemes, in which entries are often stored as linked lists with each node randomly placed on disk[7,8,10], or with the documents chained together on the basis of common attribute values[11]. Given this structure, queries are processed by using the vocabulary and index mapping to find the location of the inverted file entry for each term in the query; accessing the disk to retrieve the inverted file entries for those terms; performing any logical operations on those entries; and then using the document mapping to access the document file to retrieve the answers. If the search structure is a B-tree, typically one or at most two disk accesses will be required to find the location of the inverted file entry of each term, since the memory of current machines is large enough to hold a substantial portion of the search structure. The number of accesses to retrieve the entry itself is the number of blocks containing the entry, which in our scheme will usually be one; then, depending on whether the document mapping is in memory or on disk, one or two disk accesses will be required for each answer.

To simplify query evaluation, inverted file entries should be maintained in sorted order of document number. On insertion of new terms into existing documents, this will involve shifting large volumes of data in memory to make space for the new identifier, but such shifts are faster than retrieval of the same volume of data from disk. Since shifts of data will generally precede a write to disk, the shift will be dominated by other costs.

	Bible	*Comact*	*Trec*
Text size (Mb)	4.4	132.1	1,198.7
Number of records	31,102	261,829	511,514
Distinct terms	9,073	36,840	407,820
Distinct terms per record (av.)	23	49	165
Longest entry (bytes)	3,888	32,729	63,939
Average entry length (bytes)	60	242	154
Total number of terms	701,533	12,745,527	84,286,478
Compressed index size (Mb)	0.5	8.5	59.9

Table 1: Sizes of test databases

3 Test databases and indexes

We used the inverted files of three text databases to test our method for storing files of dynamically changing variable length records. Each database consists of documents; the indexed values were the words occurring in each document. Thus some indexed values, such as the word 'the', were frequently repeated, about half occurred more than once, and each document contained many values to be indexed. Index entries noted only whether or not a document contained the word being indexed, so that even if a document contained several occurrences of a word the inverted file entry only listed that document's number once. Before the indexes were generated, the words in the documents were stemmed—that is, case was folded and variant endings such as 'ed', 'ing', and 'lessly' were removed[12].

The databases were the complete King James edition of the Bible, or *Bible*, in which each document is a verse; the complete Commonwealth Acts of Australia, 1901 to 1989, or *Comact*, in which each document is a page; and the (first) TREC collection of articles extracted from the TIPSTER database, or *Trec*, in which each document is an article from such sources as the Wall Street Journal or Associated Press, or a legal document such as a United States Federal Regulation. The parameters of these databases are given in Table 1.

Each inverted file entry is a sorted list of ordinal document identifiers. Since the largest identifier is not known in advance, in a fixed-length representation some number of bits must be chosen in advance to store each identifier. Typically 24 or 32 bits would be suitable. As we have shown elsewhere, however, compression techniques can be used to represent these entries much more compactly, typically reducing the space required by a factor of about five while still permitting fast decoding[1,2]. With such compression, each addition of a record will add, for each term in the record, a small number of bits to the inverted file entry of that term. In our simulations we have concentrated on compressed entries; the figures in Table 1 assume that each entry is compressed using a 'local V_G' code[2].

4 Storage of records on disk

There are two difficulties in managing dynamic records on disk. The first is that they vary in length. The second is that each record can change in length over time.

We propose a space management scheme in which records are stored in large, fixed-length blocks[3]. In this scheme, records are numbered contiguously from zero. This number is used as an index into a *record mapping* indicating which disk block contains each record. Records are stored in fixed-length blocks of B bytes, where B is significantly greater than the average record length. (We consider records of more than B bytes later.) Each block contains a *block table* of addresses of records within the block, used to find the location of an record within the block once the block has been retrieved from disk. The record mapping need only store the number of the block containing each record; to retrieve a record, the whole block is fetched. With current disk performance, it only takes about twice as long to fetch a block of 64 Kb than a block of 1 Kb*, and, as we show in the next section, block sizes of around 32 Kb to 64 Kb give good results with our data.

Blocks will in general have some free space, because the records and block table do not occupy exactly B bytes, as illustrated in Figure 2. To minimise shifting of data within each block, the block table is stored at one end of the block and the records at the other, so that both grow towards the middle.

To manage free space we require a *free list*, which will generally be short, of descriptions of blocks (other than the last block of the file) whose free space is in excess of some fixed *tolerance*, typically a few percent. This list should be held in memory; if it becomes large, indicating that the file is becoming disorganised, data should be moved amongst blocks to get better space utilisation. However, the free list itself will not occupy much space: a linked list representation will require at most 12 bytes per block, to hold the number of the block, the number of free bits in the block, and a pointer to the next node in the list. For example, on a file of 1 Gb stored in 64 Kb blocks, the free list will consume at most 200 Kb, and normally much less.

The last block in the index should also be held in memory, rather than on disk, to facilitate update. The value of keeping the last block in memory is illustrated by the insertion and update algorithms shown below.

The block table can account for a significant fraction of a block's space. For example, if record numbers and record lengths are represented in 32 bits each, a block of only 128 entries will have a 1 Kb table; in the simulations described below, blocks of several hundred small records were common. A simple technique for reducing the size of the block table is to use fixed length representations of values, but keep the length of these representations as small as possible. For example, if the block size is

*We note that typical figures for disk retrieval are not very informative. For example, for the three kinds of disk drives attached to our Sun SPARCserver 2, the overheads of retrieving 64 Kb compared to retrieving 1 Kb were 30%, 45%, and 400%. Factors involved include seek, latency, caching and prefetch strategies, and disk channel speed.

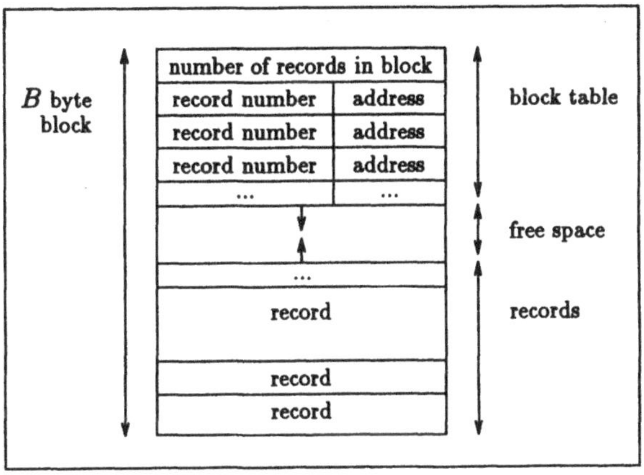

Figure 2: Block structure

16 Kb then 17 bits is sufficient to identify any bit in the block. The maximum record number can vary, but it is straightforward to let the largest record number held in the block govern the number of bits used to store each record number; for example, if the largest record number was 881,634 then $\lceil \log_2 881,634 \rceil = 20$ bits should be used. This implies that the block table must occasionally be rebuilt, but in practice rebuilds will be rare and in any case require only a few instruction cycles per record.

Another technique for reducing the size of the block table is to compress it. Since the records can easily be stored in order, the techniques we use for compressing inverted file entries can be applied to record numbers. However, compared to the fixed length scheme described above, the additional space saving would be relatively small. Space in the table might also be saved by byte or word alignment of records within the block. For example, byte alignment would waste an average of four bits per record, but would allow table pointers that were three bits shorter. Moreover, in many situations records will in fact be an integral number of bytes, or even words, long.

The final component of our scheme is an *update cache*, used to keep access costs down during insertion, update, and deletion. This cache contains a series of pairs, each pair being the number of the record to be changed and the change to be made to that record. In text databases, for example, it is common for adjacent documents to contain duplicate terms, so if updates to the index are cached then disk accesses can be saved. The *size* of the cache is the number of pairs it can contain. In our simulations, described in Section 6, we investigated a range of cache sizes.

5 Index maintenance

Given the file structures described in the previous section, file maintenance is straightforward. New records should be inserted according to the following algorithm.

1. If there is a block in the free list with sufficient free space, add the record to that block and update the free list.
2. Otherwise, if the last block has sufficient free space, add the record to the last block.
3. Otherwise, write the last block to disk, add it to the free list if necessary, create a new last block in memory, and add the record to that block.

'Adding a record to a block' consists of copying the record into the block; updating its block table; and updating the record mapping. Whichever of the above steps is used, if the record is smaller than a block, and if the record mapping is in main memory, then at most one disk read and one disk write is required to update the file; and, assuming that inserted records are small, will usually require no disk operations.

Record extension should be performed with the following algorithm.

1. Read the block containing the record to be extended, if it is not already in memory.
2. If the block contains sufficient free space for the extended record, move other records to accommodate the altered record, update the block table, and write the block to disk.
3. If there is not sufficient free space,
   (a) If moving a record in the block to either a block in the free list or the last block leaves sufficient space, then move that record, update the record mapping, and return to step (2).
   (b) Otherwise, move the extended record to the last block, creating a new last block if necessary.
4. Update the free list.

Assuming that the record is smaller than a block, at most two reads and two writes are required by this procedure, and usually one read and one write will be sufficient because only the block containing the record will be affected. Note that moving the average $B/2$ bytes sideways within a block, as required for update in place, will take considerably less time than a single disk access for reasonable values of B. For example, on a Sun SPARCserver 2, 32 Kb can be moved in about 5 milliseconds, compared to about 40 milliseconds to write a 64 Kb block.

Variations on the above procedures based on strategies such as best fit, worst fit, and so on, can be applied. Record deletion and contraction can be handled by procedures that are similar to those described above, with similar costs.

With large blocks, many records can be kept in each block and most records will fit within a block. Some records may, however, be larger than a block. There are several possible strategies for dealing with such long records. We chose to allow each block to contain, in addition to short records, up to one record that was larger than the block size and a series of pointers to overflow blocks containing the parts of the record that did not fit in the main block. There is a trade-off between choice of block size and the proportion of records that are longer than a block. Large blocks imply greater retrieval time, but the block size should be substantially greater then the size of the average record, or the average number of disk accesses required to retrieve a record will be large.

Update of long records requires that each of the blocks containing part of the record be read and written, so in practice it is desirable to store the overflow blocks contiguously, possibly in a separate file. Although dynamically maintaining contiguity would be expensive, an occasional re-ordering could be used to keep access costs down. In our simulations, we have pessimistically assumed that a separate access is required for each overflow block. Biliris[5,6] considers in detail the problem of storing dynamic records that are large compared to the block size.

6 Results

To test our space management scheme we implemented a space usage simulator that kept track of space utilisation, block table size, and number of disk accesses during creation of inverted file indexes. The parameters of this simulator were block size, tolerance, and cache size. As input, we used sequences of 'entry-num, bit-incr' pairs, where the bit-incr is the number of bits an update operation adds to the entry with identifier entry-num. These pairs were output from a program for creating inverted indexes, and so the data stream was, in effect, the sequence of term insertions that would take place if a compressed inverted index was being built during a linear pass over the document collection, assuming that the vocabulary and compression parameters had been accumulated in a pre-scan of the text.

Space utilisation

Our measure of space utilisation is the space required to store entries as a percentage of the total file size, so that a file 8,000 bits long with 7,000 bits of entries would have an 87.5% space utilisation, with the remaining 12.5% occupied by block tables and any free space†. The final space utilisation for our test databases is given in Table 2

†For consistency with previous reports[4,5,6,7,8], we have not, however, included the cost of the mapping that identifies, for each record number, the block containing the record.

in the first group of columns; the second group of columns shows the average ratio of records to blocks. The tolerance used for these experiments was 5%.

Block size (Kb)	Utilisation (%)			Records per block		
	Bible	*Comact*	*Trec*	*Bible*	*Comact*	*Trec*
4	95.5	97.5	97.3	64.3	30.7	70.3
8	94.9	97.3	96.9	127.8	46.5	101.9
16	93.5	97.4	96.7	252.0	76.8	157.6
32	93.5	97.1	96.6	504.1	131.1	249.1
64	93.5	96.7	96.8	1,008.1	261.3	409.5

Table 2: Space utilisation

As this table shows, excellent space utilisation is achieved across a range of block sizes. The utilisation does not change once the block size significantly exceeds the size of the longest entry, so that, for example, the utilisation for *Bible* does not change for blocks of 16 Kb or over; as shown in Table 1, the longest *Bible* entry is about 4 Kb. In these results, when space had to be created in a block the smallest sufficiently large entry was moved; we also tried moving the first sufficiently large entry (to minimise shifting of data within the block), but did not achieve such good space utilisation with this strategy. The entry, when moved, was placed in any block with sufficient free space; use of other strategies, such as best fit or worst fit, did not appear to make a significant difference to space utilisation.

Space utilisation as a function of index size during the construction of the *Trec* index is shown in Figure 3. The dip in the graph beginning at 15 Mb is a quirk of our data: a large number of new terms are introduced at that point. The minimum utilisation of 93%—excluding the initial index creation phase, in which utilisation is poor because the entries are very small compared to the block size and the block table size is more significant—is typical of all of the indexes and block sizes.

There was no marked relationship between cache size and space utilisation. However, we would expect use of a large cache to degrade utilisation slightly—the grouping of updates means that larger numbers of bits are being added to each record, so that fine control over allocation of entries to blocks is not possible. In our experiments, a cache of size 1,000 typically led to a 0.1% decline in utilisation. We found that space utilisation was also almost independent of tolerance for values between 1% and 10%; the main effect of changing tolerance was in the length of the free list. In our experiments, for tolerances of 5% or more the free list did not exceed 500 nodes.

We also experimented with use of run-length compression for the record numbers in the block table. This gave only a slight improvement in utilisation, however, with a typical change from 96.0% to 96.5%. Given that an uncompressed table can be searched much more rapidly, we do not believe that such compression is worthwhile.

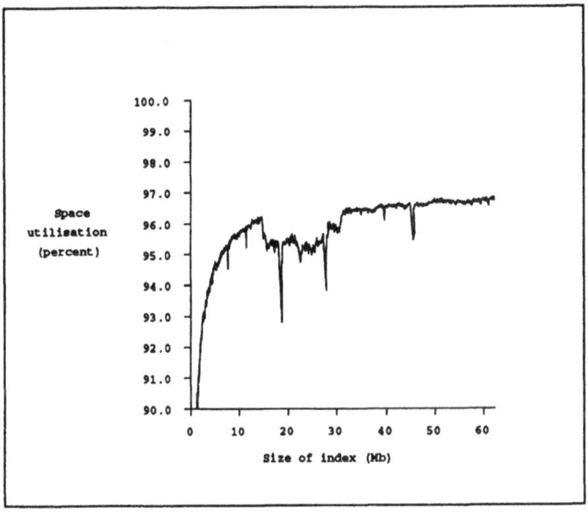

Figure 3: Space utilisation for 16 Kb blocks in *Trec*

Disk accesses

Although block size does not have much impact on space utilisation, it does affect the number of disk accesses required for an extension, as shown in Table 3. Since the longest entries will occupy many short blocks, and in our 'extension only' experiments are the entries that are accessed most frequently, the number of accesses required for an average update declines rapidly with increase in block size. Again, once the block size exceeds the length of the longest entry the cost stabilises, as expected, at less than 2 accesses per operation, assuming that the record mapping is held in main memory.

Block size	*Bible*	*Comact*	*Trec*
4	2.0	3.6	4.1
8	1.9	2.9	3.2
16	1.9	2.4	2.7
32	1.8	2.0	2.3
64	1.6	2.0	2.0

Table 3: Average disk accesses per operation

Based upon these results, block sizes of 32 Kb to 64 Kb appear to be well suited to our data; however, the best choice of block size will depend heavily on the average entry length, on the distribution of entry lengths, and the frequency with which longer entries are accessed during operations other than extension. We are currently planning experiments to test our scheme in such an environment.

The number of disk accesses needed for an update is approximately double the number required to retrieve an entry in answer to a query. Thus, although more data may have to be fetched if long blocks are used—because more entries not pertinent to the query are fetched—long blocks also imply fewer accesses, because there are fewer overflow blocks to be retrieved, and, within bounds, less access time overall.

Caching

Use of a cache of updates has, like block size, a dramatic effect on the number of disk accesses required for an average operation, as shown in Table 4. (The cache does not, of course, affect the cost of retrieving an entry.) In our simulations the cache was used in a very simple way: if the cache contained several updates to an entry then these updates were performed together. We did not attempt to order updates so that, for example, two entries residing in the same block were updated at the same time, but such an optimisation would only further improve the performance of the cache; for example, for 16 Kb blocks and a cache of size 1,000,000 we estimate that this optimisation would reduce the number of disk accesses per insertion by a factor of at least 10.

Cache size	*Bible*	*Comact*	*Trec*
1	1.9	2.4	2.7
10	1.8	2.4	2.7
100	1.3	1.7	2.6
1,000	0.6	0.6	1.7
10,000	0.2	0.2	0.7
100,000	≈0.05	≈0.07	0.2
1,000,000	<0.01	≈0.02	≈0.07

Table 4: Average disk accesses per operation with caching and 16 Kb blocks

The number of disk accesses required per operation, with and without caching, is shown as a function of index size in Figure 4. The number of disk accesses does grow slowly with the size of the index. This is because the number of entries that are longer than a block increases, and extra disk accesses are required for overflow blocks. However, for large blocks the number of disk accesses is certainly not excessive, and, given that, with our scheme, the index never needs to be rebuilt, the claim that inverted files are expensive to maintain[13] no longer holds.

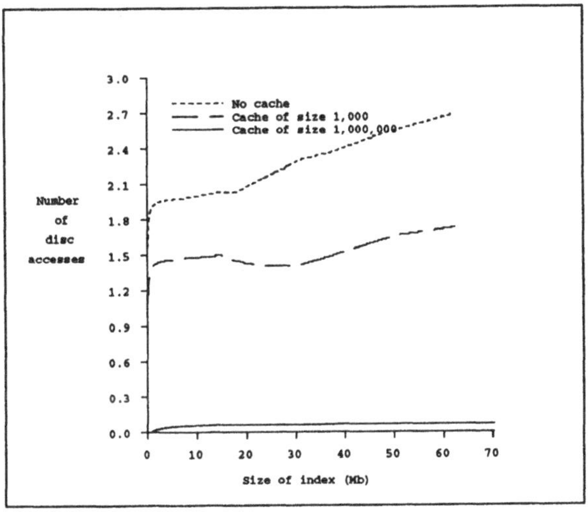

Figure 4: Number of disk accesses for 16 Kb blocks in *Trec*

We have used large caches for our experiments because a single record insertion can generate hundreds—or, in the case of one of the *Trec* records, over twenty thousand—updates to an index. For other kinds of data such large caches may not be practical, particularly if insertions are infrequent, although if insertions are infrequent their cost is not so important. With text data, small caches are unlikely to be effective, because each entry will be modified at most once per document insertion, and each document contains many distinct terms.

7 Conclusion

We have described a scheme for managing large collections of records of dynamically varying length. The application we have used to prove the technique is the storage of a compressed inverted file to a large text collection, and in this case we have achieved space utilisations in excess of 93%; update costs of less than two disk operations per operation or amendment; access costs of a little over one disk operation per retrieval; and have assumed only that the record mapping (two bytes per record) can be stored in memory, and that relatively fast access to large disk blocks is possible. To date we have applied the technique to the storage of inverted indexes for text databases through the use of a simulator, as described in this paper. However, the technique is also applicable to a variety of other application areas, such as the storage of the text of such a document collection; the storage of buckets of data in a hashed file system;

and the storage of B-tree nodes in a tree structured file system. Experiments to test the usefulness of the method in these areas with a full implementation are underway.

8 Acknowledgements

We would like to thank Neil Sharman for several suggestions and assistance with the implementation. This work was supported by the Australian Research Council.

9 References

1. A. Moffat and J. Zobel. Coding for compression in full-text retrieval systems. In *Proc. IEEE Data Compression Conference*, pages 72–81, Snowbird, Utah, 1992.
2. A. Moffat and J. Zobel. Parameterised compression for sparse bitmaps. In *Proc. ACM SIGIR International Conference on Research and Development in Information Retrieval*, pages 274–285, Copenhagen, 1992.
3. J. Zobel, A. Moffat, and R. Sacks-Davis. An efficient indexing technique for full-text database systems. In *Proc. Conference on Very Large Databases*, pages 352–362, Vancouver, 1992.
4. D.E. Knuth. *The Art of Computer Programming, Volume 1: Fundamental Algorithms, Second Edition.* Addison-Wesley, Massachusetts, 1973.
5. A. Biliris. The performance of three database storage structures for managing large objects. In *Proc. ACM-SIGMOD Conference on Management of Data*, pages 276–285, 1992.
6. A. Biliris. An efficient data storage structure for large dynamic objects. In *Proc 8'th IEEE International Conference on Data Engineering*, pages 301–308, Phoenix, Arizona, February 1992.
7. K.J. McDonell. An inverted index implementation. *Computer Journal*, 20(1):116–123, 1977.
8. C. Faloutsos and H.V. Jagadish. On B-tree indices for skewed distributions. In *Proc. Conference on Very Large Databases*, pages 363–374, Vancouver, 1992.
9. D.B. Lomet. A simple bounded disorder file organisation with good performance. *ACM Transactions on Database Systems*, 12(4):525–551, 1988.
10. G. Wiederhold. *File Organisation for Database Design.* Computer Science Series. McGraw-Hill, New York, 1987.
11. D. Grosshans. *File Systems Design and Implementation.* Prentice-Hall, New Jersey, 1986.
12. J.B. Lovins. Development of a stemming algorithm. *Mechanical Translation and Computation*, 11(1-2):22–31, 1968.
13. C. Faloutsos. Access methods for text. *ACM Computing Surveys*, 17(1):49–74, 1985.

A GUIDELINE FOR IMPLEMENTING ACCESS METHOD MODULES IN EXTENSIBLE DBMS MODUS

KAZUTAKA FURUSE
Doctoral Program in Engineering, University of Tsukuba
1-1-1 Tennoudai, Tsukuba City, Ibaraki, Japan

JEFFREY XU YU
Department of Computer Science, Australian National University
GPO Box 4, Canberra ACT 2601, Australia

KAZUNORI YAMAGUCHI
Department of Graphic and Computer Science, University of Tokyo
3-8-1 Komaba, Meguro-ku, Tokyo, Japan

HIROYUKI KITAGAWA and NOBUO OHBO
Institute of Information Sciences and Electronics, University of Tsukuba
1-1-1 Tennoudai, Tsukuba City, Ibaraki, Japan

ABSTRACT

In extensible DBMSs, users are able to implement access method modules and embed them into the systems. However, writing the access method modules is not easy task, because there is no guideline for users to follow.

In this paper, we present a specification of tree structured index mechanisms based on a model of trees. This specification is useful as a guideline for implementing access method modules. The guideline helps users to understand the behavior of index mechanisms, and it makes users' task easy. Using this guideline, users can implement each access method module straightforwardly.

1. Introduction

It has been pointed out by many researchers that conventional database management systems (DBMSs) are lacking in capability to support non-standard database applications, such as engineering design, image/voice applications, and scientific/statistical applications[1,24]. For example, in case of spatial databases, it is known that R-tree[14,20], which has similar structure to B$^+$-tree, is a useful and effective access method for storing and retrieving spatial objects. However, the conventional DBMSs are monolithic. They are designed and implemented to support only a fixed set of pre-defined (i.e., system defined) data types and a fixed set of access methods, and are not to support any other data types and access methods after they have been implemented.

In order to improve the expressive power and the efficiency of DBMSs, it is inherently required for DBMSs to support application specific data types and application specific new access methods. Recently, a couple of research projects have been coping with these issues by introducing a concept of *extensibility*. These systems are called *extensible DBMSs*[7]. In these systems, a special group of users called DBI† are allowed to extend DBMS by the following steps.

- Implementing user defined types and/or access methods, and
- embedding them into DBMS.

The extensible DBMSs currently proposed, such as EXODUS[5,6] and POSTGRES[22,23], have facility to include user defined modules. However, as we will discuss in the next section, all these projects mention the importance of extensibility but deal with it by their own ways. All the approaches in EXODUS and POSTGRES make it possible to extend systems, but it is not an easy task. There is no guideline for writing user defined extension. To make a guideline, the formal specification of such extensibility should be investigated and understood.

In this paper, as a case study, we narrow our points on design and implementation of the tree structured index access methods, and propose a guideline to make the process of embedding them into the system easy. The reason why we choose this class of access methods is because the tree structured index mechanisms are the most popular technique in supporting specific data types in engineering applications.

In our system MODUS[12,25], access method interface (AMI), is the only entrance where user defined access method modules can attach to. AMI is composed of a set of abstract functions, and its semantics is clearly specified by the formal specification of index mechanisms. In each module, a concrete version of AMI functions must be provided. The formal specification has the following two main benefits.

- The formal specification provides a precise guideline for implementing modules. It helps users to understand the behavior of index mechanisms, and thus, makes it easy to construct new access method modules.
- The formal specification helps extensible DBMS designers to establish a clear interface between the kernel of the DBMS and the modules which are implemented by users.

The remainder of this paper is organized as follows. In Section 2, we compare different three approaches for implementing extensibility and discuss their advantages and disadvantages. Section 3 presents the formal specification of tree structured index mechanisms. In Section 4, with the specification described in Section 3, we propose a guideline for implementing tree structured index mechanisms. Finally, in Section 5, we conclude this paper and discuss the remaining problems of our approach.

2. Comparison of Three Approaches to Implement Extensibility

In this section, we compare approaches adopted in EXODUS, POSTGRES and MODUS to embed new access methods into the systems, and discuss their advantages and disadvantages.

†In the extensible DBMSs, users who construct application-specific DBMSs are called as *database implementors* (DBI) or *database designers*. Note that role of DBI and that of DBA (database administrator) are quite different. The former is to construct DBMS, and the latter is to administrate the DBMS constructed by DBI.

- EXODUS: a programming approach
  In EXODUS project, a major tool provided is the programming language E and its compiler. E is an extension of C++, and is designed as a persistent language that aids users in a number of problem areas related to implementation of database systems, including interaction with persistent storage. All access methods, utility functions, and data model independent operations are written in E. By using E, experienced users are able to design and implement modules which are embedded into the system.

- POSTGRES: a practical approach
  As mentioned in [21], an access method contains only a small number of procedures that define the characteristics of the access method. In POSTGRES, some system relations are provided in the database dictionary to keep the necessary information about access methods. For example, in a system relation called **AM**, a collection of operators for access methods is registered. For each operation, its name, identifier, and other information needed for query processing are stored in this relation.

  In addition to the system relations, a generic abstract interface for each access method is provided which includes procedures such as `open`, `close`, `get-next`, `insert`, `delete`, and `replace`. Experienced programmers are possible to implement new access methods by writing these procedures. For more details, see [21,23].

- MODUS: a specification based approach
  In MODUS, users can embed tree structured index access methods by writing access method modules. Semantics of tree structured access methods based on a model of trees are provided by a formal specification. Based on the tree model and the specification of access methods, we propose, which will mention in the following sections, a fixed set of functions called *access method interface* (AMI). The specification of tree structured access methods provides the precise semantics of them, and hence provides a guideline for writing each AMI function.

Each approach we mentioned above has its advantages and disadvantages.

- In EXODUS, an object-oriented persistent programming language is provided. Based on this programming language, users are able to implement access method mechanisms. However, there is not any guideline for users to follow. And there is not any guarantee that the embedded part will work well.

- POSTGRES has adopted a more practical approach. It is clear in the system dictionary what kind of information must be kept, and what procedures such as `get-next` and `insert` are available. However, the interface seems somewhat ad hoc, and no guideline for implementing access methods is provided.

- In MODUS, the specification of a set of abstract functions based on a model of trees are provided. This specification makes the semantics and behavior of access methods clear, and provides users a guideline for writing the access method modules. The specification also helps designers of extensible DBMSs to establish a rigorous interface for the kernel and the access method modules.

	static		dynamic			
	search path	insertion path	solution to overflow	propagation of splitting	solution to underflow	propagation of consolidation
B^+-tree	1	1	splitting	needed	consolidation	needed
prefix B^+-tree	1	1	splitting	needed	consolidation	needed
Bit-tree	1	1	splitting	needed	consolidation	needed
B^{link}-tree	1	1	splitting	needed	consolidation	needed
Π-tree	1	1	splitting	needed	consolidation	needed
R-tree	n	1	splitting	needed	re-insertion	—
R^*-tree	n	1	splitting and re-insertion	needed	re-insertion	—
R^+-tree	n	n	splitting	needed	re-insertion	—
k-d-B-tree	1	1	splitting	not needed	consolidation	not needed

Table 1: Characteristics of Tree Structured Index Mechanisms

The final goal of each project is to support extensibility, that is to say, to provide users the way to implement modules for extension and to embed them into the DBMSs. To this purpose, we believe that it is necessary to specify each part of DBMS formally. In this paper, as a case study, we construct a formal specification of the tree structured access methods to make the semantics of them clear, and to provide users with a guideline for implementing access method modules.

3. Classification and Specification of Tree Structured Index Mechanisms

3.1. Brief Survey of the Existing Tree Structured Index Mechanisms

Tree structured index mechanisms are the standard for indexing data in DBMS. There are a number of mechanisms proposed, and novel mechanisms are invented perpetually. The most standard one is B^+-tree[2,8]. There are many variants of B^+-tree. Prefix B^+-tree[3] and Bit-tree[10] are designed to reduce disk space required for the tree. B^{link}-tree[15] and Π-tree[17] are designed to have extra pointers between sibling nodes to provide high concurrency.

Recently, many tree structured index mechanisms for spatial (or multidimensional) data are proposed[19]. R-tree[14], R^+-tree[20], and R^*-tree[4] are the mechanisms for indexing spatial region data. k-d-B-tree[18] is useful and effective for indexing spatial point data.

3.2. Classification of Tree Structured Index Mechanisms

In this subsection, to make the characteristics of the tree structured index mechanisms clear, we classify them. Here, we assume the followings for the sake of simplicity.

- The index is completely balanced.
- In each index, only leaf nodes have record entries.

In Subsection 3.4, we construct a specification of the tree structured index mechanisms according to the classification. As most of tree structured index mechanisms including all mechanisms mentioned in this subsection satisfy these assumptions, our approach of specification is widely applicable.

Table 1 shows characteristics of the major tree structured index mechanisms. In this table, columns are divided into two groups: "static" and "dynamic". As we will discuss later, the specification is described according to these two aspects of index mechanisms.

Columns grouped in "static" describe static nature of the index mechanisms. The column "search path" describes the number of possible paths from a root node to leaf nodes that have to be traced when searching operation is done. In conventional index mechanisms such as B^+-tree, it is sufficient to trace only one path to retrieve records in an index with a given key value. However, there are some index mechanisms (such as R-tree) that require more than one path to be traced. The column "insertion path" gives the number of record entries which are inserted when insertion operation is done. In R^+-tree, entries are possible to be inserted into more than one leaf nodes to improve searching performance. In most of all index mechanisms but R^+-tree, only one record entry is inserted into the index.

Columns grouped in "dynamic" describe dynamic nature, that is, maintenance mechanisms of the index mechanisms. The column "solution to overflow" shows the mechanism to dissolve the overflow of nodes which may occur in the course of inserting records into indices. All index mechanisms in the table use the node splitting to dissolve the overflow. R^*-tree, one of the revised versions of R-tree, uses an algorithm that combines a splitting algorithm with a re-insertion algorithm to improve searching performance. The column "solution to underflow" shows the mechanism to dissolve the underflow of nodes which may occur in the course of deleting records from indices. There are two ways to dissolve the underflow: node consolidation and re-insertion. Node consolidation is the inverse procedure of the node splitting. Some index mechanisms use re-insertion instead of node consolidation to improve searching performance. In general, re-insertion is more effective than node consolidation when the number of the search paths is larger than one.

The columns "propagation of splitting" and "propagation of consolidation" describe the necessity of rearrangement of indices when splitting or consolidation occurs. Most of index mechanisms require the propagation of node splitting and node consolidation from leaf node toward root node. k-d-B-tree is the only exception, and does not require the propagation.

With this characterization, we can classify the index mechanisms according to their static nature and dynamic nature as shown in Table 2. Rows in this table are classified according to "static," and columns are classified according to "dynamic." Index mechanisms are divided into three categories by the classification according to their static nature, and are divided into (at least) two categories† according to their dynamic nature.

The existence of some empty categories in Table 2 indicates the possibility of new types of index mechanisms. For example, if we invent a node consolidation algorithm which is more effective than re-insertion for R-tree, we will have another revised version of R-tree

†With the characterization of Table 1, we can divide the columns into more than two categories. For example, because R^*-tree is different from R-tree in the point of the solution of overflow as described earlier, we can make another category of "splitting with re-insertion, and re-insertion." However, we will ignore such insignificant difference between index mechanisms to prevent the classification and the specification from being unnecessarily complex.

	splitting and consolidation	splitting and re-insertion
search path = 1 insertion path = 1	B^+-tree prefix B^+-tree B^{link}-tree Π-tree k-d-B-tree	
search path = n insertion path = 1	(a)	R-tree R^*-tree
search path = n insertion path = n		R^+-tree

Table 2: Classification of Tree Structured Index Mechanisms

which will be placed in the category labelled as "(a)" in Table 2.

3.3. *A Model of Trees*

To give the specification of the tree structured index mechanisms, we need a model for representing trees. As a model for trees, the model based on *ranked alphabets*[9] is well known and used widely. However, this model doesn't suit out purpose. In this model, location of a node in a tree is represented by a absolute path from root node to the node. As stated in the previous subsection, the tree structured index mechanisms have dynamic nature such as node splitting and node consolidation. Since these mechanisms should be defined independently of the location of nodes, it is desired that relative location between nodes can be represented easily in model of trees.

In this subsection, we briefly introduce the $\beta\gamma$ model for specifying the structure of trees formally. In this model, a tree is represented based on the relative location between nodes and thus this model is suited for our purpose. For more details and formal definition of this model, see [13].

First of all, we define some notations. Let N be the set of all natural numbers. Sets are denoted by curly braces, such as $\{e_0, e_1, \ldots, e_n\}$. Lists and tuples are denoted by angle brackets and parentheses, respectively, such as $\langle e_0, e_1, \ldots, e_n \rangle$ and $(e_0, e_1, \ldots, e_n)$. A power set of a set S is denoted as $\mathcal{P}(S)$ and a set of all lists whose elements are elements of a set S is denoted as $\mathcal{L}(S)$.

The $\beta\gamma$ model is based on navigation operators from a node to another node of trees. There are five navigation operators: ε, β, γ, β^{-1}, γ^{-1}(see Figure 1). ε stands for empty navigation (i.e., navigation from a node to itself). γ represents navigation from a node to its first child, and β represents navigation from a node to its next sibling. β^{-1} and γ^{-1} are inverse operators of β and γ, respectively.

Composition of the navigation operators is denoted by concatenation. For example, navigation from a node to its third child is represented as $\beta\beta\gamma$ (note that the navigation operators are applied from right to left). For all $\nu \in \{\varepsilon, \beta, \gamma, \beta^{-1}, \gamma^{-1}\}$, composition of ν n

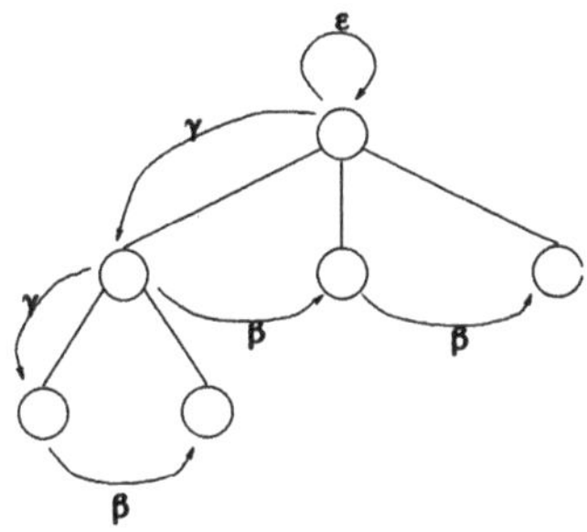

Figure 1: Navigation Operators

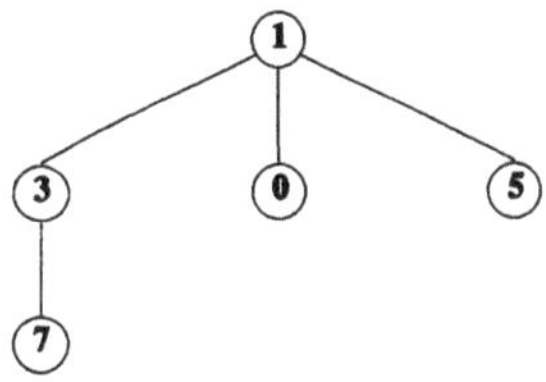

Figure 2: A Tree Labelled with Natural Numbers

times is denoted as ν^n, such as $\beta^2 = \beta\beta$ and $\gamma^3 = \gamma\gamma\gamma$.

In the $\beta\gamma$ model, the navigation operators are used to represent path from a node to another node†. In this paper, we refer the set of all paths as P††. A tree is defined as a partial mapping from P to L, where L is a set of labels of nodes. For example, consider a tree labelled with natural numbers as shown in Figure 2. In the $\beta\gamma$ model, as shown in

†As we have the empty navigation operator ε and the inverse operators β^{-1} and γ^{-1}, there are infinite number of representations for an identical path. For example, $\gamma\beta\varepsilon$, $\beta^{-1}\beta\gamma\beta$, etc. represent the paths which are inherently equal to the representation $\gamma\beta$. As this is undesirable, in [13], we introduce a reduction system which has the Church-Rosser property to define *normal form* (or reduced form) of each representation. As for the example given above, the representation such as $\gamma\beta\varepsilon$, $\beta^{-1}\beta\gamma\beta$, etc. are all reduced to the normal form $\gamma\beta$ with this reduction system. Intuitively, it can be said that a normal form represents one of the minimum (i.e., shortest) representations of a path. In this paper, we use the normal forms for representing paths.

††Roughly speaking, we may consider P the Kleene-closure of the set of the navigation operators. Precise definition of P is also described in [13].

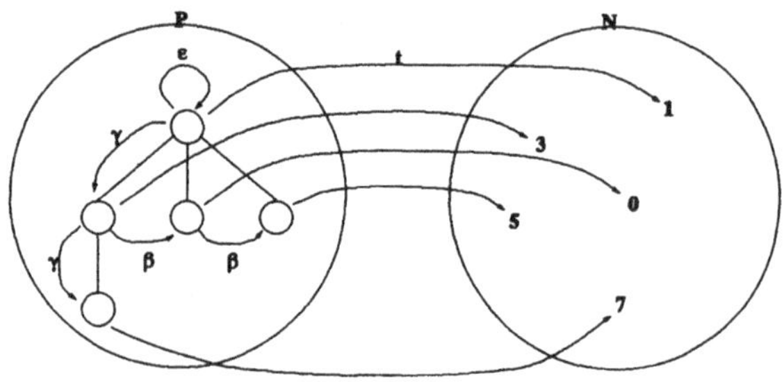

Figure 3: The representation of the tree in Figure 2 in the $\beta\gamma$ model

Figure 3, this tree is defined as a partial mapping $t : \mathsf{P} \to \mathsf{N}$ such that

$$\forall p \in \mathsf{P}, \quad t(p) = \begin{cases} 1, & \text{if } p = \varepsilon \\ 3, & \text{if } p = \gamma \\ 0, & \text{if } p = \beta\gamma \\ 5, & \text{if } p = \beta\beta\gamma \\ 7, & \text{if } p = \gamma\gamma \\ \bot, & \text{otherwise} \end{cases} \tag{1}$$

where $\bot$ means *undefined*. As shown in this example, $t(p)$ stands for a label of a node, where p is a path from the root node. As ε is the empty navigation, $t(\varepsilon)$ stands for the label of the root node.

In Subsection 3.4, we use this model of trees to specify the tree structured index mechanisms. As the $\beta\gamma$ model is based on relative location between nodes (i.e., the navigation operators, of course), this model is useful for describing dynamic aspects of indices, such as node splitting and node consolidation.

3.4. Specification of Tree Structured Index Mechanisms

In Subsection 3.2, we classify the tree structured index mechanisms by two aspects of characteristics. According to this classification, we construct a specification of tree structured index mechanisms formally. We use this specification to propose a guideline for implementing index mechanisms.

Specification of a tree structured index mechanism is defined by organization of the index and primitive operations applied to instances of the index.

Organization of tree structured indices

Organization of a tree structured index can be described with the $\beta\gamma$ model. As the model already describes basic nature of trees, all we have to do is to specify the structure of leaf nodes and non-leaf nodes of the trees. That is, an organization of a tree structured

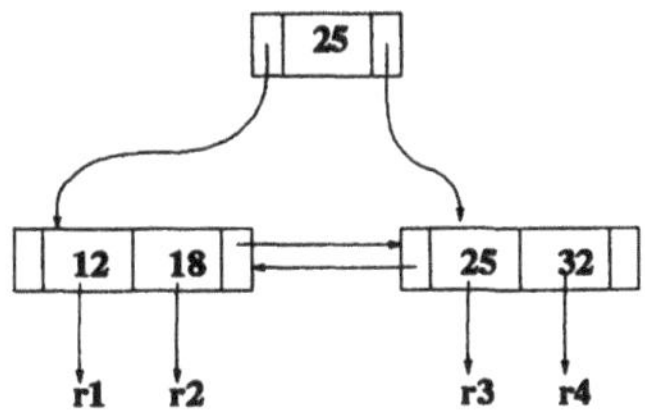

Figure 4: A B$^+$-tree

index is represented as a pair (N_l, N_n), where N_l is a set of leaf nodes and N_n is a set of non-leaf nodes.

An instance of a index (N_l, N_n) is defined as a partial mapping from P to $N_l \cup N_n$. For example, consider an instance of B$^+$-tree whose key values are natural numbers as shown in Figure 4 ($r_1, r_2, \ldots$ are record identifiers). Leaf nodes and non-leaf nodes of this tree can be modelled by lists of $\mathsf{N} \times R$ and lists of N, respectively (R is a set of record identifiers). Thus, this instance of B$^+$-tree can be represented as a partial mapping $t : \mathsf{P} \to \mathcal{L}(\mathsf{N} \times R) \cup \mathcal{L}(\mathsf{N})$ such that

$$\forall p \in \mathsf{P}, \quad t(p) = \begin{cases} \langle 25 \rangle, & \text{if } p = \varepsilon \\ \langle (12, r1), (18, r2) \rangle, & \text{if } p = \gamma \\ \langle (25, r3), (32, r4) \rangle, & \text{if } p = \beta\gamma \\ \perp, & \text{otherwise} \end{cases} \tag{2}$$

Primitive operations for tree structured indices

There are three primitive operations for manipulating tree structured indices: *search*, *insert*, and *delete*. The meanings of these operations for each index mechanism are determined by static and dynamic nature of the index mechanism as we discussed in Subsection 3.2. These primitive operations are described by the characteristics of Table 1 as follows†.

search(t : index tree, k : key value) =
  for each p in **search_path**(t, k)
    find record identifiers whose associated key value is k in the node p

insert(t : index tree, k : key value, r : record id) =
  for each p in **insert_path**(t, k)
    insert the pair (k, r) in the node p
    if overflow occurs, then call **dissolve_overflow**(t, p)
      and **propagate_overflow**(t, p)

delete(t : index tree, k : key value, r : record id) =

†In this paper, we describe the specification of the primitive operations in semi-formal style because of page limitation. Completely formal specification will be described in [11].

for each p in **insert_path**(t, k)
    delete the pair (k, r) in the node p
    if underflow occurs, then call **dissolve_underflow**(t, p)
        and **propagate_underflow**(t, p)

In this description of primitive operations, the functions written in boldface (such as **search_path**) are the characteristic functions of the index mechanisms. By describing these characteristic functions, we can construct various kind of tree structured index mechanisms. When describing the characteristic functions, we can use the $\beta\gamma$ notation to specify the relative location between nodes. This is comprehensive and useful for describing dynamic nature of the mechanisms, such as node splitting and node consolidation. For example, the characteristic functions **dissolve_overflow**(t, p) of conventional B^+-tree is described (in semi-formal style) as follows.

dissolve_overflow$(t : \text{index tree}, p : \text{path}) =$
    allocate a node and insert it at the location βp
    distribute entries of the node p into the node p and βp
        according to maintenance policy of B^+-tree
    adjust the parent node located at $\gamma^{-1}p$

Sibling node and parent node of the node located at p are represented as βp and $\gamma^{-1}p$, respectively. The $\beta\gamma$ notation makes the description of the primitive operations quite simple and comprehensive.

In this section, we have shown that each index mechanism can be specified by its organization (or structure of nodes) and its characteristics. This specification can be used as a guideline for implementing the tree structured index mechanisms as shown in the next section.

4. Implementing Tree Structured Index Mechanisms

4.1. Architecture of MODUS

This subsection briefly describes the architecture of MODUS. Major objective of the research project on MODUS is to design and implement an extensible DBMS of practical use. In MODUS, users can introduce new basic data types and new access methods with small labor. MODUS is composed of *kernel* and some components called *managers*. Each managers implements each DBMS facility. The kernel coordinates behavior of managers and provides services such as data retrieval and data manipulation to database applications. Some managers can be extended by including *modules* defined by users. As managers are independent of each other, it is possible to put new modules under control of a certain manager without any influence on other managers. For example, as *type manager* is independent of *access method manager*, inclusion of new data types does not affect the behavior of access method modules.

Figure 5 shows the architecture of MODUS. MODUS is composed of three processes: *data server*, *transaction server*, and *query processor*.

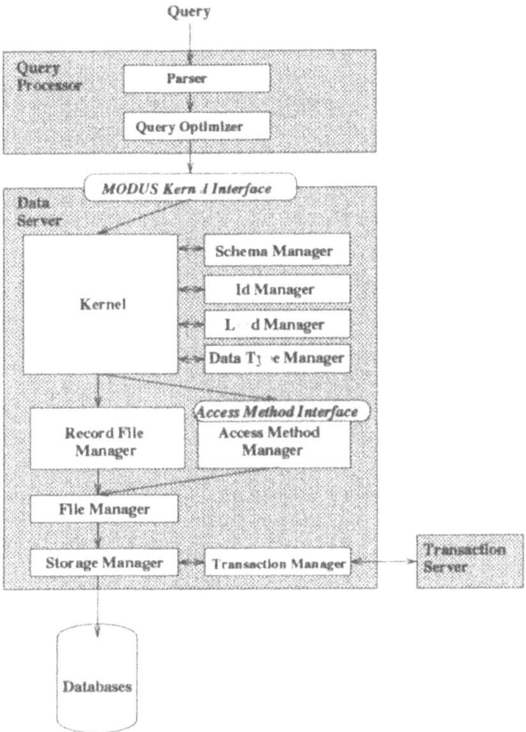

Figure 5: The architecture of MODUS

Main part of MODUS is data server. The data server is composed of *kernel* and some *managers*.

The access method manager in the data server provides indexing facility to the kernel. Each access method is defined in an *access method module* controlled by the access method manager.

Coordinating the managers, the kernel processes queries served through MODUS kernel interface. When kernel receives a query, it consults the schema manager to find out whether the query is valid. It also checks which files are needed to process the query and which data types of objects are stored in the files using the schema manager. Next, the kernel gets record identifiers in the index files from the access method manager. Records themselves are received from the record file manager by sending requests with the record identifiers. Type information is served by the data type manager. Using this information, the kernel evaluates expressions included in the query. Results are sent to the query processor. For

create	Create an index file
destroy	Destroy the specified file
open	Open the specified file
close	Close the specified file
search	Search the index to get record identifiers
insert	Insert an entry into the index file
delete	Remove the specified entry from the index file

Table 3: Access Method Interface

more details, see [12].

4.2. Implementing Access Method Modules

As described in the previous subsection, the access method manager implements the indexing mechanism of MODUS. The role of access method manager is to provide indexing service to kernel by controlling access method modules written by users. Here, the point is, from the kernel's point of view, that there must not be any difference among access method modules. In other words, to be extensible, it is necessary for kernel to control all access methods embedded into the system in uniform way. To achieve this goal, we set the interface between the kernel and the access method manager. This is called *access method interface* (AMI).

AMI is a fixed set of abstract functions. Table 3 shows the major part of AMI functions. In each access method module implementing tree structured index mechanism, a concrete set of AMI functions must be described. Users can use the specification of the primitive operations (such as *search*) described in the previous section as a guideline for implementing the AMI functions. Users are not restricted, but greatly recommended to implement the AMI functions along this guideline.

Following is an example of a part of access method module implementing R-tree index mechanism.

```
module Rtree
require "Rectangle";
type Recentry = tuple of { rec: Rectangle, id: Recid };
type Leaf = list of Recentry;
type Nonleaf = list of Rectangle;
type Node = union of { l: Leaf, n: Nonleaf };
type Rtree = tree of Node;
...
function search(t: Rtree, k: Rectangle) returns list of Recid
{
    p: Path;
    r: Leaf;
    result: list of Recid;
```

```
    foreach (p = search_path(t, k)) {
        r = node(p);
        if (overlap(r.rec, r))
            result->append(r.id);
    }
    return result;
}
...
end Rtree
```

In this module, the function **search** is implemented straightforwardly along the specification of *search* mentioned in the previous section. That is, the specification is used as a guideline, and it makes the implementation easy. In this implementation, the characteristic functions such as **search_path** are used to describe AMI functions. The characteristic functions are defined as submodules of the access method module. For example, the function **search_path** is implemented as a submodule of the module **Rtree**, as follows.

```
module search_path
function search_path(t: Rtree, k: Rectangle) returns list of Path
{
    return search_path1(t, k, EMPTY);
}

function search_path1(t: Rtree, k: Rectangle, p: Path)
    returns list of Path;
{
    path: Path;
    n: Leaf;
    r: Rectangle;
    result: list of Path;

    if (leaf(p)) {
        result->append(p);
    } else {
        path = concat(GAMMA, p);
        foreach (r = members(node(p))) {
            if (overlap(r, k)) {
                result->append_list(search_path1(t, k, path));
            }
            path = concat(BETA, p);
        }
    }
    return result;
}
end search_path
```

Functions for handling trees and paths, such as **node** (getting the entity of the node specified by the given path) and **concat** (concatenage two paths), are provided for writing access method modules as library functions.

Implementing the characteristic functions as submodules makes the description of modules clear and comprehensive. Furthermore, as submodule is implemented independently of each other, reusability of access method modules (and their submodules) is improved. For example, if we invent more effective node splitting algorithm for R-tree, we can implement a revised access method module of R-tree by simply replace the submodule **dissolve_overflow** with new one.

5. Conclusion

In this paper, we have presented the model of trees and the specification of tree structured index mechanisms based on the model. We have also presented that the specification is useful as a guideline for implementing user defined access method modules. The guideline helps users to understand the behavior of each AMI functions and it makes users' task to construct new access method modules easy. Along this guideline, users can implement each access method module rather straightforwardly.

However, uncommon operations specific to some index mechanisms are not treated in the present specification. For example, sequential access operations available in B^+-tree is not considered yet. We are now extending the current approach to specify this kind of operations by introducing the notion of cursors into the specification for traversing nodes of indices. With cursors, we can specify sequential access operations which are based on the mechanisms prepared in each index mechanism for navigating nodes. We anticipate that the introduction of cursors will shed light to the internal behavior of tree structured index mechanisms.

6. Acknowledgements

The authors are grateful to Prof. Yuzuru Fujiwara of Institute of Information Sciences and Electronics, University of Tsukuba for his helpful comments and encouragement to our research.

7. References

1. M. Atkinson, F. Bancilhon, D. DeWitt, K. R. Dittrich, D. Maier, and S. Zdonik. The Object-Oriented Database System Manifesto. in *Proc. of 1st Int'l. Conf. on Deductive and Object-Oriented Databases* (Kyoto, Japan, Dec. 1989).

2. R. Bayer and E. McCreight. Organization and Maintenance of Large Ordered Indexes. *Acta Informatica* **1(3)** (1972).

3. R. Bayer and K. Unterauer. Prefix B-trees. *ACM Trans. on Database Systems* **2(1)** (Mar. 1977).

4. N. Beckmann, H.-P. Kriegel, R. Schneider, and B. Seeger. The R*-tree: An Efficient

and Robust Access Method for Points and Rectangles. in *Proc. of the 1990 ACM SIGMOD Int'l. Conf. on Management of Data* (Atlantic City, NJ, May 1990).

5. M. J. Carey and D. J. DeWitt. The Architecture of the EXODUS Extensible DBMS. in *Proc. of the Int'l. Workshop on Object-Oriented Database Systems* (Asilomar, California, Sep. 1986).

6. M. J. Carey and D. J. DeWitt. An Overview of the EXODUS Project. *IEEE Database Engineering* **6(2)** (June 1987).

7. M. J. Carey and L. Haas. Extensible Database Management Systems. *ACM SIGMOD Record* **19(4)** (Dec. 1990).

8. D. Comer. The Ubiquitous B-Tree. *ACM Computing Surveys* **11(2)** (June 1979).

9. B. Courcelle. Fundamental Properties of Infinite Trees. *Theoretical Computer Science* **25** (1983).

10. D. E. Ferguson. Bit-Tree: a Data Structure for Fast File Processing. *Communications of the ACM* **35(6)** (June 1992).

11. K. Furuse. Formal Specification of Tree Structured Index Mechanisms (1992). (in preparation).

12. K. Furuse, Y. Ishikawa, K. Yamaguchi, H. Kitagawa, and N. Ohbo. Design and Implementation Technique of the Extensible DBMS MODUS. in *Proc. of Advanced Database System Symp.* (IPSJ, Tokyo, Japan, Dec. 1990). (in Japanese).

13. K. Furuse and K. Yamaguchi. A Model of Tree Structure Based on the Navigational Operators. Technical report, University of Tsukuba, (1992).

14. A. Guttman. R-trees: A Dynamic Index Structure for Spatial Searching. in *Proc. of Annual Meeting SIGMOD '84* (Boston, Massachusetts, June 1984).

15. P. L. Lehman and S. B. Yao. Efficient Locking for Concurrent Operations on B-trees. *ACM Trans. on Database Systems* **6(4)** (Dec. 1981).

16. G. M. Lohman, B. Lindsay, H. Pirahesh, and K. B. Schiefer. Extensions to Starburst: Objects, Types, Functions, and Rules. *Communications of the ACM* **34(10)** (Oct. 1991).

17. D. Lomet and B. Salzberg. Access Method Concurrency with Recovery. in *Proc. of the 1992 ACM SIGMOD Int'l. Conf. on Management of Data* (San Diego, CA, June 1992).

18. J. T. Robinson. The k-d-B-tree: A Search Structure for Lange Multidimensional Dynamic Indexes. in *Proc. of the SIGMOD Conf.* (Ann Arbor, MI, Apr. 1981).

19. H. Samet. *The Design and Analysis of Spatial Data Structures.* (Addison-Wesley, 1989).

20. T. Sellis, N. Roussopoulos, and C. Faloutsos. The R^+-tree: A Dynamic Index for Multi-Dimensional Objects. in *Proc. of the 13th Int'l. Conf. on Very Large Data Bases* (Brighton, England, Sep. 1987).

21. M. Stonebraker. Inclusion of New Types in Relational Data Base Systems. in *Proc. of 2nd Int'l. Conf. on Data Base Engineering* (Feb. 1986).

22. M. Stonebraker and G. Kermnitz. The POSTGRES Next-Generation Database Management System. *Communications of the ACM* **34(10)** (Oct. 1991).

23. M. Stonebraker and L. A. Rowe. The Design of POSTGRES. in *Proc. of ACM SIGMOD '86 Int'l. Conf. on Management of Data* (Washington, D. C., June 1986).

24. M. Stonebraker, L. A. Rowe, B. Lindsay, J. Gray, M. J. Carey, M. Brodie, P. Bernstein, and D. Beech. Third-Generation Database System Manifesto. *ACM SIGMOD Record*, **19(3)** (Sep. 1990).

25. X. Yu. *Supporting Suructured Objects in MODUS.* PhD thesis, University of Tsukuba (1990).

DESIGN OF OBJECT-ORIENTED DATABASES - FROM FUNCTIONAL SPECIFICATIONS TO OBJECT STRUCTURES*

JANUSZ R GETTA
Department of Computer Science, University of Wollongong,
PO Box 1144 (Northfields Avenue), Wollongong NSW 2500, Australia
Tel: [+61](0)42-214339 Email: jrg@cs.uow.edu.au

ABSTRACT

We are motivated by a strong need for more systematic approach to the design of object-oriented databases. The paper introduces the methodology of object-oriented database design which is entirely based on the functional approach to database modelling. The methodology adopts a formal model of object-oriented database where the main principle is a dual specification of the database scheme as a pair that consists of behavioural and structural scheme. The database design algorithm uses the names of object classes, the signatures of methods, and inheritance relationship specified in the behavioural scheme to generate the structural scheme, i.e. the structural definitions of object classes, and the implementations of methods. The algorithm assumes an existence of two-level memory hierarchy where a certain amount of a stable cache-like memory provides a significantly faster access to the database objects than the rest of available disc memory. The optimal design is based on the principle that the instances of object classes accessed by the methods frequently enough, and responsible for the best performance of methods are stored in a stable cache-like memory[9].

1. Introduction

The growing number of the commercially available object-oriented database systems[7,12,5,26], and the expanding range of their applications raises the question about the general, and more systematic methodology for the design of object-oriented databases. By the design methodology we mean a formal notation which is expressive enough to describe the conceptual view of the modelled domain and the collection of rules to transform the conceptual model into the declaration of the database structures. Generally the database design methodologies falls into two categories: the data analysis techniques capable to analyse the semantics of user data and to build an abstract view of the described reality, and the technical design methods to convert an abstract model into implementation of the database structures[10]. For instance the majority of existing methodologies for the relational database design are based on the semantic modelling techniques[13,23,24], and on the algorithms for decomposition, or synthesis of the relational schemes. The development of the object-oriented approach to database modelling has followed an entirely different way than the relational approach. The experiments, and early implementations preceded the theoretical efforts, and the attempts to construct a formal model of object-oriented database. A number of formal specifications that

---

* Work supported by the Australian and Overseas Telecommunications Corporation (AOTC) under contract number 7260.

appeared later[4,3,6,14,11,16,27,28] did not get a larger support and were finally overshadowed by the collection of "commandments"[1] and the commercial standard[2] of the object-oriented database model. Unfortunately both solutions provide a "look-and-feel" oriented specification of the object-oriented database model rather than its precise definition. The lack of formal definition, the discrepancies between the experimental and commercial products, and the trend to cover many different aspects of database modelling within one formalism[4] made the development of a consistent and sound methodology of the object-oriented database design more difficult then for the other database models.

The objective of our work is to propose a simplified (RISC-oriented[15]) model of the object-oriented database, and then to use such model for the development of object-oriented database design methodology. The definition of our model is based on the modular approach to object-oriented databases[8]. In order to satisfy the principles of the object-oriented approach[1] the model distinguishes two separate database schemes: *the behavioural scheme* and *the structural scheme*. The behavioural scheme includes the names of object classes, the signatures of methods available for the database users to access and to manipulate the objects and specification of the inheritance hierarchy. The existence of the behavioural scheme is justified by a need to provide a clear, and simple view of the database, and to precisely determine the collection of operators available for object manipulations. We assume that no implementation details are allowed on this level. On the other hand, the structural scheme includes the definition of object structures such as the properties of objects, the components of objects, and the implementations of methods. Contrary to the classical object-oriented approach we do not group the methods around the definitions of object classes but we allow them to be common for all classes defined within the behavioural scheme. Such approach provides more flexibility, especially in the situations when it is necessary to define the operations on the instances of many different classes. Separation of the behavioural aspects of the database scheme from its structural and implementation details suggests the methodology for the design of object-oriented databases where the behavioural scheme plays the role of the conceptual model, and the structural scheme is a final objective of the design. While the implementation details of the particular object-oriented database management system are known to a designer then it is possible to define a complete translation of the behavioural scheme into the structural scheme. In principle, our task is to construct the multilevel object structures appropriate for the efficient implementation of the methods specified in the behavioural scheme. The main objective of this paper is to provide an algorithm capable to generate the structural definition of the object-oriented database from its functional specification under assumption of the most efficient implementation of the methods. In order to make our model more practical we assume that a certain amount of a stable cache-like memory is available for storing the objects that require shorter access time, and that it is possible to estimate the maximum number of objects within each class. Our design algorithm is capable to generate the object structures, and the implementations of methods such that the instances of object classes crucial for an efficient computation of methods will fit the best within a cluster of the fast-access memory.

The generation of the hierarchical database structures has been already investigated in a number of approaches. There exists the exhaustive analysis of the problem based on the normalization theory of the nested relational structures[20,21]. Unfortunately, the results obtained there cannot be directly applied in our case because the design process was based on the information coming from the specification of the functional and multivalued dependencies among the atomic attributes. Another approach[25] introduced the conceptual design of the complex objects based on the formal model of entities on which the queries may be made. The authors proposed to define the structures of the complex objects in such a way that the optimum computation of the predefined classes of SQL-like queries would be possible. This idea is close to ours, but the proposal remained on the conceptual level only and it did not provide an algorithm capable to construct the complex objects. The problem how to implement the database structures which are sufficient to optimize the computation of the predefined database operations is typical for the implementation of database systems based on the functional database model[22]. However, the advanced methodologies of functional database design[17,18,19] are more oriented towards the optimization of the number of functions than towards the investigation of optimal object structures.

The automatic generation of the structural scheme requires a number of assumptions about the signatures of methods, and the type constructors available for specification of the structural definitions of the object classes. The set of valid signatures includes the signatures of the multiargument methods whose domains are the collections of objects, such as:

```
price: engine,chassis,BrakeSystem,TransmissionSystem →real
```

and the signatures whose codomains are the sets of object sequences - tuples like:

```
evaluation: Student → ( Course, Grade )
```

Note, that we use a shorthand notation (A) to denote the powerset of the class A instead of the traditional *P*(A).

Any method that maps single objects into the tuples of objects and/or the values of atomic attributes may be easily "hard-wired" within the structural definition of the respective object classes. In such case, implementation of the method is a piece of code that accesses the appropriate components of objects. For instance the methods:

```
wheels:     car → ( wheel )
owner:      car → person
prod-date:  car → date
```

may be implemented as the associations among the instances of a class `car` and its components. To materialize this idea a class of objects `car` should be defined as follows:

```
car = [wheels:(wheel),owner:person, pdate:date]
```

Then, it is obvious that the respective methods may be implemented as:

```
wheels(c):      [return(c.wheels)]
owner(c):       [return(c.owner)]
prod-date(c):   [return(c.pdate)]
```

Unfortunately, there exist a large class of methods that can not be implemented in such trivial way. The methods whose domains include the sequences of objects and the methods that returns the sets of object tuples requires more sophisticated structures. In such case the implementation problems are caused by the assumption about the limited number of type constructors available for a specification of complex objects. In order to make our approach more practical and consistent with the commercially available object-oriented database systems we allow to use the "collection of ..." type constructor only. The implementation of the methods that maps the tuples of objects into a set of tuples of objects needs at least the "collection of sequence ..." type constructor. For instance the methods:

```
results:    car → (race, position)
place: Student,Course,Lecturer → Room
```

cannot be directly implemented as associations between the objects and their components. However, there exist a solution to this problem. It is possible to decompose the signatures of such methods into the valid signatures i.e. the signatures of more elementary methods that can be directly implemented within the structures of objects. Moreover, it is possible to generate the implementation of the methods such that they use the elementary methods in its computations. The aim of such decomposition is to obtain a set of normalized signatures where the domains are the collections of objects and the codomains are at most the sets of tuples built of objects or collections of single objects. The decomposition rules need to use the "construction" classes of objects in order to implement the normalized methods. For instance the rule that eliminates the tuples of objects from the arguments of method transforms a signature of method `place` into the signatures:

```
m1: Student → (C)
m2: C → Lecturer,Course,Room
```

and the following implementation of a method `place`:

```
place(s,l,c):[for all t in m1(s) do
                 if  (m2(t).Lecturer = l) and
                     (m2(t).Course = c) then
                        return(m2(t).Room); ]
```

The classes: `Student` and `C should` contain the following components:

```
Student = [m1: C, ...]
C = [m2(1):Lecturer,m2(2):Course,m3(3):Room, ...]
```

Then the methods m_1 and m_2 may be implemented as follows:

```
m1(s): [return(s.m1)]
m2(c): [return(c.m2(1),c.m2(2),c.m2(3)]
```

Another decomposition rule is required for the signatures whose codomains are the sets of object tuples. The decomposition process is followed by grouping the signatures with the same domains, generating of the respective object structures for each group, and the implementations of methods.

The rest of our paper is structured as follows. Section 2 introduces the modular object-oriented database model. The decompositions rules are defined in Section 3. Section 4 presents the algorithm for the design of structural scheme. The paper is concluded in Section 5.

2. Object-Oriented Database Model

Our definition of the object-oriented database model is consistent with the main principles of the object-oriented approach to database modelling. In order to satisfy the principle of data encapsulation and information hiding the model introduces two separate views of the database: the behavioural view and the structural view. As the consequence of this approach the database scheme consists of two separate schemes: the behavioural scheme, and the structural scheme. The model enforces two extensions in respect to the classical approach to object-oriented database modelling. The names of the behavioural schemes may play the role of the names of object classes and the methods may use as its arguments the objects from several different classes included within the behavioural scheme. Interpretation of the names of behavioural schemes as the names of object classes enforces the information hiding principle, and enables the specification of the multiple levels of abstraction within the object-oriented database scheme. On a particular level a structure of database is "visible" through the behavioural scheme as a collection of object classes and operators available to access and to manipulate the objects. The structural scheme includes a specification of object properties, a specification object components, an inheritance hierarchy, and the implementations of methods.

Definition 2.1

Let N be a set of names. We define a list of names as a sequence $C_1, ..., C_k$ where each $C_i \in N$ or C_i is a parenthesized list of names $(C_{i1}, ..., C_{ip})$.

∴

Definition 2.2

A valid signature is an expression s: X → Y where s is a signature name, X is a list of names such that $X = C_1, ..., C_k$ where each $C_i \in N$ and Y is a list of names.

∴

Definition 2.3

A valid polymorphic signature is an expression s: $X_1 \rightarrow Y_1 \mid ... \mid X_k \rightarrow Y_k$ were s is a signature name and each $X_i \rightarrow Y$ is a valid signature.

∴

Example 2.1

The signatures:

```
supervised-by: student, course → ( tutor )
price: engine,BrakeSystem,wheel → real
component: car→BrakeSystem,TransmissionSystem,(wheel)
```

are valid signatures, the signature:

```
name:   student → string| ...|tutor → string
```

is a valid polymorphic signature.

∴

Definition 2.4

A behavioural scheme **B** is defined as a system (C, I, S) where

(i) C is a nonempty set of class names,

(ii) I is a set of names of imported behavioural schemes,

(iii) S is a nonempty set of valid signatures of the methods defined over $C \cup I$.

∴

It is assumed that the imported behavioural schemes are visible to a database user as the names of object classes, unless a user do not wish to reveal their internal structure. We distinguish them from the names of object classes in order to emphasize that it is possible to access their structures whenever it is necessary to move into the lower level of abstraction in the object specification By default, the set of methods available for a given class of objects includes the signatures of the generic methods to *create* and *destroy* the objects as well as the methods to *pack* (encapsulate) and to *unpack* (reveal encapsulation) the objects.

Example 2.2

Consider the following hierarchy of the behavioural schemes for `TransCompany` object database.

$C_{TransCompany}$ = `{driver}`
$I_{TransCompany}$ = `{Vehicle}`
$S_{TransCompany}$ =
```
{owns:     driver → (Vehicle)
 owner:    Vehicle → driver
 name:     driver → string|Vehicle → string
 licence: driver → string
 registration: Vehicle → string}
```

The imported behavioural scheme `Vehicle` is defined as follows.

$C_{Vehicle}$ = `{engine,wheel,chassis}`
$I_{Vehicle}$ = `{BrakeSystem,TransmissionSystem}`
$S_{Vehicle}$ =
```
{colour:          chassis → string
 safety-factor:   BrakeSystem, wheel →real
 price:           engine,BrakeSystem,wheel →real
 suitable:        BrakeSystem →engine, wheel,
                                  TransmissionSystem}
```

The imported behavioural scheme `TransmissionSystem` is defined below.

$C_{TransmissionSystem}$ = `{clutch,gearbox,propeller-shaft, differential-gear}`
$I_{TransmissionSystem}$ = $\varnothing$
$S_{TransmissionSystem}$ =
```
{ match:   gearbox → propeller-shaft
  weight:  clutch → real|
           propeller-shaft →real|
           gear-box → real
  connected-to: clutch, gear-box →
                     differential-gear    }
```

We skip the specifications of the imported behavioural scheme `Brake-System` and all behavioural schemes imported into it.

∴

Definition 2.5

A structural definition of a class C is an expression:

$$C = [\, p_1 : t_1, ..., p_n : t_n \,] \text{ is-a } C_1, ..., C_k$$

where $C_1, ..., C_k$ are the names of classes such that class C inherits its properties from, $p_1, ..., p_n$ are the names of properties and components and $t_1, ..., t_n$ are the type expressions built over the names of elementary types, the names of classes, the names of behavioural schemes and the "collection of ..." type constructor denoted by ( ).

∴

Definition 2.6

A structural scheme S is a pair (D, P) where:

(i) D is a set of the structural definitions of the object classes for the respective classes in the behavioural scheme,

(ii) P is a set of routines being the implementations of the methods declared in S component of the respective behavioural scheme.

∴

Example 2.3

The structural scheme respective to the top level of behavioural scheme `TransCompany` is as follows.

```
D = {driver =   [name: string, owns: (Vehicle),
                licence: string, birth-date: date]
     Vehicle = [owner: driver, type: string, model:string,
                regs: string,component-1: engine,
                component-2: (wheel),component-3: chassis,
                internal-system-1: BrakeSystem,
                internal-system2: TransmissionSystem]
P = {   owns(d)  : [return(d.owns)],
        owner(v) : [return(v.owner)],
        name(d)  : [ if d is-a driver then
                          return(d.name)
                     else
                          return(d.type, d.model)
                     endif],
        licence(d): [return(d.licence)],
        registration(v): [return(v.regs)]}
```

∴

3. Decompositions

The implementation of the methods as associations among the objects impose the restrictions on the signatures of methods.The signatures of the methods that map single objects into the sets of object tuples are said to be Canonical Form signatures (CF-signatures). In general, not every valid signature is a CF-signature. This section introduces the decomposition rules of the valid signatures into CF-signatures and describes the implementations of the respective methods.

Definition 3.1

We say that a signature s is a CF-signature if and only if it is consistent with the pattern: s: C → Y where C is a class name and Y is a list of names such that each member of this list is either a name or parenthesized name.

∴

Definition 3.2 (domain decomposition rule)

Consider a signature s: X → Y where X, Y are the lists of names. The <u>domain decomposition rule</u> splits the left-hand side of the signature s and converts it into:

$$s_1: X' \to (C),$$
$$s_2: C \to X'',Y$$

where X" = X - X' and C is a name of construction class.

∴

Property 3.1

Consider a signature s and its domain decomposition into s_1, s_2. Let s_1 and s_2 satisfy the conditions:

(i) s_2. is an injective mapping of the construction class C into a set of object tuples: {z: if s(x) = y then z = <x.X",y>},

(ii) if s(x) = y then $\exists c \in s_1(x.X')$ $s_2(c).Y = y$ and $s_2(c).X'' = x.X''$.

Then the following routine is a correct implementation of a method s.

$$\begin{aligned}&s(x)\text{: [for all c in } s_1(x.X') \text{ do}\\ &\quad\text{if } s_2(c.X'') = x.X'' \text{ then}\\ &\quad\quad\text{return}(s_2(c).Y);]\end{aligned}$$

∴

Example 3.1

Consider a signature :

```
place: Student,Course,Lecturer → Room
```

such that a method place satisfies the following constraints:

```
place(Peter,DB,Paul)  = 125
place(Peter,AI,Mike)  = 256
place(Peter,DB,John)  = 40
place(Mary,DB,Paul)  = 125
place(Mary,DB,John)  = 40
```

Application of the domain decomposition rule yields the signatures:

```
m1: Student → (T)
m2: T → Lecturer,Course,Room
```

Preservation of the Property 3.1 requires the following construction objects, and the materializations of the methods m_1 and m_2:

```
m1( Peter )  =  {t1,t2,t3}
m1( Mary )  =  {t1,t3}
m2( t1 )  =  <DB,Paul,125>
m2( t2 )  =  <AI,Mike,256>
m2( t3 )  =  <DB,John,40>
```

Hence, a method `place` may be implemented as follows.

```
place(s,l,c):[for all t in m1(s) do
                if  (m2(t).Lecturer = l) and
```

```
(m2(t).Course = c) then
    return(m2(t).Room);]
```

∴

Definition 3.3 (codomain decomposition rule)

Consider a signature s : X → Y(Z) where X, Y, Z are the lists of names. The codomain decomposition rule splits the right-hand side of the signature s and converts it into:

$$s_1: X \rightarrow Y(C)$$
$$s_2: C \rightarrow Z'(Z'')$$

where Z"= Z - Z' and C is a name of construction class.

∴

Property 3.2

Consider a signature s and its codomain decomposition into s_1, s_2. Let s_1 and s_2 satisfy the conditions:

(i) s_2 is an injective mapping of construction class C into a set of object tuples:

$$\{z: \text{if } s(x) = z \text{ the } \exists z' \in z.Z',\ z'' = z.Z''\quad z = <z',z''>\}$$

(ii) if s(x) = z then

$$z = \cup_{c \in s1(x).C} <s_1(x).Y, s_2(c)>,$$

Then the following routine is an implementation of a method s.

s(x): [for all c in s_1(x).C) do
for all z in s_2(c).Z" do
return(s_1(x).Y, s_2(b).Z', z);]

∴

4. Design Algorithm

The algorithm presented in this section generates the structural definitions of the object classes using the specification of: methods, class names and inheritance hierarchy. It is assumed that a certain amount of fast cache-like memory is available for storing the objects.The objective of our algorithm is to find such structural definitions of object classes that the majority of the most intensively used classes will be stored in the cache memory. The design algorithm consist of two phases. The first one finds the optimal decomposition of the signatures into CF-signatures from the point of view of the best utilization of cache memory. The second phase uses the CF-signatures to generate the structural definition of the object classes, and the implementations of methods.

Definition 4.1

Let D be a set of all left-hand sides (domains) of the signatures in S. A minimal cover of D is denoted by *cover*(D) and defined as a set of class names used in L such that for each left-hand side d∈D there exists a class name c∈*cover*(D) which is used in d.

A set of all minimal covers of D is denoted by D^*.

∴

Algorithm 4.1

Input:

(i) A behavioural scheme (C, I, S) of object oriented database,

(ii) An inheritance relationship H, $C \times C \supseteq H$,

(iii) An estimated maximum number of objects n_c in each class $c \in C$,

(iv) A size of object identifier i_c for each class $c \in C$.

Output:

(i) The structural definitions of the classes in C,

(ii) The implementations of the methods defined in S.

Method:

Step 1.

Apply the information about inheritance of the methods to the definitions of polymorphic methods. For all pairs of classes (A, B) such that A inherits the properties and methods from B check whether exists a polymorphic signature s: $A \to Y|...|B \to Y$. Remove a variant $A \to Y$ from a polymorphic signature s.

Step 2.

Replace each polymorphic signature with the respective set of single signatures. For each polymorphic signature s: $X_1 \to Y_1|...|X_k \to Y_k$ construct a collection of signatures s_1: $X_1 \to Y_1$, ...,s_k: $X_k \to Y_k$ and the following implementation of the method s.

```
s(x): [ if x is X1 then return(s1(x));
        elseif x is X2 then return(s2(a));
        ...
        else return(sk(x));]
```

Step 3.

Consider a set of all CF-signatures S_a such that its codomain a list of atomic type names. Use all such signatures with the same domain c to find a size of data part d_c for the objects of class c. Remove the signatures in S_a from set S.

Step 4.

Use the codomain decomposition rule to eliminate the sets of object tuples from the codomains of the signatures in S.

Step 5.

Consider the domains D of all signatures in S and construct the set of minimal covers D^*.

Step 6.

For each minimal cover in find the collections of domain decompositions and compute the storage cost for each of them. The storage cost of the decomposition α is computed as summation of the storage costs of individual CF-signatures in α.

$$\text{cost}(\alpha) = \Sigma_{s \in \alpha} \text{cost}(s)$$

The storage cost of a signature s: $A \to B_1, ..., B_k$ is defined as

$$\text{cost}(s) = n_A{*}(d_A + \Sigma^k_{j=1} p_{B_j}{*}i_{B_j})$$

where n_A is an estimated maximum number of objects in class S, d_A is a size of data part in each object of class A, p_{Bj} is an estimated number of references to the objects of class B_j, and i_{Bj} is a size of object identifier in class B_j. The number of references to the objects of class B_j may be estimated in the following way. If B_j is a class name then p_{Bj}= 1, else if B_j is a parenthesized class name then in the worst case $p_{Bj}= n_{Bj}$.

Step 7.

Chose the decomposition such that its storage cost fits the best in a given cluster of cache memory.

Step 8.

Use the signatures in Sa and the CF-signatures selected in the previous step to construct the structural definitions of the object classes and generate the implementations of the methods using the properties 3.1, 3.2

∴

5. Summary

In this paper we have studied the automatic generation of the object database structures using the functional specification of the database domain. We discovered that an efficient implementation of methods needs decomposition of the signatures into more elementary one (CF-signatures) and the definition of construction classes of objects. The decomposition rules, and its impact on the implementation of methods and the algorithm for the design of object structures were presented. We can not deny that there exists several other factors related to the functional specification that may be taken under the consideration in order to enhance the design process, such as: the properties of methods, specification of methods with default and optional arguments, and more detailed specification of its semantics. The other extensions of the design algorithm which seem to be necessary include the consideration of more sophisticated mulilevel storage model, and the requirements regarding object clustering. We have studied here one special approach trying to minimize the number of information that should be provided on input to the design algorithm The extensions of this methodology may be a subject of a future paper.

6. Acknowledgement

This work was carried out by the Telecommunications Software Research Centre (TSRC) at the University of Wollongong, a centre of excellence funded by the Australian and Overseas Telecommunications Corporation (AOTC).

7. References

1. G. Atkinson et al., *Object-Oriented Database Manifesto*, Proceedings of the First International Conference on Deductive and Object-Oriented Databases, Kyoto, December, pp. 223-240, 1989
2. T. Atwood, *A Model Blueprint*, SunWorld, March, 1992
3. J. Banerjee et al., *Data Model Issues for Object-Oriented Applications*, ACM Transactions on Office Information Systems, vol. 5, Jan., 1987,
4. C. Beeri , *Formal Approach to Object-Oriented databases*, Proceedings of the First Deductive and Object-Oriented Databasc Conference, Kyoto, pp. 405-430, 1989
5. P. Butterworth, A. Otis, J. Stein, *The GemStone Object Database Management*

System, Communications of the ACM, vol. **34**, no. 10, pp. 65-77, 1991
6. W. Chen, D.S. Warren, *C-logic for complex objects*, Proceedings of the ACM SIGACT-SIGMOD-SIGART Symposium on Principles of Database Systems, March, 1989,
7. O. Deux et al., *The O_2 System*, Communications of the ACM, vol.**34**, no. 10, pp. 35-48, 1991
8. J. R. Getta, *Translation of Extended Entity-Relationship Database Model into Object-Oriented Database Model*, IFIP DS-5 Conference, Semantics of Interoperable Database Systems, Lorne, Australia, November, 1992.
9. J. Gray, F. Putzolu, *The 5 minute rule for trading memory for disc access and the 10 byte rule for trading memory for CPU time*, Proceedings of ACM SIGMOD Internat. Conference on Management of Data, pp. 134-146, 1987, pp.395-399,
10. I.T. Hawryszkiewycz, *Database Analysis and Design*, 2nd ed., MacMillan Publishing Company, 1991
11. M. Kifer, G. Lausen, *F-Logic, a Higher Order Language for Reasoning About Objects, Inheritance and Schemes*, Proceedings of ACM SIGMOD Internat. Conference on Management of Data, pp. 134-146, 1989,
12. C. Lamb et al., *The ObjectStore Database System*, Communications of the ACM, vol. **34**, no. 10, pp. 51-63, 1991
13. L.A. Maciaszek, *Database Design and Implementation*, Prentice Hall, 1990
14. D. Maier, *Why Isn't There an Object-Oriented Data Model ?*, Technical Report, Oregon Graduate Centre, May, 1989
15. F. Manola, S. Heiler, *An Approach to Interoperable Object Models*, Proceedings of the International Workshop on Distributed Object Management, Edmonton, Canada, August, 1992
16. D. Maier, J. Zhu, H. Ohkawa, *Features of the TEDM Object Model*, Proceedings of the First Deductive and Object-Oriented Database Conference, Kyoto,pp. 511-530, 1989
17. L. Orman, *Design Criteria for Functional Databases*, Information Systems, vol. **10**, no. 2, pp. 207-218, 1985
18. L. Orman, *Functional Data Model Design*, Information Systems, vol. **11**, no. 2, pp. 123-135, 1986
19. L. Orman, *Redundancy in Functional Databases*, Information Systems, vol **11**, no. 3, pp. 225-234, 1986
20. Z. Ozsoyoglu, L-Y Yuan, *A Normal Form for Nested Relations*, ACM Transactions on Database Systems, vol. **12**, no. 1, pp. 111-136, 1987
21. M.A. Roth, H.F. Korth, *The Design of non-1NF Relational Databases Into Nested Normal Form*, Proceedings of ACM SIGMOD Internat. Conference on Management of Data, pp. 143-159, 1987,
22. P. Shipman, *The Functional Data Model and the Data Language DAPLEX*, ACM Transactions on Database Systems, vol. **6**, no. 1, pp. 140-173, 1981
23. V.C. Storey, *Relational Database Design Based on the Entity-Relationship Model, Data and Knowledge Engineering*, vol. **7**, no. 1, pp. 47-83, 1991
24. T. Teorey, *Database Modelling and Design, The Entity-Relationship Approach*, ed. Morgan Kaufmann, 1990

25. J.A. Thom, K. Ramamohanarao, *Schema Design for Complex Objects, Research and Practical Issues in Databases*, Proceedings of the 3rd Australian Database Conference, Melbourne, February, pp. 66-80, 1992
26. *VERSANT, Product Profile*, Versant Object Technology, 1991
27. Y. Wand, *A Proposal for a Formal Model of Objects*, in Object-Oriented Concepts, Databases, and Applications, eds. Kim W., Lochowsky F.H., pp. 537-559, 1989
28. R.J. Wieringa, *A Formalization of Objects Using Equational Dynamic Logic*, Procedings Second Internat. Conf. Deductive and Object-Oriented Databases, December, 1991, pp.431-452

Mapping One-to-One Predicates to a Relational Schema

Peter R. Ritson and Terence A. Halpin

Key Centre for Software Technology
Department of Computer Science
University of Queensland
Australia 4072

Abstract

A One-to-One dependency between two object types is often considered the simplest form of dependency; as such, its relational implementation, including the enforcement of constraints, has often been over-simplified. Traditionally, a 1:1 dependency is grouped as a 1:*n* or *n*:1 dependency with a preference to favouring fewer null values. In fact other alternatives exist each with its own set of update, query and constraint enforcement anomalies. This paper investigates various alternatives for mapping 1:1 predicates to a relational schema and the problems encountered when implementing the resulting schema; guidelines are provided to assist in choosing the preferred relational database design.

Introduction

Conceptual design methods such as ORM (*O*bject-*R*ole *M*odelling) and ER (*E*ntity *R*elationship modelling) are based on identifying object types and the relationship types (*predicates*) connecting object types; a relational database stores instances of these fact types in such a way as to *eliminate* (or at least minimise) redundancies in stored facts. The success or failure of any relational design is dependent on identifying what relations (tables) are required and the enforcement of intra-table and inter-table constraints. The determination of tables is generally based on the type of dependencies between object types.

In the case of binary predicates, these dependencies are often described as one-to-one (1:1), one-to-many (1:*n*), many-to-one (*n*:1) or many-to-many (*m*:*n*); where the terms *many* and *one* can include the *zero* case. Since there are four general cases, two object types and each can include or exclude the zero case; there is a total of 16 (4*2*2) possible classes of binary fact types as shown in Table 1 (the notation *0/1* can be read as *zero-or-one*, e.g. 0/1:1 is read as (zero-or-one)-to-one).

Figure 1 shows the FORM (*F*act-based ORM) constraint patterns for the same 16 classes of binary fact types; the four general cases (given above) are identified by the intra-fact uniqueness constraint pattern (represented as bars above a predicate role(s)), and the explicit exclusion or inclusion of the zero case is identified by the explicit addition or omission of a mandatory role dot on the arc connected to an object type.

	0/1	1	0/n	n
0/1	0/1:0/1	0/1:1	0/1:0/n	0/1:n
1	1:0/1	1:1	1:0/n	1:n
0/m	0/m:0/1	0/m:1	0/m:0/n	0/m:n
m	m:0/1	m:1	m:0/n	m:n

Table 1 Classes of relationship [after Date 1990b, p. 431]

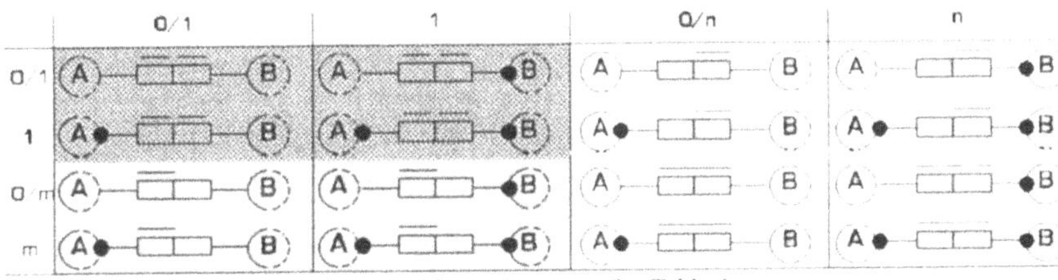

Figure 1 Classes of generic FORM binary fact types for Table 1

	0/1	1	0/n	n
0/1	A (a, b OP, ...) B (b, ...) OR A (a, ...) B (b, a OP, ...)	A (a, b OP, ...) B (b) OR A (a, ...) B (b, a)	A (a, ...) B (b, a OP, ...)	A (a, ...) B (b, a)
1	A (a, b) B (b, ...) OR A (a) B (b, a OP, ...)	A (a, b) B (b) OR A (a) B (b, a)	A (a) B (b, a OP, ...)	A (a) B (b, a)
0/m	A (a, b OP, ...) B (b, ...)	A (a, b OP, ...) B (b)	A (a, ...) AB (a, b) B (b, ...)	A (a, ...) AB (a, b) B (b)
m	A (a, b) B (b, ...)	A (a, b) B (b)	A (a) AB (a, b) B (b, ...)	A (a) AB (a, b) B (b)

Table 2 Some relational schema alternatives for Figure 1

The half-solid ellipse ◌ is a meta-symbol for any object type (in FORM solid ellipses denote entity types and broken ellipses denote value types). The optional roles shown in Figure 1 are truly optional, i.e. there must be some mandatory role (not shown) attached to the object type. Table 2 shows the relational schemas for the fact types of Figure 1; note that two alternatives are shown for 1:1 classes.

This paper focuses on the shaded portion of Table 1 since the mapping of the other classes have been well documented elsewhere [Teorey, Yang & Fry 1986; Elmasri & Navathe 1989; Date 1990a; Ritson & Halpin 1992]. In addition, the 0/1:1 class is obviously analogous to 1:0/1 (with the object types swapped); therefore three classes of the *general* 1:1 predicate will be examined: 0/1:0/1, 1:0/1 and the "*mandatory*" 1:1. The various alternatives for mapping these predicates to a relational schema are investigated; the advantages and disadvantages of each alternative is presented along with the difficulties of implementation (including the enforcement of constraints); and guidelines for selecting an alternative are given.

The unqualified notation *1:1* will be used to represent both the three *general* classes and the *mandatory* class. Where clarity or emphasis is required then the notation will be qualified. The unqualified notations 1:*n*, *n*:1 and *m*:*n* will always include the zero cases for *1*, *n* and *m*.

Mapping Alternatives for One-to-One Predicates

As shown above, there are three distinct classes of 1:1 binary predicates. Figure 2 shows examples of these where: every department is managed by *exactly one* manager and every manager manages *exactly one* department; a manager is assigned *exactly one* car and a car can be assigned to *at most one* manager (or may be generally available to any employee); and every department can have *at most one* logo (but might not have a logo) and a logo can belong to *at most one* department (or may belong to some other object type such as a local or state government). The metasymbol •! attached to Logo and Car depicts the presence of at least one mandatory role or that the object type is lazy (i.e. the object type may have instances that exist but do nothing else that we know about [Ritson & Halpin, 1992]).

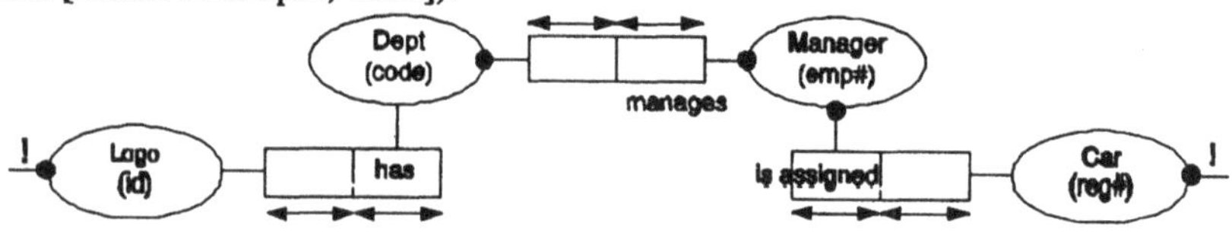

Figure 2 Three classes of 1:1 predicates

Traditionally, each 1:1 predicate is grouped as if it was a 1:n or a n:1 fact type where one object type becomes determinant and the other becomes dependent (i.e. one object type references the other object type). Which object type is "determinant" is generally based on minimising null values by favouring the object type which must participate, over the object type which may participate (Table 2 & Figure 3a & 3b). For the mandatory 1:1 and the 0/1:0/1 classes the decision is still arbitrary.

Alternatives in Figure 3, have been applied to the mandatory 1:1 predicate between Dept and Manager. The other two 1:1 predicates have been implemented in the same manner for all alternatives shown; in fact there are at least 24 distinct relational schema alternatives for Figure 2.

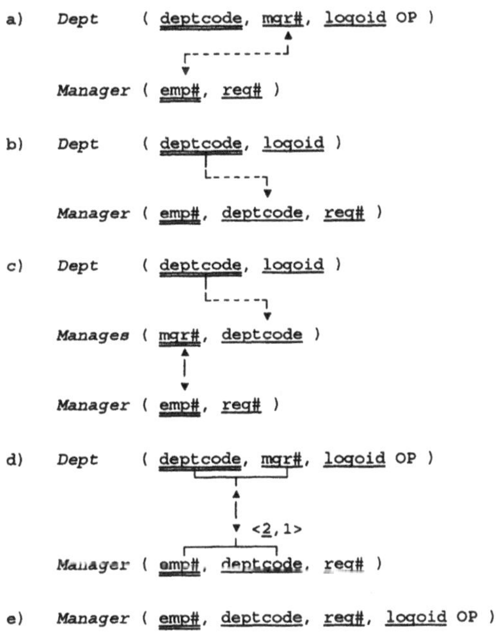

Figure 3 Relational schema alternatives for mandatory 1:1 predicate of Figure 2

One author [Shoval 1991] has identified other criteria and presented a detailed set of decision rules for handling all three classes but still restricts implementation to either a 1:n or a n:1 solution. The preference criteria identified (in decreasing order of importance) include: fewer number of tables (unless at least two additional *hierarchical links*); greater number of *hierarchical links*; determinant is also part of a primary key in another relation; and determinant is also foreign key to another relation. The decision rules are based on what other types of relationships (n:1, 1:n and m:n) are involved with each object type. Mandatory and optional roles are ignored as are the *absolute number* of different dependency types (although the *summary* does state that this last factor is probably irrelevant). If either of these factors are included then the number of links could be affected and the method invalidated; also no proof is given that the preferred alternative is in fact the best in all 64 cases examined (only a generalisation for fewer tables and more links). Appendix I gives two cases where the method is invalid.

Date [1990b] also addressed the problem and indirectly introduced two more alternatives. Firstly, for 0/1:0/1 predicates, implement as a *m:n* fact type (i.e. generate a separate table) (Figure 3c) although this seemed to be the result of simply needing to focus on the 1:1 predicate and not as a general alternative for 1:1 predicates (in fact Date referred to the resulting table as expressing '... a combination of two (zero-or-one)-to-one relationships ...'[p. 435]). Secondly, for the mandatory 1:1, implement as two fact types; one being a *n*:1 the other a 1:*n* (i.e. each object type references the other object type) (Figure 3d).

Teorey, Yang and Fry [1986] implement 0/1:0/1 and 1:1 as either *n*:1 or 1:*n* and a 0/1:1 as a 1:*n*. They also suggest the possibility of implementing a general 1:1 as two fact types (1:*n* and *n*:1).

Another alternative sometimes advocated from the point of view of minimising relations based on functional dependencies (and briefly noted by Elmasri & Navathe [1989 p. 330]) is to group *related* (via common object types) 1:1 predicates into the same table. This is demonstrated in Figure 3e where Manager is chosen as the determinant.

A more recent text [Batini, Ceri & Navathe 1992, pp318-20] advocates the grouping alternative for mandatory 1:1 predicates; and the single many-to-many alternative for the other classes of 1:1 predicates in order to avoid null values.

Five alternatives have been identified for mapping 1:1 predicates:

i) *Single many-to-one*; group 1:1 predicate as if it was a *n*:1 fact type.
ii) *Single one-to-many*; group 1:1 predicate as if it was a 1:*n* fact type.
iii) *Single many-to-many*; group 1:1 predicate as if it was a *m*:*n* fact type.
iv) *Duplicate*; group 1:1 predicate as if it was two fact types (a *n*:1 and a 1:*n*).
v) *Group*; group 1:1 predicates with a common object type(s) into the same table.

These alternatives are examined in relation to the three distinct classes of 1:1 predicates.

Towards a Preferred Relational Schema

When selecting a preferred relational schema a number of (often conflicting) criteria should be addressed in order to avoid information loss (data or constraints), data redundancy, or insertion/modification/deletion anomalies. Preference criteria include: minimum number of tables; minimum number of null values; and maximum number of easily enforced conceptual constraints.

Minimum Number of Tables

Fewer tables usually implies: fewer inter-table constraints to enforce; fewer joins to retrieve information; and fewer insertion, modification and deletion anomalies to avoid. It is assumed that the same level of normalisation and constraint enforcement is maintained.

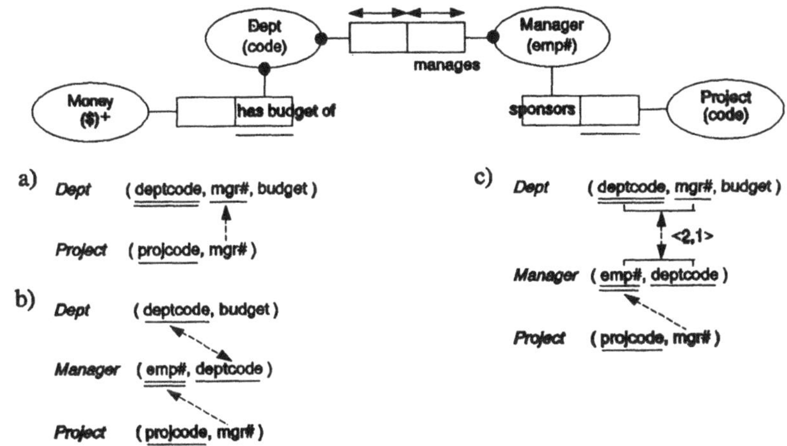

Figure 4 Minimising number of tables

Figure 4 shows three solutions for implementing the given schema. Solution (a) represents mapping alternatives (i) and (v); solution (b) represents alternatives (ii) and (iii); and solution (c) represents alternative (iv). Solution (a) offers the following advantages over solutions (b) and (c):

- The mandatory roles for Dept are enforced by intra-table constraints in (a); whereas an inter-table equality constraint needs to be enforced in (b).
- To obtain all non-project information for a department (i.e. budget and manager), only one table needs to be accessed in (a) and (c); whereas a table join is required in (b).
- To obtain all information on departments including any projects (derived fact via Manager), two tables need to be joined in (a) and (c); whereas three tables need to be joined in (b).
- To insert a new department, details are inserted into only one table for (a); whereas insertions into two tables are required for (b) and (c).
- Insertion, modification and deletion anomalies for Dept are avoided in (a); whereas (b) and (c) could lead to some departments (or department-manager combinations in the case of (c)) in Dept not existing in Manager or some departments (or department-manager combinations) in Manager not existing in Dept unless the following constraints are implemented:
  foreign key reference clause for Dept
  foreign key reference clause for Manager
  update and delete rules to enforce *cascades* or *restricted* updates and deletes in both Dept and Manager;
  Note this implies support for cyclic references; references to non-primary key columns; and, in the case of (c), references to combined columns which would require redundant unique clauses.

The number of tables can only be decreased if all functional roles for an object type are mapped to other object types either by implementing 1:1 predicates as 1:n predicates or by grouping (alternatives (i), (ii) or (v)).

Maximum Number of Conceptual Constraints Easily Enforced

Enforcement of all conceptual constraints minimises the possibility of information loss. If a constraint can not be enforced then insertion, modification or deletion anomalies may occur. Generally intra-table constraints are easier to enforce (e.g. by null support clauses, primary and unique keys, check clauses, or unique indexes) than inter-table constraints (e.g. by foreign key references, delete and update rules, and pre-tested or post-tested triggers).

Note that this criterion differs from Shoval's maximum number of hierarchical links, in that intra-table constraints are also included, not just inter-table links.

In Figure 4, Solution (a) would be preferred since most conceptual constraints are easily enforced by intra-table techniques. Enforcement of the subset constraint requires support for both foreign key references and associated rules for update and deletion (i.e. full support for referential integrity to candidate keys); or some facility to manually enforce this constraint. Enforcement of the equality constraint in Solutions (b) and (c) will also require support for cyclic references (and associated rules for update and deletion) (i.e. ANSI SQL2).

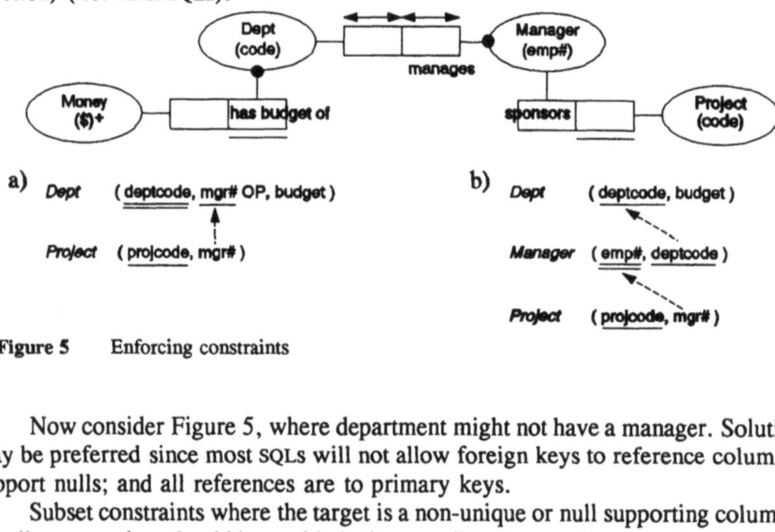

Figure 5 Enforcing constraints

Now consider Figure 5, where department might not have a manager. Solution (b) may be preferred since most SQLs will not allow foreign keys to reference columns that support nulls; and all references are to primary keys.

Subset constraints where the target is a non-unique or null supporting column, and equality constraints should be avoided when possible since enforcement is often difficult with existing SQL facilities.

Minimum Number of Null Values

By decreasing the number of null values or eliminating the need to support nulls on the foreign key, then: developer and user errors in working with nulls are reduced; equality constraints are usually replaced by subset constraints; and all anomalies related to support of null values are minimised or eliminated (see Ritson & Halpin [1991] or Halpin & Ritson [1990, 1992] for a discussion on supporting null values). In addition, storage space may also be decreased. This is generally achieved by favouring mandatory roles over optional roles as in Solution (a) of Figure 6.

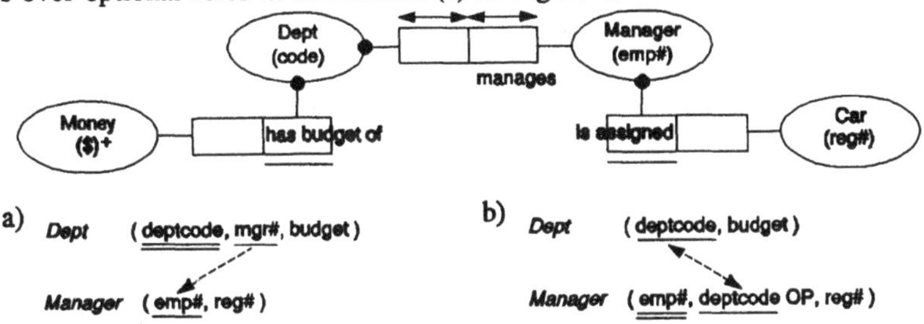

Figure 6 Minimising number of nulls

A Preferred Relational Schema

Selecting a preference based on the above three criteria is not always straight forward. For example, in Figure 5 solution (a) has fewer tables but requires support of null values and a subset constraint to a column supporting nulls; whereas solution (b) is easily implemented with foreign key reference clauses and non-null columns.

In addition to the general selection criteria given above, the target SQL may need to be considered. For example, DB2 only supports PRIMARY KEY constraints and not UNIQUE column constraints; and FOREIGN KEY specifications must reference primary keys. The ANSI SQL2 standard, on the other hand, requires any column mentioned in a PRIMARY KEY or UNIQUE clause to be declared as NOT NULL; and FOREIGN KEY clauses must reference a primary key or unique column list. Non-supported facilities need to be manually implemented and difficulties in enforcement may affect selection of alternative.

Possible 1:1 Cases

When considering a solution to a given 1:1 predicate, one must consider mandatory and optional participation in the 1:1 predicate and the existence of other mandatory or optional functional roles. It is shown later that existence of non-functional roles is generally irrelevant.

Either of the two object types involved may or may not have other functional roles attached. Since more than one additional functional role does not affect the number of tables (only the number of columns in the key-table) the possibility of more than one additional functional role need not be considered.

Where an object type has another functional role attached then either both, one or none of the roles may be mandatory; this gives 2^2 (4) possible mandatory role configurations on the object type. If an active object type has no other functional role attached then its optionality in the 1:1 predicate gives only one (1) possibility. The total number of possibilities for any 1:1 predicate is therefore 25 ($\{2^2+1\}*\{2^2+1\}$) since two object types are involved. These possibilities are shown in Figure 9 to Figure 11, where Case 1 and Cases 6-9 are symmetrical and each of the other cases represent 2 possibilities with the object types reversed.

Cases 1, 4, 5, 8, 9 and 15 represent the mandatory 1:1 class; cases 6, 7 and 10 represent the 0/1:0/1 class; the other cases (2, 3, 11-14) represent the 0/1:1 class (or the 1:0/1 class when reversed). These cases reveal a number of trends:

- When one object type has no other functional roles attached (Cases 1-5) then Option 3 (*m:n*) is identical to applying Option 2 (1:*n*) to the other object type; and Option 5 (*Group*) is identical to applying Option 1 (*n*:1) to the other object type.
- With a symmetrical structure (Case 1 and cases 6-9) Option 1 and Option 2 are equivalent with respect to number of tables and constraint pattern.
- Option 3 always avoids null values for the 1:1 predicate but produces the largest number of tables (except for Case 1) and requires a decision on primary key.
- Option 4 always increases the number of constraints; leads to possible update anomalies; and involve inter-table equality constraints.
- Option 5 is not possible with the 1/0:1/0 class (Cases 6, 7 and 10) since both candidate keys must support nulls.
- Option 5, when supported, always results in the minimum number of tables but: requires a decision on primary key; loses the fact that the two entities are distinct; and leads to more than one entity represented by a table.

Considering these trends and the previous criteria, Option 1 can be regarded as the preferred alternative in all cases as defined. For the non-symmetrical cases (cases 2-5 and 10-15) Option 2 would be the preferred alternative for the reversed possibility.

Effects of Non-functional Roles

When non-functional roles are considered then each object type may have both functional and non-functional roles attached; functional roles only; non-functional roles only; or no other non-referential roles. Since more than one non-functional role simple adds additional tables to all options, the possibility of more than one non-functional role need not be considered.

Where both a non-functional and a functional role are attached then 2^3 (8) possible mandatory role configurations exist for the object type. The total number of possibilities for any 1:1 predicate is therefore increased from 25 to 289 ($\{2^3+2^2+2^2+1\}*\{2^3+2^2+2^2+1\}$). Since the same additional tables and constraints are added to all options, the effect of non-functional roles can generally be ignored.

The only exception to this rule is where a non-functional role is attached to an active object type with no functional roles except a mandatory 1:1 predicate which is optional for the other object type Figure 7. This occurs in 12 (of the possible 289) cases which are all extensions to either Case 2 or Case 3 of Figure 9. In these cases a subset or equality constraint is required to the null supporting candidate key of Option 1; if Option 2 is chosen then the subset or equality constraint will reference a primary key.

In Figure 7 the hollow mandatory role dot is a meta-symbol for mandatory or optional role; the relational schemas shown represent optional non-functional roles and a mandatory functional role for object type A.

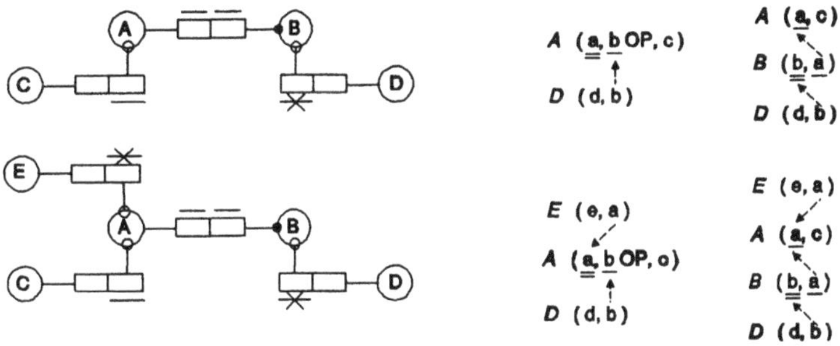

Figure 7 Generic cases for non-functional roles

Choosing a Preferred Solution

The preferred solution for a 1:1 predicate varies depending on the objectives of the relational mapping. If the objective of the mapping is simply to achieve the minimum number of tables then the preferred option for each case is shown in the following table where ● denotes preferred option; ¤ denotes comparable option ; and cases 2' and 3' refer to the extended cases involving non-functional roles.

Case	1	2	2'	3	3'	4	5	6	7	8	9	10	11	12	13	14	15
opt 1	●	●	●	●	●	●	●	●	●			●					
opt 2	¤							¤	¤								
opt 3	¤																
opt 4																	
opt 5	¤	¤	¤	¤	¤	¤	¤			●	●		●	●	●	●	●

If the objective is to avoid null values for primary and alternate keys without grouping other functional roles then the preferred options are:

Case	1	2	2'	3	3'	4	5	6	7	8	9	10	11	12	13	14	15
opt 1	●					●	●			●	●		●	●	●	●	●
opt 2	¤	●	●	●	●					¤	¤						
opt 3	¤	¤	¤	¤	¤			●	●			●					
opt 4																	
opt 5	¤	¤		¤		¤	¤										

If the objective is to achieve minimum number of tables without grouping other functional roles of different object types into the same table and to avoid foreign key references to columns supporting nulls (where possible), then the preferred options are:

Case	1	2	2'	3	3'	4	5	6	7	8	9	10	11	12	13	14	15
opt 1	●	●		●		●	●	●	●	●	●	●	●	●	●	●	●
opt 2	¤		●		●			¤	¤	¤	¤						
opt 3	¤		¤		¤												
opt 4																	
opt 5	¤	¤		¤		¤	¤										

This last objective represents the safest and can be achieved by the following decision algorithm:

If no functional roles exist for either object type then create a separate table (case 1);
else if only one object type is mandatory and it plays other roles, then group on that object type (cases 2', 3' and 11-14);
else if only one object type has functional roles then group on that object type (cases 2-5);
else if the mandatory role constraints are symmetrical then group on either object type (cases 6-9);
else group on the object type with the mandatory functional role (cases 10 and 15).

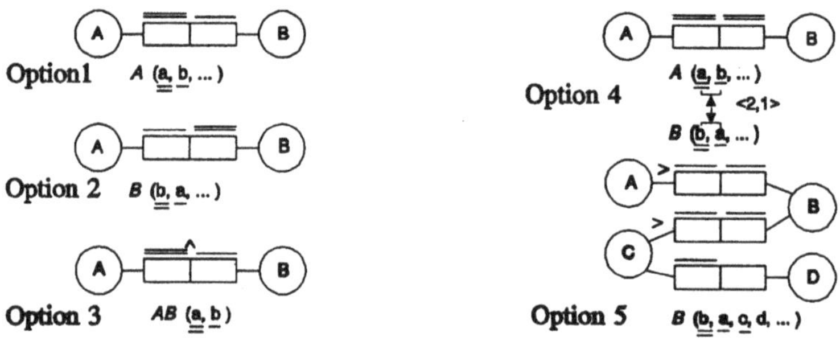

Figure 8 1:1 implementation notation

Effect on Rmap

The current Rmap algorithm [Ritson & Halpin 1992] includes a *Step 0* which is designed to prepare a conceptual schema for mapping. The following needs to be a component of this step:

- *Identify grouping preference for 1:1 predicates.*

This can be achieved by applying a decision algorithm and adding *implementation* notation (used for mapping decisions only) to a conceptual schema as shown in Figure 8. In Option 4 the notation also highlights the primary identifier. The '>' (or '<') notation in Option 5 signifies that all functional fact types of this object type are to be directed towards the other object type. This implementation notation must then be recognised during steps 1, 2 and 3 of the mapping algorithm.

Summary

This paper has presented the various alternatives for mapping 1:1 predicates to a relational schema. Problems associated with the various options have been identified and solutions given. In general:

- a mandatory 1:1 predicate can be grouped with either object type except when only one object type has no other functional roles in which case it should be grouped with the object type with additional functional role(s);
- a 0/1:0/1 predicate can be grouped with either object type except when only one object type has a mandatory functional role in which case it should be grouped for that object type; and
- a 1:0/1 predicate should be grouped with the object type that is mandatory except when only one object type has no other roles in which case it should be grouped with the object type with additional role(s).

These guidelines however, are dependent on the SQL facilities available for implementation and the personal preferences of a user. Other issues which may affect these guidelines such as the roles being played by lazy objects or being involved in other constraints (e.g. exclusion, equality or subset constraints) are the subject of further research.

References

ANSI/X3/SPARC 1975: 'Study Group on Data Base Management Systems Interim Report', *SIGMOD FDT Bull*, 7(2) 1975.

Batini, C.; Ceri, S. and Navathe, S.B. 1992: *Conceptual Database Design*, Benjamin/Cummings, Redwood CA.

Date, C.J. 1986: *Relational Database: Selected Writings*, Addison-Wesley, Reading MA.

Date, C.J. 1989: *A Guide to the SQL Standard*, 2nd edn, Addison-Wesley, Reading MA.

Date, C.J. 1990a: *Relational Database: Writings 1985-1989*, Addison-Wesley, Reading MA.

Date, C.J. 1990b: *An Introduction to Database Systems: Volume I*, 5th edn, Addison-Wesley, Reading MA.

Date, C.J. 1992a: *Relational Database: Writings 1989-1991*, Addison-Wesley, Reading MA.

Elmasri, R. and Navathe, S.B. 1989: *Fundamentals of Database Systems*, Benjamin/Cummings, Redwood CA.

Halpin, T.A. and Ritson, P.R. 1990: 'Entity Integrity: A Closer Look', *Technical Report 196*, Key Centre for Software Technology, University of Qld.

Halpin, T.A. and Ritson, P.R. 1992: 'Fact-Oriented Modelling and Null Values', *Proc. 3rd Australian Database Conference*, Melbourne (Feb).

Ritson, P.R. and Halpin, T.A. 1991: 'A Practical Approach to Nulls', *Technical Report 206*, Key Centre for Software Technology, University of Qld.

Ritson, P.R. and Halpin, T.A. 1992: 'Mapping Conceptual Constraints to a Relational Schema', *Technical Report 223*, Key Centre for Software Technology, University of Qld.

Shoval, P. 1991: 'One-to-One Dependencies in Database Design', *IEE Transactions on Knowledge and Data Engineering*, 3(3):371-9 (Sep).

Teorey, T.J.; Yang, D. and Fry, J.P. 1986: 'A Logical Design Methodology for Relational Databases Using Extended Entity-Relationship Model', *Computing Surveys*, 18(2):197-222 (Jun).

Case	FORM Configuration	Option 1 (*n*:1)	Option 2 (1:*n*)	Option 3 (*m*:*n*)	Option 4 (*n*:1 & 1:*n*)	Option 5 (group)
1	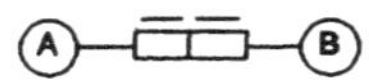	*A* (a, b)	*B* (b, a)	*AB* (a, b)	*A* (a, b) *B* (b, a)	*AB* (a, b)
2	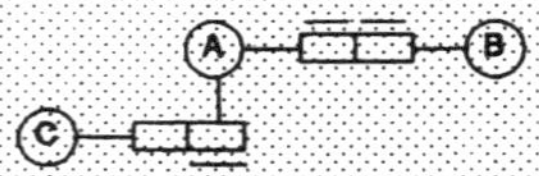	*A* (a, b OP[1], c OP[1]) [1] ∃ non-null in {b,c}	*A* (a, c) *B* (b, a)	*A* (a, c) *AB* (a, b)	*A* (a, b OP[1], c OP[1]) 2 *B* (b, a) [1] ∃ non-null in {b,c} [2] where b is non-null	*AB* (a, b OP[1], c OP[1]) [1] ∃ non-null in {b,c}
3	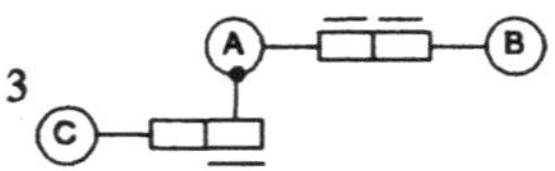	*A* (a, b OP, c)	*A* (a, c) *B* (b, a)	*A* (a, c) *AB* (a, b)	*A* (a, b OP, c) 1 *B* (b, a) [1] where b is non-null	*AB* (a, b OP, c)
4	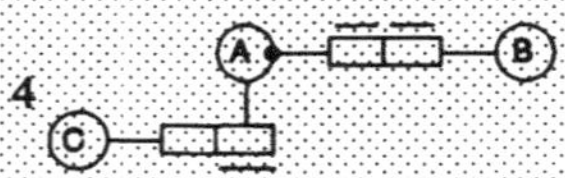	*A* (a, b, c OP)	*A* (a, c) *B* (b, a)	*A* (a, c) *AB* (a, b)	*A* (a, b, c OP) *B* (b, a)	*AB* (a, b, c OP)
5	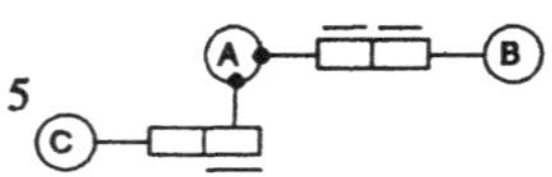	*A* (a, b, c)	*A* (a, c) *B* (b, a)	*A* (a, c) *AB* (a, b)	*A* (a, b, c) *B* (b, a)	*AB* (a, b, c)

Figure 9 Possible 1:1 cases

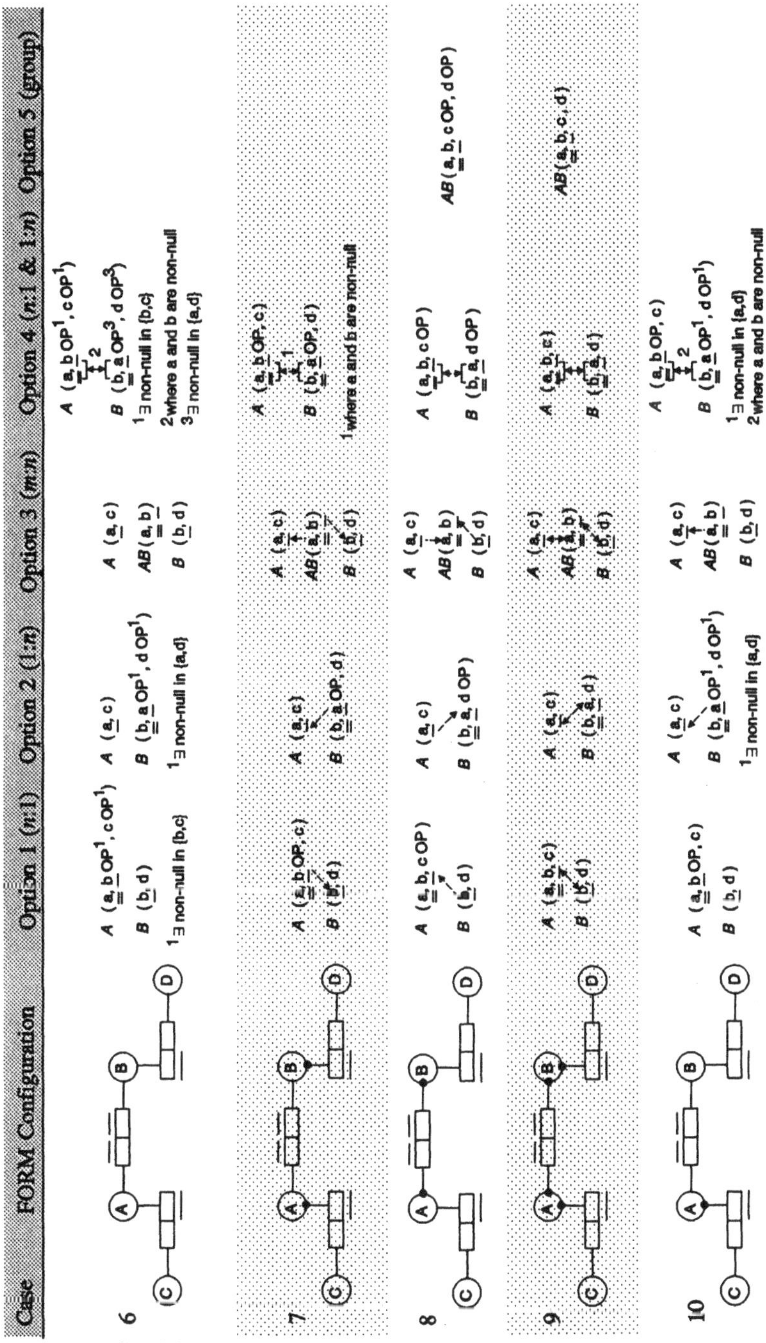

Figure 10 Possible 1:1 cases cont.

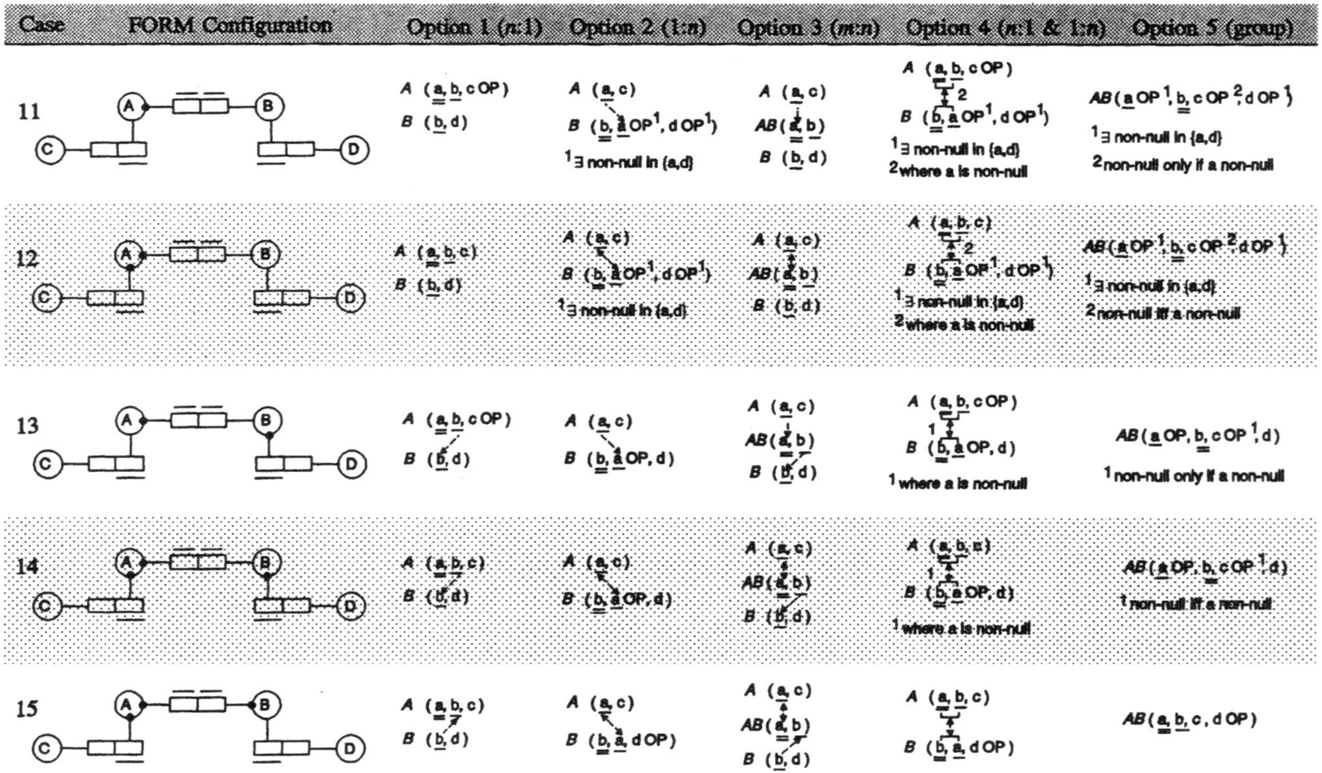

Figure 11 Possible 1:1 cases cont.

Appendix I: Shoval's 1:1 Dependencies Decision Rules

Shoval [1991] offers a detailed set of decision rules for handling 1:1 predicates based on what other types of relationships (n:1, 1:n and m:n) are involved with each object type. Besides ignoring the effect of the implementation of other 1:1 relationships, the effects of mandatory and optional roles are also ignored leading to an incomplete and in fact invalid set of results.

As an example of the effects of mandatory and optional roles, consider Shoval's Case (2) (Figure I.1) which he presents as a example of a symmetrical solution with no preference since both involve two tables and one hierarchical link. Shoval defines a hierarchical link as a connection between record types which have key to foreign key associations.

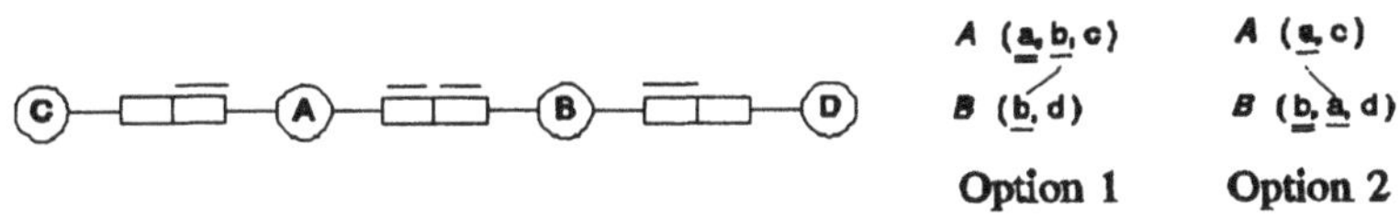

Figure I.1 Shoval's Case (2) for 1:1 fact types

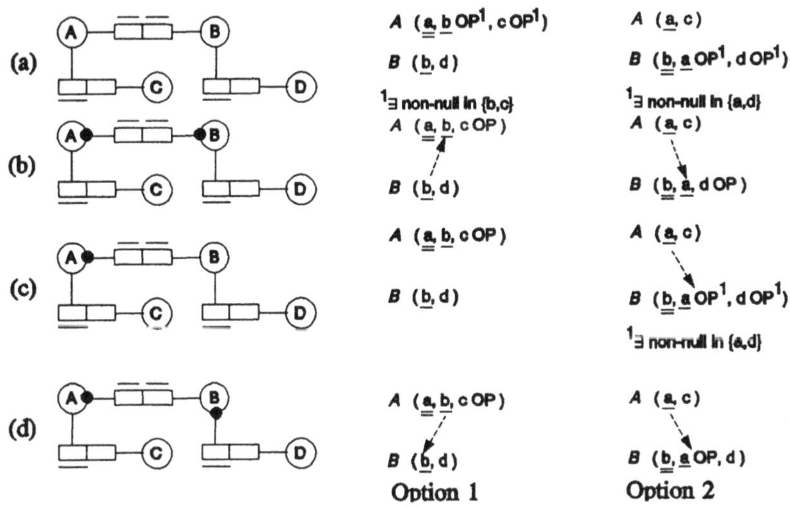

Figure I.2 Shoval's Case (2) with mandatory and optional roles

If all roles are optional and A and B are active then the correct relational solution involves the implementation of two mandatory disjunct constraints (one for each object type) as shown in Figure I.2a. If mandatory roles are included then different solutions are obtained as shown in Figure I.2. Solutions (a) and (b) are symmetrical, however solutions (c) and (d) are not (option 1 should be chosen in both cases since option 2 involves a foreign key reference to a null supporting candidate key). There are in fact 16 possible combinations of mandatory and optional roles for Shoval's Case (2) of which only 4 are symmetrical.

As a further example of the importance of mandatory and optional roles consider Shoval's Case (18) (Figure I.3) which favours option 1 since it has more links. If all roles are optional and A and B are active then the mandatory disjunctions on A and B are enforced by the table structures; therefore the links are meaningless and option 2 (Figure I.4a) may be preferred since there are fewer tables. If the 1:1 is mandatory for both A and B then option 2 (Figure I.4b) is the preferred option.

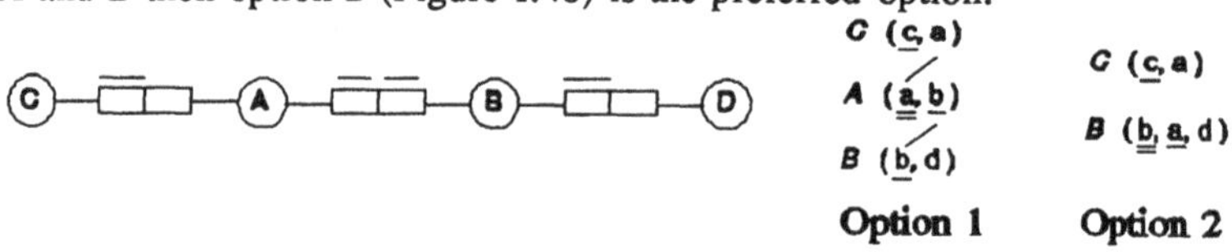

Figure I.3 Shoval's Case (18) for 1:1 fact types

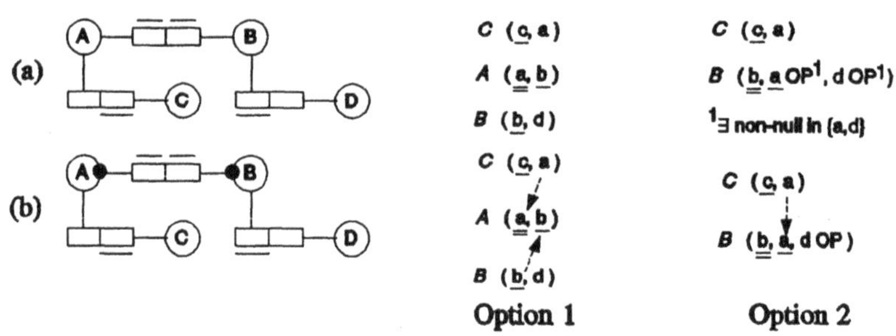

Figure I.4 Shoval's Case (18) with mandatory and optional roles

Shoval's set of decision rules has been shown to be incomplete and, in some cases, invalid. However the technique is of merit and requires further examination.

A design process of databases based on a fuzzy object-oriented approach

Annie CAVARERO
Université de Nice - Sophia Antipolis, I3S, CNRS-URA 1376
250 Avenue Albert Einstein, Sophia-Antipolis 06560 Valbonne, France

and

Carlos GONZALEZ
Instituto Tecnológico de Costa Rica
Departamento de Computación, Apartado 159-7050,Cartago, Costa Rica

ABSTRACT

A design process of databases, based upon a fuzzy object-oriented approach, is presented in this paper. The first goal of this process is to help the designer in the elaboration of a schema (object module). Each object module represents a part of an information system for a given designer. From these modules, the second goal of this process is to obtain an unified object model. If a traditional method is used, a single global representation of the information system is expected to be obtained. However, this approach is usually complex and intuitive, because the information is in many cases uncertain and imprecise. So, we introduce a design tool and an unification tool which use the inference and knowledge representation power of the fuzzy methodology approach.

1. Introduction

There are two major problems in an application design: to give a correct view of the real world and to find a consensus between the different designers.

The work reported here is a contribution to resolve these points, called respectively design process and unification of conceptual schemata. The design step is quite complex and often intuitive. We obtain most often several representations of the real world. Then, much time is spend to build one view from these representations. In the literature it is possible to find several schema unification methodologies [3, 11, 15, 16, 27] based upon common criteria such as naming and structural conflicts. All use the entity-relationship model or some extension to it. At present time, the object oriented approach is more and more used in the design process. In this paper we present a design process built upon a such approach. It includes an unification process because we want take in account all the descriptions of an application. Nevertheless, it is very hard to obtain only one sure result. To keep the different views in an unique resulting schema and to conserve the different conflicts, we use the notion of *fuzzy object class*. Like the other authors, we also retain a semantic approach. In order to facilate the process, we introduce the concepts of *general application*, that is, a set of general object classes, and *proximity coefficient* between these general classes and the different classes of object modules.

The paper is structured as follows. In section 2, we introduce the object-oriented model retained and the fuzzy logic concepts used.

Section 3 presents the principles which are the tools for the design and unification of objects modules.

We show in section 4 how we use these different concepts in the design process.

The steps which constitute the unification process are presented in section 5. This process may be automated but it must be interactive. For instance, when there are conflicts unresolved by the rules of the automatic system, the system asks for the designer's point of view. At the end of the process, we obtainied an unified object model.

Finally, the conclusions are presented in the section 6.

One important remark can be made upon the use of the different concepts. In the design of a schema, it is necessary to verify that there are no redundancies. So the concepts use in the unification process, are also used in the design process.

2. Basic concepts

In this section we present some concepts of fuzzy logic and object oriented approach.

It exists two main ways to use the fuzzy concepts in the object oriented. On one hand in the object class attributes when we associate fuzzy values to the attributes. On the other hand we can represent with the fuzzy concept, partial inheritance between objects classes. This inheritance form is used when there is multiple inheritance.

First, we introduce the concept of fuzzy set. Let X be a set, we say that $A := \{ (x, \mu_A(x)) / x \in X \}$ is a *fuzzy set* of X, where $\mu_A : X \rightarrow [0,1]$ is the *membership function*. The *possibility distribution* Π_A is the fuzzy set of the possible values of A.

Example. Let X = { Peter, Paul, George, Jean } the set of employees in an organisation. From this set we can define some fuzzy sets. For example, if we have "the age of a person", we can create the fuzzy set A : = { (Peter, 0.2), (Paul, 0.5), (George, 0.55), (Jean, 0.3) }of the age of persons. From this set, it is possible to deduce some conclusions : for example, if we consider that a person with 65 years or more has a coefficient equal to 1 and that a baby has a coefficient equal to 0, then Peter is the youngest, Paul and George have nearly the same age and so on. In addition, for this set, we can define other characteristics for these persons, for example, efficiency, charm, etc.

With this idea it is possible to translate the imprecise expression of facts, given by the users.

We now define the concept of fuzzy binary relation. Let X,Y be two subsets in U (universal set). We say that the set $R := \{ (x,y;\mu_R(x,y)) / (x,y) \in X \times Y \}$ is a *fuzzy binary relation* in $X \times Y$ [31], where $\mu_R(x,y)$ is the membership function $X \times Y \rightarrow [0,1]$

In the case where X and Y are finite sets, we can represent a relation by a matrix. If X and Y are finite sets, we can represent a fuzzy binary relation via a matrix.

Example. Let X = Y = {Ann, Beatrice, Charles, Mary}. Let R : "X is much older than Y", we can represent this situation as in Fig. 1.

In the object-oriented approach, the principal concept is the object. An *object* represents a concrete or abstract thing which is an element of a given application [23]. This object is defined by a description and a behavior. The description is made from values taken by this object in a set of *attributes* and its behaviour from values taken in a set of *operations* [14].

A *fuzzy object class (foc)* X is an object whose members have the same attributes and operations. Additionally, each foc has a *determinant*, Det_X. So, an object is an occurence of a foc described by the values of attributes and operations and located via the determinant.

Buckles and Petry [7] introduced the concept of *fuzzy relational database* (see also [18, 19, 26]), which is a set of *fuzzy* relations, each of them being a set of *fuzzy tuples*, that is, a set of tuples where each component is a set of values and not an atomic value as in relational databases. An attribute or an operation from a foc can be seen as a fuzzy tuple.

The graphic representation for a foc is presented in Fig. 2., and the textual representation for a foc X is : $X = (Det_X;\ A_1=\{...\},...,\ A_n=\{...\}\ ;\ O_1=\{...\},...,\ O_m=\{...\}\ )$.

Fig.1. Example of a fuzzy binary relation

	Ann	Betty	Charles	Mary
Ann	0	.3	0	.7
Betty	0	0	0	.2
Charles	.5	.7	0	1
Mary	0	0	0	0

Fig. 2. Representation of a foc

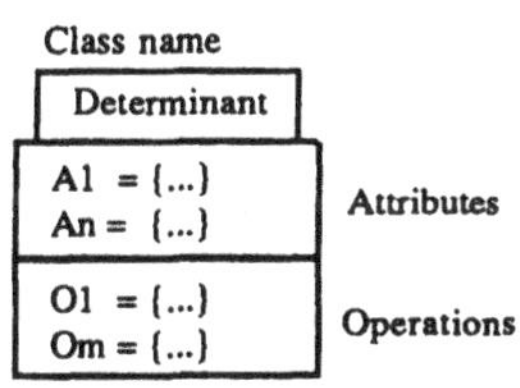

Remarks.

a) The notation $A_i = \{...\}$ means that the attribute A_i is represented by a *fuzzy tuple*, that is, a collection of subsets of values which characterize this attribute.

b) The *determinant* (Det_X) is a set of parameters which determines the characteristics of X [10].

c) The foc determinants inside an conceptual schema are unique, except in the case of a generalization where the focs have the same determinant.

Example. Consider a *Sales* system with the focs: *Supplier*, *Customer*, *Hi-fi*, *Invoice*, and *Writing-desk*. In this application we can build the determinants of the object classes with the following parameters :

Object type = {person ; artificial person ; concrete thing ; abstract thing } ;

Object communication = {input, output, invisible }

Object information support = { document, record, microfilm, file } ;

Object position = { internal to system, external to system, produced by system };

Now, according to these parameters, we find the object class determinants :

$Det_{Supplier}$ = [{person 0.2, artificial person 0.8} ; {input 1} ; { } ; {external

0.9}]

$Det_{Customer}$ = [{person 0.8, artificial person 0.2} ; {input 1 , output 1} ; { } ; {internal 0.01, external 0.9}]

$Det_{Hi\text{-}fi}$ = [{concrete thing 1} ; {invisible 1} ; { } ; {internal 1}]

$Det_{Writing\ desk}$ = [{concrete thing 1} ; {invisible 1} ; { } ; {internal 1}]

$Det_{Invoice}$ = [{concrete thing 1} ; {input 1, output 1} ; {document 1, record 0.8} ; {produced by system 1, external to system 1}].

When we compare these determinants we find that object classes *Hi-fi* and *Writing desk* have the same determinant. So, it may be possible to compare these classes (cf. Section 5) and eventually to create one object class.

The attributes of a foc are described by a set of properties named *attribute configuration* (definition domain, state (stable/ unstable), format, allowable values, simultaneous values, default values, etc ...). In the same way, the operations in a foc are described by a set of properties which is named *operation configuration*..(condition of process, complexity (sample, compound, multiple), life cycle (temporary (delay), permanent), list of related operations, etc...). These configurations allow a more precise definition. When we find attributes or operations with the same name, we can compare all the elements of the definition. So if it exists some differences, the process asks to the designer if he prefers to change the name or to put in the same sequence the different configurations.

An Information System (IS) is described by a set of classes linked to each other. As in other works ([3, 4, 17]), we retain the following logical links : *generalization* and *composition*. We complete those by *semantic connection*.

Generalizations are simples, an object of a subclass is associated with only one object of the superclass and an object of a superclass is associated with only one object of the subclass. Some authors introduce inheritance constraints to account for the fact that subclasses form or not a partition and to indicate whether the objects of the superclass are linked or not to the objects of the subclasses. We keep these inheritance constraints translating them into both graphical and textual representations. Let X be a superclass and $X_1,\ldots, X_n$ be its subclasses. If $X_i \cap Y_j = \emptyset$, $i \neq j$, the textual representation of this kind of generalization is: $[X|\text{-}\ X_1,\ldots, X_n]$.

On the other hand, if the subclasses are not disjoint, the textual representation of this situation is : $[X \mid= X_1, \ldots, X_n]$.

Another constraint type is when there exists a bijection between the objects of the superclass and those of the subclasses. In this case, we say that the superclass is the *prolongation* of the subclasses. The textual representation is : $[X[p] |\text{-}X_1,\ldots,X_n]$.

In the multiple generalization, let X = (Det_X ; $A_1,\ldots, A_m$; $O_1,\ldots,O_r$), Y = (Det_Y; $B_1,\ldots,B_n$; $S_1,\ldots, S_k$) two focs and Z a subclass of X and Y. The textual representation is : Z = (Det_X+Det_Y ; attributes from X,Y and new attributes ; operations from X, Y and new operations).

A composition (aggregation) is represented with the textual representation: $[X \| Y_1,\ldots,Y_n]$.

A *semantic connection* is a relation between independent classes. The concept of

association in the entity-relationship model is a particular case of semantic connection. Indeed, this link is caracterized by a *name*, a *direction*, a *cardinality* (1:1, 1:N, N:1, M:N), and can be *permanent*, *temporary*, *cyclic* or *exceptional*.
Remark. We have many reasons to support semantic connections. In fact, as we see in [5] "... Associations are between independent objects of equal syntactic weight. In general, it seems inappropriate to contaminate objects with knowledge of other objects..." and "... It is difficult to get multiplicity right on the few design process..."

The semantic connections representation 1:1 and 1:N is [X →Y], [X →→Y] respectively.

Most often, at the level of semantic connections 1:N, it is better to introduce attributes and operations into semantic connection and not in the classes themselves. So, a semantic connection is viewed as a foc. This situation helps us in the unification of different link types. In the case of semantic connection between three classes (or more) we prefer to create a new class and three associated semantic connections (or more).

Finally, we say that the *object module* (OM) is a logical construction which regroups classes linked by semantic connections, generalizations, and/or compositions. An *object model* is obtained from the set of OM's and represents the conceptual schema of this application. In this schema, redundancies between OM's are deleted and conflicts are resolved.

3. Principles of the design process.

In this process, we introduire a new step before the step of real world structuration in objects classes. This step allows the objects classes construction between the description of their behavior regardless the needs of a specific application. So we define applications type, sets of general fuzzy object classes. In fact the principle problem in the different object oriented method is found in these words: "find the objects!!". We want to help the designer in the research of the objects. When each designer has obtained his schema (OM), the second originality of this work is the use of an unification process of the OM's to give an object model.

3.1. General fuzzy object class

For each information system domain it is possible to define a *general application*. This general application allows us to collect the objects and their behavior which we usually find in each realization of the application. As a general rule, designers who work on the same domain do so according to a meta level. At this level, is defined a common set of properties and actions.
Example. In both private and public accountancy we find everytime: customers, suppliers, budgetary accounts, etc. Likewise, operations like registering invoices or payments, customer balance calculation, etc., are present in each realization of accountancy. In all applications it is at the implementation level, at the operation distribution in the time and at the values level, that differences exist. From this common nucleus the designers bring minor modifications (adding, deleting attributes or operations) but they keep the base structure of the general application.

From these observations, we create general applications defined among a set of general focs. Each attribute or operation is balanced by a ***necessity presence degree*** (example: in the foc *Customer* the attribute *name* has a necessity presence degree equal to 1, but the attribute *age* can have a necessity presence degree equal to 0.2) This degree is used in the step of unification process of focs. We compare also, via a *hesaurus* related to the general application domain, the attributes and the operations of each foc with the elements of general foc. When there is synonymy, we mark the equivalent elements to facilitate the unification process.
Remark. If a foc is not associated to a general foc, then we call this class *independent*. In this case we use the determinant of the class to compare with other independent classes.
Example. Let a general foc *Customer* and two focs *Buyer* and *Purchaser* in two different OM's, according to the Fig. 3.

Fig. 3. General foc Customer

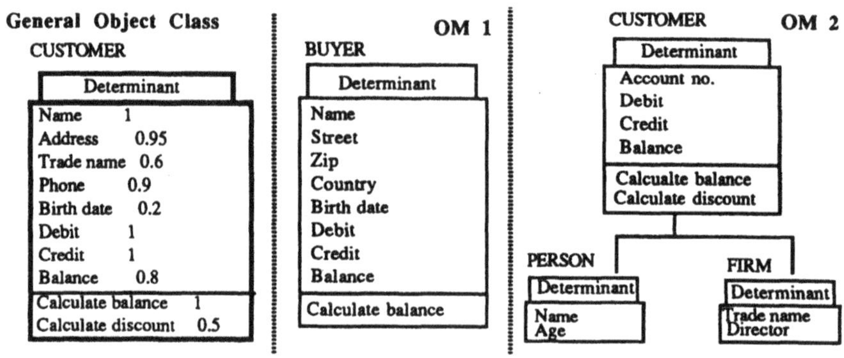

Thanks to a thesaurus of object class names, we can compare these different focs (*Buyer*, *Customer*) in relation to the general foc *Customer*, because we found the following list of synonyms : {{*Customer*}, {*Buyer*}, {*Purchaser*}}. By consultation of this same thesaurus, which is specific to the domain of accountancy general application, we translate each term (attribute or operation) found in the thesaurus into terms of the common language. For example, if we have in the thesaurus the following equivalences :{{Birth date}, {Age, current date - birth date}, {Age}, {birth year}} and {{Address}, {Street, number, Zip, City, Country}, {P.O. Box, Zip, City, Country}}, then the translation in common language gives the schema of the Fig. 4.

Fig. 4. Translation in common language

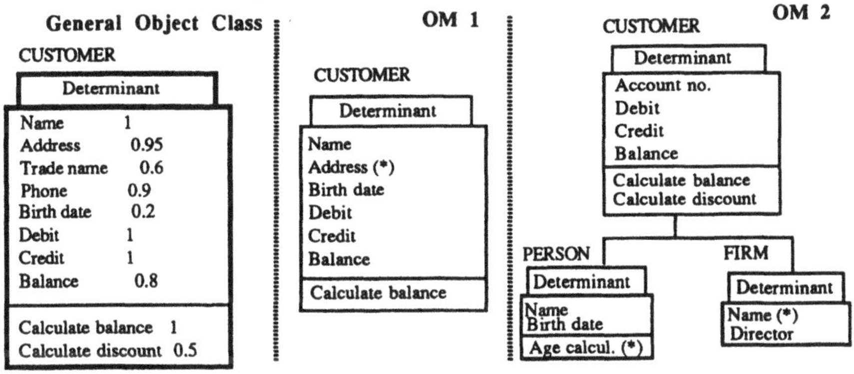

(*) Signals the term translated and/or all modifications involve by the derived attributes

Remark. The first set of terms in each list of the thesaurus is the set which we use in the translation process.

3.2 Explicit configurations of attributes and operations

In section 2, we said that the attributes of a foc are described by means of its configurations. There are two different ways to define the configuration of an attribute [12].

On the one hand, we assign these characteristics inside each attribute. The approach to the problem is to determine if two attributes are or not equivalent, that is, if we can replace only one attribute. Analysis of equivalence in the case where the configurations are implicit is very difficult.

On the other hand, we have an approach where we can define explicitly a set of attribute configurations via a hierarchy, each attribute is associated to one node of the hierarchy. In this approach, each configuration in inferior level inherits characteristics of the configuration which is in a superior level. In [12] we find the attribute hierarchy of configuration presented in Fig. 5.

Fig. 5. Hierarchy configuration of attributes

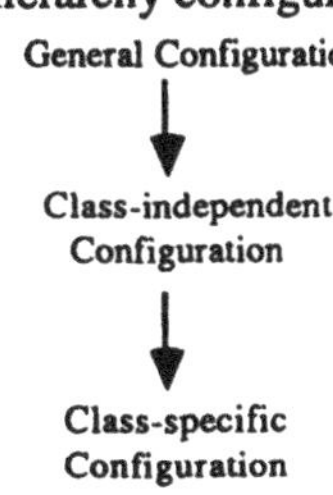

Remark. If we must compare two attributes, it is possible to use their configuration

hierarchies. In this case, if two attributes have not the same configuration hierarchy, the system cannot automatically give a response and the designer must decide.
The previous idea can be applied to operations of a foc and so, we can define an operation hierarchy configuration of operations presented in Fig. 6.

Fig. 6. Hierarchy configuration of operations

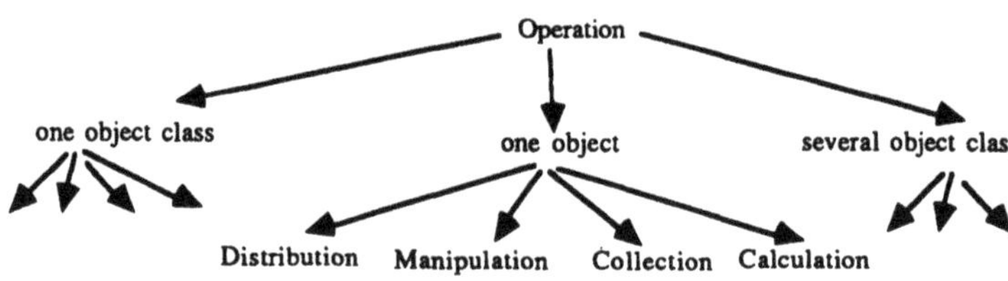

Consider two attributes, or two operations. If we know their configuration hierarchies, this can aid in the analysis of the equivalence of these concepts. These elements of comparaison are used in the design process and in the unification process. In the design process, each description of attribute or operation is compare to the others in the same OM, before to be take in account. This is made to obtain well built OM, relating to the coherence inside a description.

3.3. Equivalence of attributes and operations

Before defining the candidacy to a foc fusion, let us now analyze the configuration and the meaning of a concept (attribute or operation). The name of a concept C is represented by *name*(C); the configuration by *conf* (C) and the meaning by *mean*(C).

Let A and B two attributes (or operations). From the configurations of A and B, we can define a *fuzzy vector* : $(a_{11}, a_{22}, ..., a_{nn})$, where each component a_{ii} is an element of [0,1] and represents the *similitude degree* between A and B in the property i.
Remark. The vector of similitudes can be generalized to a matrix of priorities as in Fig. 7. In this case, a_{ij} $(i \neq j)$ represents the *priority ratio* of the property i in A over the property j in B.

This relation is dynamic and its dimensions depend of the configuration hierachies concerned. Thus, we can compare *conf*(A) and *conf*(B), via a similitude degree of n% (*conf*(A) ≅(n) *conf*(B)). This percentage may be previously determined. We say that A and B have the *same meaning* (*mean*(A) = *mean*(B) if

a) *name*(A) and *name*(B) are in the same set in the thesaurus,

b) *conf*(A) @(n) *conf*(B).

Remarks. a) If A and B do not satisfiy b) and *name*(A) = *name*(B), then the designer must replace one name.

b) It is possible to obtain that n attributes (or operations) have the same meaning to m other attributes. In this situation, two cases are possible: To verify in the thesaurus the equivalence of the two sets, or else, to ask the designer his opinion.

Fig. 7. Similitude Matrix (a_{ij} Œ [0,1])

	Identifier	Amplitude	Complexity	...
Identifier	a11	a12	a13	a1j
Amplitude	a21	a22	a23	a2j
Complexity	a31	a32	a33	a3j
...	ai1	ai2	ai3	aij

3.4. Fusioned Fuzzy Object Class

Assume that $\mathbf{A} = \{A_1,\ldots, A_n\}$, $\mathbf{B} = \{B_1,\ldots,B_k\}$, $\mathbf{O} = \{O_1,\ldots, O_m\}$ and $\mathbf{S} = \{S_1,\ldots, S_p\}$. If OM_i and OM_j are two object modules, where i<j, we say that OM_i has a *weigth more important* than OM_j (cf. section 5).

Now, let $X = (Det_X\ ;\ \mathbf{A}\ ;\ \mathbf{O})$ and $Y = (Det_Y\ ;\ \mathbf{B}\ ;\ \mathbf{S})$ two focs in OM_i, OM_j, respectively, where i<j. We say that X and Y are *fusionable* ($X \equiv Y$) if X and Y are attached with the same general foc. If on the contrary X and Y are independant focs we say that X and Y are fusionable if $Det_X = Det_Y$.

Assume that $mean(\mathbf{C_i}) = mean(\mathbf{D_i})$, $i \in [1, \min(n,k)]$, $mean(\mathbf{T_j}) = mean(\mathbf{U_j})$, $j \in [1, \min(m,p)]$, where $\mathbf{C_i} \in \mathbf{P}(\mathbf{A})$, $\mathbf{D_i} \in \mathbf{P}(\mathbf{B})$, $\mathbf{T_j} \in \mathbf{P}(\mathbf{O})$, $\mathbf{U_j} \in \mathbf{P}(\mathbf{S})$ and $\mathbf{P}$ stands for the power set, then the *fusioned foc* of X and Y is $(Det_X\ ;\ (\cup\ \mathbf{C_i} \oplus \mathbf{D_i}) \cap (\mathbf{A} \cup \mathbf{B});\ (\cup\ \mathbf{T_j} \oplus \mathbf{U_j}) \cap (\mathbf{O} \cup \mathbf{S})$

Remark. $\mathbf{C} \oplus \mathbf{D} := \mathbf{C}$ if we consider to keep **C**, else, is equal to **D**.

4. Design process.

The goals of the design process are resumed like follows:

- Use of an application type and general objects classes to make easier the description of a given application
- Development of objects classes and not description of classes.
- Optimisation of objects module.

4.1. Use of applications type.

The designer, after the choice of an applicaton type can work in two ways:

Either he uses the knowledge of the problem domain. In this case, a set of general object classes is proposed. From this set, he build his owner objects classes (possibility of adding, deleting each element (atttribute, operation, class)). To each built class, it is associated a determinant value from the concerned general class.(eventually this general class has been modified; In this case an attachement coefficient is calculate to know the degree of similitude between the created class and the general class. It is used in the unification process).

Whether he builds without help, objects classes. In this case he must define the complete configuration of each attribute and of each operation, and also a determinant value. From these objects classes and with the determinant, the system suggests to the designer, the sets of objects classes which are near.

In the description of the elements of the IS, the designer who wants to use domain expertise, must take in account conflicts created by the modification of names (homonyms, synonyms) and of structures (type conflicts, identifiant conflicts, behavior conflicts) [27]. The different thesauri, associated to each application type, give an help to resolve semantical conflicts.

4.2. Construction of objects classes.

From these objects classes and determinant values, the system using the semantic test score [28], elaborates an objects classes typology. The system works on the fuzzy determinant values. To translate the objects classes semantic, we use propositions like *X is A*. Each proposition represents an objects class. Using an explicative data base (determinant values), the system obtains a test score semantic linked to each class. With a comparison of these semantics, the system proposes to consider that the classes are next or not. In the same way, the meanings of attributes and of operations are compare. If it is necessary, they are merged. So the system builds an objects classes schema. The obtained schema has not generalization links.

4.3. Optimization of the objects classes schema.

In this step, there are many optimization types. On the one hand, the introduction of generalization - specialization, the objects classes are not in the same plane but they are put in a hierarchy of classes regardless stability and inheritance criteria. On the other hand, the distribution of objects classes, which is to group, to split structures and to share instances of objects classes, is made.

5. Unified object model

In this section we introduce the unification process. It is based upon the approach, two at time, according the Fig. 8 [2] :

If we use this approach, we must consider that each object module has a *weight* or priority vis à vis the others module. This weight can be determined by some parameters, for example, date of construction of the view, priority or hierarchy of designer in the firm, etc.

We can also define a partial order among the OM's. In the process we consider OM_1 the module with the most important weight and therefore, the first to be taker into account in the unification process.

Fig.8. Unification process

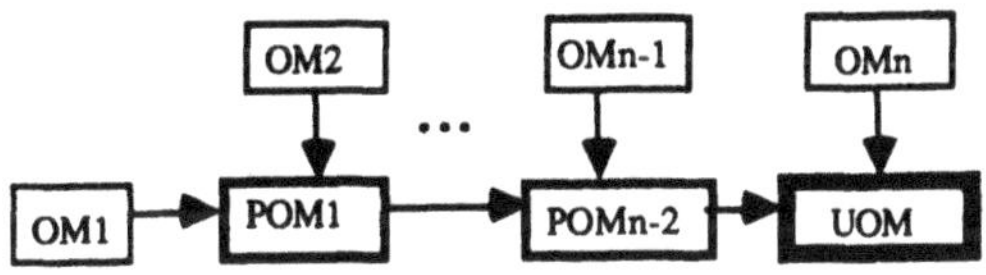

OMi ≥ OMj if i < j

OMi : Object module i
POMj: Preliminary object model j
UOM: Unified object model

Our unification process is composed of six steps: determination of the proximity of the focs, translation in common language, determination of redundancy level of focs, assembly of classes, links unification and equivalence analysis between attributes and operations.

Consider n OM's being unified, each concept (attribute, operation, class, semantic connection, generalization, and composition) in an OM will have membership label to the OM concerned. In this way, all concepts of all OM's are identifiable.

5.1. Step 0 : Focs proximity determination

The first step concerns the determination of the proximity of the focs with regard the general focs. Indeed, for each foc X in an OM, two cases are possible :

a) There is a general foc Y such as *name*(X) is in the set of the synonyms of *name*(Y) in the thesaurus. In this case, we compare the attributes and operations of X and Y. If there is not comparison, then ask the designer to change *name*(X).

b) There is not an object type Y such as *name*(X) is in the set of the synonyms of *name*(Y) in the thesaurus, then ask the designer if there is a general foc equivalent to X. In this case, change *name*(X) to *name*(Y). Otherwise, the foc X is independent of the general focs.

5.2. Step 1 : Translation to common language

In this step, we translate the focs, and also their components, in the common language used in the general focs of the specific domain (cf. Section 3.1.)

5.3. Step 2 : Determination of the redundancy level of focs

The third step of the unification process is the identification of focs which can be fusionable. For this, we compute the redundancy level of each foc X. There are two ways to compute this level. In the first case, easily the redundancy level of a foc is equal to the number of times where a general foc is involved in proximity with the focs of the OM's.So, if *lev*(X) = k, then X is attached with a general foc and there k different focs in k MO's, attached to this general foc. In the second case, where the focs are independent from the general focs, we use the determinant concept. We compare the determinant focs, two at time, and if there are k equal foc determinants to Det_X, in k differents OMs, then *lev*(X) = k.

We can partition the focs according to the redundancy level and, within each of these subsets, again, we can partition the focs according to the meaning of the determinant (cf. Section 4.2.).

5.4. Step 3 : Assembly of Objects Classes

Let X and Y be focs in POM_i and OM_{i+2} respectively, $i \in [1,n]$. Several cases are possible:

1) If *lev*(X)=*lev*(Y)=0, then X and Y are not fusionable and so they appear all together in POM_{i+1}.

2) If *lev*(X)=*lev*(Y)=1 and X ≡ Y we must put the contents (attributes and operations) of Y in that of X, and we make *lev*(X)=0. [In this case, the membership label of X changes to i+1, because X will be a foc in POM_{i+1} and we must to eliminate Y from OM_{i+2}. Each attribute and operation stays with their original membership label (we use this idea in the third step)].

3) If *lev*(X) = *lev*(Y) = k, $k \in [2,n]$, and X ≡ Y, then there are k-2 candidate focs $Z_1, Z_2, \ldots, Z_{k-2}$, in k-2 OM's, to be fusioned with X and Y. In this case, we put the contents of Y in the contents of X. So, we make *lev*(X) = *lev*(Z_1) =...= *lev*(Z_{k-2}) = k-1. (In this case, the original membership label of X changes to i+1 and we must eliminate Y from OM_{i+2}).

5.5. Step 4 : Link Unification

With regard to link unification, there are cases depending on the link type and the characteristics of focs, because a link unification can induce alterations on the concerned focs. Each case can be viewed as a set of rules belonging to a knowledge base.

1) Step 4.1 Semantic connection unification: In the previous section we established that semantic connections can be reduced to binary links. Therefore, we only consider the latter situation. In what follows, the symbol "—" represents " → " or " →→ ".

Let L=[X—Y] and K=[U—Z] two semantic connections in POM_i and OM_{i+2}, respectively, $i \in [1,n]$. Several cases are possible :

1. If X ≡ U, Y ≡ Z and L ≡ K, then keep only L=[X—Y] .
2. If X ≡ U, Y ≡ Z and L ¬≡ K, then keep L=[X—Y] and K = [X—Y].
3. If X ≡ U and Y ¬≡ Z, then keep L=[X—Y] and K=[X—Z].
4. If X ¬≡ U, Y ≡ Z, then keep L=[X—Y] and K=[U—Y].
5. If X ¬≡ U and Y ¬≡ Z, then keep L=[X—Y] and K=[U—Z].

Remarks. a) When a link unification is performed, link membership labels are to set to i+1 because links will be in OM_{i+1}.

b) If after the unification of two 1:N semantic connections we obtain a semantic connection M:N, we resolve this problem by defining a new foc and two semantic connections 1:N.

2) Step 4.2 Generalization unification: When focs candidate to the fusion are inserted in generalization structure, we can resolve the problem via the definition of an algebra over this structure. In fact, consider the symbol " | " which represents " |- " or " |= " in the textual representation of the generalization (cf. section 2).

Now, let [A_1 |...| A_i |...| A_n] and [B_1 |...| B_j |...| B_m] two *partial generalizations* in POM_i and OM_{i+2} respectively, and $A_i \int B_j$, as in Fig. 9. We can define the addition of generalizations as following : [A_1 |...| A_i |...| A_n] + [B_1 |... | B_j |...| B_m] =

[(A_1 |...| A_{i-1}) + (B_1 |...| B_{j-1}) | A_i | (A_{i+1} |...| A_n) , (B_{j+1} |...| B_m)]

Fig. 9. Fusion of generalizations

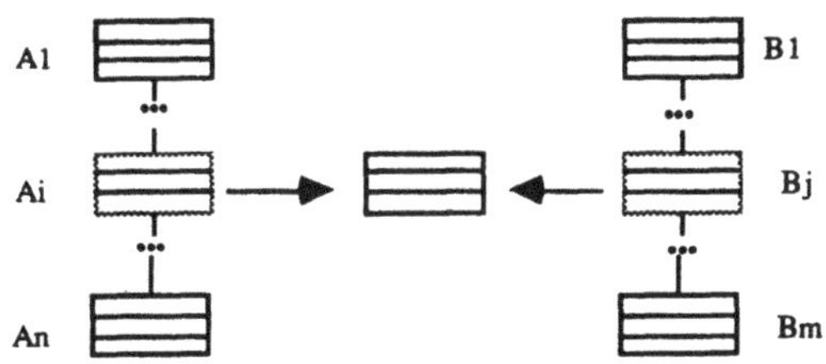

3) Step 4.3 Composition unification : When focs candidate to the fusion are inserted in composition structure, we can resolve the problem via the definition of an algebra over this structure.

Now, let [A_1 ||...|| A_i ||...|| A_n] and [B_1 ||...|| B_j ||...|| B_m] two partial compositions in POM_i and OM_{i+2} respectively, and $A_i \int B_j$. We can define the addition of compositions as follows:

[A_1 ||...|| A_i ||...|| A_n] + [B_1 ||...|| B_j ||...|| B_m] =

[(A_1 ||...|| A_{i-1}) + (B_1 ||...|| B_{j-1}) || A_i || (A_{i+1} ||...|| A_n) , (B_{j+1} ||...|| B_m)].

Remark. We can introduce other tools for the analysis of the link unification process. They are ratios given by the use of fuzzy relations which are termed *coefficients*. First, the *credibility coefficient* which gives the percentage of truthfulness about a rule in the application domain being learned. Second, the *distributivity coefficient* which gives the useage percentage of a rule by the concerned classes. These coefficients allow to evaluate a third coefficient, the *proximity coefficient*, which gives the level of inheritance for classes concerned by a given generalization (fusion or rupture of classes obtained).

5.6. Step 5 : Equivalence of Attributes and Operations:

After the third step of the unification process, that is, the assembly of focs of the model POM_i and the module OM_{i+2} in the model POM_{i+1}, $i \in [1,n-2]$, we can find classes with redundant and/or inconsistent attributes and operations. We enumerate the cases that can arise and we show the actions that need to be performed.

Let $A_1,....., A_n, B_1,..., B_m$ the attributes of the fusioned foc in POM_{i+1}, where $A_1,....., A_n$, are the original attributes of X in POM_i and $B_1,..., B_m$ are the original attributes of Y in OM_{i+2}. Let A in $\{A_1,....., A_n\}$ and B in $\{B_1,....., B_m\}$. Then

1) If *name*(A) = *name*(B) and *mean*(A) = *mean*(B), then delete B and keep A.

2) If *name*(A) = *name*(B) and *mean*(A) ≠ *mean*(B), then change *name*(B) (say C) and keep A and C.

3) If *name*(A) ≠ *name*(B) and *mean*(A) = *mean*(B), then delete B and keep A.

4) If *name*(A) ≠ *name*(B) and *mean*(A) ≠ *mean*(B), then keep A and B.

5) In general, if *mean*$(A_{i1},...,A_{ik})$ = *mean*$(B_{ji},...,B_{js})$

Remark. When we keep the attributes or operations in POM_{i+1} they must change the membership label to i+1.

6. Conclusion

The design process is based in a set of steps which can be automated via an expert system. It is the same thing to the unification process.

We can resume the different steps as follows:

a) Description by the different users, of their specific OM's. The user does not describe objects directly. In fact an approach like our gives a basic structurating of the real world. From modification of this basic structuration, the user can build his own classes. The system help him in the coherence of his descriptin. The user then, agrees to the object modules obtained. In fact thre is an interactive step to allow at the user to verify the appropriateness of the translation of the description of objects classes.

b) Use of an unification process, whose the goal is the integration of the object modules;

c) Optimization of the object module obtained; and

d) Realization of the object bases.

The advantages of a such process are:

a) several descriptions of same application can coexist;

b) an application nucleus is found (set of compatible classes between different descriptions) to eliminate the redundancies. But the incompatibilities are conserved; and

c) restructuration of the designs of an application to facilitate the implementation and maintenance. The system creates several levels of schema, levels visible (or not) to the user together with the unified object model. This is closely related to the view concept used in databases.

Finally, the process can be extended to several applications therefore obtaining the global schema of an information system.

Now we are working on two goals:

* The first one is on the construction of an ascending design method. The main idea is that the designer gives instances of objects and the system builds the classes.

* The second one is on the construction of an expert system to create application

type.

A validation of a such process is making on robotic domain, and specially on assembly of mecanical components.

References

1. S. Abiteboul, R. Hull, Restructuring hierarchical database objects, *Theoretical Computer Science*, vol. 62, pp. 3-38, 1988.
2. F. Bancillhon , W. Kim , Object-oriented database systems : In transition, *ACM Sigmod Record*, vol. 19, no. 4, pp. 49-53, December 1990.
3. C. Batini, M. Lenzerini, A methodology for data schema integration in the entity-relationship model, *IEEE Trans. Soft. Eng.*, vol. SE-10, no. 6, pp. 650-664, 1984.
4. E. Bertino, L. Martino, Object-oriented database management systems : concepts and issues, *IEEE Computer*, pp. 33-47, April 1991.
5. M. R. Blaha, W. J. Premerlani, J. E. Rumbaugh, Relational database design using an object-oriented methodology, *Communications of the ACM*, vol. 31, no. 4, pp. 417-427, 1988.
6. G. Booch, *Object oriented design : with applications*, Benjamin/cummings : California, 1991.
7. B. P. Buckles, F. E. Petry, A fuzzy representation of data for relational databases, *Fuzzy Sets and Systems*, vol. 7, no. 3, pp. 213-226, 1982.
8. A. Cavarero, C. González, La logique floue comme outil d'unification de modules d'objets, rapport de recherche équipe KI2S, Université de Nice Sophia-Antipolis-CNRS U.R.A. 1376, 92-04, 1992.
9. A. Cavarero, C. González, Principes d'un système expert comme outil d'unification de modules d'objets, *Sixièmes Journées Internationales des Sciences Informatiques (JISI'92)*, pp. 166-185, Tunis, 1992.
10. A. Cavarero, C. González, Unification des schémas conceptuels dans l'orienté objets dit flou, accepted in the *Premier Colloque Africain sur la Recherche en Informatique, INRIA et Université de Nations Unies)*, Yaoundé, Cameroun, october 1992.
11. V. Dayal , H. Y. Hwang,View definition and generalization for database integration in a multibase system, *IEEE Trans. Soft. Eng.*, vol. SE-10, no.6, pp. 628-645, 1984.
12. C. Fleming, B. von Halle, *Handbook of relational database design*, AddisonWesley : New Jersey, 1989.
13. R. George, F.E. Petry, B.P. Buckles, Uncertainty modelling in object-oriented geographical information systems, submitted to *the Conference on Database and Expert Applications*, 1992.
14. J. V. Joseph, S. M. Thatte, C.W. Thompson, D. C. Wells, Object-oriented databases : design and implementation, *Proceedings of THE IEEE*, vol. 79, no. 1, pp. 42-64, 1991.
15. W. Kim, J. Seo, Classifying schematic and data heterogeneity in multidatabase

systems, *IEEE Computer*, pp. 12-18, December 1991.
16. J. A. Larson, S. B. Navathe, A theory of attribute equivalence in databases with application to schema integration, *IEEE Trans. Soft. Eng.*, vol. SE-15, no. 4, April 1989.
17. M. Loomis, A. V. Shaw, J. Rumbaugh, An object modeling technique for conceptual design, *European Conference on Object Oriented Programming*, Paris, France, published as *Lecture Notes in Computer Science*, 276, Springer-Verlag, pp. 192-202, 1987.
18. T. A. Malyuta, V. V. Pasichnik, A.A. Stogniy, Means for management of relational fuzzy data bases-way to merging of systems of data bases and knowledge bases, Database Systems of the 90's International Symposium, Berlin, November 1990, published as *Lecture Notes in Computer Science*, 460, pp. 337-346, 1991.
19. J. M. Morressey, Imprecise information and uncertainty in information systems, *ACM Trans on Information Sys.*, vol. 8, no. 2, pp. 159-180, 1990.
20. C. V. Negoita, *Expert Systems and fuzzy systems*, Benjamin/Cummings : California, 1985.
21. C. Parent, S. Spaccaprieta, Gestion d'objets complexes avec des entités complexes, *Journées AFCET Bases de Données Deductives et Bases de Données Orientées Objets*, 13-14 décembre, 1988.
22. J. Peckman, Semantic data models, *ACM Computing Surveys*, vol. 20, no. 3, pp. 153-189, September, 1988.
23. J. Rumbaugh M. Blaha, W. Premerlani, F. Eddy, W. Lorensen, *Object-oriented modeling and design*, Prentice Hall : New Jersey, 1991.
24. U. Schiel, The time dimension in information systems, *Information Systems : Theoretical and Formal Aspects*, Elsevier Science Publishers, IFIP, pp. 67-75, 1985.
25. S. Shenoi, A. Melton, L. T. Fan, An equivalence classes model of fuzzy relational databases, *Fuzzy Sets and Systems*, vol. 38., pp. 153-170., 1990.
26. S. Shenoi, A. Melton, An extended version of the fuzzy relational database model, *Information Sciences*, vol. 52, pp. 35-52, 1990.
27. P. Shoval, S. Zohn, Binary-relationship integration methodology, *Data & Knowledge Engineering*, Noth Holland, vol. 6, pp. 225-250, 1991.
28. L. Zadeh ,Test-score semantics as a basis for a computational approach to the representatin of meaning, *Literary and Linguistic Computing* ,vol. 1, pp. 24-35, 1986.
29. L. Zadeh, *Fuzzy logic*, IEEE Computer, pp. 83-93, April 1988.
30. L. Zadeh, Knowledge representation in fuzzy logic, *IEEE Trans. on Knowledge and Data Eng.*, vol. 1, no. 1, pp. 89-99, March 1989.
31. H. J. Zimmermann, *Fuzzy set theory and its applications*, Dordrecht, The Netherlands: Nijhoff, 1987.

HORIZONTAL PARTITIONING FOR DISTRIBUTED DATABASE DESIGN : A GRAPH-BASED APPROACH*

MINYOUNG RA
Computer Science Division
Department of Mathematics
Korea Military Academy
Seoul, KOREA 139-799

ABSTRACT

Horizontal partitioning is the process that divides a global relation into subsets of tuples, called horizontal fragments. In this paper we present a graph-based algorithm for horizontal partitioning. In this algorithm horizontal fragments (mostly overlapped) are determined by using the clustering of predicates that are based on the predicate affinity. For clustering, this algorithm adopts the graphical partitioning technique developed in our previous research for vertical partitioning. Thus a relatively small number of horizontal fragments are generated. We also present a adjusting function for nonoverlapping horizontal partitioning.

1. Introduction

In a distributed database system data fragmentation is one of the major design issues. Fragmentation or partitioning is the process of subdividing a global object (entity or relation) into several pieces, called fragments. Data fragmentation is performed during the design of a database to improve the performance of transactions. In order to obtain improved performance, fragments must be "closely matched" to the requirements of the transactions.

The decomposition of a global schema into fragments can be performed in two different types of fragmentation : horizontal fragmentation and vertical fragmentation[1]. Vertical fragmentation is the process that divides a global object into groups of their attributes, called vertical fragments. In order to be able to access the same data after partitioning, it is required that each fragment include

*This research was supported in part by Korea Science & Engineering Foundation (KOSEF) Grant No. 923-1100-088-1

a key attribute of the global object. Horizontal fragmentation is the process that divides a global relation into subsets of tuples, called horizontal fragments. Each fragment is associated with a predicate which indicates the distinguishing property possessed by the instances or tuples of that fragment. Note that fragments can be overlapped. This means that fragments can have common attributes and tuples in vertical fragmentation and horizontal fragmentation respectively. This paper is concerned with horizontal fragmentation.

Ceri, Negri and Pelagatti[2] analyze the horizontal partitioning problem, dealing with the specification of partitioning predicates and the application of horizontal partitioning to different database design problems. However, since each fragment is given by the conjunction of all the predicates in the natural form or negated, thr maximum possible number of fragments can be 2^n, where n represents the number of predicates.

Ceri, Navathe and Wiederhold[3] develop an optimization model for horizontal partitioning without replication in the form of a linear integer zero-one programming problem. They modeled the logical schema of a database as a directed graph with objects as nodes and links as edges, and required the user to specify the information about: (1) the data about schema (attribute size, relationship size, cardinality), (2) tabulation of transactions (frequencies, site of origin), (3) distribution requirement (constraints). This model, however, requires pre-fragmentation.

Yu et al.[4] propose an adaptive algorithm for record clustering, which is conceptually simple and highly intuitive. However, the adaptive approach does not use the given transaction information that is useful for partitioning, thus it cannot be applied until the execution of transactions.

In the present research, we are focusing our attention on identifying all the horizontal partitions at a time based on transaction specifications. For this we propose a horizontal partitioning methodology which uses the MAKE_PARTITION algorithm developed in the previous work[5]. In order to use the MAKE_PARTITION algorithm, we consider only those transactions whose processing frequency is large. These transactions access tuples of the relations based on some predicates. These predicates are called simple predicates[2]. The syntax for a simple predicate is as follows:

simple_predicate ::= attribute_name <op> attribute_name
| attribute_name <op> value
<op> ::= < | > | <= | >= | <> | =
attribute_name ::= string
value ::= element of the domain of the attribute.

A transaction gives rise to a set of simple predicates. The WHERE clause of a database operation (say SELECT) may consist of a disjunction or conjunction or negation of a set of simple predicates. Simple predicates are easier to handle and understand. Moreover, a simple predicate splits a relation into two horizontal fragments. One horizontal fragment consists of those tuples that satisfy the simple predicate and other with those tuples that do not. We limit the scope of this paper by assuming that all simple predicates are previously known. A statistical analysis of transactions may be conducted to determine the most important transactions and the most heavily used predicates.

In this paper, the focus of this research is on single relation fragmentation. Hence join predicates (including derived predicates) of the form R1.A=R2.B which deal with a pair of relations are not considered for horizontal partitioning. They are very much a part of allocation phase and are considered for minimizing the effort and cost of joins[6]. In contrast, horizontal partitioning approaches used in systems like Bubba[7] or Gamma[8] attempt to achieve parallelism of join queries, etc. In our decomposition of the overall distribution problem, join predicates are in fact considered, but at a later stage (i.e. allocation stage).

The organization of this paper is as follows. Section 2 describes preliminaries for the proposed algorithm including the review of the graphical partitioning algorithm. In Section 3, the proposed algorithm for horizontal partitioning is described, and Section 4 describes a function for nonoverlapping horizontal partitioning. Section 5 gives conclusions.

2. Preliminaries

2.1 Overview

We developed a vertical partitioning algorithm using a graphical method[5]. That algorithm starts from the attribute affinity (AA) matrix, which is generated from the attribute usage matrix using the same method as that of the previous approach[9]. The attribute usage matrix represents the use of attributes in important transactions. Each row refers to one transaction; the "1" entry in a column indicates that the transaction "uses" the corresponding attributes. Figure 1 shows the attribute usage matrix for 10 attributes and 8 transactions.

Attribute usage matrix											Number of accesses per time period
Attributes / Transactions	1	2	3	4	5	6	7	8	9	10	
T1	1	0	0	0	1	0	1	0	0	0	Acc 1 = 25
T2	0	1	1	0	0	0	0	1	1	0	Acc 2 = 50
T3	0	0	0	1	0	1	0	0	0	1	Acc 3 = 25
T4	0	1	0	0	0	0	1	1	0	0	Acc 4 = 35
T5	1	1	1	0	1	0	1	1	1	0	Acc 5 = 25
T6	1	0	0	0	1	0	0	0	0	0	Acc 6 = 25
T7	0	0	1	0	0	0	0	0	1	0	Acc 7 = 25
T8	0	0	1	1	0	1	0	0	1	1	Acc 8 = 15

Fig. 1 Attribute usage matrix

Attribute affinity is defined as

$$aff_{ij} = \sum_{k \in \tau} acc_{kij}, \quad i \neq j$$

where acc_{kij} is the number of accesses of transaction k referencing both attributes i and j. The summation occurs over all transactions that belong to the set of important transactions τ. This definition of attribute affinity measures the strength of an imaginary bond between the two attributes, predicated on the fact that attributes are used together by transactions. Figure 2 shows the attribute affinity matrix which was formed from the Figure 1.

We consider the AA matrix as a complete graph called the affinity graph in which an edge value represents the affinity between the two attributes as shown in Figure 3. Then, forming a linearly connected spanning tree, the algorithm generates all meaningful fragments in one iteration by considering a cycle as a fragment. A "linearly connected" tree has only two ends. This approach is based on the fact that all pairs of attributes in a fragment have high "within fragment

Attributes	1	2	3	4	5	6	7	8	9	10
1		25	25	0	75	0	50	25	25	0
2	25		75	0	25	0	60	110	75	0
3	25	75		15	25	15	25	75	115	15
4	0	0	15		0	40	0	0	15	40
5	75	25	25	0		0	50	25	25	0
6	0	0	15	40	0		0	0	15	40
7	50	60	25	0	50	0		60	25	0
8	25	110	75	0	25	0	60		75	0
9	25	75	115	15	25	15	25	75		15
10	0	0	15	40	0	40	0	0	15	

Fig. 2 Attribute affinity (AA) matrix

affinity" but low "between fragment affinity". The basic procedure for the graphical algorithm for vertical partitioning is described as follows[5].

1. Start anywhere in the affinity graph.
2. Form a linearly connected spanning tree.
   - Linearly connected tree is a tree which has only two ends.
   - Edge that has the largest value is selected as a next edge.
3. Identify a "cycle" in the spanning tree.
4. Try to extend the cycle. Repeat this step as long as it applies.
5. Split a cycle off from the graph at the "cut edges" generating a fragment
6. Repeat steps 2 through 5.

The major advantages of the proposed method over the previous work[9] are as follows:

(1) There is no need for iterative binary partitioning. The major weakness of iterative binary partitioning is that at each step two new problems are generated increasing the complexity; furthermore, termination of the algorithm is dependent on the discriminating power of the objective function.

(2) The method requires no objective function. The empirical objective functions were selected after some trial and error experimentation to see that they

possess a good discriminating power. Although reasonable, they constitute an arbitrary choice. In the proposed methodology this arbitrariness has been eliminated.

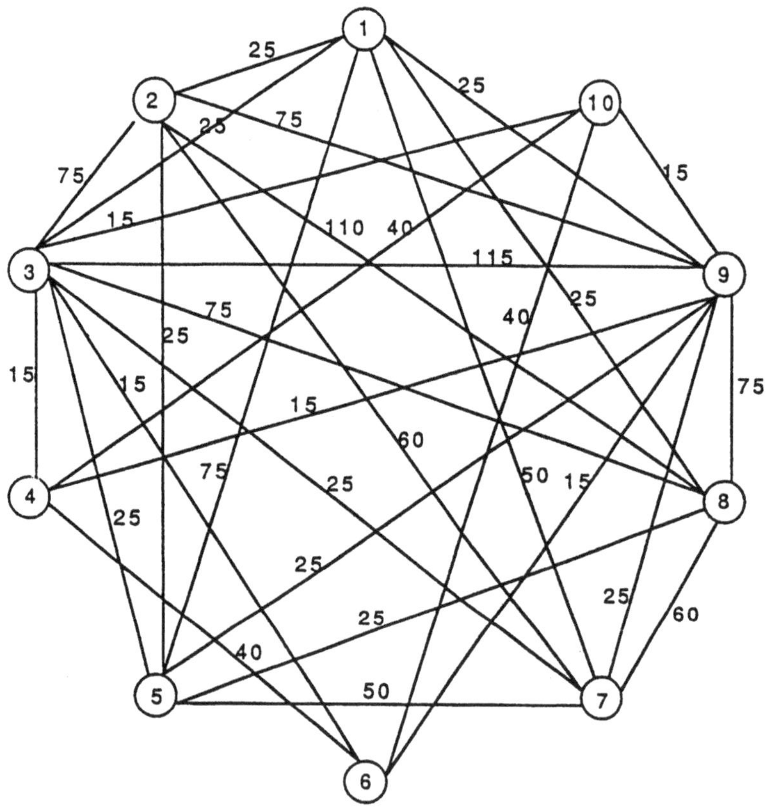

Fig. 3 Affinity graph after excluding zero-valued edges

In this paper we apply the same approach to horizontal partitioning. A simple example explains our horizontal partitioning methodology below. The inputs are a set of transactions and a corresponding set of predicates as follows (assume D#, SAL, and AGE are attributes of an example relation):

T1 : D#<10 (p1), SAL>40K (p7)

T2 : D#<20 (p2), SAL>40K

T3 : D#>20 (p3), SAL>40K, AGE<30 (p9)

T4 : 30<D#<50 (p4), SAL<40K (p8), AGE<30

T5 : D#<15 (p5), SAL<40K

T6 : D#>40 (p6), SAL<40K, AGE>30 (p10)

T7 : D#<15 (p5), SAL<40K

T8 : D#>40 (p6), SAL<40K, AGE>30

Note that the above set of predicates do not span all the tuples of the relation; tuples with SAL=40K will not be accessed by any of the above transactions.

As we can see in the previous work[3,9], it is not necessary to collect information on 100% of the expected transactions (that would of course be impossible). Since the 80-20 rule applies to most practical situations, it is adequate to supply information regarding the 20% of the heavily used transactions which account for about 80% of the activity against the database. This is an empirical observation which is well accepted by practitioners.

2.2 Predicate Usage Matrix and Predicate Affinity Matrix

The algorithm that we propose starts from the predicate usage matrix. The predicate usage matrix represents the use of predicates in important transactions. The predicate usage matrix for the above example (10 predicates and 8 transactions) is shown in Figure 4. Each row refers to one transaction: the "1" entry in a column indicates that the transaction uses the corresponding predicates. Predicate affinity is generated in a similar manner as attribute affinity. Figure 5 shows a predicate affinity matrix generated from the predicate usage matrix in Figure 4. In this matrix, there are three kinds of values: numeric for predicate affinity which represents explicit relationships, "==>" (or "<==") for implication which represents direct implicit relationships, and "*" for close usage which represents indirect implicit relationships. "==>" and "*" are introduced for the case that the affinity matrix is too sparse.

Predicates / Transactions	p1	p2	p3	p4	p5	p6	p7	p8	p9	p10	Number of accesses per time period
T1	1	0	0	0	0	0	1	0	0	0	Acc 1 = 25
T2	0	1	0	0	0	0	1	0	0	0	Acc 2 = 50
T3	0	0	1	0	0	0	1	0	1	0	Acc 3 = 25
T4	0	0	0	1	0	0	0	1	1	0	Acc 4 = 15
T5	0	0	0	0	1	0	0	1	0	0	Acc 5 = 25
T6	0	0	0	0	0	1	0	1	0	1	Acc 6 = 25
T7	0	0	0	0	1	0	0	1	0	0	Acc 7 = 25
T8	0	0	0	0	0	1	0	1	0	1	Acc 8 = 15

Fig. 4 Predicate usage matrix

Predicates	1	2	3	4	5	6	7	8	9	10
1										
2	<==, *									
3	*	*					symmetric			
4	0	0	==>							
5	0	0	0	*						
6	0	0	0	*	*					
7	25	50	25	0	0	0				
8	0	0	0	15	50	40	*			
9	0	0	25	15	0	0	25	15		
10	0	0	0	0	0	40	0	40	0	

Fig. 5 Predicate affinity matrix

The numerical value of the (i,j) element in this matrix gives the combined frequency of all transactions accessing both predicates i and j. The details of affinity calculation here are the same as in vertical partitioning. The value "==>" of the (i,j) element indicates that predicate i implies predicate j, and the value "*" represents that predicates i and j exhibit a "closeness" although they do not have an implication. Two predicates i and j are "close" when the following conditions are satisfied: (1) i and j must be defined on the same attribute, (2) i and j must be used jointly with some common predicate c, (3) c must be defined on an attribute other than the attribute used in i and j. This is reasonable because predicates i, j, and c are different from one another and thus two fragments generated by predicates i,c and predicates j,c are considered "closely related" since they both involve predicate c. In the above example, p1 and p2 are "close" because of their usage with the common predicate p7 in transactions T1 and T2. These two relationships are introduced to represent logical connectivity between predicates.

The attractive features of this approach are:

(1) Fragments are based on actual predicates; by applying implication between predicates, the number of fragments is reduced,

(2) We can make use of the pre-developed algorithm,

(3) By using clustering of predicates suggested above, a relatively small number of horizontal fragments are generated (In Ceri et al.'s work[2], the generated fragments can be up to 2^n, where n represents the number of predicates),

(4) 0-1 integer formulation is not needed.

3. The Algorithm

First a modified version of the graphical partitioning algorithm for clustering predicates will be given. Then by using this clustering, the entire steps for horizontal fragmentation will be described.

3.1 Clustering of Predicates

We will apply the graphical algorithm[5] to horizontal partitioning. However, we cannot use this algorithm directly because the predicate affinity matrix may be too sparse. Thus we introduce two more relationships which represent logical connectivity between predicates. They are "==>" for implication and "*" for close usage as explained in Section 2.2.

To obtain the modified version of the graphical partitioning algorithm, the following heuristic rules are applied.

(1) A numerical value (except zero) has higher priority than the values "==>", "<==" and "*" when selecting a next edge. This is because we place more importance on affinity values which are obtained from transaction usage rather than on logical connectivity among the predicates.

(2) In the comparisons involved in checking for the possibility of a cycle or extension of a cycle (note: a cycle in the graph defined as an "affinity cycle" generates a fragment), we ignore cycle edges with affinity values "==>", "<==" and "*". For example, in Figure 6, in comparing edge (p4,p8) with edges of the cycle (p8,p5,p6,p10) we ignore edge (p5,p6) which has affinity "*". This is because the affinity values "==>", "<==" and "*" represent implicit relationships and therefore can be collapsed.

(3) "==>" and "<==" are considered to have higher affinity value than "*" since the former indicates direct implication, whereas the latter represents only logical connectivity between the two predicates through their usage with a common predicate.

(4) If there are two "==>"s in a column corresponding to predicate p_k, one implied by predicate p_i and another implied by predicate p_j, then the entry (i,k) has higher priority than the entry (j,k), either if the entry (i,j) is equal to "<==", or if the entry (j,i) is equal to "==>". In other words,

$$p_i \Rightarrow p_j \Rightarrow p_k \quad .... \quad (a)$$

$$p_j \Rightarrow p_i \Rightarrow p_k \quad .... \quad (b)$$

in the above implication, if (a) holds, then j has higher priority than i, and if (b) holds, then i has higher priority than j.

These rules can be easily incorporated into the graphical partitioning algorithm[5]. For example, if we assume that every affinity value in predicate affinity matrix is greater than 2, then we can assign value 1 for "*" and 2 for "==>" to represent rules 1 and 3. The detailed description of the modified algorithm now follows.

```
procedure Make_Hori_Partition(L[1..n,1..n]): set of edges
        { assign value 1 for "*" and 2 for "==>" respectively in a
    predicate affinity matrix}

  { initialize flags and variables }
  B[1] <- 1
  f1 <- 1, f2 <- 0      { f1 & f2 each refer to an end of the
                               spanning tree }
  p_cycle,c_node,f_edge,candidate_p <- false
  pmin <- ∞             { minimum edge of a cycle }

  { initialize vectors }
  for i <- 2 to n do
        strongest[i] <- 1
        maxwt[i] <- L[i,1]
        B[i] <- 0
  end_for

  repeat n-1 times
     max <- -1

     { select the next node }
     for j <- 2 to n do
         if   maxwt[j] > max and (strongest[j] = f1 or strongest[j] = f2)
         then max <- maxwt[j]
              k <- j
     end_for

     { adjust the pointers for checking a primitive cycle }
     if strongest[k] = f1 then if f2 = 0 then f2 <- k
                                          else swap f1,f2
                                               f2 <- k
                               else f2 <- k
     { check if there is a primitive cycle }
     for j <- 2 to n do
        if   B[j] = k and c_node = false
        then p_cycle <- true
             if B[j-1] > 0  then f_edge <- true
     end_for


     if    p_cycle = true { primitive cycle exists }
     then  { check if it is an affinity cycle }
           if   pmin ≥ former_edge_wt or f_edge = false
           then candidate_p <- true
                c_node <- true
           else f_edge <- false
     else
           insert k into B, maxwt[k] <- -∞
           if   candidate_p = true
           then if     maxwt[k] < pmin or cycle_c_edge_wt < pmin
                then  { partition exists }
                      reinitialize variables
                      if   f_edge = false
                      then save this partition
                      else change the cycle node
                           if   former_edge_wt < pmin
```

```
                        then save this partition
                             remove k from B
                        else extend the cycle
                else  extend the cycle

    { pmin contains the minimum edge of a cycle }
    if   (maxwt[k] ≠ 1 or maxwt[k] ≠ 2) and pmin > maxwt[k]
    then pmin <- maxwt[k]

    { rearrange vectors for next selection }
    for j <- 2 to n do
        if L[k,j] > maxwt[j] then maxwt[j] <- L[k,j]
                                  strongest[j] <- k
    end_for
end_repeat
```

3.2 A Heuristic Procedure for Horizontal Partitioning

Now we describe the complete horizontal partitioning procedure by using the Make_Hori_Partition algorithm described in the previous subsection and the example introduced above.

Procedure HORIZ_PARTITIONING

Step 1. Perform clustering of predicates: It is done by using the Make_Hori_Partition algorithm presented in Section 3.1. We obtain in this step a set of subsets of predicates. In our example, we can obtain three clusters of predicates as shown in Figure 6: (p1,p2,p7), (p3,p4,p9), (p5,p6,p8,p10).

Step 2. Optimize predicates in each subset: In this step predicate inclusion and predicate implication are considered to minimize the number of predicates. In our example, the first subset {D#<10, D#<20, SAL>40K} is refined into {D#<20, SAL>40K} since D#<10 ==> D#<20. The second subset {D#>20, 30<D#<50, AGE<30} is also refined into {D#>20, AGE<30} since 30<D#<50 ==> D#>20, but the last one {D#<15, D#>40, SAL<40K, AGE>30} has no change. Note that this optimization can be done before step 1. But in this paper, we perform this step here in order to allow more detailed clustering. For example, a pair of predicates such as p1 and p2 in which one, (say, p1), implies another (say, p2), can be grouped in different clusters in step 1. The three clusters of predicates produced in this step, called "cluster sets", are listed in Figure 6.

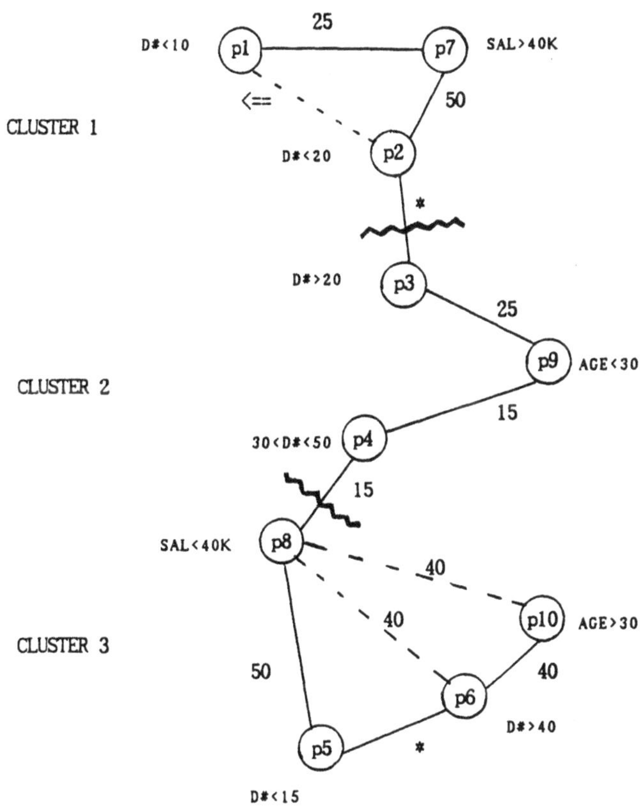

Cluster sets produced: {D#<20, SAL>40K}
{D#>20, AGE<30}
{D#<15, D#>40, SAL<40K, AGE>30}

Fig. 6 Clustering of predicates

Step 3. Compose predicate terms: Corresponding to the cluster sets (Figure 6) produced in step 2, we proceed as follows. The cluster sets are first evaluated to determine the "least common attribute". A least common attribute is an attribute that appears least commonly in cluster sets. In our example, AGE or SAL can be the least common attribute. Note that D# appears in all the three sets. A table called the "predicate term schematic table" is now constructed as follows: (1) Place in the first column the chosen attribute with its appropriate ranges to cover that attribute exhaustively. In our example, if we choose SAL as the least common attribute, we create two entries: SAL<40K and SAL>40K for the SAL attribute. (2) Then, we apply the next to least common attribute, and write its appropriate ranges that appear in the cluster sets against each entry for the first column. For example, since AGE is the next attribute, the predicate AGE>30 is coupled with SAL<40K (from cluster set 3). (3) If the considering least common attribute is opened to the attribute that is in the left column, the considering predicate must be written as many times as the number of predicates in the left column. For example, the AGE<30 predicate appearing in cluster set 2 must be written twice into the table against each entry for SAL. This resulting predicate term schematic table is shown at the left in Figure 7. Note that these ranges may be overlapping. It should be noted that if we do not use the "least common attribute", more fragments may be generated. For example, the number of fragments resulting from the schematic table formed in the order of D#, SAL, and AGE is greater than that of in the order of SAL, AGE, and D# (See Figure 7 and 8(a)). If there are more than one least common attributes, then the same number of fragments are generated regardless of the attribute order even though the schematic tables are slightly different from each other as shown in Figure 7 and 8(b). We are currently investigating the difference in effectiveness between the two tables. Now predicate terms are generated easily from the above table as follows. Each horizontal entry in the table gives rise to one predicate term. If predicates refer to the same attributes then they are ORed, otherwise they are ANDed. The resulting predicate terms for our original example are as follows (see Figure 7):

SAL>40K AND AGE<30 AND D#<20,
SAL>40K AND AGE<30 AND D#>20,
SAL<40K AND AGE>30 AND (D#<15 OR D#>40),
SAL<40K AND AGE<30 AND D#>20.

Step 4. Perform fragmentation: We have one horizontal fragment per predicate term. Thus the number of horizontal fragments will at most be the number of predicate terms plus one because there is one remaining fragment called the "ELSE" fragment, which is the negation of the conjunction of predicate terms.

Predicate term schematic table

SAL>40K (p7)	AGE<30 (p9)	D#<20 (p1,p2)
		D#>20 (p3,p4)
SAL<40K (p8)	AGE>30 (p10)	D#<15 OR D#>40 (p5) (p6)
	AGE<30 (p9)	D#>20 (p3,p4)
ELSE		

===>

Predicate terms:

SAL>40K AND AGE<30 AND D#<20
SAL>40K AND AGE<30 AND D#>20
SAL<40K AND AGE>30 AND (D#<15 OR D#>40)
SAL<40K AND AGE<30 AND D#>20

Fig. 7 Predicate term schematic table and predicate terms

D#<20	SAL>40K	AGE<30
		AGE>30
D#>20	SAL>40K	AGE<30
	SAL<40K	AGE<30
D#<15 OR D#>40	SAL<40K	AGE>30
ELSE		

(a)

AGE>30	SAL<40K	D#<15 OR D#>40
	SAL>40K	D#<20
AGE<30	SAL>40K	D#>20
		D#<20
ELSE		

(b)

Fig. 8 Other predicate term schematic tables

Note that the result of step 4 may be overlapped fragments or nonoverlapped fragments. This algorithm was implemented to demonstrate its effectiveness by slightly modifying the previous implementation of the algorithm for vertical partitioning[10].

3.3 Some Comments on the Complexity and Optimality of the Algorithm

The complexity of this algorithm is dominated by the step 1, and thus will be $O(n^2)$ for n predicates as in the vertical partitioning algorithm. A smaller value of n indicates a good understanding of the heavily used predicates by users. The smaller the n, the better will be the performance of horizontal partitioning.

Now let us consider the effect on the increase of the number of predicates and attributes. Let us define the following variables.

n: number of predicates

m: number of attributes, n>>m

thus n/m : average number of predicate per attribute

Then, as shown in step 3 and Figure 7, the number of predicate terms produced by the algorithm will at most become $(n/m)^m$. This means that the number of predicate terms does not depend on the number of predicates, but the number of attributes. Thus the number of fragments is not so large as in previous approaches (e.g. 2^n in Ceri et al.'s work[2]). However, the research on the efficiency and applicability of this algorithm in the context of the number of attributes in predicates should be continued.

The number of fragments produced by the proposed algorithm may not equal to the optimal number of fragments. Even though this algorithm does not guarantee the optimal number of fragments, we can argue that this algorithm is valuable and produces near-optimal solution. This is because the proposed algorithm incorporated the clustering technique evaluated as a meaningful approach[5].

4. Nonoverlapping Horizontal Partitioning

The result of predicate partitioning may give rise to overlapped horizontal fragments. If nonoverlapped fragments are needed, we apply the ADJUST function (described below). There may be more than one way of creating nonoverlapped fragments from overlapped fragments. Figure 9 shows the three possible ways of dealing with overlapped horizontal fragments. Among these three possible ways, the best way is selected on several different criteria, the important among them being: (1) transaction processing cost, (2) minimization of the number of fragments.

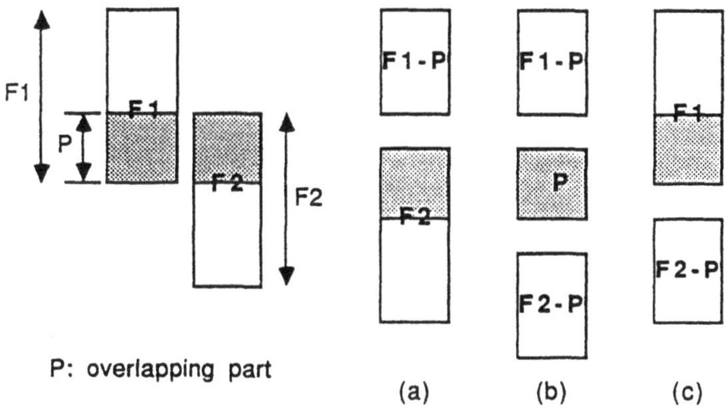

Fig. 9 Three possible ways of dealing with overlapped horizontal fragments

A heuristic procedure for generating nonoverlapped fragments is proposed based on these criteria. Let us define the following set of variables. Here, by "part" we mean that it is a potential horizontal partition (For example, there are three parts in Figure 9).

i =	1,⋯,n denote the parts.
k =	1,⋯,m denote the transactions accessing the parts.
C_{ik} =	cost of accessing part i by transaction k.
F_{ik} =	the frequency with which transaction k accesses part i.
$U_{(ij)k}$ =	cost of unioning two parts i and j into part ij required by transaction k.
$S_{(i/ij)k}$ =	cost of selecting the ith part from the merged part ij by transaction k.

The cost factors would depend on implementation details such as access methods, storage structures, use of special algorithms for duplicate elimination, etc. This level of detail is out of the present scope of our paper.

Using the above parameters and variables, we develop a heuristic adjusting procedure. The merging occurs if the overall cost is reduced because of some transactions accessing the two parts together.

Procedure ADJUST

(1) For each pair of contiguous parts i and j, find the cost of accessing these parts with and without merging respectively.

A. Cost without merging:

$$\sum_{k=1}^{m} C_{ik}F_{ik} + \sum_{k=1}^{m} C_{jk}F_{jk} + \sum_{k=1}^{m} U_{(ij)k}$$

B. Cost with merging:

$$\sum_{k=1}^{m} C_{(ij)k}F_{(ij)k} + \sum_{k=1}^{m} S_{(i/ij)k}$$

(2) Find two parts i and j that produce the maximum saving if they are merged, and then merge them.

(3) After merging two parts, only one new part is generated. Let the set of parts after step (2) be S = 1,⁻,p.

(4) Then repeat steps (1)-(3) for the parts in set S till no two contiguous parts can be merged.

Note that if no merging occurs then each part will be a horizontal fragment. Figure 10 shows an example of the final nonoverlapping fragmentation obtained by using the ADJUST function from the overlapping fragmentation generated in Section 3.2.

Predicate term schematic table

SAL>40K (p7)	AGE<30 (p9)	D#<20 (p1, p2)
		D#>20 (p3, p4)
SAL<40K (p8)	AGE>30 (p10)	D#<15 OR D#>40 (p5) (p6)
	AGE<30 (p9)	D#>20 (p3, p4)
ELSE		

——→ ADJUST

Nonoverlapping fragmentation

SAL>40K AND AGE<30 AND D#<20	H1
SAL>40K AND AGE<30 AND D#>20	H2
SAL<40K AND AGE>30 AND D#<15	H3
SAL<40K AND AGE<30 AND D#>20	H4
ELSE	H5

Fig. 10 Nonoverlapping horizontal fragmentation

5. Conclusion

In this paper we have presented a horizontal partitioning algorithm, which is based on predicate clustering by using the graphical partitioning technique developed in our previous work for vertical partitioning. The major feature of this algorithm is that a relatively small number of horizontal fragments are generated by using the clustering of predicates.

This algorithm can be used by itself or can be used in conjunction with vertical partitioning for forming a grid for "mixed" partitioning for distributed database design[11].

We are applying this work to the development of an interactive design tool. This design tool will allow users to make fragmentation and allocation decisions for distributed databases using vertical, horizontal, and mixed partitioning. Extension of the present work to incorporate cost information will also be beneficial.

References

1. Ceri, S., and Pelagatti, G., Distributed Databases: Principles and Systems, pp. 72–81, McGraw Hill, 1984.

2. Ceri, S., Negri, M., and Pelagatti, G., "Horizontal data Partitioning in Database Design," Proc. ACM SIGMOD International Conference on Management of Data, pp. 128–136, 1982.

3. Ceri, S., Navathe, S. B., and Wiederhold, G., "Distribution Design of Logical Database Schemas," IEEE Trans. on Softw. Eng. SE-9, pp. 487–504, July 1983.

4. Yu, C. T., Suen, C., Lam, K., and Siu, M. K., "Adaptive Record Clustering," ACM Trans. on Database Systems, Vol. 10, No. 2, pp. 180–204, June 1985.

5. Navathe, S. B., Ra, M., "Vertical Partitioning for Database Design: A Graphical Algorithm," Proc. ACM SIGMOD International Conference on Management of Data, pp. 440–450, May 1989.

6. Navathe, S. B., Ra, M., "An Allocation Algorithm for Mixed Fragments in Distributed Database Environment," Working Paper, Georgia Institute of Technology, October 1990.

7. Copeland, G., Alexander, W., Boughter, E., and Keller, T., "Data Placement in Bubba," Proc. ACM SIGMOD International Conference on Management of Data, pp. 99–108, 1988.

8. DeWitt, D. J., Gerber, R. H., Graefe, G., Heytens, M. L., Kumar, K. B., and Muralikrishna, M., "GAMMA – A high Performance Dataflow Database Machine," Proc. Twelfth International Conference on Very Large Data Bases, pp. 228–237, 1986.

9. Navathe, S. B., Ceri, S., Wiederhold, G., and Dou, J., "Vertical Partitioning Algorithms for Database Design," ACM Trans. on Database Systems, Vol. 9, No. 4, pp. 690–710, December 1984.

10. Sreewastav, K., "A Distributed Database Initial Design System," Master's Thesis, University of Florida, 1990.

11. Navathe, S. B., Ra, M., Varadarajan, R., Karlapalem, K., and Sreewastav, K., "A Mixed Partitioning Methodology for Distributed Database Design," UF-CIS Technical Report TR 90-17, University of Florida, February, 1990.

On Horizontal Fragmentation of Distributed Database Design

Yanchun Zhang

Department of Computer Science
The University of Queensland, QLD 4072, Australia

Abstract

In this paper, horizontal partitioning of distributed databases is addressed. The horizontal fragmentation is carried out on each relation based on the predicate affinity and the bond energy algorithm. This is a successful application of a vertical partitioning algorithm to horizontal partitioning.

1 Introduction

In a distributed database, a given relation is not necessarily stored at any single site. Its tuples may be dispersed among several sites because of performance considerations. Sometimes, the same tuples are stored at several sites. We shall term the pieces of relation that reside at each site "site fragments" of the relation. Distribution design is a phase in the development of a distributed application which is concerned with the allocation of data and operations to the various processing sites, according to the application's requirements. The goal of data distribution is to determine fragments of relations and to allocate fragments to sites.

Three kinds of fragmentations have been identified: vertical fragmentation, horizontal fragmentation and mixed fragmentation [9, 11, 12]. Vertical fragmentation is a process that subdivides a relation into subrelations called vertical fragments which are projections of the relation on the subsets of original attributes. Horizontal fragmentation is a process that divides a relation into subsets of tuples through selection operations, called horizontal fragments. Several vertical partition algorithms are well developed and implemented [2, 7, 3]. most of them are based on attribute affinity. On the other hand, horizontal partition has been addressed with the specification of partition predicates. However, as the number of predicates increases, the cost of calculation becomes too expensive (non polynomial).

In this paper, we shall adapt a well known vertical partition algorithm for a horizontal partition. Similar to the attribute affinity, we shall introduce predicate affinity which describes the closeness between two predicates. We shall group those predicates with higher affinity in a horizontal fragment. The paper is organised as follows. In Section 2, a vertical partition algorithm, which is based on the computation of attribute affinity and on the bond energy algorithm (BEA), is briefly reviewed. In Section 3, predicate affinity is introduced, and the horizontal fragmentation is proposed by adapting the BEA algorithm and a vertical partition algorithm. Finally, our conclusions are included in Section 4.

2 A Brief Review of Vertical Partitioning

Let R ={A1, A2, ..., An} be a relation schema. A vertical fragmentation schema R^V of R is a set of subsets of R, defined as $R^V = \{R_1, R_2, ..., R_m \mid R_i \in R, \cup Ri = R\}$

Most of the previous algorithms for vertical fragmentation have started by constructing an attribute affinity matrix from an attribute usage matrix. In the early work by Hoffer and Severance [4] the attribute affinity was developed. It described the degree to which pairs of attributes are accessed together, hence grouping attributes with high affinity will reduce process costs. Clustering attributes on the basis of their familiarity was achieved in [4] by applying the Bond Energy Algorithm (BEA) developed by McCormick [6] to a matrix of attribute values.

Navathe [7] extended the work of Hoffer [4] to a two phase vertical partitioning algorithm. An iterative binary partitioning method was used, based on first clustering the attributes and then applying empirical objective functions or mathematical cost functions to perform the fragmentation. In the first phase of the design, the fragmentation is based purely on intuition and does not consider any idea of cost. The second phase of the algorithm incorporates estimates of cost factors reflecting the physical environment to refine the initial fragments. The computational complexity of this algorithm is $O(n^2 log(n))$. Navathe and Ra [8] proposed a graphical algorithm for vertical partitioning. It has less complexity $O(n^2)$. However, it does not always produce reasonable partitions [5]. In some cases, the results produced by this algorithm are undesirable. Therefore, our discussions will be based on [7].

The major information required for vertical fragmentation is related to applications. Since vertical partitioning places those attributes usually accessed together in one fragment, there is a need for some measurement of "togetherness". This measure is the affinity of attributes which indicates how closely related the attributes are. The following inputs need to be provided by the user in order to come up with the vertical partition scheme.

1 Schema information: relation schemas, attributes.

Attribute usage matrix											Access Frequencies
Attribute	1	2	3	4	5	6	7	8	9	10	
T 1	1	0	0	0	1	0	1	0	0	0	Acc 1 = 25
T 2	0	1	1	0	0	0	0	1	1	0	Acc 2 = 50
T 3	0	0	0	1	0	1	0	0	0	1	Acc 3 = 25
T 4	0	1	0	0	0	0	1	1	0	0	Acc 4 = 35
T 5	1	1	1	0	1	0	1	1	1	0	Acc 5 = 25
T 6	1	0	0	0	1	0	0	0	0	0	Acc 6 = 25
T 7	0	0	1	0	0	0	0	0	1	0	Acc 7 = 25
T 8	0	0	1	1	0	1	0	0	1	1	Acc 8 = 15

(a)

Attribute	1	2	3	4	5	6	7	8	9	10
1	75	25	25	0	75	0	50	25	25	0
2	25	110	75	0	25	0	60	110	75	0
3	25	75	115	15	25	15	25	75	115	15
4	0	0	15	40	0	40	0	0	15	40
5	75	25	25	0	75	0	50	25	25	0
6	0	0	15	40	0	40	0	0	15	40
7	50	60	25	0	50	0	85	60	25	0
8	25	110	75	0	25	0	60	110	75	0
9	25	75	115	15	25	15	25	75	115	15
10	0	0	15	40	0	40	0	0	15	40

(b)

Figure 1: Attribute usage and affinity matrix

2 Transaction information: name, frequency, attribute usage, etc.

The attribute usage matrix is a matrix containing transactions as rows and attributes as columns. Element(i, j)=1 if transaction i uses attribute j, else it is 0.

Attribute Affinity (AA) matrix is an n*n matrix for the n attribute relation whose (i, j) element equals the "between-attributes" affinity that is the total number of accesses by transactions referring to both attributes i and j.

$$\text{i.e. } AA_{ij} = \textstyle\sum_{k \in T} acc_{kij}, \text{ k} \in \text{T}$$

where acc_{kij} is the number of accesses of transaction k referring both attributes i and j. The summation occurs over all transactions that belong to the set of important transactions T.

Example 1. Let R(A1, A2, A3, ..., A10) be a relation schema. Assume that T1, T2, ..., T8 are a set of applications to run on this relation. Their attribute usage matrix and frequencies are shown in Fig. 1 (a). The attribute affinity matrix is constructed in Fig. 1 (b). The fundamental task in designing a vertical fragmentation algorithm is to find some means of grouping the attributes of a

Attribute	5	1	7	2	8	3	9		10	4	6
5	75	75	50	25	25	25	25		0	0	0
1	75	75	85	25	25	25	25		0	0	0
7	50	50	50	60	60	25	25		0	0	0
2	25	25	60	110	110	75	75		0	0	0
8	25	25	60	110	110	75	75		0	0	0
3	25	25	25	75	75	115	115		15	15	15
9	25	25	25	75	75	115	115	x	15	15	15
10	0	0	0	0	0	15	15		40	40	40
4	0	0	0	0	0	15	15		40	40	40
6	0	0	0	0	0	15	15		40	40	40

Figure 2: Clustered AA

relation based on the attribute affinity values in AA. It has been suggested by [4, 7] that the bond energy algorithm (BEA) should be used for this purpose.

The BEA takes as input the attribute affinity matrix, permutes its rows and columns, and generates a clustered affinity matrix (CA). The permutation is done in such a way as to maximize the following global affinity measure (AM).

$$AM = \sum_{i=1}^{i=n} \sum_{j=1}^{j=n} A(i,j)[A(i,j-1) + A(i,j+1)]$$

where A(0, j)=A(i, 0)=(An+1, j)=A(n+1, i) =o

BEA determines an ordering of attributes, or produces a clustered AA matrix. Hoffer suggests a tentative assignment of groups of attributes to fragments. The Slip-Non-Overlap algorithm [7] partition an object into two nonoverlapping fragments. Assume that a point x is fixed along the main diagonal of a clustered AA matrix, as shown in Fig. 2. The point x defines two blocks U (for upper) and L (for lower). Each defines a vertical fragment given by the set of attributes in that block. A nonoverlapping partition is obtained by selecting a point x such that the following goal function z is maximized:

max z = CL * CU - CI^2.

where CT = $\sum_{k \in T} acc_k$, T = { k | k is a transaction }

CL = $\sum_{k \in LT} acc_k, LT = \{k \mid A(k) \in L\}$

CU = $\sum_{k \in UT} acc_k, UT = \{k \mid A(k) \in U\}$

CI = $\sum_{k \in IT} acc_k, IT = T - \{LT \cup UT\}$

A(k) is the set of attributes used by transaction k.

Note that this approach split the set of attributes two-way. For a n-way partition, it can be invoked iteratively or implemented as a recursive procedure.

The result of a repetitive application of a binary partition to Example 1 is shown in Fig.3.

Attribute	5	1	7	2	8	3	9	10	4	6
5	75	75	50	25	25	25	25	0	0	0
1	75	75	50	25	25	25	25	0	0	0
7	50	50	85	60	60	25	25	0	0	0
2	25	25	60	110	110	75	75	0	0	0
8	25	25	60	110	110	75	75	0	0	0
3	25	25	25	75	75	115	115	15	15	15
9	25	25	25	75	75	115	115	15	15	15
10	0	0	0	0	0	15	15	40	40	40
4	0	0	0	0	0	15	15	40	40	40
6	0	0	0	0	0	15	15	40	40	40

Attribute Part*	5	1	7	2	8	3	9	10	4	6	Iteration level
1	X	X	X								2
2				X	X	X	X				2
3								X	X	X	1

Figure 3: Repetitive application of binary partition

3 Horizontal Partition Algorithm

Ceri [1] analyses the horizontal partitioning problem, dealing with the specification of partitioning predicates. There are two types of horizontal fragments: primary and derived. A primary horizontal fragment depends solely on the properties of its own attributes. A derived horizontal fragment is not only based on the properties of its own attributes, but also depends on the horizontal fragments of another relation.

In this paper, we only consider primary horizontal fragmentations. Ceri and Pelagati [1] impose a frequency constraint on each resulting fragment. This constraint ensures that the probability of access to each tuple in a candidate fragment must be the same. If this property does not hold, then further horizontal fragmentation may take place; that is, the fragment has not been fully reduced.

Let us consider only simple predicates formed from the global relation, ie. attribute-name θ value, where θ is one of $\{ <, >, =, \leq, \geq, \neq \}$, the value is from the domain of the attribute. Let these predicates be denoted by pi. Each predicate forms a condition in the theta selection defined on that table.

Consider the set of all such simple predicates. Let this set be denoted by P, P={p1, p2, ..., pm}. The conjunction of these predicates (or some negatives) forms the fragment schema on this table.

A set P of predicates is complete iff any two tuples belonging to the same fragment are referenced with the same probability by any application.

The set P is said to be relevant iff each predicate in the set partitions the global relation. That is, the predicate and its negation are referenced differently at least by one application (each predicate is said to be relevant as well).

A fragment is formed by the feasible conjunction of all predicates in P, where the predicate is in natural or negated form.

Primary horizontal fragments may be constructed using the following method [1, 10]:

Method:

1 Find one relevant predicate p1.

2 Let P={p1}.

3 Find another relevant predicate and add this to P.

4 Continue until P is complete.

5 Form the fragment schema for this table

Note that the test of completeness involves the comparison of the probabilities of access by any application. As the size of set P increases, the cost of calculation might be too expensive.

In order to adopt the vertical partition algorithm [7] for horizontal fragmentation, we may consider the predicate usage. Similarly, we can define predicate affinity. The BEA algorithm could then be employed to cluster predicates, and a horizontal fragment is formed for each cluster.

We now describe the steps involved in the horizontal partitioning algorithm.

Method:

1 Input a predicate usage matrix: In the predicate usage matrix, each row represents an important transaction; each column represents a simple predicate; the "1" entry in a row indicates that the transaction uses the corresponding predicates.

2 Construct the predicate affinity matrix: Predicate affinity is generated from the predicate usage matrix in a similar manner to attribute affinity. The value of the (i, j) entry in the predicate affinity matrix represents the combined frequency of all important transactions accessing both predicates i and j.

3 Clustering predicates: By using the vertical partitioning algorithm in [7], we obtain a set of clusters of predicates.

4 Optimize predicates. In each subset, predicate inclusion and predicate implications are considered to reduce the number of predicates.

5 Construct horizontal fragments: For each refined cluster, construct a predicate term that will be used for a fragment definition. The term is constructed as follows. Simple predicates with the same attribute are ORed, and then predicates with different attributes are ANDed. Finally, add one remaining fragment which is the negation of the disjunction of predicate terms.

We demonstrate our horizontal partitioning methodology by using a simple example below.

Example 2. Let R=(Eno, Ename, Sal, Degree) be a relation schema. Let T1, T2, ..., T6, and T7 be a set of important transactions. Their corresponding predicates are shown as follows:

- T1: Eno < 10 (p1), Sal $\geq$ 50K (p3), Degree=Ph.D (p6)
- T2: Eno < 20 (p2), Sal $\geq$ 50K
- T3: Eno ≥ 20 (p4), Sal $\geq$ 50K
- T4: $30 <$ Eno < 60 (p5), Sal $<$ 50K (p9), Degree=Ph.D
- T5: Eno < 15 (p7), Sal $<$ 50K, Degree=Ph.D (p6)
- T6: Eno > 50 (p8), Sal $<$ 50K, Degree=Ph.D
- T7: Eno < 15 (p7), Sal $\geq$ 50K

Input a predicate usage matrix and construct a predicate affinity matrix . The predicate usage matrix is shown in Fig.4 (a) and its predicate affinity matrix is shown in Fig.4 (b).

Clustering predicates . By using the above rules and the split-non-overlapping algorithm [7], we can obtain two subsets of predicates as shown in Fig. 5: (p4, p1, p2, p3), (p7, p9, p6, p5, p8).

Optimize predicates . Since (Eno $< 10 \Rightarrow$ (Eno < 20), furthermore, (Eno < 20 OR (Eno ≥ 20) $\Rightarrow$ "true", the first subset (Eno < 10, Eno < 20, Eno ≥ 20, Sal $\geq$ 50K) is refined to (Sal $\geq$ 50K). The second one (Eno > 50, Eno < 15, $30 <$ Eno < 60, Sal < 50, Degree= Ph.D) is also refined into ((Eno > 30 OR Eno < 15) AND Sal < 50 AND Degree=Ph.D

Predicate usage matrix										Access Frequencies
Predicates	p1	p2	p3	p4	p5	p6	p7	p8	p9	
Transactions										
T1	1	0	1	0	0	1	0	0	0	Acc 1 = 25
T2	0	1	1	0	0	0	0	0	0	Acc 2 = 50
T3	0	0	1	1	0	0	0	0	0	Acc 3 = 25
T4	0	0	0	0	1	1	0	0	1	Acc 4 = 35
T5	0	0	0	0	0	1	1	0	1	Acc 5 = 25
T6	0	0	0	0	0	1	0	1	1	Acc 6 = 25
T7	0	0	1	0	0	0	1	0	0	Acc 7 = 25

(a)

Predicates	1	2	3	4	5	6	7	8	9
1	0	0	25	0	0	25	0	0	0
2	0	0	50	0	0	0	0	0	0
3	25	50	0	25	0	25	25	0	0
4	0	0	25	0	0	0	0	0	0
5	0	0	0	0	0	35	0	0	35
6	25	0	25	0	35	85	25	25	85
7	0	0	25	0	0	25	0	0	25
8	0	0	0	0	0	25	0	0	0
9	0	0	0	0	35	85	25	0	0

(b)

Figure 4: Predicate usage and affinity

	4	1	2	3	7	9	6	5	8
4	0	0	0	25	0	0	0	0	0
1	0	0	0	25	0	0	25	0	0
2	0	0	0	50	0	0	0	0	0
3	25	25	50	0	25	0	25	0	0
7	0	0	0	25	0	25	25	0	0
9	0	0	0	0	25	0	85	35	0
6	0	25	0	25	25	85	0	35	25
5	0	0	0	0	0	35	35	0	0
8	0	0	0	0	0	0	25	0	0

Figure 5: Clustered predicate affinity matrix

Construct horizontal fragments . For each refined set, construct a predicate term that will be used for fragmentation.

```
( Sal > 50K).
(Eno < 15 OR Eno > 30 ) AND (Sal < 50K) AND (Degree=Ph.D)
```

We have one horizontal fragment per predicate term. Thus the number of horizontal fragments will at most be the number of predicate terms plus one because there is one remaining fragment which is the negation of disconjunction of predicate terms. In this case, the remaining one is

(15 < Eno < 30 AND Sal < 50K) OR ((Eno < 15 OR Eno > 30) AND (Sal < 50K AND Degree≠Ph.D)

Remarks The complexity of the proposed approach is dominated by Step 3. Therefore, it has complexity O($n^2 log(n)$), where n is the size of the input. Our approach is based on a non-overlapping partition algorithm. It implies that at Step 3 the partition of simple predicates are nonoverlapped. It means that one single predicate can only appear in one fragment. If a predicate is allowed to appear in different fragments, it will be a overlapping fragmentation. Intuitively, in some cases, this overlapping may offer more flexibilities. This will be investigated in the future work.

The same idea of using predicate matrix for horizontal fragmentation was first proposed in Navathe's work [9], where a modified version of a graphical algorithm [8] was used to cluster predicates. However, as pointed out in Lin's work [5], the graphical partitioning algorithm in [8] has some undesirable features. It does not always produce the reasonable solutions. Therefore, our horizontal partitioning procedure is based on the vertical partition algorithm in [7]. Another feature is the simplicity. In the clustering step, we do not consider the similarity and inclusion relations between different predicates. We believe this could be incorporated in the step of optimization phase or in the late stage of the data allocation for distributed database design.

4 Conclusions

In this paper, the horizontal partitioning of distributed databases has been addressed. Vertical partitioning algorithms are well developed and implemented. In order to adapt the vertical partition algorithm for horizontal partitioning, predicate usage and predicate affinity are introduced. Then the bond energy algorithm is employed to cluster predicates. Each cluster will generate a primary horizontal fragment. This result is a successful application of a vertical partitioning algorithm to horizontal partitioning.

In future work, overlapping partitioning on the predicate affinity matrix will be addressed. Intuitively, it might produce more reasonable solutions by allowing a simple predicate to appear in different fragment definitions.

ACKNOWLEDGEMENT: The author would like to thank Professor Maria Orlowska for her constructive comments and discussions on this paper.

References

[1] S. Ceri and G. Pelagate. *Distributed Databases: Principles and Systems.* New York: McGraw-Hill, 1984.

[2] S. Ceri, B. Pernici, and G. Wiederhold. Optimization problems and solution methods in the design of data distribution. *Information Systems*, 14(3):261–272, 1989.

[3] D. Cornell and P.S. Yu. A vertical partitioning algorithms for relational databases. In *Proc. Third International Conferences on Data Engineering*, Feb. 1987.

[4] J. A. Hoffer and D.J. Severance. The use of cluster analysis in physical database design. In *Proc. First Intl. Conf on VLDB*, 1975.

[5] X. Lin and Y. Zhang. A new graphical method for vertical partitioning in distributed database design. In *Proceedings of The Fourth Australian Database Conference*, 1993.

[6] W.T. McCormick and P.J. Schwietzer. Problem decomposition and data reorganization by a clustering technique. *Opeation Research*, 20, Sep 1972.

[7] S. Navathe and S. Ceri. A vertical partitioning algorithms for database design. *ACM Trans. on Database Systems*, 9, 1984.

[8] S. Navathe and M. Ra. Vertical partitioning for database design: A graphical algorithm. In *ACM SIGMOD 89*, pages 440–450, 1989.

[9] S. Navathe, M. Ra, R Varadarajan, K Karlapalem, and K Sreewastav. A mixed partitionning methodology for distributed database design. *Technical Report, Department of Computer Science, The University of Florida*, 1990.

[10] M. Tamer Ozsu and Patrick Valduriez. *Principles of Distributed Database Systems.* Prentice Hall, 1991.

[11] Y. Zhang and M. Orlowska. Correctness issues of distributed database design. *Australian Computer Science Commun.*, 15(1), 1992.

[12] Y. Zhang, M. Orlowska, and R. Colomb. An efficient test for validity of unbiased hybrid knowledge fragmentation in distributed databases. *Intl. J. Software Engineering and Knowledge Engineering*, 2(4), 1992.

A NEW GRAPHICAL METHOD FOR VERTICAL PARTITIONING IN DATABASE DESIGN

Xuemin Lin and Yanchun Zhang

Department of Computer Science
University of Queensland
QLD 4072, Australia
e-mail: lxue@cs.uq.oz.au / yan@cs.uq.oz.au

ABSTRACT

In this paper, a graphical approach to vertical partitioning of a relation is presented. An attribute affinity graph expressed by an affinity matrix can be easily constructed from the set of important and frequently used transactions to the system. This is the input of our partitioning process. The partitioning process has two major steps. In the first phase, a set of clusters on the affinity graph is constructed, where each cluster is a vertex set of a subgraph with a "strong" connectivity between vertices. In the second phase, clusters with the "highest affinity index" are iteratively chosen as fragments. This approach overcomes most of the deficiencies of the partitioning algorithm by Navathe-Ra [Nava 89]. The overall computational complexity of this proposed approach is usually smaller than the algorithm [Nava 84].

1. Introduction

In distributed database design and in centralized database design, the partitioning of a global relational schema into fragments is crucial to the performance of transactions [Nava 84, Nava 89, Aper 88]. Three kinds of fragmentations have been identified: "vertical partitioning", "horizontal partitioning", and "mixed partitioning" [Ceri 84]. The correctness issues of these fragmentations in distributed database design have been discussed in [Zhan 92a&b, Orlo 91]. In this paper, we shall only consider *vertical partitioning*: a process that divides a global object, which is either a single relation of a normalized relational database or a universal relation, into groups of their attributes, called vertical fragments. Various applications of vertical partitioning are listed in [Nava 84], such as the partitioning of individual files in a centralized environment, data distribution in distributed databases, and the division of data among different levels of memory hierarchies.

The Bond Energy Algorithm (BEA) [McCo 72] was first used by Hoffer and Severance [Hoff 75] to cluster attributes according to their pairwise affinity. Most of the current approaches [Nava 84, Corn 87, Ceri 88] for vertical partitioning apply BEA [Hoff 75, McCo 72] as a clustering method. [Nava 84] proposes a two-phase strategy for a vertical partitioning. In the first phase, an attribute usage matrix and transaction frequencies information are used to build the attribute affinity (AA) matrix, and clustering is then performed on the AA matrix. Subsequently, an iterative binary partition is used with an empirical objective function until no further partitioning results. In the second phase, a refinement is carried out by incorporating estimated cost factors on the basis of the type of a problem being solved. This approach has been used in several systems for distributed database design [Corn 87, Ceri 88, Nava 84].

A graphical algorithm for vertical partitioning is proposed by Navathe and Ra [Nava 89]. Instead of using the BEA [McCo 72, Hoff 75] to cluster attributes, they apply graphical techniques. This graphical algorithm is based on the same intuition as in [Nava 84]:

II. all pairs of attributes in a fragment have high "within fragment affinity" but low "between fragment affinity" [Nava 89].

Experiments showed that in some cases the performance of their graphical approach is better than the performance of the algorithms in [Nava 84]. The quality of this algorithm is measured by the claimed properties [Nava 89, pp.446]. However, in general, the Navathe-Ra algorithm [Nava 89] demonstrates some serious deficiencies:

- the produced output does not necessarily satisfy the claimed properties [Nava 89, pp. 446];
- the algorithm generates a solution which depends on the input order [Nava 89, pp. 447].

We shall show two simple examples to demonstrate these features in Section 2.

The major purpose of this work is to formalize the graphical notion of pairwise affinity and to present a new algorithm for vertical fragmentation to more precisely satisfy the intuition II. In contrast to the Navathe-Ra algorithm and [Nava 84], our approach has the following important properties:

- the output produced meets an intuitive solution to the partition problem;
- the computational complexity is usually smaller than the algorithm [Nava 84] (see Section 5);
- the main body of the algorithm is easier to implement than the algorithm [Nava 84];
- the two deficiencies of [Nava 89] mentioned above have been resolved so that the claimed properties of Navathe-Ra algorithm are archived in our new algorithm.

This paper is organized as follows. In Section 2, two counter examples to the claimed properties of Navathe-Ra approach [Nava 89] are presented to justify the above claims. In Section 3, a graphical formalization of a cluster (to reflect the pairwise affinity among the attributes) is given. In Section 4, we present an algorithm, Cluster, for the generation of all clusters. In Section 5, an algorithm, NOV, developed for constructing non-overlapping fragments, and its analysis, are presented. This is followed by the conclusion.

2. Some Drawbacks of Navathe-Ra Algorithm

The major information required for vertical fragmentation is related to applications (see Section 3). A good vertical partition should have the frequently accessed attributes grouped together in a fragment of this partition. Thus, the requirement of some measurement of "togetherness" arises. The Navathe-Ra algorithm [Nava 89] attempts to find an intuitively correct vertical partition for a set of attributes by using geometric information through an "affinity graph" (defined in Section 3).

As we mentioned in the introduction, the Navathe-Ra algorithm has some undesirable features. We shall demonstrate some of them in the following simple examples. For a detailed discussion of the Navathe-Ra algorithm, we refer readers to [Nava 89].

Let the affinity between attributes *A*, *B*, *C*, *D*, *F*, *H*, *I*, *K* be given as illustrated in Figure 1, where the edges' labels intuitively correspond to the frequency of usage of the attributes.

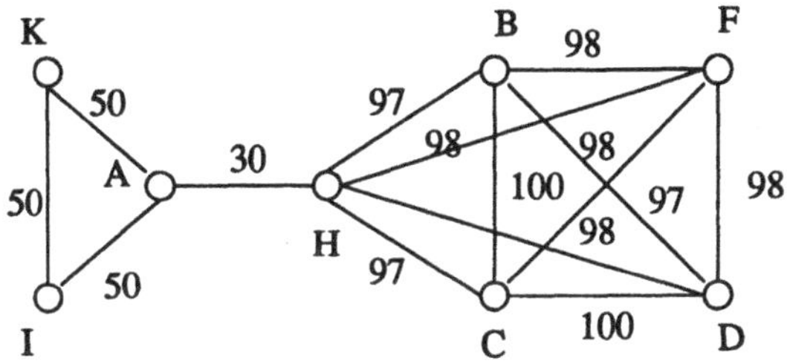

Figure 1

It should be easy to observe that the possible and intuitively correct partition of this set of attributes will be:

(*) $\{\{H,B,F,D,C\},\ \{A,I,K\}\}$.

However, when Navathe-Ra algorithm is applied to the graph in Figure 1 with the starting attribute *B*, the following partition might be produced:

(**) $\{\{B,F,D,C\},\ \{H\},\ \{A,I,K\}\}$.

We now describe how the partitioning (**) is produced by Navathe-Ra algorithm:

According to Navathe-Ra algorithm, if it starts with attribute *B* then either *BFDCB* or *BFHDCB* will become an "affinity cycle" [Nava 89] with *B* as its "cycle node" [Nava 89]. Suppose that *BFDCB* is chosen as an affinity cycle by the algorithm. This algorithm will then check if this cycle can be extended from *C*, that is, all paths *CXB* will be checked to see if one of them can be chosen to extend the cycle

BFDCB to *BFDCXB* where X is a vertex in $\{A,K,I,H\}$. In this case, the cycle *BFDCB* cannot be extended any more from C according to the condition in [Nava 89, pp.443]. Similarly, next this algorithm will check to see if the cycle *BFDCB* can be extended from B. Again in this case, this cycle cannot be extent from B. Thus, $\{B,F,D,C\}$ is cut as a fragment. Subsequently, the partitioning (**) is produced.

Our intuitive solution (*) satisfies the properties presented in [Nava 89] (see also Theorem 5 and Corollary 5), though unfortunately, in the generated solution (**) it is hard to justify $\{H\}$ as a separate fragment.

The following example in Figure 2 shows another undesired property of Navathe-Ra algorithm.

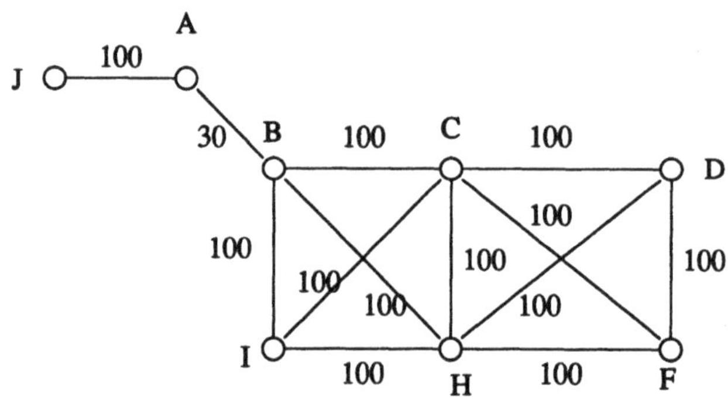

Figure 2

Similarly, an application of the graphical algorithm on the graph of Figure 2 may produce two following results depending on its input order. This contradicts the uniqueness property of the result produced by the graphic algorithm.

Result 1: $\{B,C,H,I\}$ and $\{D,F\}$ and $\{A,J\}$ form a partition.

Result 2: $\{B,C,H,I,D,F\}$ and $\{A,J\}$ form a partition.

Clearly, the partition of Result 2 is intuitively correct.

3. Basic Notation and the New Cluster Model

In this section, we introduce some basic notations, and then present a cluster model.

Given a finite set V, a *partition* of V is a set $F=\{f_i: 1 \le i \le l\}$ such that each f_i is a subset of V called a *fragment* of V, and $\bigcup_{i=1}^{l} f_i = V$. A partition $\{f_i: 1 \le i \le l\}$ of V is *nonoverlapping* if for each pair f_i and f_j of distinct fragments, $f_i \cap f_j = \emptyset$. Note that if V is a set of attributes in a relation schema then a partition of V is a *vertical partition* schema in relational database design.

We now introduce an affinity graph over a set V of attributes and a set of *important transactions* [Nava 84]. Here V consists of either

(1) the attributes in a single relation schema R, or

(2) a universal set of attributes, that is, the set of attributes in the universal relation schema **R**.

In case (1), we assume that V contains all the attributes of R; once a partition is obtained, we simply append the primary key to every fragment [Nava 84]. In case (2), once a partition F of V is obtained, we can normalize F in two ways:

(a) each fragment generated can be normalized to a relation schema [Nava 89], or

(b) for each fragment f_i of V, we subgroup the attributes of f_i to several new fragments $f_{i,j}$ so that each $f_{i,j}$ is in a relation schema, while $j \neq k$, $f_{i,j}$ and $f_{i,k}$ are in two different relation schemata. Then we add the corresponding primary key to every $f_{i,j}$.

For a given set V of n attributes to be partitioned, the following information can be obtained from the user requirements:

- A set of m important transactions with some statistical information, such as the frequency u_i of transaction i $(1 \leq i \leq m)$ and each attribute usage.

Thus, the attribute usage matrix $[a_{i,j}]_{m \times n}$ is constructed as follows. For $1 \leq i \leq m$, $1 \leq j \leq n$, $a_{i,j} = 1$ if transaction i uses attribute j, otherwise $a_{i,j} = 0$.

The attribute affinity matrix $AA = [A_{i,j}]_{n \times n}$ is constructed as follows. For $1 \leq i, j \leq n$, each element $A_{i,j}$ is equal to the "between-attributes" affinity, that is, the total number of access of the transactions referring to both attributes i and j:

$$A_{i,j} = \sum_{k=1}^{m} u_k a_{k,i} a_{k,j}.$$

Navathe and Ra use the affinity matrix $[A_{i,j}]_{n \times n}$ to generate the *attribute-affinity graph* $G = (V, E, p)$ where V is the vertex set of G, E is the edge set, (V,E) is a complete graph, and the mapping p assigns each edge $e_{i,j} = (v_i, v_j)$ $(i \neq j)$ with the value $p(e_{i,j}) = A_{i,j}$. For each edge e, $p(e)$ is its *affinity value*.

An *affinity graph* is a representation of an attribute-affinity graph through the removal of the edges with the affinity value 0.

Let I denote the set of all positive integers. We now give a mathematical description of an affinity graph. An affinity graph is represented by a *positive weighted* graph $G = (V, E, p)$ consisting of a *simple graph* (V, E) [BM] and a mapping p: $E \rightarrow I$.

The following basic graph notation will be used in the rest of the paper.

In a graph (V,E), $(u,v) \in E$ is *incident to* u and v. A graph (V',E') is a *subgraph* of (V,E) if $V' \subseteq V$ and $E' \subseteq E$. (V,E) is *connected* if for each pair u,v of distinct vertices, there is a *path* [BM] connecting u and v. (V,E) is *2-connected* if $|V| \geq 3$, and if after the removal of an arbitrary vertex, the resultant graph is still connected. (Note that we exclude the case that there is a 2-connected graph with 2 vertices).

Suppose that V' is a subset of V. A subgraph (V', E') of (V, E) is *induced* by V' if E' is the set of those edges which are incident to a pair of vertices in V'. A *connected component* of (V,E) is a connected subgraph (V',E') of (V,E) with the property that for each vertex u of V' and each vertex v of $V-V'$, there is no path from u to v in (V, E). A vertex u of (V, E) is *isolated* if there is no edge incident to u.

All the above concepts can be immediately applied to an affinity graph $G=(V, E, p)$ if we ignore the mapping p.

A *cluster* V' of an affinity graph $G=(V, E, p)$ is a subset of V such that either

(3.1) $|V'|>1$, and there is a connected subgraph (V', E') of (V, E) with the property that for each edge e of E', $p(e)$ is larger than the affinity values of those edges "going out from V'" (for example, in Figure 3 edges (B,H), (C,B), and (D,B) go out from $\{D, H, C\}$); or

(3.2) V' consists of an isolated vertex of G.

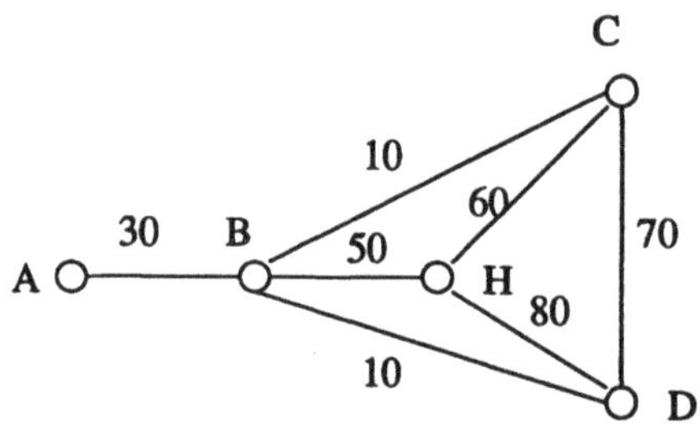

Figure 3

Figure 3 gives an example, where $\{A,B,C,D,H\}$, $\{B,C,D,H\}$, $\{C,D,H\}$, and $\{D,H\}$ are clusters.

Lemma 1: The relationship between two clusters V_1 and V_2 of an affinity graph G is that either they are disjoint or there is a complete inclusion.

Proof: We only need to prove that if $V_1 \cap V_2 \neq \emptyset$ then

(3.3) either $V_1 \subset V_2$ or $V_2 \subset V_1$.

Suppose that (3.3) does not hold, that is, there is a $v_1 \in V_1$ and a $v_2 \in V_2$ such that v_1 and v_2 are not in $V_1 \cap V_2$. Because V_1 and V_2 are clusters, there are two connected subgraphs G_1 and G_2 respectively with V_1 and V_2 as their vertex sets so that (3.1) holds with respect to both G_1 and G_2. Thus, there an edge e_1, which is on a path from v_1 to $V_1 \cap V_2$ in G_1 and goes out from both $V_1 \cap V_2$ and V_2, such that $p(e_1)$ larger than the affinity values of those edge going out from V_1. Similarly, there is another edge e_2, which is in a path from v_2 to $V_1 \cap V_2$ and goes out from both $V_1 \cap V_2$ and V_1, such that $p(e_2)$ larger than the affinity values of those edge going out from V_2. Hence $p(e_1)>p(e_2)$ and $p(e_2)>p(e_1)$. Contradiction! □

From Lemma 1, by using mathematical induction on the number of vertices, it immediately follows that:

Theorem 1: Given an affinity graph $G=(V, E, p)$, there are at most n clusters where n is the number of vertices of G. □

4. A Cluster Algorithm

In this section, we describe an algorithm, Cluster, which takes an affinity graph $G=(V, E, p)$ as an input, and generates all the clusters. The main idea is as follows. First, the edges are grouped according to their affinity values. Therefore, E is partitioned into a list M of disjoint subsets $M_1, M_2, ..., M_k$ in a decreasing order of edge affinity values. Then we form a subgraph (V, M_1), and generate all connected components. The vertex sets with a size larger than 1 of the generated connected components will be the first group of clusters, since all other edges connected to a component above in the original graph will have an affinity value smaller than that of the edges in the components. Similarly, considering the subgraph $(V, M_1 \cup M_2)$, we generate all connected components in this subgraph. The vertex sets with a size larger than 1 of the components are to be another group of clusters, where the affinity values of the remaining edges in the original graph are smaller than the edge affinity value in $M_1 \cup M_2$. Similarly it is possible to generate all possible clusters. This algorithm is presented more precisely below.

Algorithm Cluster (G, Var T)
Input $G=(V,E,p)$: affinity graph;
Output T: a set of clusters of V
Begin
  Step 1. Sort on E to generate a list M of subsets of E: $\{M_1, M_2, \cdots M_k\}$
    such that all edges in the same M_i have the same value
    of $p(e)$, and if $e_i \in M_i, e_j \in M_j, i<j$ then $p(e_i)>p(e_j)$;
  Step 2. For $i=1$ to k
    Begin
    Let $G_i=(V, \bigcup_{j=1}^{i} M_j)$;
    Find all connected components of G_i;
    End
  Step 3. Let T_1 be the set of the vertex sets of all elements
    with at least two vertices generated at Step 2;
    Let T_2 consist of the isolated vertices;
    $T=T_1 \bigcup T_2$;
End

The correctness of the algorithm Cluster follows from the above discussion. Here we state the following theorem which can be easily proved.

Theorem 2: After applying Cluster on an affinity graph, the output T consists of all clusters of G. □

In Cluster, the sorting process of Step 1 could be finished in time $O(m\log n)$ [Sed], where m is the number of edges, and n is the number of vertices. It seems that Step 2 is much more complicated, since it involves many redundant or repetitive computations in finding components relating to G_1, G_2, ..., G_k. However, if a proper data structure is used, the redundant computations could be avoided. Consequently, Steps 2 and 3 can be finished in $O(n^2)$. The implementation details and its analysis are included in the Appendix. Here we state the time complexity of the algorithm Cluster.

Theorem 3: The algorithm Cluster takes $O(m\log n + n^2)$ time where m is the number of edges, and n is the number of vertices. □

5. Vertical Partition Algorithms

In this section, we present an algorithm, NOV, which produces a non-overlapping partition of a set of attributes.

To present our algorithm, we introduce some notation.

Given an affinity graph G, our main aim is to find a partition $\{f_i\colon 1 \le i \le l\}$ to precisely follow the intuition II. The algorithm NOV iteratively finds a fragment f_i with the property of f_i being a cluster and having the highest "affinity index" (defined below).

Given an affinity graph $G=(V, E, p)$ and a cluster V' of G, we define a subset $E(V')$ of E as follows. If $|V'|>1$ then

- $E(V')=\{e\colon e$ incident to two vertices of V' and $p(e)$ is larger than affinity values of the edges going out from $V'\}$.

If V' consists of an isolated vertex of G then $E(V')=\emptyset$. The subgraph $G(V')=(V', E(V'))$ is called the *associated graph* of the cluster V'. From the fact that V' is a cluster, it follows that $G(V')=(V', E')$ is connected if $|V'|>1$.

Now a quadruple $(c(V'), x(V'), d(V'), w(V'))$ is used to denote the *affinity index* of V' where if $|V'|>1$, then

- $c(V')=2$ if $G(V')$ is 2-connected and $c(V')=1$ otherwise,
- $x(V')=\dfrac{1}{|V'|}$,
- $d(V')=\dfrac{2|E(V')|}{|V'|(|V'|-1)}$,
- $w(V')=\dfrac{\sum_{e\in E(V')} p(e)}{|E(V')|}$,

and if $|V'|=1$ then $c(V')=1, x(V')=0, d(V')=0$, and $w(V')=0$.

For two affinity indices $a=(c, x, d, w)$ and $\overline{a}=(\overline{c}, \overline{x}, \overline{d}, \overline{w})$, $a>\overline{a}$ if either

- $c>\overline{c}$, or
- $c=\overline{c}$ and $x>\overline{x}$, or
- $c=\overline{c}$, $x=\overline{x}$, and $d>\overline{d}$, or
- $c=\overline{c}$, $x=\overline{x}$, $d=\overline{d}$, and $w>\overline{w}$.

5.1. Algorithm NOV

Given an affinity graph $G=(V, E, p)$ where $|V|=n$ and $|E|=m$, we present NOV.

In NOV, the procedure CLUSTER($G=(V, M, p)$, Var T) is used where G is the input affinity graph and M is a list of ordered subsets of E as described in the last section, and procedure CLUSTER is a slight modification of Algorithm Cluster such as the removal of the procedure SORT from Algorithm Cluster. It should be clear that CLUSTER takes $O(n^2)$ time.

In NOV, given a set T of clusters, the procedure OBTAIN(T, Var $S(T)$) outputs the set $S(T)$ of affinity indices of the elements of T. Because the 2-connectivity of a graph $(\overline{V}, \overline{E})$ can be checked in $O(|\overline{E}|)$ time [Sed], the associated graph of a cluster can be found in $O(m)$ time, and there are at most $O(n)$ clusters in G. Thus OBTAIN takes $O(nm)$ time.

Further in NOV, a procedure CHOOSE(T, $S(T)$, Var f) is used to choose an element f with the highest affinity index from T. CHOOSE takes $O(n)$ time.

The algorithm NOV is described as follows.

Algorithm NOV (G; Var F;)
Input G: affinity graph; Output F: set of fragments;
Begin
 $F:=\emptyset$; $j:=0$; SORT(G,M,k) ($M=\{M_i: 1\le i\le k\}$);
 $V_0:=V$; $E_0:=M$;
 While $V_j\ne\emptyset$ **do**
  Begin
   CLUSTER((V_j, E_j, p), T);
   OBTAIN(T, $S(T)$);
   CHOOSE(T, $S(T)$, f);
   $F:=F\cup f$;
   $j:=j+1$; $T:=\emptyset$;
   $V_j:=V_{j-1}-f$;
   delete the edges incident to a vertex of f from E_{j-1} to form E_j;
  End
End

The consequence of the above discussion is as follows:

Theorem 4: Given an affinity graph, NOV runs in time $O(lnm)$, where l is the number of fragments. □

5.2. Analysis of the Algorithm NOV

In this section, we present some properties of NOV; and then we show that this algorithm may overcome some of the disadvantages of the graphic algorithm of [Nava89].

Properties of NOV

To show some properties of NOV, we now introduce two classes of affinity graphs. An affinity graph $G=(V, E, p)$ is *distinguishable* if it has the following properties:

(1) there is a nonoverlapping partition $\{f_{i,j}: 1 \le j \le l_i, 1 \le i \le k\}$ of V (note here the two dimensional subindex is used to label a fragment) such that each $f_{i,j}$ has at least 3 vertices;

(2) for $1 \le j \le l_1, f_{1,j}$ is a cluster of G, the associated graph of $f_{1,j}$ is a complete graph, and there is no cluster which is a proper subset of $f_{1,j}$ and its associated graph is 2-connected;

(3) iteratively from $x=1$ to $k-1$, let G_x denote the resultant graph after the removal of $\{f_{i,j}: 1 \le j \le l_i, 1 \le i \le x\}$, then for $1 \le j \le l_{x+1}, f_{x+1,j}$ preserve the property (2) with respect to G_x.

One can immediately prove that there is only one partition with the properties (1), (2) and (3) in a distinguishable affinity graph G; such a partition is called the *outstanding partition* of G.

An affinity graph $G=(V,E,p)$ is *strongly distinguishable* if it has the following properties:

(4) $\{f_i: 1 \le i \le l\}$ is a nonoverlapping partition of V such that each f_i has at least 3 vertices; and

(5) for $1 \le i \le l, f_i$ has the property as described in (2) with respect to G.

Note that a strongly distinguishable affinity graph is also distinguishable. One may easily prove that there is only one partition with the properties (5), (6) in a strongly distinguishable affinity graph G; such a partition is also called the *outstanding partition* of G.

From NOV, it is easy to show the following:

Theorem 5: Suppose that G is a distinguishable affinity graph. Then the partition F on the vertex set of G produced by Algorithm NOV is the outstanding partition of G. □

Corollary 1: Suppose that G is a strongly distinguishable affinity graph. Then the partition F on the vertex set of G produced by NOV is the outstanding partition of G. □

Remarks

As well as the above properties, from our experiments we can state that:

- the attributes of a fragment obtained by NOV are intuitively grouped together in the affinity graph.

Navathe and Ra [Nava 89] believe from their experiments that their graphical algorithm will produce some significant fragments which cannot be found by the algorithm in [Nava 84]. The quality of the graphical algorithm [Nava 89] was measured by Theorem 5 and Corollary 1 which are claimed to be true for their algorithm. As shown in Figure 1, their algorithm generally does not follow Theorem 5 and Corollary 1. In contrast, the algorithm NOV will produce the intuitive correct partitions respectively with respect to Figures 1 and 2.

We should mention that the non-overlapping algorithm of [Nava 84] has no such performance guarantees as stated in Theorem 5 and Corollary 1. After obtaining the attribute affinity matrix, the non-overlapping algorithm in [Nava 84] runs in $O(Ln^2 \log n)$ time, where L is the number of important transactions and n is the number of attributes. It should be clear that usually L is $\Omega(m)$ where m is the number of edges of the affinity graphs. Subsequently, the non-overlapping algorithm in [Nava 84] runs in $\Omega(mn^2 \log n)$ time in the worst case. In contrast, after obtaining the attribute affinity matrix, it takes $O(n^2)$ to construct an affinity graph; and NOV takes $O(lmn)$ where l is the number of fragments, m is the number of edges, and $l = O(n)$. Thus, we can expect that our approach is more efficient than [Nava 84].

In general, we believe that NOV will find all significant partitions. However the algorithm NOV, like the nonoverlapping algorithm in [Nava 84], suffers from the restriction of non-overlapping partitions. This can be improved by developing an algorithm OVE (stands for overlapping algorithm) which produces overlapping partitions. This enhancement will be discussed in a separate paper.

6. Conclusion

In this paper, a new cluster model and a graphical vertical partitioning algorithm NOV are presented. This approach overcomes some deficiencies found in the algorithm of [Nava 89]. The algorithm NOV has a time complexity $O(lmn)$, where m is the number of edges, n is the number of vertices, and l is the number of fragments. It is more efficient than the algorithm in [Nava 84] and more effective than [Nava 89].

References

[Aper 88] Peter M. G. Apers, "Data Allocation in Distributed Database Systems", *ACM Transactions on Database Systems*, Vol. 13, No. 3, September 1988, page263-304.

[BM] J. A. Bondy and U. S. R. Murty, *Graph Theory with Applications*, The Macmillan, 1978.

[Ceri 87a] S. Ceri, B. Pernici, and G. Wiederhold, "Distributed Database Design Methodologies", *Proceedings of the IEEE*, Vol. 75, No. 5, May 1987, page533-546.

[Ceri 87b] S. Ceri, B. Pernici, G. Wiederhold, "Optimization Problems and Solution Methods in the Design of Data Distribution", *Information Systems* vol. 14, No. 3, pp261-272, 1989.

[Hoff 75] J. A. Hoffer and D.J. Severance, "The Use of Cluster Analysis in Physical Database Design", *Proc. First Intl. Conf on VLDB*, 1975.

[McCo 72] W.T. McCormick, P.J. Schwietzer, "Problem Decomposition and Data Reorganization by a Clustering Technique", *Operations Research*, Vol. 20, Sep. 1972.

[Nava 84] S. Navathe, etc., "Vertical Partitioning Algorithms for Database Design", *ACM Transactions on Database systems*, Vol.9, No.4, December 1984.

[Nava 89] S. Navathe and M. Ra, "Vertical Partitioning for Database Design: A Graphical Algorithm", *Proc. of ACM SIGMOD*, 1989.

[Orlo 91] M. Orlowska, Y. Zhang and J. Szymczyk, "An Extensible Tool for a Distributed Database Environment", *Proc. of Distributed Database Workshop, Hong Kong*, December 1991.

[Sacc 85] D. Sacca and G. Wiederhold, "Database partitioning in a cluster of processors", *ACM Transactions on Database Systems*, Vol. 10, No. 1, March 1985, page 29 -56.

[Sed] R. Sedgewick, *Algorithms*, Addision-Wesley, 1988.

[Zhan 92a] Y. Zhang and M. Orlowska, "Correctness Issues of Distributed Database Design", ACSC Vol. 15, No.1, 1992.

[Zhan 92b] Y. Zhang, M. Orlowska and B. Colomb, "An Efficient Test for the Validity of Hybrid Knowledge Fragmentation in Distributed Databases", *Intl. J. of Software Engineering and Knowledge Engineering*, Vol.2, No.4, 1992.

APPENDIX: Implementation of the Algorithm Cluster & Its Complexity

To implement the algorithm Cluster efficiently, a proper data structure is required. Given an affinity graph $G=(V, E, p)$, the procedure SORT(G, M, k) outputs a nonoverlapping partition $\{M_i: 1 \le i \le k\}$ of E such that for each edge e of M_i, $p(e)=a_i$, and $a_i > a_j$ if $i<j$.

For $1 \le i \le k$, let $M_i=\{e: p(e)=a_i\}$. We may assume that SORT(G, M, k) outputs a linked list M of E by linking M_i from $i=1$ to k. Further in our data structure, we assume that each edge (u,v) is double linked to its two ends u and v.

Given an order of the vertices, the vertex set can be represented as $\{v_i: 1 \le i \le n\}$. We use an array to store the vertices of G according to the given order.

A set $F=\{f_i: 1 \le i \le n\}$ of group identifiers is used in the implementation of Cluster. We propose that for each vertex u, there is a link pointing to a f_i from u. Let $V(f_i)=\{u: u \text{ point to } f_i\}$. We establish a link from each f_i to $V(f_i)$.

Given a subset F' of F and an element f of F', procedure GROUP(V, F', f, Var T) proceeds as follows:

G.1 for each element f' of F', add $V(f')$ to T if $|V(f')| > 1$; and

G.2 for each $V(f')$ where $f' \neq f$ and $f' \in F'$, replace the link of each vertex v of $V(f')$ to f' by the link to f, and then add v to $V(f)$; and

G.3 for each $V(f')$ where $f' \neq f$ and $f' \in F'$, $V(f') := \emptyset$.

Clearly, the procedure GROUP can run in time $O(n)$ where n is the number of the vertices.

Another procedure CREATE(M, $G'=(V', E')$) is used in the implementation. It constructs a graph G' without isolated vertices from the input edge set M as follows:

C.1 for each edge e of M, if e connects a vertex u pointing to f_i and a vertex v pointing to f_j with $i \neq j$, then respectively add f_i (if it is not in V') and f_j (if it is not in V') to V', and add (f_i, f_j) to E'.

Clearly, CREATE(M_i, G') takes $O(|M_i|)$ and there are at most $|M_i|$ edges in G'.

Further, a standard procedure COMPONENT(G', S) can be found in [Sed], which outputs the set S of the vertex sets of the connected components of G'. It follows from [Sed] that if G' has no isolated vertices then COMPONENT takes $O(|E'|)$ where E' is the edge set of G'. Hence the algorithm Cluster can be implemented as follows, given $V=\{v_i: 1 \le i \le n\}$:

```
Algorithm Cluster(G=(V, E, p): affinity graph; Var T: a set of subsets of V)
Begin
 T:=∅;
 SORT(G, M, k); (M={M_i: 1≤i≤k})
 From i=1 To k Do
 Begin v_i points to f_i;
       V(f_i):={v_i}
 End;
 From i=1 To k Do
 Begin CREAT(M_i, G');
       COMPONENT(G', S);
       For each element s of S Do
       Begin Choose an element f from s;
             GROUP(V, s, f, T)
       End;
       G':=∅
 End;
 T:=T∪{V(f): V(f)≠∅}
End
```

Theorem 3: The algorithm Cluster takes $O(m\log n+n^2)$ time where m is the number of edges, and n is the number of vertices.

Proof: First, it is clear that the procedure SORT(G, M, k) takes $O(m\log m)=O(m\log n)$ time. It is also clear that the procedure CREAT(M_i, G') is executed k times in Cluster, and each call of CREATE(M_i, G') takes $O(|M_i|)$ time. Thus, overall the procedure CREATE(M_i, G') takes $O(m)$ time in this Algorithm.

It is clear that COMPONENT(M_i, G') is executed k times, and that each call of COMPONENT(G', S) takes $O(|E'|)$ time (because G' is either empty or it contains no isolated vertices) where E' is the number of the edges of G' and $E' \subseteq M_i$. Thus, overall COMPONENT takes $O(m)$ time in this algorithm.

We should note that in the algorithm Cluster, GROUP groups several fragments into one fragment and then adds the original fragments to T. Thus GROUP at most is executed $O(n)$ times (because initially we have n non-disjoint fragments) and each time GROUP takes $O(n)$ time. The procedure Group takes a total time of $O(n^2)$.

Hence the algorithm Cluster takes $O(m\log n+n^2)$ time. □

Acknowledgement: The work of the first author is partially supported by GIRD grant. We would like to thank Professor M. Orlowska for the extensive discussion and the detailed comments on the presentation. We also would like to thank Mr. J. Szymczyk for an implementation of the algorithm in this paper.

Improving integrity checking by compiling derivation paths

Matilde Celma[†], Juan Carlos Casamayor[†] and Hendrik Decker[‡]

[†] DSIC, Universidad Politécnica, PO box 22 012, E-46020 Valencia, {mati, carlos}@dsic.upv.es

[‡] Siemens AG, PO box 83 09 53, D-8000 München 83, hendrik@ztivax.zfe.siemens.de

Abstract

We propose a method for integrity checking in deductive databases. It improves the method of Lloyd, Sonenberg and Topor if the update does not propagate through negation. Integrity is checked after each update. Two phases are distinguished: Generation and Evaluation. Without accessing stored facts, two sets of tuples that focus on the difference of consecutive database states are computed, in the generation phase. Each such tuple consists of an atom, instances of which may either be inserted or deleted, and an expression in which information about derivations that possibly lead to inconsistency is compiled. Evaluation of some of such expressions in the evaluation phase suffices for determining satisfaction or violation of integrity. This is less expensive than the evaluation of simplified integrity constraints in methods which, after generation, do not focus any more on derivation paths that have led to the simplified instances.

Introduction

We adopt the foundations of deductive databases as described in [Ll]. An *integrity theory* is a finite set of closed first order formulae, called *integrity constraints* (or simply *constraints*), that are required to be satisfied in any given database state. Integrity is *satisfied* if each constraint is a logical consequence of the completion of the database, and is *violated* otherwise. We assume that each constraint is represented as a denial, as proposed in [SK]. Using transformations described in [Ll] [De2], such a representation is always possible. Function symbols of any arity are permitted to occur.

Each pair of consecutive database states ("old" and "new") is linked via an *update* (which we use as synonymous to *transaction*), i.e. two disjoint finite sets of clauses, to be inserted to and, resp., deleted from the old state, by an indivisible operation. (The terminology of "consecutive states" is due to [Kü].) The "blind" way of integrity checking is to query each constraint after each update. Since this can be very costly, all known methds for integrity checking take advantage of the fact that integrity is satisfied in the old state, and hence, any violation of integrity in the new state must be due to the update or consequences derived from it.

In all methods for integrity checking that we know of, two phases may be distinguished, viz. *generation* and *evaluation*. They are executed either separately and sequentially or stepwise and interleaved. Generation consists of two subphases (that may also be separated or interleaved). First, elements of some Δ, i.e. a set of atoms ("facts") that capture the difference between old and new state, are computed. Following [Ni], such facts are then applied to those integrity constraints that are affected by the update. As a result, possibly simplified instances of affected constraints are obtained. Evaluation of such instances in the new state turns out to be sufficient for checking satisfaction or violation of integrity. The procedure employed for evaluation in our method is *SLDNF resolution* [Cl] [Ll].

In various implementations, the generation phase either accesses stored facts of base relations or it doesn't. For example, the methods in [De1] [SK] [DW] [Ol] [NDCC] need to access facts for generation, while those in [LST] [BDM] [AIM] don't. Also [Kü] describes a way of computing a Δ (in a separate phase) without fact access. In this paper, we also separate generation from evaluation, and generation goes without fact access.

Similar to [AIM], we describe, in section 1, a Δ consisting of two sets of tuples. One focuses on the difference of old and new state in terms of what is deleted, and the other, of what is inserted. More precisely, the first component of each tuple is a (not necessarily ground) atom such that instances of that atom may either be deleted or inserted. The second component is an expression containing compiled information about derivation paths that possibly lead to violation of integrity. Evaluation of some of such expressions then suffices for determining satisfaction or violation of integrity. Section 2 contains soundness and completeness results for our method. In section 3, we illustrate our approach by some extended examples.

Inspired by [AIM], we aim at improving the method of [LST]. The main difference to [LST] is that, in effect, we evaluate constraints by focusing on the derivation paths via which they are affected by the update. In this sense, we use the Δ not only to simplify the constraints, but also to evaluate them. As opposed to that, the Δ of [LST] (which in fact is the projection of our Δ on its first component) is only applied to the constraints, which are then evaluated without further focus. For each tuple in the Δ of [AIM], the first component coincides with ours; the second component only contains information about at most one database clause with non-empty body ("rule") through which a derivation that may lead to integrity violation goes, while our Δ typically compiles several of such rules. Thus, the Δ of [AIM] is often less focused than ours. (In fact, the Δ of [AIM] is unsound in many cases, but that could be fixed.)

1 Focusing on the difference between consecutive database states

The Δ to be specified in this section is of syntactic nature. In fact, it only focuses on a reasonably tight cover of what has actually changed, rather than capturing the precise difference of derivable facts (which, in general, is not computable anyway). A semantic description of the *precise difference* between consecutive states D and D', in terms of the well-known *completion* semantics of deductive databases [Cl] [Ll], is given by the follwing two sets.

$$DEL_{D,D'} = \{ L \ : \ L \text{ is a ground literal, } comp(D) \models L, comp(D') \not\models L \}$$

$$INS_{D,D'} = \{ L \ : \ L \text{ is a ground literal, } comp(D) \not\models L, comp(D') \models L \}$$

In words, the precise difference between consecutive states is defined by the ground literals that are either logical consequences of the old state but not of the new ($DEL_{D,D'}$), or logical consequences of the new state but not of the old ($INS_{D,D'}$). Since a literal is either positive or negative, it may seem at first that, for each literal L in $DEL_{D,D'}$, the opposed literal would be in $INS_{D,D'}$ and vice-versa. However, this is not necessarily the case, as shown below. Let D consist of the following clauses (x and y are variables, p, q, r, s, t are predicates and digits are constants):

$p(x) \leftarrow q(x) \,\&\, r(x)$	$q(1) \leftarrow$
$s(x) \leftarrow t(x) \,\&\, \neg p(x)$	$q(2) \leftarrow$
$r(x) \leftarrow r(x)$	$t(3) \leftarrow$

Suppose that the update consists of the insertion of $q(3) \leftarrow$. Then, $s(3)$ and $\neg p(3)$ are literals in $DEL_{D,D'}$, but neither $\neg s(3)$ nor $p(3)$ is in $INS_{D,D'}$. So, this example illustrates that the computation of the precise difference of consecutive states is difficult, if some predicates are defined recursively. In fact, the precise difference may not even be computable, in the presence of functions. (Similar problems would arise with other semantics.) Hence, it is justified to focus on a reasonably tight cover, such as the Δ described below.

As already indicated, the Δ of [LST] only focuses on the difference of derivable facts in consecutive states. That of [AIM] attempts to go a step futher by also taking into account a possibly simplified instance of the last rule through which some derivation that may lead to violation of integrity goes. (When we say "last", we see derivations as starting from the bottom up, along the forward direction of rules.) As opposed to that, the Δ specified below compiles a possibly simplified instance of each rule (not only the last) such that the update propagates through a positive literal in the body of that rule.

From now on, let us suppose that the integrity theory is always included in the database, in the following way: For each constraint of form $\leftarrow W$ in the theory, the clause violated $\leftarrow W$ is included in the database, where violated is a distinguished 0-ary predicate that is not used otherwise. Clearly, integrity is violated if there is an SLDNF refutation of $D \cup \{\leftarrow \text{violated}\}$; integrity is satisfied if there is a finitely failed SLDNF tree of $D \cup \{\leftarrow \text{violated}\}$.

For a pair D, D' of consecutive database states that is linked by an update U $= U_{ins} \cup U_{del}$, such that $D' = (D \backslash U_{del}) \cup U_{ins}$, we define the set $pos_{D,D'}$ inductively, for $n \geq 0$, as shown below. As in [LST], computation of $pos_{D,D'}$ does not need to access the extensional part (i.e., stored facts) but only the intensional part (i.e., deduction rules) of the database.

For convenience, let true represent the empty conjunction. For an expression E and a substitution θ, let Eθ denote application of θ to all variables in E. Instead of "Δ", we use "pos" and "neg", for facilitating comparison with [LST].

$$pos^0 = \{(A, W) : \text{there is a clause } A \leftarrow W \text{ in } U_{ins}\}$$

$$neg^0 = \{(A, true) : \text{there is a clause } A \leftarrow W \text{ in } U_{del}\}$$

$$\begin{aligned} pos^{n+1} = \; & \{(A, New \,\&\, W')\theta : A \leftarrow W \in D', \; B \text{ is a positive literal in } W, \\ & \quad (A', New) \in pos^n, \; \theta \text{ is mgu of } A' \text{ and } B, \\ & \quad W' \text{ is obtained by dropping } B \text{ from } W\} \\ \cup \; & \\ & \{(A, New \,\&\, W)\theta : A \leftarrow W \in D', \; \neg B \text{ is a negative literal in } W, \\ & \quad (A', New) \in neg^n, \; \theta \text{ is mgu of } A' \text{ and } B\} \end{aligned}$$

$$\begin{aligned} neg^{n+1} = \; & \{(A, New)\theta : A \leftarrow W \in D, \; \neg B \text{ is a negtive literal in } W, \\ & \quad (A', New) \in pos^n, \; \theta \text{ is mgu of } A' \text{ and } B\} \\ \cup \; & \\ & \{(A, New)\theta : A \leftarrow W \in D, \; B \text{ is a positive literal in } W, \\ & \quad (A', New) \in neg^n, \; \theta \text{ is mgu of } A' \text{ and } B\}. \end{aligned}$$

$$pos_{D,D'} = \bigcup_{n \geq 0} pos^n$$

Note the asymmetry between sets pos^n and neg^n ($n \geq 0$): Intuitively, $pos_{D,D'}$ contains more (compiled) information about derivations that may lead to the insertion of atoms in the new state than the tuples in neg^n contain information about deletions from the old state. This is justified, since we are foremostly interested in the possible insertion (!) of the atom violated. (In [CCD], we define a Δ that further sharpens the focus on the precise difference, as given by $INS_{D,D'}$ and $DEL_{D,D'}$, and captures insertions and deletions symmetrically. However, the efficiency of evaluation is not necessarily improved, that way.)

Similar to the Δ in [LST], the generation of $pos_{D,D'}$ involves, in principle, the calculation of infinitely many sets pos^n and neg^n, for $n \geq 0$. However, in many practical cases, we can use a stopping rule to terminate the generation phase after finitely many steps, as in [LST]. One such rule involves computing sets of tuples P^n and N^n rather than pos^n and neg^n, respectively. P^n and N^n are defined and used in much the same way as pos^n and neg^n, except for the following (simplifying) step. We omit any tuple of form $(A, New \,\&\, W)$ from P^n

(resp., N^n) for which there is another tuple (A', New') in P^k (resp., N^k), for some $k \leq n$, such that (A, New) is an instance of (A', New'). If, after such omissions, some P^n and N^n both become empty, then terminate the iteration and use the union $P_{D,D'}$ (say) of all sets P^i ($i \leq n$), in place of $pos_{D,D'}$. The results in section 2 remain valid for $P_{D,D'}$ used in place of $pos_{D,D'}$. A further refinement is to delete from $P_{D,D'}$ any tuple of form (A, V & W) for which there is another tuple (A', W') in $P_{D,D'}$ such that (A, W) is an instance of (A', W'). Similar to the stopping rule in [LST], the one above eventually may not work in the presence of functions. Then, a remedy as proposed in [LST] (replacing possibly infinitely many elements in Δ by a single, subsuming one) helps, in many cases.

2 Soundness and completeness

We distinguish between soundness and completeness of the generation phase, on one hand, and of the evaluation phase, on the other. For the soundness and completeness theorems below, we need the following definition.

Definition

a) For a database D and a query $\leftarrow W$, SLDNF is *complete* if each of the following two points holds.

- For each ground substitution θ such that comp(D) $\models W\theta$, there is an SLDNF refutation of $D \cup \{\leftarrow W\}$ with computed answer subsuming θ.
- If comp(D) $\models \leftarrow W$, then there is a finitely failed SLDNF tree of $D \cup \{\leftarrow W\}$.

b) For a database D and a query $\leftarrow W$, SLDNF is *conclusive* if SLDNF is complete for D and $\leftarrow W$, and each fair SLDNF derivation of $D \cup \{\leftarrow W\}$ is either successful or failed.

c) For a database D, SLDNF is *complete* (resp., *conclusive*) if, for each atom A, SLDNF is *complete* (resp., *conclusive*) for D and $\leftarrow A$.

Sources of sufficient conditions for completeness or even conclusivity of SLDNF resolution are, e.g., [Ll] [CL] [Ku] [DC] [De3] [Ca]. Improvements w.r.t. conclusivity may be obtained, e.g., by enhancing SLDNF with loop trapping (cf. [KT]).

Intuitively, soundness of generation means that, for each tuple in $pos_{D,D'}$, its second component contains information about derivations in the new state that may lead to the insertion of instances of the atom in the first component. Conversely, completeness of generation means that each inserted fact is captured in $pos_{D,D'}$. In essence, soundness and completeness of generation together means that $pos_{D,D'}$ captures a superset of positive (negative) literals in $INS_{D,D'}$ (resp., $DEL_{D,D'}$). It is easily seen that $pos_{D,D'}$ is more in focus than corresponding sets in [LST] and [AIM], in terms of approximating $INS_{D,D'}$ and $DEL_{D,D'}$.

Note that [LST] compute their Δ in two steps, by first applying all deletions in U_{del} to D, yielding a database D'', and then applying all insertions in U_{ins} to D'', yielding D'. Then, D is always used in the definition of pos^{n+1}, instead of D', which possibly improves the Δ, and thus the evaluation phase. However, the same improvement (and more) can be achieved by the simplifications mentioned at the end of section 1. It is easy to compute and apply our Δ to constraints precisely as in [LST].

More formally, soundness of generation is expressed in part *a*, completeness of generation in part *b* of theorem 1, below. The proofs, details of which can be found in [Ce], essentially are by induction on the definition of $pos_{D,D'}$. Actually, theorem 1 is a proper consequence of a stronger result in [Ce], showing that, roughly, each refutation of any atom in the new state that does not exist in the old one is captured in $pos_{D,D'}$.

Theorem 1 (Soundness and completeness of generation)
Let D, D' be a pair of consecutive database states. Then, the following holds.

a) For each tuple (A, New) in $pos_{D,D'}$, each computed answer θ of D' ∪ {← New} and each ground instance A' of Aθ, comp(D') ⊨ A' holds.

b) If SLDNF is complete for D', then, for each ground atom A such that comp(D) ⊭ A and comp(D') ⊨ A, there is a tuple (A', New) in $pos_{D,D'}$ and a computed answer θ of D' ∪ {← New} such that A is an instance of A'θ.

Intuitively, soundness of evaluation as expressed in theorem 2, below, means: If there is a tuple (violated, New) in $pos_{D,D'}$ such that evaluation of

New determines the existence of an SLDNF refutation of D′ ∪ {← violated} (as in theorem 1*a*), then integrity is violated in D′; under the condition that SLDNF is conclusive for D′, integrity is satisfied in D′, otherwise. Conversely, completeness of evaluation means: If integrity is violated, then there is a tuple (violated, New) in $pos_{D,D'}$ such that evaluation of New determines an SLDNF refutation of D′ ∪ {← violated}. In other words, integrity can be checked by evaluating components New of tuples (violated, New) in $pos_{D,D'}$.

It is easy to show that, if the update does not propagate through negation, then evaluating simplifications obtained by applying the Δ of [LST] or [AIM] to affected constraints means to search trees that (often properly) contain the trees searched for evaluating components New. So, for that case, and hence particularly for the definite case, evaluation in our method is often less and never more expensive than evaluation in [LST] or [AIM] (which, in turn, is often less and never more expensive than checking integrity blindly, by running SLDNF on D′ ∪ {← violated}).

Soundness of generation is expressed more formally in parts a_1 and a_2, completeness of evaluation in parts b_1 and b_2 of theorem 2, below. The proofs, details of which can be found in [Ce], essentially use theorem 1 and the easily shown lemma that, for a pair of consecutive states D, D′ such that SLDNF is conclusive for both, it follows that SLDNF is conclusive for both D and D′ and each component of each tuple in $pos_{D,D'}$.

Theorem 2 (Soundness and completeness of evaluation)
Let D, D′ be a pair of consecutive database states, and integrity be satisfied in D. Then, the following holds.

a_1) Integrity is violated in D′ if there is a tuple (violated, New) in $pos_{D,D'}$ such that there is an SLDNF refutation of D′ ∪ {← New}.

a_2) Integrity is satisfied in D′ if there is no tuple as specified in a_1 and SLDNF is conclusive for D′.

b_1) If integrity is violated in D′ and SLDNF is conclusive for D′, then there is a tuple (violated, New) in $pos_{D,D'}$ such that there is an SLDNF refutation of D′ ∪ {← New}.

b_2) If integrity is satisfied in D′, then there is no tuple as specified in b_1.

Note that conclusivity is required in a_2 and b_1 since, otherwise, integrity may be violated even if there is no tuple as specified in a_2 and b_1, respectively. For example, the integrity theory {← p} is satisfied in D = {violated ← p}. By inserting p ← p, we obtain (violated, p) in $pos_{D,D'}$. Integrity is violated in the new state D', since ← p is not a logical consequence of comp(D'). However, there is no SLDNF refutation of D' ∪ {← p}, nor any other SLDNF refutation that would indicate violation.

3 Examples

We illustrate the method presented in this paper by two examples of a database and an integrity theory, first by one taken from [NDCC] (see next page): Each fact in the room relation consists of the number of a room (first component) belonging to a certain department (second). Facts about course consist of subject names (first) and the organizing department (second). Each fact in the lecture relation contains course subject (first), room number (second), weekday (third) and start time (fourth). The r-equipment relation specifies pieces of equipment (second) in rooms (first), and c-equipment specifies equipment (second) that is necessary for certain courses (first).

The three rules declare certain rooms to be either inadequate or acceptable for certain courses. Note that (perhaps because of scarcity of space) a room may have to be considered acceptable for some course, even though it might qualify as inadequate for that course. Also note that the maths and the computer science departments may use each other's rooms if acceptable. The first constraint denies that there may be two different lectures in the same room at the same time of the same day. The second one forbids that any lecture be held in a room that is not acceptable for the respective course. It is easy to see that integrity is satisfied in the given state.

All variable symbols are represented by (possibly subscribed) capital letters. All constants are strings of digits or lower case characters. The symbol "←" is omitted in clauses that are either facts or appear in one of the updates U_1, U_2, U_3. An expression of form $E \neq F$, as used in one of the rules below, is an abbreviation for the literal ¬equal(E, F), where the predicate equal is supposed to be defined by the (possibly built-in) clause equal(E, E) ←.

room(27, maths)	course(logic, maths)	lecture(logic, 27, mo, 10)
room(36, maths)	course(prolog, comp-sc)	lecture(prolog, 36, tue, 10)
room(43, comp-sc)	course(lisp, comp-sc)	lecture(lisp, 43, wed, 11)

r-equipment(27, board)	c-equipment(logic, board)
r-equipment(27, coffee-machine)	c-equipment(logic, coffee-machine)
r-equipment(36, board)	c-equipment(prolog, overhead)
r-equipment(36, overhead)	c-equipment(prolog, board)
r-equipment(43, video)	c-equipment(lisp, overhead)

inadequate(R, C) ← room(R, X) & course(C, Y) & c-equipment(C, E) & ¬r-equipment(R, E)

acceptable(R, C) ← room(R, X) & course(C, X)

acceptable(R, C) ← ¬inadequate(R, C)

violated ← lecture(C_1, R, W, S) & lecture(C_2, R, W, S) & $C_1 \neq C_2$

violated ← lecture(C, R, W, S) & ¬acceptable(R, C)

U_1 = {lecture(prolog, 27, wed, 11)} U_2 = {¬ r-equipment(43, video)}

U_3 = {¬ r-equipment(36, overhead)}

Note that the second rule about the predicate acceptable is not allowed [Ll]. However, the union of the database above and {← violated} is allowed, in the sense of the weak allowedness condition of [Ll], since acceptable never occurs in a positive literal of the body of any rule or constraint.

The update U_1 leads to an inconsistent state. On the other hand, U_2 does not violate integrity. Both can be shown straightforwardly by our method, since the respective Δ's are figured out easily. Somehow, U_3 (removing the overhead projector from room number 36) is more interesting, since the update is propagated through negation in rules several times, during the generation phase; thus, the resulting Δ is less immediate. Generation of the Δ according to the definition in section 1 is shown below. (An example for the case that the update is not propagated through negation is given later-on.) Let r, c, le, r-e, c-e, in, ac, ov stand for identifiers with respective initials above.

$pos^0 = \emptyset$

$neg^0 = \{(\text{r-e}(36, ov), true)\}$

$pos^1 = \{(in(36, C),\ r(36, X)\ \&\ c(C, Y)\ \&\ \text{c-e}(C, ov)\ \&\ \neg \text{r-e}(36, ov))\}$

$neg^1 = \emptyset$

$pos^2 = \emptyset$

$neg^2 = \{(ac(36, C),\ r(36, X)\ \&\ c(C, Y)\ \&\ \text{c-e}(C, ov)\ \&\ \neg \text{r-e}(36, ov))\}$

$pos^3 = \{(violated,\ r(36, X)\ \&\ c(C, Y)\ \&\ \text{c-e}(C, ov)\ \&\ \neg \text{r-e}(36, ov)\ \&\ le(C, 36, W, S)\ \&\ \neg ac(36, C))\}$

Since each of neg^3, pos^4 and neg^4 is empty, computing the Δ above stops with the union of pos^i, $i = 1, 2, 3$. Evaluation of the second component of the tuple in pos^3 yields a refutation, indicating that U_3 violates integrity.

The Δ of [LST] is obtained by projecting the tuples above on their first component. If constraints are not represented as denials but as first-order formulae without occurrence of ← at the front, as in [LST], then the generation of the Δ of [LST] terminates already at stage 2. Instead of generating pos^3, the second constraint is identified as affected and then is instantiated with an mgu of a fresh variant of ac(36, C) and ac(R, C). Then, the simplified constraint $\forall C\, \forall W\, \forall S\ \neg le(C, 36, W, S) \vee ac(36, C)$ is evaluated. The resulting finitely failed tree indicates that integrity is violated. As an alternative to querying the constraint, the simplified denial $\leftarrow le(C, 36, W, S)\ \&\ \neg ac(36, C)$ may be evaluated. Note that the simplified denial is properly contained in the second component of pos³. This indicates that evaluation according to the Δ of [LST] may be more efficient in case the update is propagated through negation. However, if, e.g., there were lectures of several courses in room 36, then binding C to prolog, by evaluating the second component of pos³ from left to right, as done in our method, may yield a better focus than evaluating only the denial.

If the update propagates through negation and the database is free of multiple (not necessarily successful) derivation paths of the same updated facts, then the Δ of [LST] may be better than ours. Still, failure, i.e. detection that integrity is satisfied, is sometimes reached earlier with our Δ than with the one of [LST] (by failing on a subgoal which is not contained in the search space of [LST]). Conversely, if there are such multiple derivations (which is quite frequent in deductive databases), then our Δ typically is better, since evaluation in our method focuses on the paths that may lead to violation, while evaluation in [LST] may also search many other paths, superfluously. For instance, let the database D contain the four clauses $p \leftarrow q$, $p \leftarrow \neg r$, r and violated $\leftarrow p$, among others. Then, deleting r will have (violated, $\neg r$) in $pos_{D,D'}$. While our method only needs to evaluate $\neg r$, also all derivations leading to p via q are in the search space of [LST].

For comparing our Δ also to the one of [AIM] (which is unsound, for the example above), we consider another example. Let the database now contain the rules and the constraint below, as well as the same facts about room, course, lecture and c-equipment as above, but nothing about r-equipment.

inadequate(R, C) ← c-equipment(C, E) & missing-equipment(R, E)

no-good(R, C) ← inadequate(R, C) & room(R, X) & course(C, Y) & X ≠ Y

unreasonable(R, C) ← lecture(C, R, W, S) & no-good(R, C)

violated ← unreasonable(R, C)

Clearly, inserting missing-equipment(36, overhead) violates integrity. Comparing the Δ of [AIM] and [LST] to ours, as shown below, reveals that ours is more focused, and renders evaluation more efficient. For distinguishing the Δ of [AIM], we use "$\underline{pos}^i$" ($i \geq 0$) and adapt the syntax without changing the contents. The Δ of [LST] again consists of the first components of the tuples in Δ, and thus needs not be shown explicitly. All sets neg^i are empty and are therefore omitted. Again, we use appropriately shortened identifiers.

$$pos^0 = \{(\text{m-e}(36, ov),\ true\}$$
$$\underline{pos}^0 = \{(\text{m-e}(36, ov),\ true\}$$

$$pos^1 = \{(in(36, C),\ \text{c-e}(C, ov))\}$$
$$\underline{pos}^1 = \{(in(36, C),\ \text{c-e}(C, ov)\ \&\ \text{m-e}(36, ov))\}$$

$$pos^2 = \{(\text{n-g}(36, C),\ \text{c-e}(C, ov)\ \&\ r(36, X)\ \&\ c(C, Y)\ \&\ X \neq Y)\}$$
$$\underline{pos}^2 = \{(\text{n-g}(36, C),\ in(36, C)\ \&\ r(36, X)\ \&\ c(C, Y)\ \&\ X \neq Y)\}$$

$$pos^3 = \{(un(36, C),\ le(C, 36, W, S)\ \&\ \text{c-e}(C, ov)\ \&\ r(36, X)\ \&\ c(C, Y)\ \&\ X \neq Y)\}$$
$$\underline{pos}^3 = \{(un(36, C),\ le(C, 36, W, S)\ \&\ \text{n-g}(36, C)\}$$

Next, we show pos^4 and $\underline{pos}^4$, which terminate the generation of the respective Δ. Originally, constraints are not represented as denials in [AIM], but as formulae without ← at the front, as in [LST]. However, we deliberately (but faithfully) adapt the last step of computing the Δ of [AIM], as follows.

$$pos^4 = \{(violated,\ le(C, 36, W, S)\ \&\ \text{c-e}(C, ov)\ \&\ r(36, X)\ \&\ c(C, Y)\ \&\ X \neq Y)\}$$
$$\underline{pos}^4 = \{(violated,\ le(C, 36, W, S)\ \&\ \text{n-g}(36, C)\}$$

At each step except the last (from $\underline{pos}^3$ to $\underline{pos}^4$), the Δ of [AIM] loses some focus of knowledge acquired in the previous step. For example, the knowledge in $\underline{pos}^0$ that m-e(36, ov) holds in the new state is lost in $\underline{pos}^1$, since the condition m-e(36, ov) appears unnecessarily in the second component of the tuple in $\underline{pos}^1$; the knowledge in $\underline{pos}^1$ that some instance of c-e(C, ov) may lead to violation of integrity is lost in $\underline{pos}^2$ (where it is replaced by the less unfolded, hence less precise knowledge that some instance of in(36, C) may lead to violation). Unlike all other steps, the last step in [AIM] (of identifying, instantiating and simplifying affected constraints) does not lose the focus compiled in the previous step (but is more circumstantial than the adaption above).

While it may take some effort to figure out that the Δ of [AIM] (and also the Δ of [LST]) is in fact less focused than ours, in terms of theorem 1, it is comparatively easy to see that the search space of detecting violation of integrity by evaluating the second component of $\underline{pos}^4$ properly contains the search space of evaluating the second component of pos^4. Hence, the latter is more efficient than the former. Also, it is easily seen that the search space of evaluating the simplified constraint $\forall C\ \neg un(36, C)$ (or, alternatively, the denial $\leftarrow un(36, C)$) according to the Δ of [LST] properly contains the search space of evaluating the second component of pos^4.

Concluding remarks

We proposed a possible improvement of the integrity checking method described in [LST]. The efficiency of evaluation of simplified constraints in our method is never worse and often better than in [LST], in case the update does not propagate through negation. In the other case, the method of [LST] may perform better than ours if there is no updated ground fact which is at the root of multiple derivations. Currently, we work on a modification of our method that always compares favourably to [LST] and also converges with an improvement of the method of [SK].

Having followed the lines of [LST] to a large extent, we also adopted the *theoremhood view* of integrity checking, as opposed to the *consistency view*, as proposed in [SK]. The theoremhood view requires constraints to be logical consequences of the completion of the database, while the consistency view only requires the consistency of the union of the completion and the integrity theory. Requiring consistency is weaker than requiring theoremhood. Theorem 1, above, is independent of both views. However, if the consistency view is adopted, then theorem 2, above, can be strengthened by replacing "conclusive" in parts a_2 and b_1 with the weaker requirement of "complete". Yet, conclusivity should not be neglected anyway, since it is useful for ensuring the termination of the generation phase, and also for deciding whether SLDNF refutations such as those specified in theorem 2 actually do exist or not.

Acknowledgements We thank Prof. Franz Guenthner, head of CIS (Centrum für Informations- und Sprachverarbeitung, Ludwig-Maximilians-Universität München, Germany) for his hospitality during a stay of the first two authors at his centre, where part of the work on this paper was done. The stay was supported by a grant from Conselleria de Educación y Ciencia de la Generalidad Valenciana. We also thank Laura Mota at DSIC, for many useful discussions on the subject of this paper. Moreover, we appreciate reviewers' comments which have been useful as well. The third author was supported by the national project REMO, #01 ES 202 E, funded by the German Federal Ministry of Research and Technology.

References

[AIM] P. Asirelli, P. Inverardi and A. Mustaro, Improving integrity constraint checking in deductive databases, in M. Gyssens, J. Paredaens and D. van Gucht (eds), *Proc. 2nd Int'l Conf. Database Theory (ICDT '88)*, 72-86, Springer LNCS 326, 1988.

[BDM] F. Bry. H. Decker and R. Manthey, A uniform approach to constraint satisfaction and constraint satisfiability in deductive databases, in J. Schmidt et al (eds), *Proc. 1st Int'l Conf. Extending Database Technology (EDBT)*, 488-505, Springer LNCS 303, 1988.

[Ca] L. Cavedon, Acyclic logic programs and the completeness of SLDNF-resolution, *Theoretical Computer Science* 86, 81-92, 1991.

[CCD] M. Celma, J.C. Casamayor and H. Decker, Improving integrity checking by compiling derivation paths, long version, Siemens AG, München (Germany), 1992.

[Ce] M. Celma, *Comprobacion de la Integridad en Bases de Datos Deductivas*, PhD thesis, DSIC, Universidad Politécnica de Valencia, 1992.

[CL] L. Cavedon and J.W. Lloyd, A completeness theorem for SLDNF resolution, *J. Logic Programming* 7, 177-191, 1989.

[Cl] K.J. Clark, Negation as failure, in H. Gallaire and J. Minker (eds), *Logic and Databases*, 293-322, Plenum Press, 1978.

[DC] H. Decker and L. Cavedon, Generalizing allowedness while retaining completeness of SLDNF-resolution, in E. Börger et al (eds), *Proc. 3rd Workshop on Computer Science Logic*, 98-115, Springer LNCS 440, 1990.

[De1] H. Decker, Integrity enforcement on deductive databases, in L. Kerschberg (ed), *Expert Database Systems*, 381-395, Benjamin-Cummings, 1987.

[De2] H. Decker, The range form of databases and queries, or: How to avoid floundering, in J. Retti und K. Leidlmair (Hrsg.), *Proc. 5. Österreichische Artificial-Intelligence-Tagung (ÖGAI)*, 114-123, Springer Informatik-Fachberichte 208, 1989.

[De3] H. Decker, On generalized cover axioms, in K. Furukawa (ed), *Proc. 8th ICLP*, 693-707, MIT Press, 1991.

[DW] S.K. Das and M.H. Williams, A path finding method for constraint checking in deductive databases, *Data & Knowledge Engineering* 4, 233-244, North-Holland, 1989.

/KT/ D.B. Kemp and R.W. Topor, Completeness of a top-down query evaluation procedure for stratified databases, in R.A. Kowalski and K.A. Bowen (eds), *Proc. 5th ICLP*, Vol.1, 178-194, 1988.

[Ku] K. Kunen, Signed data dependencies in logic programs, *J. Logic Programming* 4, 289-308, 1987.

[Kü] V. Küchenhoff, On the efficient computation of the difference between consecutive database states, in C. Delobel, M. Kifer and Y. Masunaga (eds), *Proc. DOOD '91*, Springer LNCS 566, 1991.

[Ll] J.W. Lloyd, *Foundations of Logic Programming*, 2nd edition, Springer, 1987.

[LST] J.W. Lloyd, E.A. Sonenberg and R.W. Topor, Integrity constraint checking in stratified databases, *J. Logic Programming* 4, 331-343, 1987.

/NDCC/ G. Nüssel, H. Decker, M. Celma and J.C. Casamayor, A complete proof procedure for efficient integrity checking, in A. Olivé (ed), *Proc. 3rd Int'l Workshop on the Deductive Approach to Information Systems and Databases*, 199-216, UPC Barcelona (Spain), Report de recerca LSI-92-19, 1992.

[Ni] J.M. Nicolas, Logic for improving integrity checking in relational data bases, *Acta Informatica* 18, 227-253, 1982.

[Ol] A. Olivé, Integrity constraints checking in deductive databases, *Proc. 17th VLDB*, 1991.

[SK] F. Sadri and R.A. Kowalski, A theorem-proving approach to database integrity, in J. Minker (ed), *Foundations of Deductive Databases and Logic Programming*, 313-362, Morgan Kaufman, 1988.

Using Weakest Preconditions to Simplify Integrity Constraint Checking

Michael Lawley Rodney Topor
School of Computing and Information Technology
Griffith University, Nathan, Qld 4111, Australia

and

Mark Wallace
European Computer-Industry Research Centre
Arabellastraße 17, W-8000 München 81, Germany

ABSTRACT

We present a procedure for deriving the weakest precondition for a database update and an integrity constraint. We show how to simplify the weakest precondition to produce a condition to be evaluated before the update is performed. This provides an efficient means to ensure that database updates maintain integrity constraints.

Keywords Database, update, integrity constraint, weakest precondition

1 Introduction

In this paper we apply program derivation techniques [4, 5] to the task of efficiently checking the safety of database updates. Unlike many integrity constraint checking papers [2, 8, 10], we deal with the update "programs" themselves rather than just the resulting inserted and deleted tuples. In this sense our work is related to verification of transaction safety [11].

A database update is *safe* if it is guaranteed to maintain the truth of the database's integrity constraints [11]. We present a procedure for deriving the weakest precondition for an update and a constraint. This new condition can be combined with the update to form a conditional update. If the condition is true in the initial state, the constraint is guaranteed to be true after the update is performed. If the constraint is also true in the initial state, the conditional update is safe with respect to the constraint. In this case, we can further simplify the condition to be evaluated before the update is performed. Because the derivation of the weakest precondition and subsequent simplification is independent of the current database state, it only needs to be performed once, as a preprocessing step to produce the safe conditional update.

This provides a method for efficiently checking that updates maintain integrity constraints before performing them.

We consider a set oriented update language, based on that given by Wallace [12], and first-order conditions and integrity constraints. The update language is equivalent in power to SQL updates and more expressive than those considered by Bry et al. [2], Lloyd et al. [8], and Nicolas [10], We present a formal description of the effect of an update. We then show how to transform a constraint with respect to an update to produce a new condition. We prove that this new condition is the weakest precondition of the update and constraint, and show how to simplify the condition to be checked before performing the update.

2 Definitions

Let $\mathcal{U}$ be a *universal domain* consisting of a countably infinite set of constants. A *database* is a tuple $\langle R_1, \ldots, R_n \rangle$, where each R_i is a finite named relation over $\mathcal{U}^{k_i}$ for some $k_i \geq 0$. A *database update* U is a mapping from one database, $B = \langle R_1, \ldots, R_n \rangle$, to another, $U(B) = \langle R'_1, \ldots, R'_n \rangle$, where each R_i and R'_i have the same arity. We require the mapping to be partially recursive and C-generic for some finite set of constants C. (See [1] for an explanation of the C-genericity condition.)

A *formula* (resp., *sentence*) is a first-order, function-free formula (resp., sentence) in some fixed language. If R, $R_1, \ldots$ are relations, then r, $r_1, \ldots$ are the corresponding predicate symbols.

A *valuation* for a formula F is a mapping of the free variables of F to elements of $\mathcal{U}$. For a database B, formula F (resp., sentence G) and valuation ν for F, $B \models_\nu F$ (resp., $B \models G$) is defined as usual in model theory to mean F (resp., G) is true in B with respect to the valuation ν. We say a valuation ν' extends another valuation ν ($\nu' \geq \nu$) if the domain of ν' is a superset of the domain of ν and the restriction of ν' to the domain of ν is identical to ν.

A sentence F is a *precondition* for an update U and a sentence H if, for every database B, $B \models F$ implies $U(B) \models H$. A precondition F for U and H is a *weakest precondition* for U and H if, for every precondition G for U and H, and for every database B, $B \models G$ implies $B \models F$.

For later use in describing the effects of statements in our update language, we introduce the following notation and two simple lemmas. Let R be a relation in a database B, and $\Phi(\overline{x})$ a first-order formula with free variables $\overline{x} = x_1, \ldots, x_n$. Then $B' = B[R \mapsto R']$ denotes the result of replacing the relation R in B by R'. In practice, R' is either $R \cup \{\overline{x} \mid B \models \Phi(\overline{x})\}$ or $R - \{\overline{x} \mid B \models \Phi(\overline{x})\}$, i.e. $\Phi(\overline{x})$ is evaluated in the current database B and the resulting tuples are added to (resp., deleted from) R.

Lemma 2.1 $B[R \mapsto R \cup \{\overline{x} \mid B \models \Phi(\overline{x})\}] \models_\nu r(\overline{u})$ if and only if $B \models_\nu r(\overline{u}) \vee \Phi(\overline{u})$.

Lemma 2.2 $B[R \mapsto R - \{\overline{x} \mid B \models \Phi(\overline{x})\}] \models_\nu r(\overline{u})$ if and only if $B \models_\nu r(\overline{u}) \wedge \neg\Phi(\overline{u})$.

3 Updates

Our update language is adapted from Wallace [12]. It is syntactically simpler but can be shown to have the same expressive power [7]. Let R be a named relation, and $\Phi(\overline{x})$ a first-order formula with free variables $\overline{x}$. Then **foreach** $\overline{x} : \Phi(\overline{x})$ **do** $insert_R(\overline{x})$, and **foreach** $\overline{x} : \Phi(\overline{x})$ **do** $delete_R(\overline{x})$ are statements in our language. If $S_1, \ldots, S_n$ are statements in our language then $(S_1 \ ; \ \ldots \ ; \ S_n)$ is a statement in our language. For example, adding the tuple $\overline{a}$ to the relation R would be written **foreach** $\overline{x} : \overline{x} = \overline{a}$ **do** $insert_R(\overline{x})$. Sometimes we will abbreviate this statement as $insert_R(\overline{a})$.

The effect of a statement in our language is given informally as follows. The statement **foreach** $\overline{x} : \Phi(\overline{x})$ **do** $insert_R(\overline{x})$ (resp. **foreach** $\overline{x} : \Phi(\overline{x})$ **do** $delete_R(\overline{x})$) is executed by evaluating $\Phi(\overline{x})$ to produce a set of bindings for $\overline{x}$ and then adding to (resp. deleting from) R each $\overline{x}$ tuple. The statement $(S_1 \ ; \ \ldots \ ; \ S_n)$ is executed by first executing S_1, then executing S_2, and so on.

Example 3.1 To give a salary increase of 10% to all employees who earn over \$10,000 we could write the following statement sequence.

> **foreach** $e, s : emp(e, s) \wedge s > 10000$ **do** $insert_T(e, s)$;
> **foreach** $e, s : t(e, s)$ **do** $delete_{Emp}(e, s)$;
> **foreach** $e, s, snew : t(e, s) \wedge snew = s \times 1.1$ **do** $insert_{Emp}(e, snew)$

where T is a suitable, initially empty, temporary relation. □

The update defined by a statement S in our update language is denoted $[\![S]\!]$ and is given as follows.

1. $[\![$**foreach** $\overline{x} : \Phi(\overline{x})$ **do** $insert_R(\overline{x})]\!](B) = B[R \mapsto R \cup \{\overline{x} \mid B \models \Phi(\overline{x})\}]$
2. $[\![$**foreach** $\overline{x} : \Phi(\overline{x})$ **do** $delete_R(\overline{x})]\!](B) = B[R \mapsto R - \{\overline{x} \mid B \models \Phi(\overline{x})\}]$
3. $[\![S_1 \ ; \ \ldots \ ; \ S_n]\!](\mathrm{B}) = [\![S_n]\!](\ldots [\![S_1]\!](\mathrm{B}) \ldots)$

Clearly, for every statement S, the mapping $[\![S]\!]$ is a database update.

Lemma 3.1 *Let S be a statement and H a sentence. Then a sentence F is a weakest precondition for $[\![S]\!]$ and H if, for every database B, $B \models F$ if and only if $[\![S]\!](B) \models H$.*

Proof Suppose that, for every database B, $B \models F$ if and only if $[\![S]\!](B) \models H$. Clearly, F is a precondition for $[\![S]\!]$ and H. Further, for all databases B and preconditions G for $[\![S]\!]$ and H, $B \models G$ implies $[\![S]\!](B) \models H$, as G is a precondition for $[\![S]\!]$ and H, and hence, by assumption, $B \models F$. That is, F is a weakest precondition for $[\![S]\!]$ and H. □

4 Constraint transformation

In the context of program derivation, Dijkstra [4] defined a predicate transformer wp as follows. For any command S and predicate H, $wp(S, H)$ denotes another predicate F such that execution of S in a state satisfying F guarantees that S will terminate in a state satisfying H.

Similarly, in our database context, we define a constraint transformer wp for a statement S and a formula H. Informally, execution of S in a state satisfying $wp(S, H)$ guarantees that S will terminate in a state satisfying H.

Let H be a (possibly open) formula, Φ a formula with k free variables and r a k-ary predicate symbol, for some $k \geq 0$. We write $H[r \mapsto r \cup \Phi]$ (resp., $H[r \mapsto r - \Phi]$) for the formula resulting from the replacement of every occurrence of $r(\overline{s})$ in H by $(r(\overline{s}) \vee \Phi(\overline{s}))$ (resp., $(r(\overline{s}) \wedge \neg\Phi(\overline{s}))$).

Definition Let S be a statement in normal form and H a (possibly open) formula. Then $wp(S, H)$ is defined as follows:

1. $wp(\textbf{foreach } \overline{x} : \Phi(\overline{x}) \textbf{ do } insert_R(\overline{x}), H) = H[r \mapsto r \cup \Phi]$
2. $wp(\textbf{foreach } \overline{x} : \Phi(\overline{x}) \textbf{ do } delete_R(\overline{x}), H) = H[r \mapsto r - \Phi]$
3. $wp(S_1 \ ; \ \ldots \ ; \ S_n), H) = wp(S_1, \ldots wp(S_n, H) \ldots)$

Note that these equations define wp, and not the semantics of statements as in [5].

The following example illustrates how to construct $wp(S, H)$ according to the definition above.

Example 4.1 Let H be the constraint $\forall \overline{x}\ (p(\overline{x}) \rightarrow q(\overline{x}))$, and S the statement $S1 \ ; \ S2$, where $S1$ is the statement **foreach** $\overline{x} : r(\overline{x})$ **do** $delete_P(\overline{x})$, and $S2$ is the statement **foreach** $\overline{y} : s(\overline{y})$ **do** $insert_P(\overline{y})$. Then,

$$\begin{aligned} wp(S, H) &= wp(S1; S2, H) \\ &= wp(S1, wp(S2, H)) \\ &= wp(S1, \forall \overline{x}\ ((p(\overline{x}) \vee s(\overline{x})) \rightarrow q(\overline{x})) \\ &= \forall \overline{x}\ (((p(\overline{x}) \wedge \neg r(\overline{x})) \vee s(\overline{x})) \rightarrow q(\overline{x})) \end{aligned}$$

□

We now present a series of lemmas leading to a proof that $wp(S, H)$ is the weakest precondition for $[\![S]\!]$ and H.

Lemma 4.1 *Let S be the statement* **foreach** $\overline{x} : \Phi(\overline{x})$ **do** $insert_R(\overline{x})$, *H a formula with free variables $\overline{z}$, and ν a valuation for $\overline{z}$. Then, for every database B, $B \models_\nu wp(S, H)$ if and only if $[\![S]\!](B) \models_\nu H$.*

Proof The proof is by induction on the structure of H. Lemma 2.1 is used in the base case, $H = r(\overline{x})$. Simple induction is used when $H = H_1 \wedge H_2$, $H = H_1 \vee H_2$, or $H = \neg H_1$. The only nontrivial case is $H = \forall \overline{y}\ H'$, which is given in full below. (By renaming, we can assume that $\overline{x}$ and $\overline{y}$ are disjoint.)

$$\begin{array}{lll} B \models_\nu wp(S, \forall \overline{y}\ H') & & \\ \iff & B \models_\nu (\forall \overline{y}\ H')[r \mapsto r \cup \Phi] & \text{(definition of } wp\text{)} \\ \iff & \text{for all } \nu' \geq \nu,\ B \models_{\nu'} H'[p \mapsto p \cup \Phi] & \text{(semantics of } \forall\text{)} \\ \iff & \text{for all } \nu' \geq \nu,\ B \models_{\nu'} wp(S, H') & \text{(definition of } wp\text{)} \\ \iff & \text{for all } \nu' \geq \nu,\ [\![S]\!](B) \models_{\nu'} H' & \text{(induction hypothesis)} \\ \iff & [\![S]\!](B) \models_\nu \forall \overline{y}\ H' & \text{(semantics of } \forall\text{)} \end{array}$$

□

Lemma 4.2 *Let S be the statement* **foreach** $\overline{x} : \Phi(\overline{x})$ **do** $delete_R(\overline{x})$, *H a formula with free variables $\overline{z}$, and ν a valuation for $\overline{z}$. Then, for every database B, $B \models_\nu wp(S, H)$ if and only if $[\![S]\!](B) \models_\nu H$.*

Proof As for Lemma 4.1, but using Lemma 2.2 in place of Lemma 2.1. □

Lemma 4.3 *Let S be the sequential statement $(S_1\ ;\ \ldots\ ;\ S_n)$ and H a sentence. Then, for every database B, $B \models wp(S, H)$ if and only if $[\![S]\!](B) \models H$.*

Proof Assume inductively that, for every database B, sentence H', and statement sequence $S_1\ ;\ \ldots\ ;\ S_i$, $1 \leq i < n$, we have $B \models wp((S_1\ ;\ \ldots\ ;\ S_i), H')$ if and only if $[\![S_1\ ;\ \ldots\ ;\ S_i]\!](B) \models H'$. Then

$$\begin{array}{lll} B \models wp((S_1\ ;\ \ldots\ ;\ S_n), H) & & \\ \iff & B \models wp((S_1\ ;\ \ldots\ ;\ S_{n-1}), wp(S_n, H)) & \text{(definition of } wp\text{)} \\ \iff & [\![S_1\ ;\ \ldots\ ;\ S_{n-1}]\!](B) \models wp(S_n, H)) & \text{(induction hypothesis)} \\ \iff & [\![S_n]\!]([\![S_1\ ;\ \ldots\ ;\ S_{n-1}]\!](B)) \models H & \text{(induction hypothesis)} \\ \iff & [\![S_1\ ;\ \ldots\ ;\ S_n]\!](B) \models H & \text{(definition of update)} \end{array}$$

Lemmas 4.1 and 4.2 (with ν empty) provide the base cases. □

Theorem 4.1 *Let S be a statement, and H a sentence. Then $wp(S, H)$ is the weakest precondition for $[\![S]\!]$ and H.*

Proof The result follows immediately from Lemmas 3.1, 4.1, 4.2,and 4.3. □

To apply Theorem 4.1 we construct $wp(S, H)$ and evaluate it before performing the statement S. In the next section we describe how $wp(S, H)$ can be simplified before it is evaluated.

5 Simplification

To simplify the condition $wp(S, H)$ we take advantage of the fact that H is already true in the initial database B. In this case we show how to construct a simpler formula wp' such that wp' is true in B if and only if $wp(S, H)$ is true in B.

The following example illustrates the derivation of a weakest precondition and its subsequent simplification.

Example 5.1 Let H be the constraint $\forall\overline{x}\ (p(\overline{x}) \rightarrow q(\overline{x}))$, and S the statement **foreach** $\overline{x} : r(\overline{x})$ **do** *insert* $p(\overline{x})$. Then,

$$\begin{aligned} wp(S,H) &= \forall\overline{x}\ (p(\overline{x}) \vee r(\overline{x}) \rightarrow q(\overline{x})) \\ &\equiv \forall\overline{x}\ (p(\overline{x}) \rightarrow q(\overline{x}))\ \wedge\ \forall\overline{x}\ (r(\overline{x}) \rightarrow q(\overline{x})) \\ &\equiv H\ \wedge\ \forall\overline{x}\ (r(\overline{x}) \rightarrow q(\overline{x})) \end{aligned}$$

Given that H is true in B, we thus need only check $wp' = \forall\overline{x}\ (r(\overline{x}) \rightarrow q(\overline{x}))$ to determine whether $wp(S, H)$ is true in B and, hence, whether performing S will cause the new database to satisfy the constraint H. Checking $\forall\overline{x}\ (r(\overline{x}) \rightarrow q(\overline{x}))$ in the current database is simpler than checking H in the new database because we only need to check $q(\overline{x})$ for the new values of $\overline{x}$ that will be added to P. □

We have the following results describing some circumstances under which a constraint of a certain form is simplifiable with respect to an update of a certain form, given that the constraint is true in the current database. Without loss of generality we consider constraints in prenex conjunctive normal form.

Clearly, an update which only inserts into (resp., deletes from) predicates appearing positively (resp., negatively) in a constraint cannot cause the constraint to be violated in the updated database if it was true in the current database.

More interestingly, the following lemma gives a further condition under which $wp(S, H)$ can be simplified.

Lemma 5.1 *Let B be a database, D_i a disjunction of literals l_{ij}, H a constraint of the form $\forall\overline{x}\ (D_1 \wedge \ldots \wedge D_n)$, and S a statement. Suppose that the constraint H is true in B and that some predicate that S inserts (resp., deletes) occurs negatively (resp., positively) in H. Then there exists a simpler formula, wp' such that wp' is true in B if and only if $wp(S, H)$ is true in B.*

Proof For simplicity of presentation, we assume S is a single *foreach* statement and the updated predicate appears only once in the constraint H. Let S be the statement **foreach** $\overline{x}' : r(\overline{x}')$ **do** *insert* $p(\overline{x}')$, and l_{ij} be $\neg p(\overline{s})$. Then,

$$\begin{aligned} wp(S,H) &= \forall\overline{x}\ (D_1 \wedge \ldots \wedge (l_{i1} \vee \ldots \vee \neg(p(\overline{s}) \vee r(\overline{s})) \vee \ldots \vee l_{ik_i}) \wedge \ldots \wedge D_n) \\ &\equiv \forall\overline{x}\ (D_1 \wedge \ldots \wedge (l_{i1} \vee \ldots \vee (\neg p(\overline{s}) \wedge \neg r(\overline{s})) \vee \ldots \vee l_{ik_i}) \wedge \ldots \wedge D_n) \\ &\equiv \forall\overline{x}\ (D_1 \wedge \ldots \wedge D_n \wedge (l_{i1} \vee \ldots \vee l_{ij-1} \vee \neg r(\overline{s}) \vee l_{ij+1} \vee \ldots \vee l_{ik_i})) \\ &\equiv H \wedge \forall\overline{x}\ (l_{i1} \vee \ldots \vee l_{ij-1} \vee \neg r(\overline{s}) \vee l_{ij+1} \vee \ldots \vee l_{ik_i}) \\ &\equiv \forall\overline{x}\ (r(\overline{s}) \rightarrow l_{i1} \vee \ldots \vee l_{ij-1} \vee l_{ij+1} \vee \ldots \vee l_{ik_i}) \end{aligned}$$

given that H is true in B. This last formula is simpler to check than $wp(S, H)$ because it consists of only one of the two conjuncts in a formula equivalent to $wp(S, H)$. □

Both referential integrity constraints and functional dependencies can be expressed as constraints in the form required by Lemma 5.1. Hence they can be simplified in this manner.

Depending on the form of S and H, greater simplifications than Lemma 5.1 suggests may be possible.

Example 5.2 Let H be the constraint $\forall\overline{x}\ (p(\overline{x}) \rightarrow q(\overline{x}))$, and S the statement **foreach** $\overline{x} : r(\overline{x})$ **do** $insert_P(\overline{x})$; **foreach** $\overline{x} : r(\overline{x})$ **do** $insert_Q(\overline{x})$. Then,

$$\begin{aligned} wp(S,H) &= \forall\overline{x}\ (p(\overline{x}) \vee r(\overline{x}) \rightarrow q(\overline{x}) \vee r(\overline{x})) \\ &\equiv \forall\overline{x}\ (p(\overline{x}) \rightarrow (q(\overline{x}) \vee r(\overline{x}))) \ \wedge\ \forall\overline{x}\ (r(\overline{x}) \rightarrow (q(\overline{x}) \vee r(\overline{x}))) \\ &\equiv \forall\overline{x}\ (p(\overline{x}) \rightarrow (q(\overline{x}) \vee r(\overline{x}))) \\ &\equiv true \end{aligned}$$

given that H is true in B. Thus S may be performed safely without checking $wp(S,H)$ at all. □

It is worth noting that for this example, the methods described in [2], [8], and [10] would all require checks equivalent to $\forall\overline{x}\ (r(\overline{x}) \rightarrow q(\overline{x}))$.

Under certain circumstances, notably when inserting and deleting facts, we may also simplify the weakest precondition when the constraint contains an existential quantifier following the outermost universal quantifier.

Example 5.3 (See [9, p. 58].) Let H be the constraint $\forall x\exists y\ (p(x) \rightarrow q(x,y))$, and S the statement $delete_Q(a,b)$. Then,

$$\begin{aligned} wp(S,H) &= \forall x\exists y\ (p(x) \rightarrow q(x,y) \wedge x,y \neq a,b) \\ &\equiv \forall x\exists y\ (x \neq a \rightarrow (p(x) \rightarrow q(x,y) \wedge x,y \neq a,b)) \wedge \\ & \forall x\exists y\ (x = a \rightarrow (p(x) \rightarrow q(x,y) \wedge x,y \neq a,b)) \\ &\equiv \forall x\exists y\ (x \neq a \rightarrow (p(x) \rightarrow q(x,y))) \wedge \exists y\ (p(a) \rightarrow q(a,y) \wedge y \neq b) \\ &\equiv \forall x\exists y\ (p(x) \rightarrow q(x,y)) \wedge \exists y\ (p(a) \rightarrow q(a,y) \wedge y \neq b) \\ &\equiv H \wedge \exists y\ (p(a) \rightarrow q(a,y) \wedge y \neq b) \\ &\equiv \exists y\ (p(a) \rightarrow q(a,y) \wedge y \neq b) \end{aligned}$$

given that H is true in B. □

Furthermore, because we treat updates as a whole, we can also simplify some constraints whose outermost quantifier is existential.

Example 5.4 Let H be the constraint $\exists\overline{x}\ p(\overline{x})$, and S the statement sequence $delete_P(\overline{a})$; $insert_P(\overline{c})$. Then,

$$\begin{aligned} wp(S,H) &= \exists\overline{x}\ (p(\overline{x}) \wedge \neg(\overline{x} = \overline{a})) \vee \overline{x} = \overline{c} \\ &\equiv \exists\overline{x}\ (p(\overline{x}) \wedge \neg(\overline{x} = \overline{a})) \vee \exists\overline{x}\ \overline{x} = \overline{c} \\ &\equiv \exists\overline{x}\ (p(\overline{x}) \wedge \neg(\overline{x} = \overline{a})) \vee true \\ &\equiv true \end{aligned}$$

given that H is true in B. □

Of course, it is not always possible to simplify $wp(S, H)$.

Example 5.5 Let H be the constraint $\exists \overline{x}\ p(\overline{x})$, and S the statement $delete_{\,p}(\overline{a})$. Then,

$$wp(S, H) \quad = \quad \exists \overline{x}\ (p(\overline{x}) \wedge \neg(\overline{x} = \overline{a}))$$

which cannot be simplified. □

At present, we are unable to completely characterise the conditions under which a constraint is simplifiable with respect to an update. However, we can identify certain important special cases including constraints expressing referential integrity and functional dependencies. Also, we note that the problem of simplifying $wp(S, H)$ given that H is true in B, is a special case of semantic query optimisation [3]. Hence, the techniques applicable to semantic query optimisation are also applicable here and offer further avenues for simplification.

6 Conclusion

The ability to compute the weakest precondition of a database update and a first-order sentence leads to an efficient method to ensure that database updates maintain the truth of integrity constraints.

In the context of relational databases, our method of constraint simplification is at least as good as, and offers the following advantages over, the methods described in [2], [8], and [10].

- The simplified constraints can be evaluated before the update is performed.
- The update is considered as a whole rather than just a set of separate updates. This allows simpler constraints to be generated.
- A more powerful update language is considered which allows parameterised, set at a time, updates.

In contrast to the method described in [6] and [9] we describe a simple method for constructing the weakest precondition (for a more expressive update language) and explicit conditions under which it can be simplified. These include the common constraints expressing referential integrity and functional dependencies.

McCune and Henschen [9] describe a method for integrity constraint simplification which effectively calculates $wp(S, H)$. An incomplete method for simplifying $wp(S, H)$ is described but no claims about its effectiveness are made.

Stemple and Sheard [11] describe a method of integrity constraint simplification which also operates on the update procedure. Their update language is less powerful than ours and it is not clear how much simplification is possible with their method which is based around a modified Boyer-Moore theorem prover.

We believe our approach to be both simpler in presentation and more general in scope than the above methods. We treat a more powerful update language and derive simpler conditions to check. Our method can be applied without change to derived relations defined by non-recursive rules.

Wallace [12] describes a method for compiling integrity constraints into update procedures. He deals with an equivalent update language and also handles recursive rules. His method extends the methods based on "recursive update consequences" [2] by considering a more powerful update language and a transformation similar to *wp*. It produces simplifications similar to our method.

Extending the generation of weakest preconditions to deductive databases with recursive rules and integrity constraints is a straightforward task. It remains to be done to apply the semantic query optimisation techniques extended for recursive rules described in [3] to help simplify weakest preconditions with recursion.

References

[1] S. Abiteboul and V. Vianu. Procedural languages for database queries and updates. *Journal of Computer and System Sciences*, 41(1):181–229, 1990.

[2] F. Bry, H. Decker, and R. Manthey. A uniform approach to constraint satisfaction and constraint satisfiability in deductive databases. In *Proc. FirstInternational Conference on Extending Database Technology*, pages 488–505, Venice, Italy, Feb. 1988.

[3] U. S. Chakravarthy, J. Grant, and J. Minker. Logic-based approach to semantic qury optimization. *ACM Transactions on Database Systems*, 15(2):162–207, June 1990.

[4] E. W. Dijkstra. Guarded commands, nondeterminacy and formal derivation of programs. *Communications of the ACM*, 18(8):453–457, Aug. 1975.

[5] D. Gries. *The Science of Programming*. Texts and Monographs in Computer Science. Springer-Verlag, New York, 1981.

[6] L. J. Henschen, W. W. McCune, and S. A. Naqvi. Compiling constraint-checking programs from first-order formulas. In H. Gallaire, J. Minker, and J.-M. Nicolas, editors, *Advances in Data Base Theory*, pages 145–169. Plenum Press, New York, 1984.

[7] M. Lawley. On the power of database update languages. In G. Gupta and C. Keen, editors, *Proc. Fifteenth Aust. Computer Science Conf.*, pages 517–528, Hobart, Australia, Jan. 1992.

[8] J. W. Lloyd, E. A. Sonenberg, and R. W. Topor. Integrity constraint checking in stratified databases. *Journal of Logic Programming*, 4(4):331–343, Dec. 1987.

[9] W. W. McCune and L. J. Henschen. Maintaining state constraints in relational databases: A proof theoretic basis. *Journal of the ACM*, 36(1):46–68, 1989.

[10] J.-M. Nicolas. Logic for improving integrity checking in relational database. *Acta Informatica*, 18:227–253, 1982.

[11] T. Sheard and D. Stemple. Automatic verification of database transaction safety. *ACM Transactions on Database Systems*, 14(3):322–368, Sept. 1989.

[12] M. Wallace. Compiling integrity checking into update procedures. In *Proc. Twelfth International Joint Conference on Artificial Intelligence*, pages 903–908, Aug. 1991.

Integrity Preserving Updates in Object-Oriented Databases*

Klaus–Dieter Schewe[1], Bernhard Thalheim[2], Ingrid Wetzel[1]

[1] University of Hamburg, Dept. of Computer Science, Vogt-Kölln-Str. 30, D-W-2000 Hamburg 54, FRG
[2] University of Rostock, Dept. of Computer Science, Albert-Einstein-Str. 21, D-O-2500 Rostock, FRG

Abstract

Integrity with respect to static and dynamic constraints is a crucial property of database application systems, especially in OODBs, where structurally defined constraints such as inclusion and referential constraints have to be preserved. In this paper we solve this problem for basic *update operations* that are determined by the schema. We present a framework on rewriting of generic operations in dependence on the structural and semantical information of the schema. We show how consistency-preserving, basic update operations can be generated. Moreover, we analyse distinguished classes of user-defined constraints and generalize our result to them.

1 Introduction

One of the primary benefits that database systems offer is automatic enforcement of database integrity. One type of integrity is maintained through automatic concurrency control and recovery mechansms; allmost all commercial systems provide this. Another is the automatic enforcement of user-specified integrity constraints. Most commercial database systems, especially relational database management systems enforce only a bare minimum of constraints, largely because of the performance overhead associated with updates. A database system should be designed to automatically take methods (specified by the user or generated by the system) upon checking integrity constraints upon occurrence of certain database operations. The *maintenance problem* is the problem how to ensure the database satisfies its constraints after certain actions. There are at present two approaches to this maintenance problem. The first one, more classical is the modification of methods in accordance to the specified integrity constaints [6,9,12,21,26]. The second approach

*This work has been supported in part by research grants from the E.E.C. Basic Research Action 3070 FIDE: "Formally Integrated Data Environments".

uses generation mechanisms for the specified events [17,24,25]. Upon occurrence of certain database events like update operations the management component is activated for integrity maintenance. The first research direction was not succeeding because of limitations within the approach. The second one is at present one of the most active database research areas. One of the objectives of this paper is to show that the first approach can be extended to object-oriented databases using stronger mathematical fundamentals. Most of the research on the maintenance problem was using the relational approach.

The shortcomings of the relational database approach encouraged much research aimed at achieving more appropriate data models. It has been claimed that the ***object-oriented approach*** to be the key technology for future database systems and languages. Several systems such as O_2 [1], EXODUS [4], VISION [5], IRIS [8], ORION [11] and Gemstone [15] arose from these efforts. Current research in object oriented databases (OODBs) often addresses the outstanding formal foundation of OODBs [2,3,18,19].

Accuracy is an obviously important and desirable feature of any database. To this end, ***integrity constraints***, conditions that data must satisfy before a database is updated, are commonly employed as a means of helping to maintain consistency. In relational databases the specification and enforcement of integrity constraints has a long tradition [22], whereas in OODBs the integrity problem has only recently drawn attention [6,20]. This was the motivation for the research work reported in this paper.

In object-oriented databases, integrity maintenance can be based on two different approaches. The first one uses blind update operations. In this case, any update is allowed and the system organizes the maintenance [13]. The second approach is based on methods rewriting. This approach is more effective. Assuming an consistent database state the modified method can not lead to an inconsistent state. In contrast to the relational model the fundamental concepts of ***object identity*** [10] and ***inheritance*** imply inevitably the existence of ***inclusion*** and ***referential constraints*** that are specified with each OODB schema. Integrity with respect to these constraints must be preserved by all database updates, especially by basic ***insert-***, ***delete-*** and ***update***-operations. As usual in OODBs such operations are modeled by ***methods***. Due to the main result in [18] such operations are only uniquely determined by the schema in the case of ***value-representable*** classes. We shall outline these methods and draw specific attention to the type of the required input-value.

In relational databases distinguished classes of static integrity constraints have been discussed such as ***inclusion***, ***exclusion***, ***functional***, ***key*** and ***multi-valued dependencies***. All these constraints can be generalized to the object oriented case. Then the result on the existence of integrity preserving methods can be generalized to capture also these constraints. We shall also describe the resulting methods.

The objective of the paper is to propose a framework for supporting consistency-preserving updates in object-oriented database systems. The paper makes two contributions. We show how the generation of update methods can be based on the schema definition for the given object-oriented database. This framework can be used for deriving and implementing algorithms for enforcing static integrity constraints through update operations.

The remainder of the paper is organized as follows. In Section 2 we introduce a "light" version of the object oriented datamodel (OODM) in [18,20]. The restriction is due to a simplified fixed type system, whereas the original OODM uses arbitrary algebraic type specifications. The decision for this simplification is due to the fact that we want to demonstrate integrity preservation whithout burdening the reader with the hard mathematics of type algebras.

In Section 3 we the address the integrity preservation problem. We introduce distinguished classes of static constraints and show, how basic updates must be defined in order to preserve integrity. The presentation is mainly done on the basis of examples. However, a clear mathematical formalization and justification has been achieved based on results from [18,20]. We conclude with a short outlook on an intended generalization of the presented results.

2 Fundamentals of an Object Oriented Data Model

Relational approaches to data modelling are called value-oriented since in these models real world entities are completely represented by their values. In the object-oriented approach we distinguish between objects and values. Values can be grouped into types. In general, a type may be regarded as an immutable set of values of a uniform structure together with operations defined on such values. Subtyping is used to relate values in different types.

Whereas values are encoded by themselves [3], objects have to be encoded by object identifiers regardless of the content, location or addressability [10]. In our approach each object consists of a unique, immutable *identifier*, a set of values of possibly different types, *references* to other objects and *methods* associated with the object. This is formally expressed by

$$o \quad = \quad (i, \{v_j, T_j\}, \{\text{ref}_k, o_k\}, \{\text{meth}_l\})$$

for an object o with identifier i, values v_j of types T_j, references ref_k to objects o_k and methods meth_l.

2.1 The Class Concept as a Structural Primitive

The class concept provides the grouping of objects having the same structure which uniformly combines aspects of object values and references. Moreover, generic operations on objects such as object creation, deletion and update of its values and references are associated with classes provided these operations can be defined unambigously. Objects can belong to different classes, which guarantees each object of our abstract object model to be captured by the collection of possible classes. As for values that are only defined via types, objects can only be defined via classes. Thus, a design consists of ***type*** and ***class definitions***.

Type Definitions.

Assume the existence of ***basic types*** $STRING$, NAT, INT and $BOOL$ with the usual operations on them. Additionally, there exist a basic type ID that will be used to model object identifiers and a trivial type $\perp$ with only one element and no operations.

In this paper we only use fixed type constructors, the ***tagged tuple*** constructor denoted by $(\cdot)$, the ***finite set*** constructor denoted by $\{\cdot\}$ and the ***union*** constructor denoted $\cup$. We use concatenation on tuple types denoted by the $\circ$-operator.

Types and type constructors in general are defined by nesting of these constructors. These types can be organized in a ***subtype*** hierarchy with the subtype relation defined as usual. $\perp$ is a supertype of every type.

As a last structuring feature recursive type definitions are allowed. They only occur as input-types for generated update methods, where ***rational tree*** values are required.

Example 1 The set and the tuple type constructors are both used in the declaration for PERSONNAME:

$$PERSONNAME = (\,\text{FirstName} : STRING,\ \text{SecondName} : STRING,\ \text{Titles} : \{STRING\})$$

The definition for the type PERSON uses the type PERSONNAME and the type ADDRESS defined elsewhere:

$$PERSON = (\,\text{PersonIdentityNo} : NAT,\ \text{Name} : PERSONNAME,\ \text{Address} : ADDRESS\,)$$

The following example defines $STUDENT$ as a subtype of $PERSON$:

$$STUDENT = PERSON \circ (\,\text{StudNo} : NAT, \text{Faculty} : NAT\,)$$

□

Class Definitions.

Each object in a class consists of an identifier, a collection of values and references to objects in other classes. Identifiers can be represented using the unique identifier type ID. Values and references can be combined into a representation type, where each occurence of ID denotes references to some other classes. Therefore, we may define the structure of a class using type constructors.

- Let t be a type constructor with parameters $\alpha_1, \ldots, \alpha_n$ such that ID does not occur in t. For distinct reference names $r_1, \ldots, r_n$ and class names $C_1, \ldots, C_n$ the expression derived from t by replacing each α_i in t by $r_i : C_i$ for $i = 1, \ldots, n$ is called a ***structure expression***.

- A *class* consists of a class name C, a structure expression S, a set of class names $D_1, \ldots, D_m$ (in the following called the set of *superclasses*) and a set of methods. We call r_i the ***reference*** named r_i from class C to class C_i. The type derived from S by replacing each reference $r_i : C_i$ by the type ID is called the ***representation type*** T_C of the class C.

- A *schema* $\mathcal{S}$ is a finite collection of classes $C_1, \ldots, C_n$ closed under references and superclasses together with a collection of constraints $\mathcal{I}_1, \ldots, \mathcal{I}_n$.

Example 2 Let the types $PERSON$ and $STUDENT$ be as in Example 1. In addition assume a type $PROFESSOR$ defined as elsewhere as another subtype of $PERSON$. Then the following is a simple schema for a university application. For the moment methods are omitted.

```
Schema University
  Class PersonC
    Structure PERSON
    Methods ...
  Class MarriedPersonC
    Structure PERSON∘ (Spouse : MarriedPersonC)
    IsA PersonC
  Class StudentC
    Structure STUDENT∘ (Supervisor : ProfessorC)
    IsA PersonC
  Class ProfessorC
    Structure PROFESSOR
    IsA PersonC
  Constraint Unique(PersonC,PERSON)
  Constraint EXCL(StudentC,ProfessorC)
```

□

The notation Unique(C,T) means that values of type T do not occur twice in the class C. EXCL(C_1,C_2) states that the classes C_1 and C_2 are disjoint. Constraints will be discussed in detail in Section 3.

At each time, C is given by a finite set of objects. More precisely, C is a set of pairs (i, v), where i is of type ID and v is of type T_C such that identifiers are unique in this set. This defines an ***instance*** $\mathcal{D}$ of a schema $\mathcal{S}$.

Moreover, C gives rise to ***referential constraints*** defined by the structure S and ***IsA constraints*** defined by the set of superclasses of C, i.e.

- whenever an identifier $j :: ID$ occurs in v and this occurrence corresponds to the reference $r_k : C_k$, then there must exist an object in C_k with identifier j (*referential integrity*), and
- for each superclass D_k there exist an object with identifier i (and some value $w :: T_{D_k}$ in D_k) (*inclusion integrity*). Moreover, if T_C is a subtype of T_{D_k}, there v must correspond to w.

Note, that we do not require classes to be disjoint nor that IsA relations require a subtype relation on the corresponding representation types.

2.2 Methods as a Basis for Behaviour Modeling

Methods in general can be described operationally with the usual control constructs. Assignments are only allowed on the class C or on a selective expression on C. Therefore, we dispense with introducing a specific method language here.

Let us now concentrate on basic update methods, i.e. insertion, deletion and update of a single object on a classes C. In contrast to the relational datamodel such update operations can not always be derived in the object-oriented case, because the abstract identifiers have to be hidden from the user. However, in [18] it has been shown that for ***value-representable*** classes these operations are uniquely determined by the schema and consistent with respect to the implicit referential and inclusion constraints.

Value-representability of all classes in a schema is implied, if we define a trivial ***uniqueness constraint*** for each class. Such a constraint requires the values of type T_C in the class extension C to be unique, which is similar to a (trivial) key definition in the relational case. In Section 3 we generalize this notion.

Example 3 Let us describe the insert-method for the class PERSONC of Example 2.

insert$_{PersonC}$ (in: $P :: PERSON$, out: I :: ID) $=$
  IF $\exists\, O \in$ PERSONC . value(O) $= P$
  THEN $I :=$ ident(O)

ELSE I := NewId ;
    PersonC := PersonC $\cup$ { (I,P)}
ENDIF

For the insert on the class MarriedPersonC we need a more complex input type V recursively defined as

$$V = PERSON \circ (V \cup ID)$$

For each $P :: V$ let $f(P) :: PERSON$ be the projection onto $PERSON$ corresponding to the subtype relation between V and $PERSON$. Then we have

insert$_{MarriedPersonC}$ (in: $P :: V$, out: $I :: ID$) =
    I := insert$_{PersonC}$($f(P)$) ;
    IF $\forall O \in$ MarriedPersonC . ident(O) $\neq I$
    THEN P' := substitute(I,P,Spouse(P)) ;
        IF $P' :: ID$
        THEN $J := P'$
        ELSE J := insert$_{MarriedPersonC}$(P')
        ENDIF ;
    MarriedPersonC := MarriedPersonC $\cup$ { (I,$f(P) \circ (J)$)}
    ENDIF

We used the global method NewId to denote the selection of a new identifier. The expression substitute(I,P,T) denotes the result of replacing the value I for P in the expression T. □

3 Static Integrity in the OODM

Let us now introduce some kinds of explicit static constraints that are generalizations of constraints known from the relational model, e.g. functional and key constraints, general inclusion and exclusion constraints and multi-valued dependencies. Our aim is to show that basic update operations can be derived that also preserve such explicit constraints. In some cases an arbitrary value of some proper value type is required. We then extend the input-type.

In the following we restrict ourselves to the case of a single explicit constraint in addition to the one (trivial) uniqueness constraint that is required to assure value-representability and that has been used in [18] to construct *canonical update operations*.

3.1 Inclusion and Exclusion Constraints

Basically an *inclusion constraint* on classes C_1 and C_2 states that the values of objects in class C_1 also occur as values of objects in C_2. More generally this needs only be true for some "projections" of values. For this purpose assume the representation types T_{C_1} and T_{C_2} to be subtypes of a common type T. This can be expressed by functions $c_i : T_{C_i} \to T$ $(i = 1, 2)$. Then an inclusion constraint can be written as a first-order formula of the form

$$(I_1, V_1) \in C_1 \;\Rightarrow\; \exists\, (I_2, V_2) \in C_2.\; c_1(V_1) = c_2(V_2)\,.$$

Let $\mathcal{I}$ be such an inclusion constraint. Then each insertion into C_1 requires an additional insertion into C_2 whereas a deletion on C_2 requires a deletion on C_1. Update on one of the C_i requires an additional update on the other class.

Let us first concentrate on the insert-operation on C_1 (for an insert on C_2 there is nothing to do). Insertion into C_1 requires an input-value of type V_{C_1}; an additional insert on C_2 then requires an input-value of type V_{C_2}. However, these input-values are not independent, because the corresponding values of type T_{C_1} and T_{C_2} must satisfy the inclusion constraint.

However, in [20] it has been shown that in general the required input-type V_{C_1,C_2} must be a subtype of (V_{C_1}, V_{C_2}). We omit the details.

An *exclusion constraint* on C_1, C_2 is a constraint of the form

$$(I_1, V_1) \in C_1 \;\wedge\; (I_2, V_2) \in C_2 \;\Rightarrow\; c_1(V_1) \neq c_2(V_2)\,,$$

where c_1, c_2 are as in the inclusion case. Note that this generalizes the constraint EXCL(C_1,C_2) used in Example 2.

The handling of exclusion constraints is analogous to the handling of inclusion constraints. This means that an insert (update) on one class may cause a delete on the other, whereas delete-operations remain unchanged.

Example 4 We concentrate on the insert-operation for the class STUDENTC of Example 2. Let the exclusion constraint be defined by $T = PERSON$, where c_1 corresponds to the subtype

$$V = STUDENT \circ (\text{ Supervisor} : PROFESSOR)$$

and c_2 corresponds to the subtype $PROFESSOR$. Then we get

```
insert_StudentC (in: S :: V , out: I :: ID) =
    I := insert_PersonC(c1(S)) ;
    IF ∃ O ∈ PROFESSORC . ident(O) = I
    THEN  PROFESSORC := PROFESSORC − { O}
```

ENDIF

Note that the selected object O in the class PROFESSORC (if it exists) is the only one with $c_2(\text{value}(O)) = c_1(\text{value}(O'))$, where O' is the new object in STUDENTC. □

3.2 Functional and Uniqueness Constraints

A *functional constraint* on a class C can be defined by two functions $c^i : T_C \to T_i$ $(i = 1, 2)$. Written as a first-order formula it has the form

$$(I, V) \in C \wedge (I', V') \in C \wedge c^1(V) = c^1(V') \Rightarrow c^2(V) = c^2(V') .$$

A functional constraint defines a restriction on object values. It is called a *value constraint* iff neither T_1 nor T_2 contains ID.

A *uniqueness constraint* on C is a constraint of the form

$$(I, V) \in C \wedge (I', V') \in C \wedge c^1(V) = c^1(V') \Rightarrow I = I' ,$$

hence restricts objects. A uniqueness constraint on C is called *trivial* iff $T_C = T_1$ and $c^1 = id$ hold.

A uniqueness constraint defined via $c^1 : T_C \to T_1$ is equivalent to a functional constraint defined via c^1 and $c^2 = id : T_C \to T_C$ plus the trivial uniqueness constraint. Since trivial uniqueness constraints are already enforced by the canonical update operations, there is no need to handle separately arbitrary uniqueness constraints.

Now let $\mathcal{I}$ be a functional constraint on C. In this case nothing is required for the delete operation whereas for inserts (and updates) we have to add a precondition.

Example 5 Let us concentrate on the insert-method on class PERSONC of Example 2. Let $\mathcal{I}$ be the functional constraint defined by $T_1 = (\text{PersonIdentityNo} : NAT)$ and $T_2 = PERSON$, where c^1 corresponds to the subtype relation and $c^2 = id$. Then we get

insert$_{PersonC}$ (in: $P :: PERSON$, out: I :: ID) =
  IF $\exists\, O \in$ PERSONC . $c^1(\text{value}(O)) = c^1(P)$
  THEN $I := \text{ident}(O)$
  ELSE $I :=$ NewId ;
    PERSONC := PERSONC ∪ { (I,P)}
  ENDIF
□

3.3 Object Generating Constraints

An *object generating constraint* on a class C is intended to generalize multi-valued dependencies. It has the form

$$(I_1, V_1) \in C \wedge (I_2, V_2) \in C \wedge c^1(V_1) = c^1(V_2) \Rightarrow$$
$$\exists\, (I, V) \in C.\, c^1(V) = c^1(V_1) \wedge c^2(V) = c^2(V_1) \wedge c^3(V) = c^3(V_2)\,,$$

where $c^i : T_C \rightarrow T_i$ $(i = 1, 2, 3)$ are functions. Preserving such a constraint $\mathcal{I}$ requires to add additional inserts (deletes, updates) to each insert- (delete-, update-) method. We omit the details [20].

3.4 Finiteness Constraints

Let us now address the general case of cyclic references. An example of such cycle is the recursive definition of MARRIEDPERSONC in Example 2. According to our definitions two objects in a class C are identical iff they have the same identifier. By the use of constraints, especially uniqueness constraints, we could restrict this notion of equality. This leads to the characterization of those classes, the objects in which are completely representable by values, i.e. we could drop the object identifiers and replace references by values of the referred object. We shall see now that in case of such value-representable classes we are able to preserve an important advantage of relational databases, i.e. the existence of structurally determined update operations. The basic idea is that there is always only a finite number of objects in a database. Assuming the database being consistent with respect to inclusion and referential constraints yields that there can not exist infinite cyclic references. This will be expressed by the *finiteness property*. In [18] it is shown that this property implies the decidability of value-representability provided the type system allows recursive types to be defined in such a way that all their values are finitely representable, i.e. representable as rational trees. Furthermore, for value-representable classes the update operations are uniquely determined by the schema and consistent with respect to the implicit referential and inclusion constraints.

Example 6 Example 3 used the finiteness of the database for the derivation of the generic insert operation. This operation is able to accept any value of type V. In [18,19] we have shown that the input value type can be restricted using additional integrity constraints. For instance, assuming that the spouse of the spouse of some person is the person itself and that the spouse of a person is not the person itself the insert method can be refined to another method using the validity of

substitute(I',P',Spouse(P')) :: ID

for P' := substitute(I,P,Spouse(P)) and I' := $\text{insert}_{PersonC}(f(P'))$.

The insert method in Example 3 is now equivalent to:

insert$_{MarriedPersonC}$ (in: $P :: V$, out: $I :: ID$) $=$
  $I :=$ insert$_{PersonC}(f(P))$;
  IF $\forall\, O \in$ MARRIEDPERSONC . ident(O) $\neq I$
  THEN $P' :=$ substitute(I,P,Spouse(P)) ;
    $I' :=$ insert$_{PersonC}(f(P'))$
    IF $\forall\, O \in$ MARRIEDPERSONC . ident(O) $\neq I'$
      THEN MARRIEDPERSONC := MARRIEDPERSONC $\cup$ { $(I', f(P') \circ (I))$}
      ENDIF
    MARRIEDPERSONC := MARRIEDPERSONC $\cup$ { $(I, f(P) \circ (I'))$}
  ENDIF .

Therefore, the insert operation which is made visible to the user is now
  insert$_{MarriedPersonC}$ (P :: $PERSON \circ$ Spouse : $PERSON$) .
The corresponding delete operation for married persons is based on the uniqueness constraint for the person class $PersonC$:
  delete$_{MarriedPersonC}$ (P :: $PERSON$) . □

3.5 Transforming Static Constraints into Transactions

Let us now consider the case of arbitrary methods which can be used to model transactions. We concentrate on the question whether it is possible to achieve general consistent methods as combinations of consistent primitive operations as for explicit constraints. Regard the following simple example:

Example 7
ACCOUNTCLASS ==
  `Structure` (Person : PERSON, Account : NAT, CreditLimit : NAT)
End ACCOUNTCLASS

`Constraints`
  $(I, V) \in$ ACCOUNTCLASS $\Rightarrow V.Account + V.CreditLimit \geq 0$
  $(I, V) \in$ ACCOUNTCLASS $\wedge$ $(I', V') \in$ ACCOUNTCLASS $\wedge$
    $V.Person = V'.Person \Rightarrow I = I'$

Let $transfer(P_1, P_2, T)$ be the transfer of the amount T from P_1 to P_2, i.e.

$transfer(P_1 :: PERSON, P_2 :: PERSON, T :: NAT)$ ==
  $I_1, I_2 :: ID, N_1, N_2, M_1, M_2 :: NAT$ |
      $(I_1, (P_1, N_1, M_1)) \in$ ACCOUNTCLASS $\wedge$
      $(I_2, (P_2, N_2, M_2)) \in$ ACCOUNTCLASS $\rightarrow$
    $update_{AccountClass}(P_1, (P_1, N_1 - T, M_1))$;
    $update_{AccountClass}(P_2, (P_2, N_2 + T, M_2))$

In this case the precondition to be added is simply the weakest precondition, i.e. $N_1 + M_1 - T \geq 0$. Now regard the operation

$$S = transfer(P_1, P_2, T_1);\ transfer(P_2, P_1, T_2)\ .$$

The precondition to be added to S in order to enforce the first constraint simply is $N_1 + M_1 - T_1 + T_2 \geq 0 \wedge N_2 + M_2 - T_2 + T_1 \geq 0$, which is trivially satisfied if $T_1 = T_2$. However, for large values of $T_1 = T_2$ this condition is weaker then adding the three preconditions separately. Therefore, the weakest precondition of the transaction is not semantically equivalent to the union of the preconditions. □

4 Conclusion

In this paper we addressed the problem of integrity preserving basic update operaions in object-oriented databases. Our analysis is based on a formally defined object-oriented datamodel (OODM) that includes inclusion and referential constraints implicitly in a schema and allows in particular explicit constraints to be defined. We concentrate on particular classes of explicit constraints that have relational counterparts such as inclusion, exclusion, functional, uniqueness and object-generating constraints. We show that integrity preservation for basic update operations is possible for these constraints.

It is well known that the trigger approach can cover only enforcement of simple classes of integrity constraints for special database schemes. For instance, deriving generic operations using the trigger approach [6] for the schema

```
Schema Problematic
    Class C2
      ...
    Class C3
      ...
    Class C1
      ...
      IsA C2
      IsA C3
    Constraint EXCL(C2, C3)
```

we obtain two different solutions for the operation insert_{C_1}:

$\text{insert}_{C_1}(v_{C_1})$, $\text{insert}_{C_2}(v_{C_1}|_{C_2})$, $\text{delete}_{C_3}(v_{C_1}|_{C_3})$, $\text{delete}_{C_1}(v_{C_1})$

$\text{insert}_{C_1}(v_{C_1})$, $\text{insert}_{C_3}(v_{C_1}|_{C_3})$, $\text{delete}_{C_2}(v_{C_1}|_{C_2})$, $\text{delete}_{C_1}(v_{C_1})$.

However, the weakest insert operation for this schema is the operation

skip

since the class C_1 is empty according to the definitions.

In general, however, it is not sufficient to regard only basic update operations and a single explicit constraint. Although there exists an encouraging theoretical result on the possibility of integrity enforcement in general [20], it is still an open problem how to generate the corresponding methods. Hence the idea to replace each update operation (methods in the OODM) by a *Greatest Consistent Specialization* (GCS). It can be shown that such GCSs always exist and are uniquely determined by the operation and the constraints up to semantic equivalence. Moreover, they are compatible with the conjunction of constraints, inheritance and refinement. Unfortunately, a GCS in general is non-deterministic, but a suitable maximal deterministic branch can be selected via refinement.

Extending the research reported in this paper in this direction is one of our next goals. An unsolved open problem is the general structure of a GCS including the problem of its computation. One idea is to exploit the structure of a constraint that must involve constructor- and selector-expressions on state variables (classes in the OODM). However, this idea is still two vague to be discussed in this paper. Another open problem concerns the generalization to arbitrary dynamic constraints. Lipeck has shown in [14] that dynamic constraints expressed in some generalized propositional temporal logic give rise to transition graphs. It should be possible to derive a suitable proof obligation in the predicate transformer calculus [16] also for such constraints. Then the idea of GCS construction should carry over even to this class of constraints that comprises static and transition constraints.

For the case of the OODM we achieve more specific results for a wide class of static constraints that occur as generalizations of kinds of constraints known from the relational model. We show that integrity enforcement for primitive update operations is possible. Moreover, part of the non-determinism can be removed in a canonical way by extension of the required input-type. In general, however, this is not sufficient, since it is not possible to construct the GCS as a combination of the GCSs of primitive operations.

References

[1] F. Bancilhon, G. Barbedette, V. Benzaken, C. Delobel, S. Gamerman, C. Lécluse, P. Pfeffer, P. Richard, F. Velez: *The Design and Implementation of O_2, an Object-Oriented Database System*, Proc. of the ooDBS II workshop, Bad Münster, FRG, September 1988

[2] C. Beeri: *Formal Models for Object-Oriented Databases*, Proc. 1st DOOD 1989, pp. 370 – 395

[3] C. Beeri: *A formal approach to object-oriented databases*, Data and Knowledge Engineering, vol. 5 (4), 1990, pp. 353 – 382

[4] M. Carey, D. DeWitt, S. Vandenberg: *A Data Model and Query Language for EXODUS*, Proc. ACM SIGMOD 88

[5] M. Caruso, E. Sciore: *The VISION Object-Oriented Database Management System*, Proc. of the Workshop on Database Programming Languages, Roscoff, France, September 1987

[6] S. Ceri, P. Fraternali, S. Paraboschi, L. Tanca: *Automatic Rule Generation for Constraint Enforcement in Active Databases*, in U. Lipeck (Ed.): Proc. 4th Int. Workshop on Foundations of Models and Languages for Data and Objects "Modelling Database Dynamics", Volkse (Germany), October 19-22, 1992 (to appear)

[7] S. Ceri, J. Widom: *Deriving Production Rules for Constraint Maintenance*, in Proc. 16th Conf. on Very Large Data Bases, 1990, Morgan Kaufman Publishers, pp. 566–577

[8] D. Fishman, D. Beech, H. Cate, E. Chow et al.: *IRIS: An Object-Oriented Database Management System*, ACM ToIS, vol. 5(1), January 1987

[9] M. Gertz, U.W. Lipeck: *Deriving Integrity Maintaining Triggers from Transition Graphs*, University of Hannover, 1992, submitted for publication

[10] S. Khoshafian, G. Copeland: *Object Identity*, Proc. 1st Int. Conf. on OOPSLA, Portland, Oregon, 1986

[11] W. Kim, N. Ballou, J. Banerjee, H. T. Chou, J. Garza, D. Woelk: *Integrating an Object-Oriented Programming System with a Database System*, in Proc. OOPSLA 1988

[12] W. Kim: *A Framework for Supporting Triggers in Object-Oriented Database Systems*, Int. Journal of Intelligent and Cooperative Information Systems, 1, 1, 1992, 127–143

[13] C. Laasch, M.H. Scholl: *Generic Update Operations Keeping Object-Oriented Databases Consistent*, in Proc. 2nd GI-Workshop on Information Systems and AI, Ulm, 1992

[14] U. W. Lipeck: *Dynamische Integrität von Datenbanken* (in German), Springer IFB 209, 1987

[15] D. Maier, J. Stein, A. Ottis, A. Purdy: *Development of an Object-Oriented DBMS*, OOPSLA, September 1986

[16] G. Nelson: *A Generalization of Dijkstra's Calculus*, ACM TOPLAS, vol. 11 (4), October 1989, pp. 517 – 561

[17] J.M. Nicolas, K. Yazdanian: *Integrity Checking in Deductive Databases*, in Logic and Databases, H. Gallaire and J. Minker (eds.), Plenum Press, 1978

[18] K.-D. Schewe, J. W. Schmidt, I. Wetzel: *Identification, Genericity and Consistency in Object-Oriented Databases*, in J. Biskup, R. Hull (Eds.): Proc. 3rd International Conference on Database Theory, ICDT '92, Berlin (Germany), October 14-16, 1992, Springer LNCS (to appear)

[19] K.-D. Schewe, B. Thalheim, and I. Wetzel: *Foundations of Object-Oriented Concepts*, Technical Report, Computer Science Department, Hamburg University, Aug. 1992.

[20] K.-D. Schewe, B. Thalheim, J. W. Schmidt, I. Wetzel: *Integrity Enforcement in Object-Oriented Databases*, in U. Lipeck (Ed.): Proc. 4th Int. Workshop on Foundations of Models and Languages for Data and Objects "Modelling Database Dynamics", Volkse (Germany), October 19-22, 1992, Springer WICS (to appear)

[21] M. Stonebraker: *Implementation of Integrity Constraints and Views by Query Modification*, in Proc. ACM SIGMOD Int. Conference on Management of Data, 1975, 65-78

[22] B. Thalheim: *Dependencies in Relational Databases*, Teubner Leipzig, 1991

[23] S.D. Urban, A.P. Karadimce, and R.B. Nannapaneni: *The Implementation and Evaluation of Integrity Maintenance Rules in an Object-Oriented Database*, in Eighth Int. Conf. on Data Engineering, 1992, 562-572.

[24] J. Widom, R.J. Cochrane, and B. Lindsay: *Implementing Set-Oriented Production Rules as an Extension to Starburst*, in G.M. Lohmann, A. Sernadas, and R. Camps (eds.), Proc. 17th Int. Conf. on Very Large Data Bases, 1991, Morgan Kaufman Publishers

[25] M. Winslett: *Updating Logical Databases*, Cambridge University Press, Cambridge 1990

[26] Y. Zhou, M. Hsu: *A Theory for Rule Triggering Systems*, in Proc. 2nd Int. Conf. Extending Database Technology, Lecture Notes in Computer Science, 416, 1990, 407-421

Querying Heterogeneous Databases: A Case Study

Alexandre Lefebvre Peter Bernus Rodney W. Topor

School of Computing and Information Technology
*Griffith University, Nathan QLD 4111, Australia**

{ajl,bernus,rwt}@cit.gu.edu.au

Abstract

Data can be retrieved from several heterogeneous databases by regarding them as a single global database, and expressing queries using the schema of this global database. We review the problems that arise when the local databases have data and schema conflicts, describe necessary query and data mappings between the global and local databases, and present a possible implementation of these mappings using a simple object-oriented language.

1 Introduction

A common approach to integrating heterogeneous databases is to design a global schema for the existing databases. When accessing integrated databases from a global schema, using a global query language, each global query has to be translated to a set of local queries onto the existing databases, and the answers have to be translated onto the global schema after the local queries have been answered. The problem of query and answer translation is a common problem, not only relevant in centralized architectures based on a predesigned global schema, but in all architectures involving heterogeneous databases, such as federated databases [9].

Various types of conflicts between the databases may exist [6, 7]. Some of them concern the data conflicts themselves, such as domain conflicts, or simple schema conflicts (the same information can be represented as one or as several attributes in different databases). Data conflicts have been studied quite intensively, and solutions exist to solve them. Another type of conflict is that of *schema conflict* [7]: it occurs when an attribute value in one database appears as a relation name or an attribute name in another database.

In this paper, we analyze the problems arising when the local databases present some schema conflict, and when the relational model is chosen to represent the schemas of the global and local databases. We base our study on an example of a *stock database* inspired from [7].

We show that a simple translation of SQL queries on the global database to SQL queries on the local databases is not always possible. Higher-order information about the local databases has to be manipulated at the level of the global database. We

*This was done as part of a project for the CRC for Distributed Systems Technology.

also show that some control over the query evaluation has to be performed within the global database. We analyze the need for three types of *mapping information*: view definitions of the global relations in terms of the local ones, data mapping functions between the global database and the local databases, and domain definitions of the entities present in the local databases. Finally, we present algorithms using these data structures for translating the queries. We propose a representation of the mapping information and of the translation process using a simple object-oriented language, F-logic [4], and show its expressive power and convenience.

The work presented here extends that of [3, 7]. The use of the F-logic language allows us not only to represent the data mappings in the case of data and schema conflicts, but also to express the query translation algorithm in this same language. This way, uniformity is achieved for solving the data mapping and the query translation problems.

The structure of the paper is as follows. In the remainder of this section, we give some definitions, and present the stock database example. In section 2, we analyze the data and schema conflict problems. In section 3, we present the F-logic language, analyze the requirements for query translation and present a solution for a query translation algorithm using F-logic. Finally, we present our conclusions.

1.1 Definitions and motivating example

We consider a set of heterogeneous, autonomous databases. Each database has its own *local conceptual schema* (LCS). Each local database is supposed to be used by its local users, or application programs, which refer to the LCS. The integration of the local databases defines a *global schema*, or *common conceptual schema* (CCS). When querying the integrated databases, the global queries are expressed in terms of the CCS.

In this paper we investigate the case where the LCSs and the CCS are all expressed using the relational model, and we suppose that the query language used in the local databases, as well as in the global database is SQL. We do not deal with the problems of updates, integrity constraints, and data distribution in this paper.

Let us introduce the following motivating example, inspired from [7].

Example Consider three databases representing information about stock prices, all describing the closing price of stocks on each day in the stock market. The local schemas are as follows:

database b_1 $\quad$ r_1(date, stock, price)

database b_2 $\quad$ r_2(date, $\text{stock}_1, \ldots, \text{stock}_n$)

database b_3 $\quad$ stock_1(date, price)

...

stock_m(date, price)

In b_1, there is one single relation, with one tuple per day and stock storing the closing price. In b_2, there is one single relation, with one tuple per day, and one attribute per stock, named by the stock name, and storing its closing price. Finally, b_3 has one relation per stock, named by the stock name; each relation has one tuple per day storing the closing price. □

Several problems have to be solved when trying to integrate these three databases. First, a CCS has to be chosen. This issue has been studied in the literature [1]. In our particular case, one can identify three types of information: stocks, dates and prices. If global queries are going to be issued, asking for values of any of these entities, then the three entities have to appear in the global schema as attribute values. Therefore, the CCS should be similar to the one of b_1, where *date*, *stock* and *price* are attributes of a ternary relation r. As a justification, consider the query: *"What are the stocks which closed at 200 on the 31 July 1992?"* If the CCS had the form of the LCS of b_2 or b_3, this query could not be expressed as a relational query, because, in neither of these two LCSs, is *stock* an attribute value.

From now on, the CCS is considered to be as follows:

CCS r(date, stock, price)

2 Problems of query translation

Once the CCS has been chosen, queries of the global database have to be translated to queries of the local databases. Let us first present the translation of a simple query of the stock database.

Example (cont.) Consider the following query: *"What is the closing price of IBM on the 31 July 1992?"* Expressed in SQL on the CCS, it has the following form:

In CCS:
```
select price
from   r
where  stock=IBM and date="31 July 1992"
```

After translation, this query expressed on b_2 and b_3 has the forms:

In b_2:
```
select IBM
from   r2
where  date="31 July 1992"
```

In b_3:
```
select price
from   IBM
where  date="31 July 1992"
```

In b_2, *IBM* is the name of the attribute storing the closing price for *IBM*. In b_3, *IBM* is the name of the relation storing the closing prices for *IBM*. □

Considering the global database as a *view* over the local databases, we require answers to a global query of a (hypothetical) global database to correspond to the answers obtained by answering the translated query onto local databases, and then translating these local answers back onto the global database.

In this paper, we do not deal with the problem of distributing the global query onto the local databases, nor do we deal with the problem of integrating the answers coming from the local databases. Instead, we focus on how a given query formulated within the CCS can be translated to a local query for a given LCS.

2.1 Data conflicts

When mapping constants in a global query to constants in a local query, or translating back answers in a local database onto the global database, data may have to be converted. Several types of conflicts between the data in the global database and the data in the local databases are possible, and mapping functions have to be provided in order to solve the conflicts.

The problem of data conflicts is one of the most studied problems in the area of heterogeneous databases [1, 6, 8]. There is no general solution to this problem, but simple solutions exist for the simple cases, mainly for the case of domain mapping, or single attribute mapping (see for example [8]). A classification of possible conflicts can be found in [6]. Note that, even though [6] describes some of the data conflicts as *schema conflicts*, it does not deal with what we describe as schema conflicts, which involve attribute and relation *names*.

Data conflicts are usually solved by the use of *mapping functions*. Let us denote by $\mu^d_{b_i,b_j}$ the mapping function for domain d from database b_i to database b_j. In the remainder, we make the simplifying assumption that all data conflicts have been identified, and that the corresponding mapping functions for the data between the global database and the local databases are available.

2.2 Schema conflicts

Let us now study another query of the stock database, involving a particularly difficult schema conflict.

Example (cont.) Consider the following *query* q of the stock database: *"What are the dates and stocks for which the stock closes over 200?"*. The SQL expression corresponding to this global query of the global database is:

q in CCS:
```
select date, stock
from   r
where  price > 200
```
□

As we already mentioned in section 1.1, such a query is not expressible as a simple SQL query of b_2 or b_3, as it ranges over the attribute *stock*. Stocks are represented as attribute names in b_2 and relation names in b_3, but do not appear as attribute values in either. This type of conflict, known as *schema conflict* [7], has recently been considered in the literature. It is characterized, as in our example, by the fact that an *attribute value* in some schema corresponds to an *attribute name*, or a *relation name*, in another schema.

We now consider the translation of query q to a *set* of SQL queries on b_2, and then on b_3. Analyzing the problem, we see that we need to ask as many queries as there are stocks in b_2: for each stock value $stock_i$, a query should ask for the date, with the condition that the value of the attribute named $stock_i$ must be greater than 200, and collect these dates together with the name of the stock $stock_i$ (as a constant) into some temporary relation. The union of all intermediate answers constitutes the answer to the global query of b_2, i.e. a binary relation, one attribute being the stock name, and the other attribute, the date.

We denote by $names(stock, b_2)$ the set of stock names in b_2, and we assume that this information has been made available at the level of the global database. The value of $names(stock, b_2)$ could be obtained, for example, by querying the data dictionary of b_2. The translation of q to SQL queries of b_2 and b_3 is shown below.

Example (cont.) The translation of query q onto b_2 consists of the following query plan, containing a parametric SQL query of b_2.

For b_2:
```
foreach $stock in names(stock, b2) do
    insert into tmp
    select date, '$stock'
    from   r2
    where  $stock > 200
```

Here, **$stock** is a variable ranging over the possible values of stocks in b_2. The overall expression[1] is evaluated within the global database, and the SQL queries are sent for evaluation to b_2. A similar translation onto b_3 leads to the following query plan:

For b_3:
```
foreach $stock in names(stock, b3) do
    insert into tmp
    select date, '$stock'
    from   $stock
    where  price > 200
```
□

Note that, in addition to schema conflicts, data conflicts can also occur. In this case, mapping functions will be needed, to be applied to the constants in the query, or to the tuples of the result relation.

The study of query q shows that a query of the global database might have to be translated to a set of queries of the local databases. It shows the need for a control structure in order to issue several local queries, manipulating the local domains within the global database. In order to automate the translation of queries of the global database onto a local database, there is a need for information about the schemas of the local databases, and about the correspondence between tuples in the global database and tuples in local databases.

In [7], the authors propose a high order language to express the definition of tuples in the common schema by means of views over the local databases. In [3],

[1]The creation of the tmp relation is not presented here.

the use of *integration functions* allows the authors to express, in a similar way, the information in the global database in terms of expressions in the local databases. However, neither of these papers provides a mechanism to translate queries of the global database to queries of local databases. We show how to do this in this paper.

3 Query translation

In order to represent the view definitions and the query translation algorithm, we have to manipulate high-order concepts such as attribute and relation names, domains, and mapping functions. Therefore, a higher-order language is required. Among other features, object-oriented languages give us the possibility to manipulate attributes, relations and domains as objects, and to associate values to them by means of methods. The deductive object-oriented language F-logic [4] was introduced to provide a logical foundation for object-oriented systems. The high-order syntax of F-logic and its object-oriented nature makes it a particularly well-suited language. In the next section, we briefly present the syntax and semantics of F-logic[2].

3.1 Presentation of F-logic

In F-logic, the *instance term* $o : c$ means that the object o is an instance of class c. A *data term* $o[m@a_1, \ldots, a_n \rightarrow v; m'@a_1, \ldots, a_p \twoheadrightarrow \{v', v''\}]$ means that the value of the functional method m with arguments a_1 to a_n for the object o is v, and the value of the set-valued method m' with arguments a_1 to a_p for the object o is a set containing the values v' and v''. If a method m has no arguments, "@" will be omitted. A double-headed arrow indicates a set-valued method. Note that other values could be member of this set, and that the expression above does *not* restrict the value of m' for o to be $\{v', v''\}$: it only indicates *some of* the values of the corresponding set. An object can be denoted by a constant, or a term. For example, $dept(cs)$ is a valid object identifier. An *atomic data term* is a data term referring to only one method. Notational conventions allow us to write $o[m' \twoheadrightarrow v]$ instead of $o[m' \twoheadrightarrow \{v\}]$ for a single element of a set-valued method; the expression $o[m \rightarrow v; n \rightarrow v']$ is equivalent to $o[m \rightarrow v] \wedge o[n \rightarrow v']$; the expression $o[m \rightarrow o'[n \rightarrow v]]$ is equivalent to $o[m \rightarrow o'] \wedge o'[n \rightarrow v]$; the expression $o : c[m \rightarrow v]$ is equivalent to $o : c \wedge o[m \rightarrow v]$.

An F-logic program consists of a set of data declarations (data or instance terms) and a set of *deduction rules*. A deduction rule has a *head*, which is a data term, and a *body*, which is a conjunction of data and instance terms. Disjunction and negation are allowed in the body of rules. Deduction rules can be used in a way similar to Datalog rules (or Prolog clauses): the head of a rule defines a derived method, the value of which can be found by evaluating the body.

We follow the Prolog convention in which variable symbols start with an upper case letter and constant symbols with a lower case letter (unless they are quoted).

[2]We do not discuss here the signature (typing) aspects of F-logic, as they are not relevant to this paper.

As an example, the following rule defines the *name* N of a *person* X to be the name of his or her father F:

$X[name \rightarrow N] \leftarrow X : persony[father \rightarrow F[name \rightarrow N]]$.

We have implemented a simple interpreter in Prolog for a subset of F-logic, which excludes typing, inheritance and overriding. Evaluating an F-logic query using this interpreter uses the top-down resolution of Prolog on F-logic deduction rules. The interpreter has been implemented in MegaLog [2], a ypersistent Prolog system developed at ECRC. The clauses corresponding to F-logic declarations are stored on secondary storage in the knowledge base.

3.2 Mapping information

We now present the necessary mapping information for translating a query of the global database to queries of a given local database. We suppose that the input is an SQL query of the global database, and a target local database onto which the original SQL query should be translated. The output should consist of a (set of) SQL queries $\mathcal{S}_q$ of the target database, a control structure over $\mathcal{S}_q$, and a mapping function, translating the local answers to global answers.

We will not consider nested SQL queries here, as they can be rewritten using a separate query for the subexpression, and replacing the nested subquery by a join with the corresponding temporary relation [5].

In such a context, an SQL query can be represented as:

1. a set of output attributes (from the `select` part);
2. a set of relations (from the `from` part) and
3. a set of constraints, i.e. join conditions, equalities and inequalities (from the `where` part).

We assume, at the level of the global database, the existence of a set of view definitions for each relation of the global database. A *view definition* here is similar to a view definition in deductive databases: it represents, for a given local database, the definition of a given tuple of a global relation in terms of tuples of local relations. View definitions could be defined using the language of [7], or integrator functions of [3]. As an example, the view definition of relation r in terms of relation r_2 of b_2 is expressed as follows in [7]:

$$.gb.r(.stock = X,\ .date = D,\ .price = P,\ .database = b_2)$$
$$\leftarrow .b_2.r_2(.date = D,\ .X = P),\ X \neq date.$$

We also assume the existence of *mapping functions*, for data mapping. They will be used in order to translate the initial query constants, or to construct the mapping function translating the answers from the LCS format to the CCS format. Finally, in the case of schema conflict, the *domain definitions* of the corresponding relation names or attribute names of the local databases should be available.

Figure 1 shows the process of translating a query of the global database onto a given local database.

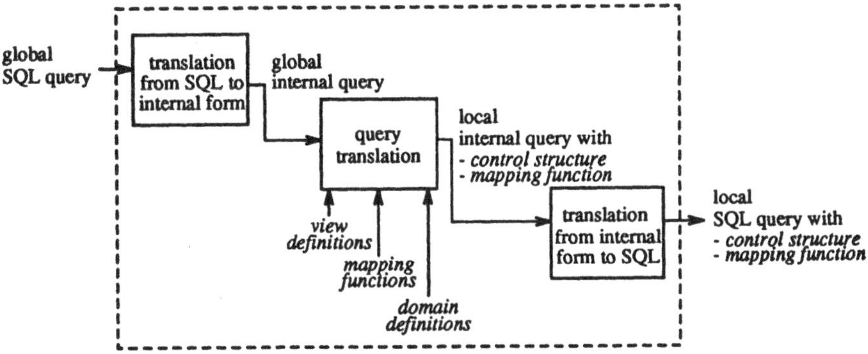

Figure 1: Query translation onto a local database

3.3 Query translation algorithm

The algorithm transforms the internal representation of a global query to the internal representation of the local query of a given local database.

Let Q be a query of a global database B. Q is represented as an object. The method *relations* associated with Q contains the set of global relation names that occur in Q using the CCS. Let $l(Q, B_i)$ be the object identifier for the local query of the local database B_i obtained by translating Q. Then, the method *relations* associated with $l(Q, B_i)$ contains the set of relation names that occur in $l(Q, B_i)$ using the LCS of B_i. Similarly, the method *attributes* contains the set of output attributes that occur in Q (resp. in $l(Q, B_i)$) using the CCS (resp. using the LCS of B_i), and the method *constraints* contains the set of join conditions, equalities or inequalities, that occur in Q (resp. in $l(Q, B_i)$) using the CCS (resp. using the LCS of B_i).

The F-logic representation of query q (*"What are the dates and stocks for which the stock closes over 200?"*) can be expressed as follows:

(1) $q[relations \twoheadrightarrow r; attributes \twoheadrightarrow \{date, stock\}; constraints \twoheadrightarrow (>, price, 200)]$

The view definitions consist of objects $view(r, b_i)$, each of which represents the definition of a global relation r using the LCS of b_i. Each view definition has two methods: *lcs_relations*, whose value is a set of *relation mapping objects* of class *rels_names*, and *lcs_attributes*, which takes a global attribute a as argument, and whose value is a set of *attribute mapping objects* of class *rels_names*, *atts_names* or *atts_values*. We represent the relation mapping objects by $relations(r, b_i)$ and the attribute mapping objects by $map(a, r, b_i)$. Each mapping object has a method *names*, whose the value is an object of class *set* or *singleton*, which represents the names of the mapped relation or attribute. These names are accessible through the method *elt* in case of a singleton, and the method *elts* in case of a set.

Example (cont.) The view definition $view(r, b_2)$ representing r in terms of relations in b_2 can be described as follows:

$view(r, b_2)[lcs\_relations \twoheadrightarrow relations(r, b_2);$
$\quad lcs\_attributes@date \twoheadrightarrow map(date, r, b_2);$
$\quad lcs\_attributes@stock \twoheadrightarrow map(stock, r, b_2);$
$\quad lcs\_attributes@price \twoheadrightarrow map(price, r, b_2)\}]$
$relations(r, b_2) : rels\_names[names \rightarrow names(r, b_2) : singleton[elt \rightarrow r_2]]$
$map(date, r, b_2) : atts\_values[names \rightarrow names(date, b_2) : singleton[elt \rightarrow date]]$
$map(stock, r, b_2) : atts\_names[names \rightarrow names(stock, b_2)]$
$names(stock, b_2) : set[elts \twoheadrightarrow \{stock_1, \ldots, stock_n\}]$
$map(price, r, b_2) : atts\_values[names \rightarrow names(price, b_2) : singleton[elt \rightarrow price]]$
□

Let us first define two auxiliary methods for local query objects. The method *rels* takes a relation of the global query as argument and returns the corresponding relation mapping objects. The method *atts* takes an attribute of the global query as argument and returns the corresponding attribute mapping objects.

$$l(Q, B)[rels@R \twoheadrightarrow M] \leftarrow Q[relations \twoheadrightarrow R] \wedge view(R, B)[lcs\_relations \twoheadrightarrow M]$$

$$l(Q, B)[atts@X \twoheadrightarrow M] \leftarrow Q[relations \twoheadrightarrow R; attributes \twoheadrightarrow X] \wedge view(R, B)[lcs\_attributes@X \twoheadrightarrow M]$$

When there is no schema conflict, the mapping names in the view definitions are all singletons, and the values of the methods *attributes* and *relations* for the local query can be obtained from the following rules:

$$Q[relations \twoheadrightarrow R] \leftarrow Q[rels@R1 \twoheadrightarrow M[names \rightarrow S : singleton[elt \rightarrow R]]]$$

$$Q[attributes \twoheadrightarrow X] \leftarrow Q[atts@Y \twoheadrightarrow M : atts\_values[names \rightarrow S : singleton[elt \rightarrow X]]]$$

In the case of a schema conflict, a range has to be constructed over which a (new) variable v should take its corresponding values. This range, represented by $range(v, S)$, will be added to the set of ranges associated with $l(Q, B_i)$, contained in the value of the method *ranges*.

The computation of the output attributes for the translated query depends on the class of the mapping objects. If the class of an attribute mapping object is:

1. *atts_names*, then the domain of the output attribute in Q corresponds to a set of local attribute names in $l(Q, B_i)$ (this is the case with b_2, if *stock* is an output attribute of the global query).

2. *rels_names*, then the domain of the output attribute in Q corresponds to a set of local relation names in $l(Q, B_i)$ (this is the case with b_3, if *stock* is an output attribute of the global query).

In these two cases, one of the output attributes will be an SQL constant. This constant is the value of a parameter, which ranges over the corresponding set. We represent the SQL expression `'val'` by *quoted(val)*.

3. *atts_values*, then the domain of the output attribute in Q corresponds to the domain of a local attribute value in $l(Q, B_i)$, for which the *attribute name* ranges

over a set (this is the case with b_2, if *price* is an output attribute of the global query: the name of the attribute corresponding to *price* in b_2 ranges over the set of stock names).

The representation of the local query $l(q, b_2)$ in F-logic has the form[3]:

$$(2)\ l(q,b_2)[relations \twoheadrightarrow r_2; attributes \twoheadrightarrow \{date, quoted(v))\}; \\ constraints \twoheadrightarrow (>, v, 200); \\ ranges \twoheadrightarrow range(v, names(stock, b_2))]$$

In the case of a schema conflict, we assume the existence of a method *newvar* for each domain name delivering a new object representing a variable. We also assume that the mapping functions can be evaluated calling a method *mapping_function* for each domain, with three arguments: the input database, the output database, and the value to be mapped. The atom *gb* denotes the global database.

The following F-logic rules represent the query translation algorithm in the case of schema conflicts.

% the relation name is a variable ranging over a set
$$l(Q,B)[relations \twoheadrightarrow Variable; ranges \twoheadrightarrow range(Variable, S)] \leftarrow \\ l(Q,B)[rels@R \twoheadrightarrow M : rels\_names[names \rightarrow S : set]] \wedge \\ not(view(R,B)[lcs\_attributes@X \twoheadrightarrow M] \wedge Q[constraints \twoheadrightarrow (=, X, \_)]) \wedge \\ R[newvar \rightarrow Variable]$$

% the relation name is a variable ranging over a set, and is an output value
$$l(Q,B)[relations \twoheadrightarrow Variable; ranges \twoheadrightarrow range(Variable, S); \\ attributes \twoheadrightarrow quoted(Variable)] \leftarrow \\ l(Q,B)[rels@R \twoheadrightarrow M : rels\_names[names \rightarrow S : set]; atts@X \twoheadrightarrow M] \wedge \\ not(Q[constraints \twoheadrightarrow (=, X, \_)]) \wedge R[newvar \rightarrow Variable]$$

% same as above, but the relation name is constrained to a given value
$$l(Q,B)[relations \twoheadrightarrow Mapped\_value] \leftarrow \\ l(Q,B)[rels@R \twoheadrightarrow M] \wedge view(R,B)[lcs\_attributes@X \twoheadrightarrow M] \wedge \\ Q[constraints \twoheadrightarrow (=, X, Value)] \wedge \\ Name[mapping\_function@gb, B, Value \rightarrow Mapped\_value]$$

% the output value is a variable ranging over a set
$$l(Q,B)[attributes \twoheadrightarrow quoted(Variable); ranges \twoheadrightarrow range(Variable, S)] \leftarrow \\ l(Q,B)[atts@X \twoheadrightarrow M : atts\_names[names \rightarrow S : set]] \wedge \\ not(Q[constraints \twoheadrightarrow (=, X, \_)]) \wedge X[newvar \rightarrow Variable]$$

% the name of the output attribute is a variable ranging over a set of values
$$l(Q,B)[attributes \twoheadrightarrow Variable; ranges \twoheadrightarrow range(Variable, S)] \leftarrow \\ l(Q,B)[atts@X \twoheadrightarrow M : atts\_values[names \rightarrow S : set]] \wedge \\ not(S[constrained@Q, R, B, \_Att \rightarrow \_Value]) \wedge$$

[3]Because of space restriction, we only present the translation of q onto b_2. Similar rules can be written for b_3. Note that the algorithm presented below would construct $l(q, b_3)$ as well.

$X[newvar \rightarrow Variable]$

% same as above, but the attribute name is constrained to a given value
$l(Q,B)[attributes \twoheadrightarrow Mapped\_value] \leftarrow$
$l(Q,B)[atts@X \twoheadrightarrow M : atts\_values[names \rightarrow S : set]] \wedge$
$S[constrained@Q, R, B, Y \rightarrow Value] \wedge$
$Y[mapping\_function@gb, B, Value \rightarrow Mapped\_value]$

where a set S of attribute names is constrained to a value $Value$ if there is a global constraint "$Y = Value$", and Y maps to a set of local attribute names which range over the set S:

$S[constrained@Q, R, B, Y \rightarrow Value] \leftarrow$
$view(R,B)[lcs\_attributes@Y \twoheadrightarrow M : atts\_names[names \rightarrow S]] \wedge$
$Q[constraints \twoheadrightarrow (=, Y, Value)]$

For brevity, the deduction rules defining the method *constraints* are not presented in this paper.

We have implemented and tested these rules on the F-logic interpreter mentioned before. The evaluation of the query "?- $l(q, b_2)[relations \twoheadrightarrow R; attributes \twoheadrightarrow X; ranges \twoheadrightarrow Y; constraints \twoheadrightarrow C]$" returns the expression (2) as an answer. □

The translation algorithm expressed with F-logic is more declarative and modular than an algorithm written in a conventional procedural programming language. When new mapping rules have to be added, a new deduction rule can simply be added to the program. One can question the generality and extensibility of such a framework. For example, we have not introduced the treatment of joins yet. In the full version of this paper, we present examples of join queries and of complex data mismatches, and show how our framework is suited to solve such problems.

4 Conclusion

We have presented a case study involving query evaluation in heterogeneous databases, where the schemas of the global and the local databases are represented using the relational model. The *stock* database example presented here shows possible data *and schema* conflicts, characterized by the fact that a global attribute domain ranges over a set of attribute or relation names in local databases.

We have studied the problem of translating queries of the global database onto the local databases, and demonstrated that some simple SQL queries can not be translated to any SQL query. Instead, when a schema conflict occurs, a set of parametric queries might have to be issued. We have shown that there is a need, at the level of the global database, to manipulate higher-order information about the local databases. This information, composed of view definitions, domain definitions and data mapping functions, is used to translate global queries to local queries.

We have presented a solution to the query translation problem, in the case of data and schema conflicts, using the simple object-oriented language F-logic. Previous work use high-order languages to express the data mappings in the case of data and schema conflicts [7, 3]. We have shown that the data mappings *and* the query translation algorithm can be expressed in the same object-oriented language, leading to a uniform solution to the data mapping and the query translation problems.

Further work remains to be done in order to investigate the additional problems arising when updating the global database, considering arbitrary application programs involving complex transactions, and taking integrity constraints into account. We also need to determine whether natural extensions of F-logic are adequate for handling these new problems, or whether a more complex language is required.

References

[1] S. Ceri, B. Pernici, and G. Wiederhold. Distributed Database Design Methodology. *Proceedings of the IEEE*, 75(5):533–546, May 1987.

[2] T. Horsfield, J. Bocca, and M. Dahmen. MegaLog User Guide. Technical report, ECRC, Munich, Germany, 1989.

[3] W. Kent. Solving Domain Mismatch and Schema Mismatch Problems with an Object-Oriented Database Programming Language. In *Proc. of the 17th VLDB Conference*, pages 147–160, Barcelona, September 1991.

[4] M. Kifer, G. Lausen, and J. Wu. Logical Foundations of Object-Oriented and Frame-Based Languages. Technical Report 90/14, SUNY at Stony Brook, August 1990.

[5] W. Kim. On Optimizing an SQL-like Nested Query. *ACM Transactions on Database Systems*, 7(3):443–469, September 1982.

[6] W. Kim and J. Seo. Classifying Schematic and Data Heterogeneity in Multidatabase Systems. *IEEE Computer*, pages 12–18, December 1991.

[7] R. Krishnamurthy, W. Litwin, and W. Kent. Language Features for Interoperability of Databases with Schematic Discrepancies. In *Proc. of the ACM SIGMOD Conference on Management of Data*, pages 40–49, Denver, Colorado, May 1991.

[8] J. A. Larson, S. B. Navathe, and R. Elmasri. A Theory of Attribute Equivalence in Databases with Application to Schema Integration. *IEEE Transactions on Software Engineering*, 15(4):449–463, April 1989.

[9] A. P. Sheth and J. A. Larson. Federated Database Systems for Managing Distributed, Heterogeneous, and Autonomous Databases. *ACM Computing Surveys*, 22(3):183–236, September 1990.

Design and Implementation of the Omega Object-based System*

Shahram Ghandeharizadeh, Vera Choi, Clifford Ker, Kai-Ming Lin

Computer Science Department
University of Southern California
Los Angeles, California 90089

Abstract

Omega is a parallel object-based system that supports a functional data model and implements the following constructs: unique object identifiers, complex objects, a type hierarchy, inheritance, and user-defined methods. This paper describes the design of the Omega database machine and the techniques employed in its implementation. In addition, it presents performance numbers from the system to demonstrate the feasibility of a parallel object-based system.

1 Introduction

In the 1990s, next-generation database management systems (DBMSs), sometimes termed *object-based* DBMSs, have become an essential component of many application domains: Computer-Aided Design (CAD) and Manufacturing (CAM), office information systems, scientific and medical applications to name a few. This is because these systems provide a rich set of semantic constructs that can represent and manipulate structurally complex inter-relationships among data found in these application domains. However, a limitation of these systems is their low performance as they are both CPU and disk intensive. The current technological trends is unlikely to resolve this limitation because while the speed of the CPU has increased rapidly over the past decade[1], the speed of the magnetic disk drive which typically serves as the secondary storage device for these systems has not kept pace[2]. Moreover, this technological trend is not expected to change in the near future [10]. The overall performance of a system will not improve significantly when only one component of the system (e.g., the CPU) is improved while the other components (e.g., the disk) remain unchanged [1]. One approach to resolve this limitation is to employ parallelism and use multiple disk drives and processors to execute a query.

*This research was supported in part by the USC FRIF grant 22-1509-9440, the NSF grant IRI-9110522, and the NYI award IRI-9258362.

[1]The speed of CPU has improved by approximately a factor of two each year since 1984 [8].

[2]The raw seek time has only improved at a rate of 7% per year [10].

In this paper, we present the design and implementation of a parallel object-based DBMS, Omega. Omega supports a functional data model [12] and implements the following object-based constructs:

- Unique object identifier: The DBMS assigns each object a unique identifier in order to enable the user to distinguish between two or more objects independent of their state or attribute values.
- Complex objects: An object may reference (or contain) several other objects in the database by having the value of a function be another object which is an instance of the range of that function. Typically, *inter-object references* are used to represent the containment or composite/component relationship among objects.
- Types: Objects that have similar properties can be grouped in a type.
- Inheritance: Types can be organized as a hierarchy in order to support inheritance of properties, simplifying the description of complex data schemas.
- User-defined methods: The system supports both derived and stored methods. With a derived method, the user defines an arbitrary query as the definition of the method. With a stored method, the user defines a function that takes one or more objects (or values) as input arguments and produces zero or more objects (or values) as output.

Ideally, a parallel system should be scalable, i.e., the response time of the system should improve proportional to the number of processors and disk drives in the system. Omega is based on a shared-nothing architecture [13] and employs several techniques to scale to a large number of processors. First, objects of an application are horizontally declustered [11, 9] across multiple disk drives, enabling the system to employ multiple processors to execute a query. Second, an object in Omega is physically independent from its sub-objects and the objects it references or contains. This enables the database administrator (DBA) to analyze the workload of an application and fine tune the placement of its objects, the sub-objects that constitute an object, and the objects which are referenced by a complex object across the processors in order to maximize the performance of the system for that application. This capability is important because in parallel database systems, a query executes where the data resides. If the physical design of the system does not allow the DBA to fine tune the placement of the data, then either 1) a single processor of a thousand processor system might become a bottleneck, reducing the overall performance of the system (and result in an expensive sequential system with many under utilized processors and disk drives) or 2) the overhead of parallelism might become significant and diminish the capability of the system to scale to a large number of processors.

The rest of this paper is organized as follows. In Section 2, we describe Omega's hardware platform. Section 3 describes how Omega implements the object-based constructs. Section 4 describes our techniques for processing a query. In Section 5, we analyze the performance of Omega when its processing capability is increased from one to eight processors for processing navigational style queries (i.e., queries that traverse the subcomponents of a complex object). The results demonstrate the feasibility of a scalable parallel object-based system. Our conclusions and future research directions are contained in Section 6.

2 Hardware Platform

Architecturally, Omega is based on a shared-nothing architecture [13] in which processors do not share disk drives or random access memory and can only communicate with one another by passing messages through a high speed communication network. Mass storage in such an architecture is generally distributed among the processors by connecting one or more disk drives to each processor.

Presently, Omega's hardware platform consists of eight HP 700/720 workstations, each with sixteen megabytes of memory, a PA/RISC CPU (60 MIPS), and a 400 megabyte disk drive (SCSI II interface). A 10 megabits/second Ethernet[3] is used to connect the workstations with one another and to another HP 700/720 workstation serving as the host machine to Omega. In this paper, we refer to each workstation as a processor.

3 Omega: A Software Object-based System

Omega consists of four process types:
Schema Manager (SM): The SM maintains the schema information for a database. This information is stored permanently in a *meta-data* file on the host and is loaded into memory when a database is first opened. This file maintains the structure of the type hierarchy and the declustering information of each type (see Section 3.1 for a more detailed description of the meta-data file). In addition, for each user registered with the system, it maintains that user's name space. A user may name an object arbitrarily as long as it is unique within his/her name space.
Query Manager (QM): One QM process is associated with each active user. The QM caches schema information and the user's name space locally, providing an ad-hoc interface for submitting queries. It supports a variant of the OSQL [5, 14] query language.
Scheduler Processes: The execution of a query that requires the participation of multiple processors is controlled by a scheduler process. This process traverses the operators of a compiled query tree and activates the Operator Processes on behalf of each operator.
Operator Processes: One operator process is employed at each processor that participates in the execution of each operator in a query tree. The different operators supported by Omega are described in Section 4.

The SM and QM processes reside at the host processor. The scheduler processes may execute on any processor (even the host). The current implementation requires the identity of the processor executing the scheduler to be revealed to the QM in advance. The operator processes execute only on the backend processors.

Given a query, the QM parses the query, constructs an internal representation of it (i.e., a query tree), and replaces user-defined names by their corresponding object identifiers. The query tree contains information such as the file each operator should iterate over, the processors containing the relevant fragments of this file, the offset and length of each

[3]While the definition of a shared-nothing architecture calls for a fast communication network, the Ethernet is by no means considered fast. However, it is sufficient for an eight processor configuration and the database sizes considered in the evaluation section of this paper. As a part of our future research directions, we intend to replace the Ethernet with a 100 megabits/second Fiber Distributed Data Interface (FDDI).

function value, etc. Next, the QM sends the query tree to a scheduler process and awaits for the query to complete execution. The scheduler process traverses the query tree and schedules each operator on the appropriate processor for execution. Finally, the QM receives the results of the query and returns them through the ad-hoc interface to the user.

3.1 Object-based Constructs

The Wisconsin Storage Structure [4], WiSS, was used to implement the object-based constructed supported by Omega. WiSS provides file services that include structured files, byte stream files as in UNIX, B^+ indices, a hash index, long data items, a sort utility, and a scan mechanism similar to that of System R's RSS [2]. A sequential file consists of a sequence of records. Records may vary in length, and may be inserted and deleted at arbitrary locations within a sequential file. WiSS views records as black boxes. Each record has a unique Record Identifier (RID) which identifies its physical location on a secondary storage device.

Omega uses three types of files to implement the object-based constructs: 1) a *meta-data* file, 2) a *Sub-object Directory (SubDir)* file, and 3) a *t-file* for each type in the system. In order to demonstrate the relationship between these files, we use the following type hierarchy for illustration purposes:

create type person **properties** (name *string*, spouse *person*);
create type emp **subtype of** person **properties** (salary *integer*);
create type stud **subtype of** person **properties** (gpa *float*);

Omega represents a type as a record in the meta-data file. This record contains: the name of a type, its immediate subtypes (supertypes), the identity of processors that contain its fragments, relevant declustering information, number of functions, name of each of its functions, internal organization of a function, available indices on a function, etc. By maintaining the sub/supertype relationships between the types, this file maintains an internal representation of the type hierarchy. This information is used by the QM to detect illegal function references when building an internal representation of a query, e.g., when a query is posed against the emp type and references a function neither local to this type nor defined on its supertypes (i.e., person).

Logically, a single object may be a member of several types. To implement this, we represent an object as a collection of sub-objects, where each sub-object represents the membership of that object in a type. Each sub-object is represented as a record in a t-file. An entry in the SubDir maintains the different sub-objects that represent a single object. Both the SubDir file and the t-files are **horizontally declustered** [9, 11] across multiple processors. The physical address of a record in the SubDir file constitutes the identifier that uniquely distinguishes one object from another (i.e., the *unique Object IDentifier* (OID) consists of the pair: <processor id, RID>).

To illustrate this implementation, consider two objects: Joe and Mary. Both are of type person, and are married to each other. While Joe works in a company (of type emp), Mary is a student. Figure 1 presents the physical organization of this database for a two processor system. In this figure, the SubDir file is declustered into two fragments and each object is represented as a record in a fragment. The physical location (<processor id, RID>) of the

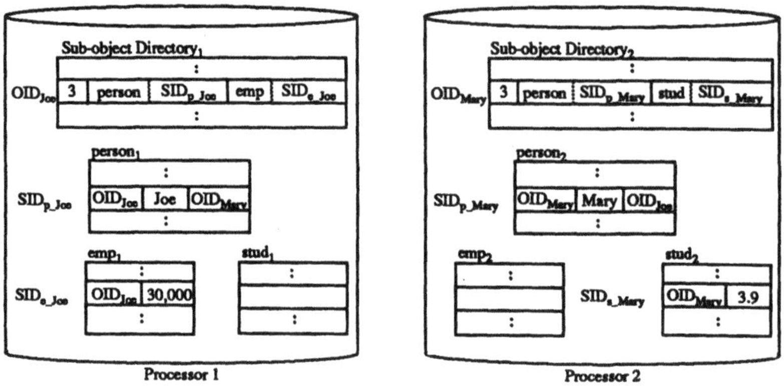

Figure 1: Example database

record representing Joe (i.e., OID_{Joe}) constitutes the identifier that uniquely distinguishes Joe from Mary (or any other object).

A sub-object which represents the membership of object x in type y is represented as a record in the t-file corresponding to y. This sub-object is uniquely identified from the other sub-objects by its Sub-object IDentifer, SID. Similar to an OID, a SID consists of the pair: <processor id, RID>. In our example, Joe is of type person and emp. Consequently, there is a record representing Joe in each of the t-files corresponding to these two types. In Figure 1, the address of each sub-object is denoted as SID_{y_x} where y is the first character of the type this SID belongs to and x is the name of the object.

A record representing object x in the SubDir file contains: 1) a reference count[4], 2) the identity of each t-file that includes x as a member, and 3) its SID. For example, Joe's record in the SubDir file contains (person, SID_{p_Joe}) and (emp, SID_{e_Joe}) to capture the fact that Joe is a member of both the person and emp types. Given the OID of an object x (say OID_x), Omega can retrieve the sub-object representing x in type y in three steps (or two random disk I/Os): 1) retrieve the record that resides on OID_x.processor-id, physical location OID_x.RID in the SubDir file, 2) extract the (y, SID_{y_x}) from this record, and 3) retrieve the record that resides on SID_{y_x}.processor-id, physical location SID_{y_x}.RID in the t-file corresponding to y.

A record in a t-file contains: 1) the OID of the object it corresponds to, and 2) the value of each function defined on that type. The OID field is used to access the value of an inherited function when executing a query (explained in Section 4). The remaining fields of a record may be of the following four types: 1) *integer*, 2) *float* (or real), 3) *character string*, and 4) user-defined type. The implementation of the first three types is straightforward. Omega implements fields that are of user-defined type by saving the OID of an object in that field. In our example, each object of type person is complex as the spouse function is object-

[4]The reference count is described in the following paragraphs.

valued. As shown in Figure 1, Mary's OID is stored in Joe's spouse field (in the person t-file) to capture the spouse relationship between these two objects. By storing OID_{Mary} in Joe's spouse field, the system can access any one of Mary's sub-objects using the spouse field of Joe. However, this is not to imply that Omega is loosely typed because, when processing a query that invokes a function on Joe's spouse field, during the construction of the query tree, the QM ensures that the invoked function is one of those defined on the person type[5] (or person's supertypes).

Omega implements multi-valued functions (or attributes) by requiring the user to define that function as a stored method (see Section 3.2 for details).

The reference count in each entry of the SubDir file represents the number of sub-objects that reference this entry. In Figure 1, the reference count for object Joe is three because two of its own sub-objects (from the person and emp type), and the sub-object corresponding to Mary in the person type (using its spouse function) reference it. As additional sub-objects reference this entry, its reference count is incremented. Similarly, as sub-objects that reference this entry are deleted, its count is decremented. An entry in the SubDir file may be deleted only when its reference count is zero (effectively destroying an object).

In summary, Omega separates an object from (1) its sub-objects in different types, and (2) its subcomponents (in the case of complex objects) in order to provide a great degree of control on the placement of the data. For example, an object and its sub-objects in different t-files may be grouped and assigned to a single processor (see Figure 1). An alternative might have been to group each sub-object and the objects it references and assign them to a single processor. The software that implements the query-processing functionality of Omega is independent of the physical location of the data (physical data independence). This flexibility is useful because different applications may require a different physical database organization in order to obtain the best performance from the system.

3.2 User-defined Methods

Omega supports two types of user-defined methods: derived and stored. With derived methods, the user describes a method as an OSQL query. Omega parses the query and stores its query tree representation in the meta-data file. When the method is invoked (or referenced), its query tree is executed to produce objects (or values).

In order to define a stored method, the user specifies its: 1) input arguments and the type of each argument, and 2) output parameters and their types. For example, one may define the children of each person as a stored method:

`create function` children (arg *person*) `->` (output *person*) `as stored`

This results in a method that takes an object of type person as input and produces zero or

[5]An alternative implementation might have been to store SID_{p_Mary} in the spouse field of Joe. We decided against this implementation because if Mary is removed from the type person (i.e., SID_{p_Mary} is removed from the person t-file), the overhead of locating all sub-objects that contain SID_{p_Mary} in any of their object-valued fields and removing them (i.e., removing the dangling pointers) would have degraded the performance of the system significantly. By storing OID_{Mary} in Joe's spouse field, when SID_{p_Mary} is removed, her record in the SubDir file is updated and the pair (person, SID_{p_Mary}) is removed from this record. The next time Joe's spouse field is referenced, the system attempts to find (person, SID_{p_Mary}) in Mary's object record. This attempt will be unsuccessful and the system returns with a null value.

more objects of this type as output. The user may assign or add values to a stored method by specifying its input and output argument values. For example, Joe's child may be set to Bob (**set** children (Joe) = Bob) and other objects may be added to this stored method (add children (Joe) = Kathy). Omega maintains a table for each user-defined method and stores the OID of each input and output object (or values of each input and output argument in the case of literals) as a record in this table. In our example, it maintains a table for the children method and stores (OID_{Joe},OID_{Bob}) as a record in this table. In the case of the add command, the record (OID_{Joe},OID_{Kathy}) is inserted into this table. Given a query that references a stored method and specifies values for its input arguments, Omega searches this table for matching values to determine the output values. To process these queries efficiently, Omega maintains a composite hash index on the value of the input arguments of a stored method in order to retrieve the output values in a few disk accesses.

4 Query Processing

Omega is customized with the standard relational algebra operators and two novel operators to process an OSQL query. It employs a data flow execution paradigm where the data is pipelined through several operators. This requires an active operator process per processor on behalf of each operation in the query tree. We start by describing the different operators. Next, we use an example to illustrate these operators and how they interact with one another.

The different operators supported by Omega are:

1. A Compute and Route SID (C&R-SID) operator. The input to this operator is an OID and its output is a SID. During the construction of the query tree, this operator is tagged with the identity of a type (say y). Given an OID, it retrieves the record residing at OID.RID, extracts its (y, SID) pair, and forwards the resulting SID to SID.processor-id. A C&R-SID operator may only appear as an intermediate node of a query tree.

2. A standard relational algebra operator (select, project, etc.). The input to this operator type is either a record or a SID. If its input is a SID, then it first retrieves the record that resides on SID.RID before performing its computation. An assumption here is that a relational operator is executing on the same processor as the SID.processor-id of its input SID (a C&R-SID operator typically proceeds this operator type in order to ensure this assumption). A relational operator may either produce a record or an OID as output. If the output of this operator is an OID and this is an intermediate node of the query tree, then the OID is forwarded to the next operator executing on OID.processor-id. Otherwise, the record is routed based on the information provided by the QM during the construction of the query tree (e.g., a hash function).

3. A multi-valued function or a stored method operator. This operator is for processing either a multi-valued function or a user-defined stored method. Its input and output parameters correspond to those defined by the user for a method (OID for the multi-valued function). This operator produces output values by using its input values to

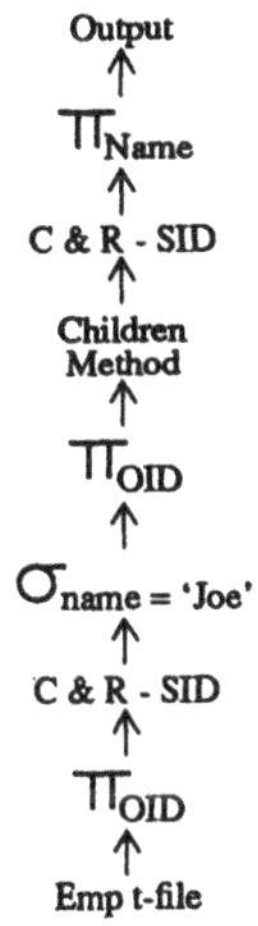

Figure 2: A query tree

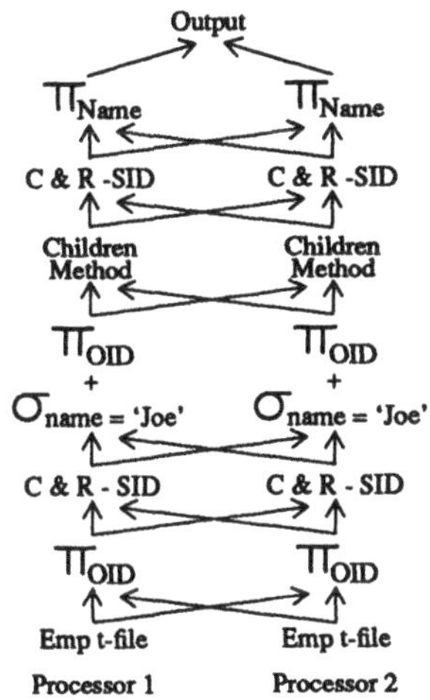

Figure 3: Parallel execution of a query tree

probe the composite hash index of a table for either a multi-valued attribute or a stored method. Its output value is either an OID or a record; if it is an OID and this is an intermediate node of the query tree, then it is sent to the next operator executing on OID.processor-id. Otherwise, the output records are routed based on the information provided by the QM during the construction of the query tree.

To illustrate these operators and how they interact, recall the schema described in Section 3.1 and the children method defined on the person type. Next, consider the following OSQL query which retrieves the name of Joe's children:

```
select name(children(e))
for each Emp e
where name(e) = 'Joe'
```

Logically, this query references an inherited function (name) for each object of the emp type in order to select those objects whose name is Joe. Next, it invokes the children stored method using each qualifying object as its input argument. For each object produced by this method, its name is evaluated and returned to the user as the final output.

Figure 2 shows the internal representation of this query (i.e., its query tree). With this query tree, a project operator (π) scans the Emp t-file (type) and projects the OID field of each record (object). For each OID, a Compute and Route SID (C&R-SID) operator evaluates the SID of the person sub-object. For each SID, a select operator (σ) retrieves the record at SID.RID and compares its name with the constant 'Joe'. If a record satisfies this selection predicate, a project operator extracts its OID field and forwards it to the children stored method operator. This operator uses its input argument to probe the hash index of the children table in order to produce output values (OID_{Bob} and OID_{Kathy}). For each produced OID, a C&R-SID operator evaluates the SID of its person sub-object. A project operator consumes each SID, retrieves the record residing at SID.RID, and produces its name as the final output.

The query tree of Figure 2 can be optimized using a subset of the standard relational algebra optimization techniques (e.g., the select and project operators can be combined and performed at the same time, see Figure 3).

Figure 3 demonstrates the parallel execution of this query tree on a two processor system. An assumption here is that the SubDir file and all the t-files are declustered across both processors. The operators of the query tree are activated in a top-down manner. Thus, the project operator that scans each fragment of the Emp t-file (in parallel on each processor) and initiates the pipeline is the last operator to be activated. This operator retrieves the OID value of each record and forwards it to a C&R-SID operator executing on OID.processor-id. This may result in inter-processor communication should the OID.processor-id be different than the identity of the processor executing the project operator. The execution of the remaining operators is the same as before except that each produced SID and OID is routed to the next operator executing on SID.processor-id and OID.processor-id respectively.

5 Performance Evaluation

In this section, we evaluate Omega using the USC benchmark [6]. We start by providing a brief description of the synthetic database used for this evaluation. Next, we analyze the scalability characteristics of the system for processing navigational queries.

5.1 The USC benchmark

The USC benchmark consists of a synthetic database and a suite of queries. The database contains only one type hierarchy and can be used to benchmark both small and large systems. The root of this type lattice consists of MAXOBJS objects.

Table 1 contains the functions defined on the root (LV0-T-ROOT) of the type hierarchy. The first nine functions can be used to model queries with a wide range of selectivity factors. The name of each function reflects its range of values. A contribution of the USC database is the definition of last three functions. The *one-to-one* function maps one object to another randomly selected object of type LV0-T-ROOT which is unique and different than itself. The *one-to-five* function maps an object to five other randomly selected objects. The *one-to-0.1p* (one to point one percentage) function maps a single object to 0.1% of randomly selected objects of type LV0-T-ROOT (0.1% of MAXOBJS) which are also unique and different than the object that contains them. Thus, each object of LV0-T-ROOT is complex and consists of three object-valued functions that identify its subcomponents. Each subcomponent is also a complex object and consists of the functions defined in Table 1.

We use the root of the type hierarchy and its functions to evaluate Omega. We refer the interested reader to [6] for a description of the structure of the type hierarchy, the functions defined on the intermediate types of the lattice, and the suite of benchmark queries.

Function Name	Type	Range of Values	Order
Unique IDentifier (UID)	Integer	0-(MAXOBJS - 1)	Sequential
Shuffled UID (SH-UID)	Integer	0-(MAXOBJS - 1)	Random
Unique Float (UF)	Float	0-(MAXOBJS - 1)	Random
Unique String1 (USTR1)	String (52 bytes)	'**...*UID'	Sequential
Shuffled String2 (SH-USTR2)	String (52 bytes)	'**...*SH-UID'	Random
one-percent	Integer	0-99	Random
ten-percent	Integer	0-9	Random
even	Integer	0,2,4,...,198	Random
odd	Integer	1,3,5,...,199	Random
one-to-one	LV0-T-ROOT (Object-valued)	-	Random
one-to-five	LV0-T-ROOT (Object-valued)	-	Random
one-to-0.1p	LV0-T-ROOT (Object-valued)	-	Random

Table 1: Functions defined on the root of the type lattice.

5.2 Performance Results

In this experiment, the database consisted of 100,000 objects (MAXOBJS = 100,000), and Omega was configured with a four kilobyte disk page size and a buffer pool size of two hundred kilobytes. All queries consisted of a simple qualification list (e.g., UID(p) = 1) and a target list that traverses the object-valued function of each qualifying object twice in a transitive manner (e.g., UID(one-to-one(one-to-one(p))))[6]. Figure 4.a presents the average response time of Omega for 1 object, 1% and 10% object selection queries as a function of the number of processors in the configuration. For each configuration, the database was evenly declustered across the processors. Moreover, the database was designed such that each object and the objects it references were assigned to the same processor (no cross processor reference).

The speedup curve corresponding to Figure 4.a is presented in Figure 4.b. In this figure, the dotted line and box represent the theoretical linear speedup curve. The performance of the one object selection is sub-linear due to the overhead of scheduling the query across a larger number of processors and the low speed of our communication network. On the other hand, the performance of the system for processing the 10% selection query is superlinear. One would expect a linear speedup because the number of random I/Os performed by each processor decreases linearly as a function of the number of processors in the system. The superlinear speedup is due to the significant difference in time the various configurations spend seeking. With one processor, the database occupies approximately 25% of the disk. When this database is declustered across eight processors, it occupies about 3% of each disk. The 10% selection performs approximately 40,000 random seeks, and the range of each random seek decreases as a function of the number of processors. Since the seek time is proportional to the square root of the distance traveled by the disk head [7], reducing the size of the database fragments on each disk significantly reduces the amount of time the query spends seeking.

[6] We assume that an OSQL query has the following structure:

```
select target list
for each object variable
where qualification list
```

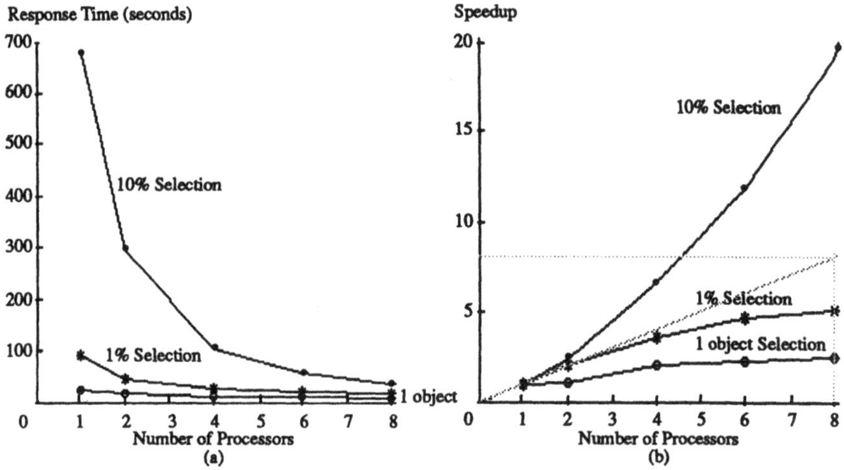

Figure 4: Performance of Omega as a function of the number of processors

In addition to this experiment, we have evaluated the performance of Omega as a function of: 1) the number of transitive traversals performed by a query, 2) the percentage of inter-object references that span multiple processors, and 3) the inheritance distance of a referenced function. The following observations were made. First, for queries that reference an inherited function, the performance of Omega is insensitive to the relative distance of a type in the hierarchy. Second, the performance of the system degrades as a function of the number of transitive traversals performed by a query due to a proportionally higher number of random I/Os performed by the system. Third, the average percentage of object references that span multiple processors impacts the scalability of the system only if it causes the workload of a query to be unevenly distributed across the processors. Finally, if a query has a low processing requirement (e.g., the one object selection query), the overhead of activating, controlling, and terminating the query across a large number of processors may outweigh the benefits of parallelism, causing the performance of the system to become sublinear as a function of the number of employed processors. For large configurations, the execution of these queries should be directed to a subset of processors.

6 Conclusion and Future Research Directions

Omega is a parallel object-based system that supports the following constructs: unique-object identifiers, a type hierarchy, inheritance, complex objects, and user-defined methods. In addition, it supports a variant of the OSQL query language for accessing and manipulating the database. In this paper, we described the physical design of the system, the operators used for processing object-based queries, and a dataflow query processing technique. In addition, we presented initial performance results from the system to demonstrate its scalability characteristics.

We intend to extend the current implementation of Omega by replacing: 1) the Ethernet with FDDI to speedup the network interface in order to simulate a multi-computer such as a hypercube, and 2) the current storage manager with EXODUS [3] in order to support large objects. With respect to the design of Omega, we intend to: 1) develop indexing techniques for a more efficient processing of the queries, 2) investigate the role of parallelism for the other object-based constructs, 3) analyze the alternative declustering techniques for a parallel object-based system and introduce techniques to localize the execution of a query to a subset of processors while distributing the workload of the database evenly across all the processors, 4) investigate the alternative clustering techniques in order to minimize the number of I/Os performed by a processor, 5) quantify the benefits and costs of replication techniques in a parallel environment for efficient processing of queries that traverse the object-valued functions.

References

[1] G. M. Amdahl. Validity of the single processor approach to achieving large scale computing capabilities. In *AFIPS 1967 Spring Joint computer conference*, 1967.

[2] M. M. Astrahan, et al. System R: Relational Approach to Database Management. *ACM Transactions on Database Systems*, 1(2):97–137, June 1976.

[3] M. Carey, D. DeWitt, J. Richardson, and E. Shekita. Storage management for objects in EXODUS. In W. Kim and F. Lochovsky, editors, *Object-Oriented Concepts, Databases, and Applications*, pages 341–371. Addison Wesley, 1989.

[4] H. T. Chou, D.J. DeWitt, R. Katz, and T. Klug. Design and implementation of the Wisconsin Storage System. *Software Practices and Experience*, 15(10), 1985.

[5] D. H. Fishman, et al. IRIS: An Object-oriented Database Management System. *ACM Transactions on Office Information Systems*, 5(1):48–69, January 1987.

[6] S. Ghandeharizadeh, V. Choi, and G. Bock. Benchmarking object-based constructs. Technical Report USC-CS-92-514, University of Southern California, 1992.

[7] J. Gray, H. Sammer, and S. Whitford. Shortest seek vs shortest service time scheduling of mirrored disks. In *Tandem Computers*, December 1988.

[8] B. Joy. Presentation at ISSCC 1985 panel session. February 1985.

[9] M. Livny, S. Khoshafian, and H. Boral. Multi-disk management algorithms. In *Proceedings of the ACM SIGMETRICS Conference*, May 1987.

[10] D. Patterson, G. Gibson, and R. Katz. A case for Redundant Arrays of Inexpensive Disks (RAID). In *Proceedings of the 1988 ACM SIGMOD Int'l Conf.*, May 1988.

[11] D. Ries and R. Epstein. Evaluation of distribution criteria for distributed database systems. UCB/ERL Technical Report M78/22, UC Berkeley, May 1978.

[12] D. Shipman. The Functional Model and the Data Language DAPLEX. *ACM Transactions on Database Systems*, 6(1):140–173, 1981.

[13] M. R. Stonebraker. The case for Shared-Nothing. In *Proceedings of the 1986 Data Engineering Conference*. IEEE, 1986.

[14] K. Wilkinson, P. Lyngbaek, and W. Hasan. The Iris architecture and implementation. *IEEE Transactions on Knowledge and Data Engineering*, 2(1):63–75, March 1990.

REPLICATED FRAGMENT ALLOCATION USING A CLUSTERING TECHNIQUE

GEORGE SEMECZKO*
Department of Computer Science,
University of Queensland,
St. Lucia Brisbane, Queensland 4072,
Australia
e-mail: g.semeczko@qut.edu.au

ABSTRACT

The problem of replicated fragment allocation in a distributed relational database is a difficult task. This is particularly the case when our goal is to minimise the overall communication cost. Current methodologies for carrying out this task use either simplistic assumptions about the network or provide a heuristic with no measure of success. We clarify the situation regarding allocation within a simple network and then show a heuristic that can be applied to complex networks. This heuristic is both efficient and results in an optimal solution for certain networks. We show how this algorithm can be applied to any network by using clustering techniques to create a more uniform approximation. The results can then be shown in the form of upper and lower bounds for the optimal solution with respect to the total communication costs.

1. Introduction

Research into the design of distributed databases has been significant to date[7,8,9,10] and usually concentrated on one of several areas. The major areas of concern have been fragmentation design, fragmentation allocation, and query optimisation.

Few solutions to the distributed database design problem have encompassed all areas. Those that have encompassed more than one area have usually made over-simplistic assumptions about the network communication costs[7] or fixed aspects relating to query processing. Without such restrictions though, the problem of distributed database design, encompassing all areas, is intractable.

While the solutions to such restricted problems can be carried out in polynomial time and present optimal solutions, more complex problems tend to present heuristics that provide "good" results. Although these more complex problems are also carried out in polynomial time, it is difficult to measure their success or optimality.

The purpose of this paper is to address the issue of network communication costs and explore the optimality of fragment allocation in networks of varying

---

* George Semeczko is currently a Lecturer in the Faculty of Information Technology at the Queensland University of Technology

complexity. We investigate optimal allocation strategies for two topologies. One of these being a complex layering of uniform communication costs. This may be found in a wide area network, designed to incorporate local area networks in a uniform manner. As these local area networks may use different communication technology, varying communication costs are catered for. Such investigations would not be complete if we could not apply these techniques to non-uniform networks. These networks tend to be ones created by the federation of independently designed networks.

The paper is organised in the following manner. In section 2, we cover the assumptions made throughout the paper in order to avoid confusion later. In section 3, we cover the network configurations that we are going to investigate with a detailed discussion on the construction and properties of the more complex network configurations.

In section 4, we cover the cost functions used to measure the total communication costs in any network, a simple network and finally a complex network. In section 5, we consider a heuristic for solving the allocation problem for the simple network and then a variation for the complex network. In section 6 we consider the implication of the heuristic for the complex network for any network. Finally, in section 7, we conclude with some remarks about this research and future directions.

2. Problem Description

Throughout this paper when we refer to a fragment, we assume that it is part of a valid fragmentation schema for a relational database, with no particular bias. That is, the fragmentation schema can be created by horizontal fragmentation, vertical fragmentation, or a combination of both. The validity of a fragmentation schema is described by Zhang and Orlowska[6].

The problem that we address in this paper is the specification of an optimal allocation schema. Optimal here referring to the minimisation of total communication costs. We assume that we are given:

(i) a fragmentation schema in the form of a set of fragments,
(ii) a fixed network with known communication costs between sites,
(iii) a set of transactions,
(iv) statistical information about the use of transactions at all sites ,
(v) a cost function for calculating total communication costs

We specify (iii) and (iv) by usage volumes. These are specified for each site, for all fragments needed to satisfy the transactions called from that site. This is specified in two parts: update and query volumes. Update volumes refer only to write operations where query volumes refer only to read operations.

The two components to the allocation problem are the specifications of accesses and update propagations. How these are carried out will influence the cost function and is covered along with the cost functions.

3. Network Configurations

Throughout this paper, we represent the network configuration with an undirected graph[1] G where $G = <V,E,w>$, such that:

$V = \{v_1,...,v_n\}$	where v_i is a vertex in the graph representing a site in the network
$E = \{e_1,...,e_m\}$	where e_j is an undirected edge between two vertices represented by an unordered pair $[v_a,v_b]$ where the vertices v_a and v_b are joined by e_j
$w: E \rightarrow R^+$	where w is a function that returns a positive weighting for all edges in E.*

Throughout this paper we will use the terms graph and network interchangeably. We will assume that the networks are fully connected and obey the triangle rule for a metric space.

3.1. Simple Network

We define a Simple Network (SN) as a network with an identical, constant communication cost between all sites. We represent this network with the graph $G^k = <V^k,E^k,k>$ where $\forall\ e_i \in E^k$, $w(e_i) = k$, where k is the constant communication cost. We say that this network has a diameter with the value k.

3.2. Complex Network

In order to represent more complex network configurations, we define a network that has more complex communication costs, but still retains some uniformity. In order to define a Complex Network (CN), we will define clustering. This will be the basis for our definition.

3.2.1. Clusters

We define a cluster G^k, as a fully connected subgraph of G that is a SN. We say that the cluster has a diameter k.

To represent a cluster in a network, we can coalesce all the vertices in a cluster into a single vertex. Thus also replacing all edges, from the vertices in the cluster to the same vertex outside the cluster, with a single edge. We calculate the weight of this new edge by one of three methods: simple averages, weighted averages, or minimum weight. We discuss these methods in a later section and assume that unless otherwise stated that simple averaging is used. In the next section we also show how we build a tree structure so that we do not lose the information relating to the vertices that are coalesced to form a cluster.

As a vertex in a graph may represent a cluster, we define the diameter function that may be applied to any vertex as follows:

$\text{diameter}(v_i) = k$	where v_i is a vertex representing cluster G^k with a diameter of value k

As many networks can be found that do not have clusters as defined here, we

---

* - It should be remembered that edges in a network graph may have a weighting that has no relationship to the Euclidean distance between the vertices being joined. This is because the weightings are artificial and may relate to the technologies used as well as the distance covered.

allow for the construction of clusters using existing clustering techniques. Clustering is a large field of study and is described in many texts[3,4]. We use a simple hierarchical technique based on centroid cluster analysis[4]. The procedure for finding all clusters in a graph of diameter no greater than k can be found as follows:

Cluster Procedure

INPUTS: Graph G, diameter k
OUTPUTS: Graph G', sets of clusters L

Step 1. Initialisation
- G' = G
- L = { }

Step 2. Iteration
- 2.1 Find smallest w(e) where $e \in E'$
- 2.2 If $w(e) \leq k$ then
- 2.2.1 merge(G',v_i,v_j) where $e = [v_i,v_j]$
- 2.2.2 add v_i,v_j to cluster list L

Step 3. Termination
- 3.1 If $w(e) > k$
- 3.1.1 terminate and return G' and L
- 3.2 else Repeat Step 2.

In the above algorithm, the merge() function, combines the two vertices v_i and v_j in graph G' combining any duplicated edges and recalculating the weight of these by simple averaging. With reference to step 2.2.2, if v_i or v_j are clusters formed during this cluster operation, then only the vertices that form that cluster are stored in L. That is, the elements already stored in L for v_i or v_j are combined into set of vertices making up the new cluster. Otherwise, both v_i and v_j are added to L as a set of two vertices.

For each cluster created from the above algorithm, the precise diameter can be calculated by the same methods used to calculate the weight of combined edges described above. We again assume that unless otherwise stated we will use simple averaging. This step could be added into the above algorithm as follows:

3.1.0 Calculate the diameter for each newly formed cluster using average of edge weights between vertices in the cluster

The effect of clustering is to form a new graph G'. Here, edge weights have been altered to allow the formation of clusters as defined at the start of this section. Although G' has single vertices representing newly formed clusters, it is assumed that the edge weights from this cluster to all other vertices is inherited by the vertices making up the cluster. In doing so, we create an approximation of the original graph. As we wish to alter the graph as little as possible, we can define an error factor that measures how much the approximation varies from the original graph. We define this accumulative error factor ε as :

$$\varepsilon = \sum_{v_i, v_j \in V} \mathrm{abs}(w'([v_i, v_j]) - w([v_i, v_j])) \quad (1)$$

In the above formulation, abs() returns the absolute value so that the error factor is never negative. We assume that w'() returns the weights from G' where edges that were combined due to clustering inherit the weight assigned to the merged edge.

3.2.2. Constructing and Defining a CN

Construction of a CN from the graph G, is carried out by the reduction of this graph by the iterative use of clustering. As the network graph is reduced through clustering, we maintain information relating to the structure of the clusters by constructing a cluster tree (CT). We define the CT as a directed graph $U = <N,A>$ where:

$N = \{n_1,...,n_m\}$	where N is the set of nodes in the CT representing vertices and clusters in G, such that n_i represents the vertex v_i in G.
$A = \{a_1,...,a_p\}$	where A is the set of directed arcs between pairs of nodes in N such that: if $a_i = [n_p,n_m]$ then diameter(n_p) < diameter(n_m) and n_p is a vertex in the cluster n_m

From this definition it is obvious that leaf nodes represent the initial vertices from the graph and all non-leaf nodes represent clusters of vertices. All CT nodes are labelled with the same identifiers as used in the network graph. Cluster diameters may be shown as weights on the arcs We describe how the CT is constructed by looking at how we construct a CN in the algorithm *CN Construction* shown below.

The search diameter and the incrementing factor will be set to values that represent appropriate scales of increase in communication costs for clusters. In the case below we set SEARCH_DIAMETER to be 1 and the INCREMENT_FACTOR to be 2, a 100% increase in the current value. In *CN Construction*, Update_CT() updates the CT structure according to the cluster sets in L.

If *CN Construction* returns a non-zero error factor, then G' is an approximation of the original graph G. We can show this approximation by mapping the CT to a network graph. Using the original network graph, the only change is to the edge weightings. These will take on the weights that are inherited from the edges connecting their parent clusters in the CT.

If a zero error factor is returned by *CN Construction*, then the graph G' would map to the graph G with no changes to any of the original weightings on edges.

CN Construction Procedure:

INPUTS: Graph G ,
n single node CT's(one for each vertex in G)

OUTPUT: Graph G' with a single vertex,
one CT U, showing all clusters used to create G',
An accumulative error, ε'

PROCEDURE:

Step 1. Initialisation

1.1	SEARCH_DIAMETER = 1	
1.2	INCREMENT_FACTOR = 2	
1.3	G' = G	/* set graph */
1.4	U = V	/* separate leaf nodes */
1.5	ε' = 0	/* set error to zero*/

```
Step 2. Iteration
        2.1     Cluster(G',SEARCH_DIAMETER) →G", L, ε  /* Cluster procedure */
        2.2     IF L ≠ Ø THEN
        2.3       G' = G"
        2.4       ε' = ε' + ε
        2.5       Update_CT(U,L)
                ELSE
        2.6       SEARCH_DIAMETER = SEARCH_DIAMETER *
                                              INCREMENT_FACTOR
                END-IF
Step 3. Termination
        3.1     IF |V'| = 1 THEN
        3.2             Return(G',U,ε)
        3.3             Terminate
                ELSE
        3.4             repeat Step 2
                END-IF
```

The example we show is represented as a table due to the complexity of the graph. The table shows the weights of the edges and the query and update volumes. The columns marked "CA" and EX" will be discussed later. The graph that follows this table shows the CT that was produced by *CN Construction* and the network graph that it maps to.

Table I - A network represented as a table, CN Constructed in figure 1

G	1	2	3	4	5	6	7	8	9	10	q	u	CA	EX
1	0	10	24	13	10	4	14	12	12	12	10	10	0	0
2	10	0	5	24	10	28	16	8	4	24	6	0	0	0
3	24	5	0	12	9	2	10	20	24	8	5	0	0	0
4	13	24	12	0	10	8	12	10	20	30	10	10	0	0
5	10	10	9	10	0	14	18	6	9	10	6	0	0	0
6	4	28	2	8	14	0	10	12	20	8	5	0	0	1
7	14	16	10	12	18	10	0	15	5	8	14	6	0	0
8	12	8	20	10	6	12	15	0	14	8	2	0	0	0
9	12	4	24	20	9	20	5	14	0	5	20	10	0	1
10	12	24	8	30	10	8	8	8	5	0	25	10	1	1

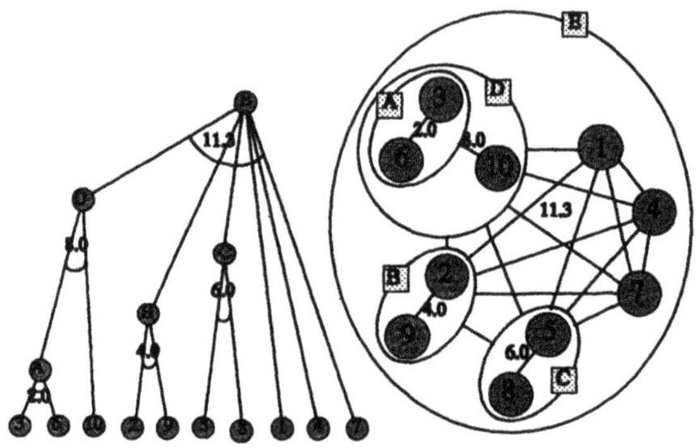

Figure 1 - The CT created for graph from Table I and the graph that the CT maps to.

We say that a network is a CN if when we apply the the *CN Construction Procedure*[*] to it the error factor that is returned is zero. If the error factor is non-zero, then we say that that network is a Non-Uniform Complex Network (NUCN).

3.2.3. Properties of a CN

There are several properties that result from the above definition of a CN. Firstly, if two clusters are connected by an edge of weight k, then any vertex that is an element of one cluster is connected to any vertex in the other cluster by an edge of weight k. In figure 1, we summarised this information by only showing the connection between clusters. For example, in figure 1, vertex 2 is connected to vertex 5 by an arc of length 11.3 and vertex 4 is connected to vertex 3 by an arc of length 11.3.

Secondly, directly related to the construction principles of a CN and clusters, the weight of arcs between vertices contained in a cluster will always be less than the weight of any arc to a vertex outside of the cluster.

Thirdly, the triangle rule for a CN is not correct. That is, for a graph to be a CN, all paths between any two vertices, consisting of more than one arc, will have a total weight greater than the weight of the path consisting of one arc.

4. Cost Functions

As we are attempting to find optimal solutions to the allocation problem, we must define our cost functions and any assumptions used in their formulation. The two components of the cost functions are the site operations and the update propagations. The site operations relate to operations for carrying out the transactions at each individual site whereas the update propagation relates to maintaining consistency between copies of the same fragment. In this section we cover the cost

---

[*] - Different sequences of SEARCH_DIAMETERS may produce different error factors. We do not cover these here due to limited space. Further research is currently being done in this area.

function as it applies to three classes of networks. The first relates to all networks, the second to SN's and the third to CN's.

4.1 A Cost Function for Any Network

The site operations consist of the transmission of all the query volumes (read operations) for each site and fragment, as well as the update volumes (write operations) to a copy of a fragment. As we assume that all transaction operations are carried out at the site of calling, we will assume that each site will access that copy of a fragment that is closest*.

We can define the site operations cost function for any network with the following function Ψ^o:

$$\Psi^o = \sum_{fij} ((u_{fi} + q_{fi})\, C_{ij}\, a_{fij}) \tag{2}$$

Where $i,j \in V$,
$f \in F$, where F is a set of fragments
u_{fi} update volumes from site i for fragment f
q_{fi} query volumes from site i for fragment f
$C_{ij} = w(\,[i,j]\,)$ the cost of communication between site i and j

$$a_{fij} = \begin{cases} 1 & \text{if all requests at site i, for access to fragment f, are fulfilled by accessing the copy of f located at site j} \\ 0 & \text{otherwise} \end{cases}$$

subject to:

$$l_{fi} = \begin{cases} 1 & \text{if fragment f is stored at site i} \\ 0 & \text{otherwise} \end{cases}$$

$a_{fij} \le l_{fj}$ site j must have a copy of fragment f
$\sum_p a_{fip} = 1$ site i accesses fragment f from only one site

The update propagation is the propagating of all update volumes for a fragment to all sites that store that fragment. Therefore, as we wish to find the optimal** method for this propagation we use a Minimal Spanning Tree (MST) as the path for the propagation. There will be a MST for each fragment, covering only the sites where a copy of that fragment is stored. The cost function for update propagation, Ψ^u, is:

$$\Psi^u = \sum_{fij} (u_{fi}\, C_{ij}\, p_{fij}) \tag{3}$$

---

* - *closest* refers to the weight of an edge connecting two sites and may not be the Euclidean distance

** We do not take into account any overhead costs involved the retransmission of an update message

Where

$$p_{fij} = \begin{cases} 1 & \text{if site i propagates all updates directed to it to site j for fragment f, that is, i and j are part of the MST for fragment f} \\ 0 & \text{otherwise} \end{cases}$$

Subject to: $p_{fij} \leq l_{fj}$ and $p_{fij} \leq l_{fi}$ both i and j must store copies of fragment f

The same result could be calculated by using the sum of all update volumes and the sum of all arcs in the MST as follows:

$$\Psi^u = \sum_f (\sum_i (u_{fi}) \sum_{ij} (C_{ij} \; p_{fij})) \tag{4}$$

Therefore, we state the total cost function, Ψ, as follows:

$$\Psi = \sum_{fij} ((u_{fi} + q_{fi}) \; C_{ij} \; a_{fij} + u_{fi} \; C_{ij} \; p_{fij}) \tag{5}$$

4.2 Cost Function for a SN

As a SN has a constant communication cost, we can simplify the cost function as it relates to both the site operations and the update propagations. Obviously, the first simplification is to replace the cost for communication between sites with the constant value. We now look at simplifying the two cost components of the SN.

4.2.1. Site Operation Costs

Accessing the closest copy of a fragment in a SN is reduced to a question of whether the calling site has a copy of the fragment or not. That is, if a site does not have a copy, then the cost of accessing any site having a copy of the fragment is the same no matter which is selected. We can restate the site operation component of this cost function as:

$$\Psi_S^o = K \sum_{fi \mid l_{fi} = 0} ((u_{fi} + q_{fi})) \tag{6}$$

4.2.2 Update Propagation

Calculation of the MST for a fragment in a SN is equally simple, as any tree that contains only those sites storing a copy of the fragment will result in the MST. The cost function for update propagation costs is reduced to a function based on the number of sites storing a copy of each fragment. This is shown in the update propagation cost component below:

$$\Psi_S^u = K \sum_f (\sum_i (u_{fi}) \;\; (\sum_{i \mid l_{fi} = 1} (l_{fi}) \; - 1)) \tag{7}$$

We can now state the cost function for a SN as follows:

$$\Psi_S = K \sum_{fi \mid l_{fi} = 0} (u_{fi} + q_{fi}) + K \sum_f \left(\sum_i (u_{fi}) \left(\sum_{i \mid l_{fi} = 1} (l_{fi}) - 1 \right) \right) \tag{8}$$

4.3. Cost Function for a CN

We now treat the CN in a similar manner to the SN, by looking at the two cost components and how they may be simplified based on its properties. When considering allocation of fragments in a CN, l_{fi} , is defined as follows:

$$l_{fi} = \begin{cases} 1 & \text{if diameter}(v_i) = 0, \text{ and fragment f is allocated to site i OR} \\ & \quad \text{diameter}(v_i) > 0, \exists\, j \text{ such that } [n_j,n_i] \in A \text{ and } l_{fj} = 1 \\ 0 & \text{otherwise} \end{cases}$$

We also define a function min_G as follows:

$min_G(n_i,f) = k$ where $\exists$ j such that $k = \text{diameter}(v_j)$ where n_j is the root of the smallest tree U' where $n_i \in N'$ and $l_{fj} = 1$.

The value k, is the cost of accessing the closest copy of the fragment f from site i. This can easily be found in the CT by traversing the tree from the leaf node n_i towards the root until the first node, n_j , is found where l_{fj} is one.

4.3.1 Site Operation Costs in a CN

Based on the definition of min_G, we can specify the site operations for a CN as follows:

$$\Psi^o_C = \sum_{fi \mid l_{fi} = 0 \,\wedge\, n_i \in N \,\wedge\, \text{diameter}(v_i) = 0} ((u_{fi} + q_{fi})\ min_G(i,f)) \tag{9}$$

In this formulation we are trying to find the diameter of the smallest cluster that a site belongs to, where it can find a copy of the required fragment. The following holds true based on the above formulation:

$$\text{if } l_{fi} = 0, \text{ where diameter}(v_i) > 0 \text{ then}$$
$$\sum_{j \mid [n_j,n_i] \in A} (u_{fj} + q_{fj})\ min_G(f,j) = (u_{fi} + q_{fi})\ min_G(f,i) \tag{10}$$

The above statement is for any given fragment f and is also due to the fact that because l_{fi} is zero then the function min_G returns the same value for i as it does for all j. But, for any node that does not store a copy of the fragment and is an element of a cluster that has had the fragment allocated to it has the min_G function returning the diameter of the cluster that it is in. This last case is exactly the same as the SN access costs from Eq.(6) where we replace the constant k with the function min_G which can be restated as follows:

$$\Psi^o_S = \sum_{fi \mid l_{fi} = 0} ((u_{fi} + q_{fi})\ min_G(f,i)) \tag{11}$$

Therefore, if we pass as a parameter to the function Ψ^o_C the cluster that we are calculating the access costs for, then we can restate Eq.(9) using the SN function for each fragment f, as follows:

$$\Psi^{o}_{C}(i,f) = \Psi^{o}_{S}(i,f) + \sum_{j \mid [n_j,n_i] \in A \wedge l_{ij}=1} \Psi^{o}_{C}(j,f) \qquad (12)$$

The first execution of this function will always be on the root node of the CT. Note that when we use the SN cost functions with parameters, we assume that we are calculating the cost function for a given cluster using its diameter as the constant k and only for the fragment passed as a parameter .

4.3.2 Update Propagation Costs in a CN

Update propagation is still based on finding a MST for each fragment. Here, though, we can find the cost of the MST by examining the number of nodes in each cluster that are allocated a fragment. Therefore, we can treat each cluster in the similar manner to that for the SN.

At each cluster, we consider the number of elements of the cluster allocated a fragment and compute the MST as we did for the SN. We represent this MST cost function in a similar manner to that shown for the access costs in Eq.(12) for each fragment f :

$$\Psi^{u}_{C}(i,f) = \Psi^{u}_{S}(i,f) + \sum_{j \mid [n_j,n_i] \in A \wedge l_{ij}=1 \wedge \text{diameter}(v_j) > 0} \Psi^{u}_{C}(j,f) \qquad (13)$$

With this function we can now state the total cost function for a CN as follows:

$$\Psi_{C} = \sum_{f} (\Psi^{o}_{C}(f,i) + \Psi^{u}_{C}(f,i)) \text{ where } \nexists\, j \text{ such that } [n_i,n_j] \in A \qquad (14)$$

5. Allocation and the Benefit Function

We now discuss how to find the optimal allocation solution for a given fragmentation schema and network. As stated earlier, our goal is to find the optimal allocation schema with respect to our cost function. To find this solution exhaustively requires the cost calculation for $2^{(n-1)} * f$, where n is the number of sites and f the number of fragments to allocate. Obviously, this is an unacceptable solution[5].

The solution to this problem is to use a greedy heuristic. The heuristic that we base our solution on comes from work by Ceri and Pelagatti[2] and is called the *all beneficial sites* heuristic. In the next sections we see how this greedy heuristic applied to an SN results in the optimal solution. We then adapt the heuristic for the CN for a similar result.

5.1 The Benefit Function for a SN

Due to the properties of an SN, it is possible to use a greedy heuristic to attain an optimal solution to the allocation problem. This is due to the fact that each site may be considered in isolation to other sites. That is, the local optimisation will result in the global optimisation. This being the requirement for an optimal solution via a greedy heuristic.

The benefit function is applied to each site for each fragment and is based on the comparison of costs for accessing the fragment. That is, it compares the cost of accessing the fragment from another site as opposed to having a copy allocated to the site and hence incurring update propagation costs. The benefit function, B_{fi}, for site i accessing fragment f, can be formulated by finding the difference between these costs and results in:

$$B_{fi} = (q_{fi} + u_{fi}) - \sum_{j} u_{fj} \qquad (15)$$

Note that as the communication cost is constant it is not shown. If the result is positive then allocating the fragment being considered to that site will result in cheaper communication cost than if it accessed it from another site. Conversely, if the result is negative then it is cheaper for the site to access the fragment from elsewhere. The situation of a zero result, means that no difference in cost will be noticed if the site had a copy or not. We take the position here that for a site to have a copy it must show a benefit and therefore must return a positive number before it is allocated to a site.

We state the heuristic *Allocate-SN* that uses this function as follows:

Allocate-SN Procedure

```
FOR EACH FRAGMENT f DO:
        nr_alloc = 0                    /* nr of copies allocated */
        largest_b = LARGEST_NEGATIVE
        largest_site = 0   /* in case no +ve Bfi */
        FOR EACH SITE i DO
                IF Bfi > 0 THEN  /* allocate f to site i */
                        lfi = 1
                        nr_alloc = nr_alloc + 1
                ELSE IF nr_alloc == 0 AND  /* check in case no */
                        Bfi > largest_b THEN  /* +ve Bfi          */
                        largest_b = Bfi
                        largest_site = i
                END-IF
        END-FOR

        IF nr_alloc == 0 THEN /* no +ve Bfi  - allocate to largest */
                i = largest_site
                lfi = 1
        END-IF
END-FOR
```

Let us look at an example for the allocation of one fragment in the following SN. From the following example, it is obvious that more than one optimal solution exists, but with the same communication cost it does not matter which we choose.

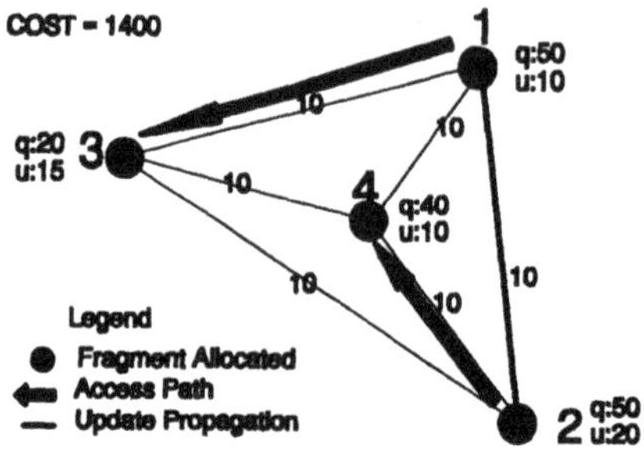

Figure 2 - An example optimal solution for a SN where the total update volume is 55

Theorem 5.1

For the optimal allocation solution for the SN the following is true for fragment f:

1) if $B_{fi} > 0$ then $l_{fi} = 1$

2) if $\exists$ j such that $B_{fj} > 0$, $\forall$ i if $B_{fi} \leq 0$ then $l_{fi} = 0$

3) if $\nexists$ j such that $B_{fj} > 0$, $\exists^1$ i such that $\forall h$ $B_{fi} \geq B_{fh}$ and $l_{fi} = 1$

Proof:

We consider only a fragment at a time as we do not consider query optimisation for joins . We consider the following function for optimisation:

$$\Psi_S(f) = K \sum_{i \mid l_{fi} = 0} (u_{fi} + q_{fi}) + K \sum_{i} (u_{fi}) \left(\sum_{i \mid l_{fi} = 1} (l_{fi}) - 1 \right) \tag{16}$$

But the optimal solution for this function will give the optimal answer to the following function as well:

$$\varphi = \frac{\Psi_S(f)}{K} + P_f \tag{17}$$

Where P_f is the total of all update volumes for fragment f, which is constant as is the communication cost K. Therefore we try to find the optimal solution to this function which can be stated as :

$$\varphi = \sum_{i \mid l_{fi} = 0} (u_{fi} + q_{fi}) + \left(\sum_{i \mid l_{fi} = 1} P_f \right) \tag{18}$$

From this, it can easily be seen that for each site i, we choose between the cost of $(u_{fi} + q_{fi})$ and P_f. Therefore, to minimise the whole function we must minimise for each site. Therefore, if $(u_{fi} + q_{fi})$ is greater than P_f, , we must allocate to site i to minimise the cost, otherwise we do not. But, if no site exists such that $(u_{fi} + q_{fi})$ is greater than P_f, then to minimise the cost we allocate to one of these sites where there is the least difference between P_f and $(u_{fi} + q_{fi})$. As the benefit function B_{fi} , is the comparison of these two costs , $(u_{fi} + q_{fi})$ and P_f., then our original statements hold true.■

5.2 The Benefit Function for a CN

In the CN situation, we must take into account the effect of allocating a fragment to a site on nearby sites. That is, due to the communication costs between sites, allocating a fragment to a site may now make it cheaper for other sites to access this copy than the one they previously accessed. Therefore, we cannot consider each site independently as in the SN case.

But, due to the structure of the CN, as stated in section 3.2.3, the communication cost for a site to access the closest copy of a fragment is the diameter of the smallest cluster that it belongs to that has a fragment allocated. For us to consider the cost of allocating a fragment to a cluster and hence whether it is cheaper than accessing a remote copy, we state a new benefit function for the CN. We state the benefit function for a CN as follows:

$$B_{fi} = \text{diameter}(v_j)\ (\ (u_{fi} + q_{fi}) - \sum_i u_{fi})\ ) - \Psi_C(i,f) \qquad (19)$$
$$\text{where } [v_i, v_j] \in A$$

In the specification for B_{fi} in Eq.(19), we cater for local accesses to a copy of a fragment by considering the optimal solution if we did allocate a copy of fragment f to site i. But to find an optimal solution for an allocation to a cluster v_i, we need to calculate the benefit function for each site in cluster v_i. Obviously, allocation and cost benefit calculation is a recursive procedure. We are guaranteed that it does terminate, as the recursion follows our CT structure in a post-order traversal.

Allocate and Calculate Benefit Procedure (ACB)

INPUTS: f - fragment to be allocated
i - v_i cluster to allocate to

OUTPUTS: ALL - Optimal Cost if f allocated to this cluster
NOA -Cost if f not allocated to this cluster, but allocated to another cluster that belongs to the same parent cluster

PROCEDURE:

```
/* Note, that P_f below is the total of all update volumes for the current fragment.*/
IF diameter(v_i) = 0 THEN              /*zero level cluster */
        ALL = 0
        NOA = (u_fi + q_fi)
ELSE  /* cluster with elements */
        /* INITIALISATION */
                ALL = 0
                NOA = 0
                Alloc_i = 0          /* number of clusters allocated to  */
                largest_b = LARGE-VE_NUMBER
                largest_i = 0
```

```
/* ITERATION */
        FOR EACH j where [n_j,n_i] ∈ A /* for each vertex in cluster v_i */
                ACB(j-ALL,j-NOA)
                B_fj = diameter(v_i) * (j-NOA - P_f) - j-ALL      /* Eq.(19) */
                IF B_fj > 0  THEN
                        ALL = ALL + j-ALL
                        alloc_i = alloc_i + 1
                ELSE
                        ALL =ALL + j-NOA * diameter(v_i)
                        IF B_fj > largest_b THEN  /* as in SN case    */
                                largest_b = B_fi
                                largest_site = j
                        END-IF
                END-IF

                NOA = NOA + j-NOA /* sum all accesses */

                IF alloc_i == 0 THEN          /* no +ve B_fj */
                        j = largest_site
                        ALL = ALL - j-NOA * diameter(v_i)
                        ALL = ALL + j-ALL
                        alloc_i = alloc_i + 1
                END-IF

                ALL = ALL + (alloc_i  - 1) * P_f /* Update propagation costs*/
                                                 /* within this cluster       */
        END-FOR
        return(ALL, NOA)
END-IF
```

This procedure carries out allocation calculations for each cluster as if it were a SN. The only difference being that the Benefit function is calculated differently. The update propagation costs are calculated only for each cluster as we only need to consider this cost between duplicate copies and the cost between them is found only where there is more than one copy within a cluster. As we always begin by applying this procedure to the top-most cluster, then the cost of the MST joining all copies of a fragment is guaranteed to be included in the final costs.

We do not show the structures here to maintain the data relating to the allocations and MST specifications, but this is easily done given the structure that we use to find the optimal cost.

Theorem 5.2

The greedy allocation method using the benefit function as defined in Eq.(19), when applied to a CN, produces an optimal solution where the following hold true:[*]:

1) if $B_{fi} > 0$ then $l_{fi} = 1$

2) if $\exists$ j such that $B_{fj} > 0$, $\forall$ i if $B_{fi} \leq 0$ then $l_{fi} = 0$

---

[*] - as the root node has all fragments allocated to it if they are used at all in the network, then this claim is a recursive claim on the CT tree.

3) if $\nexists$ j such that $B_{fj} > 0$, $\exists^1$ i such that $\forall h$ $B_{fi} \geq B_{fh}$ and $I_{fi} = 1$

Proof:

We prove this by induction based on the diameters of vertices making up a cluster, v_i. When referring to the CT, we will reference the vertices using the identifiers v_j rather than n_j to avoid confusion, as they reference the same site but in different graphs.

Case 1: $\forall$ v_j where $[v_j,v_i] \in A$ and diameter(v_j) = 0

This case simplifies to the SN situation where v_i is a SN and therefore holds true.

Case 2: Assume holds true for all v_j where $[v_j,v_i] \in A$, prove holds true for v_i. Considering the allocation in v_i is similar to that in any SN, as each vertex in v_i can be considered independently. This is due to the properties of the CN discussed earlier. That is, the difference in allocating and not allocating to a site is the benefit factor. This is due to the fact that any site will only access the closest copy of a fragment stored in the same cluster as it. Therefore, if a fragment is not allocated to a vertex in v_i, then all sites that are represented by this vertex (cluster) will access a copy stored in any other vertex in v_i for exactly the same cost.

The Benefit factor shown in Eq.(19) shows this difference. Note that it is similar in structure to Eq.(15) in showing the difference between update propagation and accessing from a remote site. Therefore using similar justification to that shown for theorem 5.1, the benefit function and the procedure using it, would provide the optimal allocation for allocating a fragment to v_i.

Therefore by induction, the use of the benefit function and the procedure using it, provides the optimal solution for the allocation problem with respect to overall communication cost minimisation. By similar aguement to that for theorem 5.1, we can also show that statements 1, 2, and 3 hold true. ■

To see an example of the application of this algorithm, see the example shown in table II. In this example, the columns q and u show the query and update volumes with the columns CA showing the ACB results with a 1 indicating allocation and the exhaustive result in the EX column. The exhaustive result is the optimum and matches that for the CA result.

6. Non-Uniform Communication Networks

We have already shown how to create clusters in any network and hence find a CN approximation for a NUCN. Using the benefit function for CN's we can find the optimal solution for the CN approximation. THe question is how does this relate to the optimal solution for the original NUCN.

The solution for the CN can be considered in most cases as a suboptimal solution. If the accumulative error factor from the *CN Construction Procedure* is very large then the CN approximation varies greatly from the NUCN and hence there may be a cheaper solution than the optimal solution for the CN. This largely depends on how the CN was approximated. Using the simple averaging method we introduce a high error factor and hence the solution for the CN,using CN costings, may provide an upper bound for the NUCN.

Table II - A "good" result of the Clustering and Allocation Algorithms

G	1	2	3	4	5	6	7	8	9	10	q	u	CA	EX
1	0	2	2	10	10	12	12	15	12	12	32	10	1	1
2	2	0	2	12	12	12	12	12	12	12	6	0	0	0
3	2	2	0	12	12	12	12	15	12	12	5	0	0	0
4	10	12	12	0	4	4	12	12	12	12	8	2	0	0
5	10	12	12	4	0	4	12	12	12	12	3	2	0	0
6	12	12	12	4	4	0	12	15	12	12	2	0	0	0
7	12	12	12	12	12	12	0	3	3	3	14	6	0	0
8	15	12	15	12	15	12	3	0	3	3	2	0	0	0
9	12	12	12	12	12	12	3	3	0	3	20	10	0	0
10	12	12	12	12	12	12	3	3	3	0	25	10	1	1

If we use weighted averages, based on the usage volumes, we get a better solution. This method is more inline with the intuition used for the allocation method based on allocation to those sites with the greatest need. Therefore, as each error in edge weights is multiplied by the volumes that are assumed to use it, it is better that sites with high useage have edges leaving them that are closer to the original. Conversely, it is less important if sites with little usage have edges that vary significantly to the orignal leaving them.

Therefore, using weighted edges we can find an optimal solution for the CN approximation and state this cost as an upper bound for the NUCN as a cheaper solution may exist. To establish how low the optimal solution for the NUCN may be, we now discuss the formulation of a lower bound.

The lower bound can be found by using the smallest edge rather than averaging. That is, we take the closest vertex edge weights for each egde that we are trying to recompute weights for. Using this CN, we can find the lower bound. Obviously, for a network that is already a CN, the upper and lower bounds are equal to the optimal solution.

7. Conclusions and Future Directions

In this paper we have shown how we can find the optimal allocation of a fragment in both a SN and a CN. These were done with a complexity of 2m and m^2 respectively, where m is the number of sites in the network. The assumptions on communication cost configurations are too great to be of universal use, but will be of great benefit in the design of complex wider area networks that encompass smaller local area networks. For existing networks that are not so uniform, we described a method that creates a CN approximation. This approximation can then be allocated to optimally. If the NUCN does not vary too greatly from a CN, as indicated by an error factor, then the result from allocating in the approximation may still be useful. If the NUCN varies too greatly from a CN, then we can use different weight calcualtion methods for the CN creation to find an upper and lower bound for hte optimal solution for the NUCN.

Further research in this area centres on several different approaches. Firstly, different clustering methods will be investigated to see if improvements can be made in the cluster approximation. This may also have an effect on the calculation and usefulness of the error factor in the final result. Secondly, improvement algorithms may be investigated to take the results from the current method and apply simple heuristics to alter the CN allocations to better fit the NUCN. Again, this may not lead to an optimal solution, but it may present a result that is adequate for the cost of calculation. Thirdly, we intend to continue the use of clustering as a basis for the combined problem of fragmentation and allocation. This problem will be solved using clustering and transaction optimisation techniques in an iterative process.

Acknowledgements

I would like to thank the many people in the Transaction Management Group and Conceptual Issues Group at the University of Queensland who have provided feedback and insite into the problems covered in this paper. In particular I would like to thank Maria Orlowska for the many hours of help and support in my research.

References

1. T.B.Boffey, *Graph Theory in Operations Research*, MacMillan Press, 1982
2. S.Ceri & G.Pelagatti, *Distributed Databases Principles & Systems*, McGraw Hill, 1985
3. B.S.Duran & P.L.Odell, *Cluster Analysis* , Springer-Verlag, 1974
4. B.Everitt, *Cluster Analysis*, Heinenmann Educational Books, 1981
5. B.M.E.Moret & H.D. Shapiro, *Algorithms from P to NP - Volume 1 Design and Efficiency*, Benjamin/Cummings, 1990
6. Y.Zhang & M.E.Orlowska, *An Efficient Test for the Validity of Unbiased Fragmentations for Distributed Database Design*, Tech. Report No.204, Computer Science Dept., University of Queensland, April 1991
7. S.Navathe, et al., *Vertical Partitioning Algorithms for Database Design*, ACM Trans. on Database Systems, Vol 9, No 4, December 1984, 680-710
8. P.M.G.Apers, *Data Allocation in Distributed Database Systems*, ACM Trans. on Database Systems, Vol 13, No 3, September 1988, 263-304
9. S.Ceri, S. Navathe, G.Wiederhold, *Distribution Design of Logical Database Schemas*, IEEE Trans. on Software Engineering, Vol SE-9, No 4, July 1983, 487-504
10. S.Ceri, B.Pernici, G.Wiederhold , *Optimization Problems and Solution Methods in the Design of Data Distribution*, Information Systems, Vol 14, No 3, 1989, 261-272

INTERCONNECTION TOPOLOGIES FOR SHARED NOTHING DBMS ARCHITECTURES

M. Hitz
T.A. Mueck

Dept. of Information Systems
University of Vienna
Liebigg. 4/3-4
1010 Vienna, Austria
{ hitz | mueck }@ifs.univie.ac.at

ABSTRACT

Parallel database management systems operating on shared nothing platforms use virtual point-to-point communication paths between any two processing elements. A routing algorithm has to provide $p(p-1)$ virtual paths between p processing elements engaged in DBMS processing. Such an algorithm simulates virtual paths by sequences of low level data transfer operations between several pairs of interconnected processing elements. Consequently, a particular data transfer volume used to process a set of DBMS tasks will be transferred using S low level data transfer operations simulating the existence of $p(p-1)$ virtual paths. S is proportional to the total time needed to transmit the data. Minimizing S for a given p represents a major performance issue for shared nothing DBMS.

A group theoretic approach, namely the Cayley graph model, is used to generate a large number of different hardware interconnection topologies. For those candidates, a virtual path workload distribution is assumed and subsequently used to minimize S. In particular, we choose candidates with small average communication path lengths in such a way that efficient routing algorithms can be provided. The resulting best Cayley graphs are presented and compared to several well-established alternatives.

1. Introduction and Rationale

Disk I/O bandwidth, CPU processing power and physical memory size are known to be the most relevant *hardware dependent* factors determining the overall performance of database management systems. Confronted with the model inherent limitations of conventional, i.e. von Neumann computer architectures and the advent of non-von Neumann hardware, several major DBMS research efforts (like [DeWi86], [CABT88] and [HoSt90], to give some prominent examples) focused on the efficient utilization of different types of parallel architectures. In particular, disk arrays were used to speed up disk I/O bound DBMS operations by an increase of the overall disk I/O bandwidth (see [PaGK88]) whereas coarse grain to medium grain multiprocessor systems were engaged to yield better performance for CPU intensive tasks (see [ScDe89]). In the context of those research projects, a large number of different non-von Neumann prototypes (shared memory as well as message passing architectures) were used as hardware platforms for the development and evaluation of appropriate DBMS prototypes. However, the practical relevance of message passing, or in other words *shared nothing* hardware systems was severely reduced by the comparatively weak communication bandwidth of virtually all available interprocessor link technologies. Considering the vast data transfer volumes occurring during query execution, a typical interprocessor communication bandwidth absolutely sufficient for typical NIC applications was prohibitively narrow for data intensive tasks. Consequently, during the 1980-ies, a shared memory configuration not yet hitting the internal bus bandwidth had good chances to outperform any message passing configuration with comparable hardware resources. As a result, only a small number of research papers published in the past decade favoured shared nothing architectures. An early shared nothing proposal in despite of weak interprocessor communication facilities can be found in [Ston86].

Since the beginning of the present decade, the situation has been changing. Facing a decisive technological breakthrough in the field of communication hardware (see [Frie90]), the interest in shared nothing architectures for data intensive applications is increasing. At the present moment, appropriate shared nothing DBMS design approaches are of prime interest compared to their shared memory counterparts following the standard scale up and speed up considerations for massively parallel architectures (see [DeGr92]). Several papers contain important results on query decomposition and parallelization ([Grae90], [ScDe90] and [WoDY90]), as well as on mass storage retrieval policies with regard to physical clustering and index maintenance ([LiKB87] and [GhDe90]). In general, most of those approaches aim either explicitly or at least implicitly at a near-uniform workload distribution for all critical hardware components, in particular at a reasonable workload distribution for

- all processing elements and attached floating point units,
- all disk controllers and their data transfer channels to main memory and
- all point-to-point interprocessor communication paths.

In this paper, a complementary question is addressed, namely the problem of finding attractive *hardware interconnection topologies* for shared nothing DBMS architectures. Assuming a parallel DBMS to use *virtual point-to-point communication paths* between any two processing elements, a firmware routing algorithm has to provide $p(p-1)$ virtual paths between p processing elements. Such a routing algorithm simulates virtual paths by sequences of *atomic transmission steps*, i.e. by data transfer operations between several pairs of interconnected processing elements. Consequently, a total data transfer volume *DTV* used to process a set of DBMS tasks will be transferred using S atomic transmission steps in order to simulate $p(p-1)$ virtual paths. Basically, S is proportional to the total time needed to transmit *DTV* and therefore represents a major performance issue for shared nothing DBMS.

The central idea of this paper can be described as follows. A group theoretic approach is used to generate a large number of different hardware interconnection topologies. For these candidates, a virtual path workload (*VPW*) distribution is assumed and subsequently used to minimize S. In particular, relying on the previously referenced results and on some recent empirical studies for the PARABASE project ([KoMV92]), a near-uniform workload distribution can be assumed with regard to all virtual point-to-point communication paths. In other words, each virtual path is used for the transmission of the $p(p-1)$-th fraction of the total volume *DTV*. With these premises in mind, we choose an appropriate evaluation framework focusing on the average virtual path length. Replacing the uniform *VPW* would change the evaluation criteria and require additional formal treatment, but would not change the methodological approach.

Assuming a *VPW* distribution and a hardware-determined maximum number of links per processing element, the question is how to find an optimal interconnection topology for a given number of processing elements, i.e. a topology yielding a minimal S. A reasonable answer to this question relies on several basic assumptions with regard to the hardware facilities. At first, the topology is assumed to be static, i.e. we do not consider dynamic reconfigurations during any operational period of the DBMS. Secondly, the hardware platform is assembled from identical processing elements, in particular from processing elements with an identical number of bidirectional interconnection links. Thirdly, each processing element may be connected to any other processing element in the configuration as long as an interconnection link is vacant, i.e. we assume that no possible interconnection between any two processing elements is inhibited by their geometric distance in a particular hardware configuration. Fortunately, neither of those assumptions causes a loss of generality with respect to popular message passing hardware platforms.

The basic rationale for such considerations is easy to state. For a particular *DTV* related to the set of query/update operations currently processed by the DBMS an interconnection topology yielding a minimum number $S_{\min}$ of atomic transmission steps for *DTV* will yield minimal response times and maximum throughput for a given shared nothing DBMS. The optimization objectives are straightforward. Since the expected value of S for a particular *DTV* and for a uniform *VPW* depends on the average node-to-node communication path length as well as on the efficiency of the corresponding routing algorithm, we have to focus on those two points.

Our optimization approach is related to a group theoretical concept known as *group graphs* or *Cayley graphs* (see [AkKr86]), which allows systematic generation and evaluation of large families of node symmetric graphs[1]. Using this theoretical concept, an operational Cayley graph production and evaluation environment is described in this paper. This environment is used to identify particular Cayley graphs with attractive properties, i.e. Cayley graphs with small average node-to-node communication path lengths allowing efficient routing and therefore bringing S close to $S_{\min}$. In general, we do not expect S to reach $S_{\min}$ even for optimal Cayley graphs, since other graphs,

[1] Informally, a graph is said to be node symmetric, if the structure of the graph viewed from any arbitrary node of the graph is always the same. This property is of practical relevance, since it makes considerable improvements with regard to routing algorithms (outlined in Section 2) possible.

in particular asymmetric graphs[2], could yield better S. However, within the category of node symmetric graphs, we did not find any topology yielding smaller S. It is possible to find punctual examples for asymmetric graphs producing smaller S than the corresponding best Cayley graph, but to our knowledge, a computationally tractable systematic generation of superior asymmetric graphs is still an unsolved problem.

In order to justify our claims, we compare selected Cayley graphs to other topologies. It is shown that those graphs clearly outperform prominent applied topologies like the binary hypercube as well as recently proposed alternatives like deBruijn graphs and star graphs.

The paper is organized as follows. In Section 2, Cayley graphs and the relationships to permutation groups are described. This sections contains a number of definitions and a discussion of some relevant properties following from the group theoretic background of the Cayley graph model. Section 3 deals with the specification of an operational generation and evaluation environment. All proofs relevant for Section 2 and 3 have been omitted in order to save space but can be found in [HiMu92]. The practical evaluation of the candidate sets together with a brief comparison to some prominent interconnection topologies can be found in Section 4. Our conclusions and an outlook at the research agenda are given in Section 5.

2. Cayley Graphs - Properties and Relationship to Permutation Groups

Theoretical research in interconnection topologies has been motivated by a strong need for attractive communication network structures to be used in technological key areas. Exemplary applications appear, for example, in the construction of massively parallel supercomputers (see [Hill87]) or in the structural layout of large distributed systems, e.g. telecommunication networks. Presently, the importance of adaptable graph generation and evaluation frameworks for interconnection topologies even increases as novel applications very likely either post new requirements or change the priorities of existing requirements for such topologies. This paper deals with the latter case, i.e. with an example for changing requirement priorities. In particular, the communication load pattern imposed by shared nothing DBMS architectures increases the relevance of the *average* node-to-node path length as evaluation criterion. In other words, with this type of application in mind, the graph theoretically motivated main focus on the graph diameter, i.e. the longest shortest path in a graph, has to be complemented by considerations about the average path length. This example should illustrate the close relationship between a presumed type of application (e.g. a link communication balanced data intensive application) and a resulting change in an evaluation framework for possible interconnection topologies (e.g. a stronger emphasis on the average path length).

Following these considerations, any methodological approach in the context of interconnection topologies has to support two intrinsically different goals, namely

[2] The term *asymmetric* is used as the opposite to node symmetric in the following.

- the *systematic generation* of a large number of different topologies within a tractable computational complexity in order to obtain a reasonable set of candidates for subsequent evaluation and
- the *algorithmic evaluation* of the candidate set based on a number of possibly conflicting evaluation criteria with possibly changing priorities according to different requirements imposed by different types of applications.

An appropriate approach originating from group theory is proposed in [AkKr86] and used for a systematic evaluation in [HiMu92] as outlined below.

In the following, $S_n = (P_n, \bullet)$ with $P_n = \{\pi_1, \pi_2, \ldots, \pi_{n!}\}$ denotes the permutation group of order $n!$. As usual, a specific permutation $\pi \in P_n$ will be denoted by strings of n digits $\pi(1)\pi(2)\ldots\pi(n)$, with the special case of the identical permutation $12\ldots n$ denoted by I. For example, S_3 corresponds to the group ({123, 132, 213, 231, 312, 321}, •) and $\pi = 231$ is used as a notational abbreviation for

$$\pi = \begin{bmatrix} 1\,2\,3 \\ 2\,3\,1 \end{bmatrix}$$

Consequently, 321•231 is an abbreviation for the composition of the two bijective functions π_1 and π_2 to be resolved from right to left, namely

$$\pi_1 \bullet \pi_2 = \begin{bmatrix} 1\,2\,3 \\ 3\,2\,1 \end{bmatrix} \bullet \begin{bmatrix} 1\,2\,3 \\ 2\,3\,1 \end{bmatrix} = \begin{bmatrix} 1\,2\,3 \\ 2\,1\,3 \end{bmatrix} = 213$$

In a next step, let us consider an arbitrary subset G of P_n, i.e. $G = \{g_1, g_2, \ldots, g_k\}$ with $G \subseteq P_n \setminus \{I\}$. G and g_i will be called *generator set* and *generator*, respectively. Informally, a generator set is used to produce a group by iterative application of the group operation to a set of group members (the generators) until the result is closed under •. More precisely, the following procedure is applied to a generator set G:

```
Generate (G)
(     T ← G
      PreviousCardinality ← 0
      while | T | > PreviousCardinality do
            PreviousCardinality ← | T |
            T1 ← { }
            for each e ∈ T do
                  for each g ∈ G do
                        T1 ← T1 ∪ { e • g }
            T ← T ∪ T1
      return T
)
```

We observe that the inner for-loop will run k times therefore producing k elements of P_n for each element of T. The outer for-loop will run $|T|$ times whereas the while-loop will terminate iff the previous step did not produce additional elements of P_n. Termination is guaranteed, since P_n is closed under •, therefore at most $n!$ permutations can be put into T. *Generate*(G) will always produce S_n or a subgroup thereof.

This leads to the following

Theorem 1: Result of *Generate*

$$(Generate(G), \bullet) \text{ is a subgroup of } S_n \text{ for an arbitrary } G \subseteq P_n$$

Consequently, the computation *Generate*(G) will be called *algebraic generation* of a permutation group, no matter if the group itself or a particular subgroup is produced.

The key idea for the understanding of the Cayley graph model is the interpretation of an algebraic generation *Generate*(G) as graph $C^{n,k}(V, E)$ with

$$V = Generate(G) \quad \text{and} \quad e(v_i, v_j) \in E \iff v_i \bullet g = v_j \text{ for any } g \in G$$

Informally, the nodes of such a graph correspond to the permutations resulting from the algebraic generation, whereas each edge $e(v_i, v_j)$ corresponds to one generation step yielding permutation v_j by the application of one of the generators to another group element v_i. For example, let $G = \{1243, 1324, 2134\} \subset P_4$. The resulting Cayley graph is depicted in Figure 1(a) below. Considering the leftmost node 3421, generator 1243 yields 3412, generator 1324 yields 3241 and finally generator 2134 yields 4321. Figure 1(b) shows the Cayley graph produced by *Generate*({321, 312}). The interpretation of Figure 1(b) is straightforward, as it depicts a Cayley graph in standard representation. Figure 1(a) shows an important special case, namely a Cayley graph in which any two adjacent nodes are connected by both, a forward and a backward edge. In this case, the graph is drawn with simple undirected lines replacing the edge pairs. We elaborate on this property in Subsection 3.2.1.

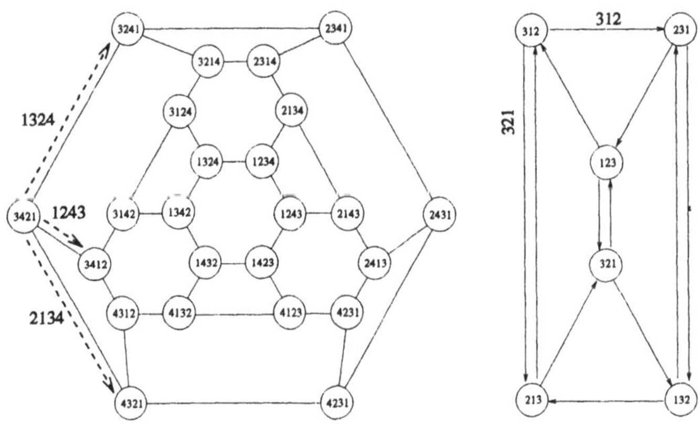

(a) (b)

Figure 1: Cayley graphs spanned by {1243, 1324, 2134} and by {321, 312}

After the specification of the Cayley graph generation model, we can focus on the resulting graphs. Cayley graphs have a number of properties which turn out to be useful in the context of interconnection topologies. In particular, in any Cayley graph $C^{n,k}(V, E)$,

- each node in V has an outdegree of k, since G contains k elements and each generator has been applied to each node in V during the algebraic generation. We conclude that all Cayley graphs are regular. This property is desirable since we want to use Cayley graphs to model interconnection topologies for sets of *identical* processing elements with an identical number of communication links per processing elements.
- the number of nodes has a trivial upper bound of $n!$. This upper bound is reached iff *Generate* (G) produces the corresponding permutation group S_n, in which case $C^{n,k}(V, E)$ is called *complete.* However, if *Generate* (G) produces a proper subgroup, the number of nodes in the Cayley graph is restricted by Lagrange's theorem. In particular, since S_n is finite, the number of nodes in a Cayley graph $C^{n,k}(V, E)$ equals a divisor of $n!$ (of course including $n!$ for complete Cayley graphs). This allows for an application of the Cayley graph framework for a reasonable number of different configuration sizes like for example 4, 6, 8, 12, 16, 18, 24, 36, 72, 120, 240, 360, 720, 5040, etc.
- for each pair of nodes $v_i, v_j \in V$ there exists an automorphism $Aut(C^{n,k}(V, E))$, such that $Aut(v_i) = v_j$ and $Aut(v_j) = v_i$. This is exactly the definition of node symmetry, hence we conclude that all Cayley graphs are node symmetric. Node symmetry provides major simplifications as far as routing algorithms are concerned. For Cayley graphs, we can handle arbitrary routing requests $(v_i \rightarrow v_j)$ by simple algebraic transformations. In particular, an optimal route for $(v_i \rightarrow v_j)$ corresponds to the minimal generation sequence $v_i \bullet g_l \bullet \cdots \bullet g_p = v_j$; multiplying both sides of the equation from left by the inverse of the target node v_j yields $v_j^{-1} \bullet v_i \bullet g_l \bullet \cdots \bullet g_p = I$. Consequently, any routing request $(v_i \rightarrow v_j)$ can be transformed to a routing request $(v_j^{-1} \bullet v_i \rightarrow I)$ which allows efficient routing heuristics (see Section 3).

The crucial point is that the mapping of algebraic generations to directed graphs enables a systematic production of a large variety of different graphs. Referring to this framework, we consider attractive Cayley graphs stemming from the permutation groups S_4, S_5, S_6 and S_7 as well as from several subgroups thus covering a set of network configurations ranging from 6 to 5040 nodes per network. Additionally, the number of communication links per processing element (i.e. the cardinality k of the generator set) is varied from 3 to 8 also covering a broad range of hardware facilities.

In a first approach, one could try to produce all Cayley graphs of a particular family (n, k), for example the family *Cayley* (6,4) of all Cayley graphs belonging to the permutation group S_6 with 4 generators. In such a complete enumeration schema, each possible generator set G yields one candidate for subsequent evaluation, i.e.

$$\begin{bmatrix} n!-1 \\ k \end{bmatrix} = \frac{(n!-1)!}{k!(n-1-k)!}$$

possible generator sets must be expanded and checked. The reduction from $n!$ to $n!-1$ in the binomial coefficient results from the decision to omit I from generator sets. This is straightforward, since the identity is just useless as a generator. The following table contains the number of possible generator sets for S_4, S_5, S_6, S_7 and for generator set cardinalities ranging from 3 to 8.

Table 1: Number of generator sets for particular families of Cayley graphs

	k=3	k=4	k=5	k=6	k=7	k=8
n=4	1771	8855	33649	100947	245157	490314
n=5	273819	7940751	1.8×10^{8}	3.5×10^{9}	5.6×10^{10}	7.8×10^{11}
n=6	6.2×10^{7}	1.1×10^{10}	1.6×10^{12}	1.9×10^{14}	1.9×10^{16}	1.7×10^{18}
n=7	2.1×10^{10}	2.7×10^{13}	2.7×10^{16}	2.3×10^{19}	1.6×10^{22}	1.0×10^{26}

The intention of this table is to demonstrate the computational intractability of complete enumeration schemes for larger Cayley graph families. Suppose for example, the generation and subsequent evaluation of one member of *Cayley*(7,8) takes 10^{-3} seconds on a fast CPU, which is not a bad value for the generation of a graph with 5040 nodes and 40320 edges and a typical evaluation run the resulting complete enumeration for *Cayley*(7,8) would take $\approx 3\times10^{24}$ years. We conclude that considerable effort has to be put into operational generation and evaluation frameworks in order to obtain practically usable results within days or at least weeks. The next section gives an outline of such a simple generation and evaluation framework designed to compute attractive topologies without using complete enumeration schemes for large families.

3. Generation and Evaluation of Cayley Graphs - An Adaptable Framework

In the previous section, Cayley graphs have been introduced and described from an algebraic point of view. However, despite of several theoretically interesting properties, the model is still lacking an operational environment for the systematic generation and subsequent application dependent evaluation of Cayley graph families. Table 1 shows that the systematic generation via brute-force enumeration schemes is quickly loosing tractability with increasing n and k. Consequently, this section is devoted to the *practical* generation and evaluation of Cayley graphs[3].

[3] All considerations with regard to fast generation and evaluation as well as all evaluation *results* presented in Section 4 are derived from a set of closely interacting generation and evaluation procedures currently operational on a SPARC workstation cluster.

3.1 Approximative Bottom Up Generations

It has been mentioned that all kinds of enumeration schemes are out of question beyond particular (n,k) combinations practically determined by the type of hardware equipment currently in use. On the other hand, *below* hardware specific (n,k) bounds, optimal[4] topologies can be found by complete enumeration. For example, employing the application dependent search space reduction described in Subsection 3.2 below and a standard 25 MHz i386 box, *Cayley*(5,4) and *Cayley*(4,5) are the largest families to be tackled in an easy manner. Switching to a SPARC IPX, *Cayley*(5,5) and *Cayley*(6,3) are no problem any more and *Cayley*(7,3) is the new challenge. Consequently, an *approximation schema* is needed which allows to produce new results starting from the largest optimal topology found by complete enumeration. In general, an approximation for increasing k and a fixed n (i.e. a "horizontal left to right" approximation with respect to Table 1) and a possibly different approximation for increasing n (i.e a "vertical top down" approximation) has to be found.

At the moment, we use a fast and simple approximation schema for increasing k and fixed n, since complete enumeration succeeded for $k=3$ up to $n \leq 7$. Therefore an approximation for increasing n values is not needed as far as less or equal 5040 processing elements have to be connected. Consequently, we focus on an approximation for $k \geq 4$ for a fixed $n \leq 7$ which can be described as follows.

Let $C_{opt}^{n,k}(V,E)$ denote the best Cayley graph of *Cayley*(n, k) found by complete enumeration and let $G_{opt}^{n,k}$ denote the corresponding generator set. In the present approximation schema, $\tilde{C}_{opt}^{n,k+1}(V,E)$ denoting the approximate optimum for *Cayley*(n, k) is derived either from $G_{opt}^{n,k}$ or from $\tilde{C}_{opt}^{n,k}(V,E)$ as starting value. In particular, let $<G_{opt}^{n,k}, P_n>$ denote the set of all $n!-k-1$ generator sets which results if $G_{opt}^{n,k}$ is extended by each permutation not equal to I and not already in $G_{opt}^{n,k}$. Consequently, $\tilde{C}_{opt}^{n,k+1}(V,E)$ is chosen as the optimal graph produced by any member of $<G_{opt}^{n,k}, P_n>$ in the context of an algebraic generation. More precisely,

$$<G_{opt}^{n,k}, P_n> = \{\dot{G} \mid \dot{G} = G_{opt}^{n,k} \cup \{\pi\} \textit{ with } \pi \in P_n \setminus \{I\} \text{ and } \pi \notin G_{opt}^{n,k}\} \text{ and}$$
$$\tilde{C}_{opt}^{n,k+1}(V,E) = \text{optimal graph} \in \{Generate(G) \mid G \in <G_{opt}^{n,k}, P_n>\}.$$

Optimistically, one might assume, that $\tilde{C}_{opt}^{n,k+1}(V,E)$ equals $C_{opt}^{n,k+1}(V,E)$, or in other words, that the optimal expansion of $C_{opt}^{n,k}(V,E)$ graphs yields $C_{opt}^{n,k+1}(V,E)$. Unfortunately, this is not the general case as far as average path length and diameter are concerned. However, it holds for a surprisingly large number of cases. For all other cases, the relative suboptimality is marginal. Interestingly, there are even cases where the approximation leaves the optimum in a particular step (i.e. for a particular $\dot{k} > 3$) but finds an optimal solution in a subsequent step (i.e. for a particular $k > \dot{k}$).

---

[4] This means *optimal* with respect to the evaluation schema presented in Subsection 3.2 below.

3.2. *Application Dependent Evaluations - Search Space Reduction and Evaluation Criteria*

Basically, there are two different directions with regard to application dependent graph evaluation. On the one hand, several criteria including average path length and number of nodes relative to diameter have to be applied to a large number of graphs. The resulting key values have to be compared to the key values of previously published topologies. On the other hand, several Cayley graphs can be discarded *even before generation* due to application dependent considerations. In other words, several generator sets can be considered inappropriate with respect to the field of application thus saving reasonable computational effort. The latter is addressed as *search space reduction* in the following Subsection 3.2.1, whereas the former is deferred to Subsection 3.2.2.

3.2.1 Search Space Reduction

In the previous section, Table 1 containing the numbers of all possible generator sets for a systematic graph generation and evaluation gives a rather devastating impression with regard to computational tractability. However, one of our basic assumptions about the relevant target hardware facilities, i.e. about the structure of the processing elements to be interconnected, yields a drastic reduction of the search space. Recalling our assumption concerning *bidirectional* interconnection links, we want to consider only those Cayley graphs $C^{n,k}(V,E)$, for which

$$e(v_i, v_j) \in E \iff e(v_j, v_i) \in E$$

holds. In other words, we want to model hardware topologies containing only bidirectional links by Cayley graphs containing forward *and* backward edges for any two connected nodes[5]. Figure 1(a) depicts a Cayley graph for which the above condition holds (edge directions have been omitted already in this figure), whereas Figure 1(b) shows a Cayley graph to be excluded from the evaluation runs following the assumption of bidirectional links.

The condition given above allows to decide whether or not a given Cayley graph is relevant in the given application domain. However, producing all possible graphs and subsequently eliminating irrelevant candidates would not reduce the time consumption. Consequently, a modified condition defined over the generator set has to be found. Basically, a Cayley graph will fulfill the condition stated above, iff the corresponding generator set is closed under inversion, or more precisely, for a graph $C^{n,k}(V,E)$ with generator set G

$$e(v_i, v_j) \in E \iff e(v_j, v_i) \in E \text{ is equivalent to } \bigwedge g \in G : g^{-1} \in G$$

[5] This is an example for a search space reduction stemming exclusively from the application domain, since different applications of Cayley graphs in the context of different modelling requirements could easily lead to different conclusions.

Deriving the number of generator sets fulfilling the second condition shows a decisive reduction in the number of evaluation candidates. Prior to this derivation, a few prerequisites are needed. In particular, each generator set which is closed under inversion may contain self-inverse generators as well as pairs of inverse generators. For example, $G_1 = \{1243, 2143, 2134\}$ contains only self-inverse generators, $G_2 = \{1243, 4312, 3421\}$ contains one self-inverse and one pair, whereas $G_3 = \{3421, 4312, 4312, 3421\}$ contains two pairs. For the $n!$ permutations of a particular S_n, we get a yet unknown number $Inv(n)$ of self-inverse permutations and $(n! - Inv(n)) \div 2$ possible pairs.

To obtain $Inv(n)$, we construct the set of self-inverse permutations of n elements as follows. We start by choosing $\pi(n)$ freely from among the n possible places. In the case of $\pi(n)=n$, $n-1$ places are left which can be filled by all $Inv(n-1)$ self-inverse permutations of $n-1$ elements. In the $n-1$ cases where $\pi(n) \neq n$, there are only $n-2$ places left, as $\pi(n)$ also determines $\pi(\pi(n))=n$. Thus, filling these $n-2$ free places with all possible $Inv(n-2)$ self-inverse permutations, we end up with $(n-1)Inv(n-2)$ possibilities. In total, we have

$$Inv(n) = \begin{cases} Inv(n-1) + (n-1)Inv(n-2) & \text{if } n > 2 \\ n & \text{if } n \leq 2 \end{cases}$$

The two special cases in this formula are easily verified:

$$Inv(1) = |\{1\}| = 1 \quad \text{and} \quad Inv(2) = |\{12, 21\}| = 2$$

Next we can use $Inv(n)$ to derive a formula for the number of generator sets closed under inversion. Let $GI(n, k)$ denote this number for particular n and k values.

Trying to construct a subset of P_n with k elements which is closed under inversion as discussed above, we observe that we can either use k self-inverse elements only, or $k-2$ self-inverse elements and a pair π, π^{-1}, etc. In general, we can combine $k-2j$ self-inverse elements with j pairs of inverse elements. We have

$$\begin{bmatrix} Inv(n)-1 \\ k-2j \end{bmatrix}$$

possibilities to select $k-2j$ generators out of $Inv(n)-1$ self-inverse generators (excluding I), and

$$\begin{bmatrix} (n!-Inv(n)) \div 2 \\ j \end{bmatrix}$$

possibilities to select j generator pairs from the remaining $n!-Inv(n)$ non-self-inverse permutations. Combining these two independent choices and summing over all possible values for j, we obtain

Theorem 2: Number of generator sets closed under inversion

$$GI(n, k) = \sum_{j=0}^{\lfloor k \div 2 \rfloor} \begin{bmatrix} Inv(n)-1 \\ k-2j \end{bmatrix} \times \begin{bmatrix} (n! - Inv(n)) \div 2 \\ j \end{bmatrix}$$

Similar to Table 1, the following table contains $GI(n, k)$ for S_4, S_5, S_6, S_7 and for 3 to 8 generators.

Table 2: Number of generator sets closed under inversion

	k=3	k=4	k=5	k=6	k=7	k=8
n=4	147	399	903	1757	2997	4538
n=5	3475	27831	188255	1112165	5869485	2.8×10^{7}
n=6	91675	2160681	4.3×10^{7}	7.4×10^{8}	1.1×10^{11}	1.6×10^{12}
n=7	2583119	1.8×10^{8}	1.1×10^{10}	5.5×10^{11}	2.5×10^{14}	1.0×10^{15}

With regard to the approximative generation described in Subsection 3.1, the crucial point is obviously the tractability of *Cayley*(7, 3). Recalling the run time estimation following Table 1, we modify the example and assume that the generation and subsequent evaluation of one member of *Cayley*(7, 3) takes 1 second total elapsed time on a SPARC station (this is a conservative assumption even with respect to our present nonoptimized implementation), the resulting complete enumeration of *Cayley*(7, 3) would take roughly one month thus yielding a practically reachable starting point for the approximative generation of $\tilde{C}_{opt}^{n,\,k>3}(V,E)$.

3.2.2. Evaluation Criteria Selected for Shared Nothing DBMS

In Subsection 3.1, the terms "optimal graph" and "leaving the optimum" have been used. Consequently, we have to discuss under what circumstances a Cayley graph is considered *optimal* with respect to our application domain. As stated in the introduction, the prime goal is to route a particular data transfer volume *DTV* through the interconnection network using as few atomic link transfer steps S as possible. It is assumed that previously published workload balancing approaches achieve a near uniform communication workload for all $p(p-1)$ virtual point-to-point communication paths. At this point, $S_{\min}$ depends on the average node-to-node communication path length, in the following denoted by $ACPL$, and on the routing algorithm. Prior to the actual discussion, a few notational conventions have to be added. Let a communication path $pa_{v_i,v_j} = \langle v_i, r_1, ..., r_t, v_j \rangle$ represent a virtual point to point connection from node v_i to node v_j where $r_1, ..., r_t$ denote intermediate relay nodes. Let $|pa_{v_i,v_j}| = t+1$ denote the corresponding number of atomic routing steps. Clearly, the shortest communication path spa_{v_i,v_j} representing the best virtual point to point connection from node v_i to node v_j is a pa_{v_i,v_j} with minimal $|pa_{v_i,v_j}|$. Facing at least two different definitions of the average communication path length, let it be defined in a Cayley graph as

$$ACPL = \frac{1}{n!-1} \sum_{v \in V \setminus \{I\}} |spa_{I,v}| \quad \text{with } n! = |V|$$

This definition is sufficient, since all Cayley graphs are node symmetric and therefore any node may be chosen to be origin of the communication path. However, some authors propose a normalized $ACPL$, namely $ACPL$ multiplied by k. This normalized $ACPL$ is appropriate if graphs with different k are compared, since it cancels the effect of larger k on $ACPL$.

At this point, the *interaction* between the $ACPL$ of a Cayley graph and the routing algorithm has to be considered. Obviously, an inefficient routing algorithm might fail to reach S_{min}, even if $ACPL$ is at a minimum. On the contrary, also an optimal routing algorithm, i.e. an algorithm always finding the shortest path between any two nodes, will be unable to approach S_{min}, if $ACPL$ is suboptimal. Thus, the effect of several routing techniques has to be taken into account. In particular, we investigate three scenarios:

- In Scenario 1, the presence of routing tables containing the precomputed shortest paths between any two nodes is assumed. Thus the routing algorithm trivially consists of subsequent table lookup steps. In this case, the routing algorithm will never fail to follow any shortest path. Consequently, a Cayley graph $C^{n,k}(V, E)$ will be optimal, iff no other Cayley graph exists in $Cayley(n, k)$ with a smaller $ACPL$. This scenario yields a main focus on $ACPL$ and allows easy evaluations, however, storing routing tables for several thousand processing elements in their main memory is almost prohibitive for the realization of this scenario.
- In Scenario 2, the use of a path finding algorithm (for example Dijkstra's single source shortest path algorithm) to compute the shortest path *upon request* guarantees shortest path routing through the network. Once again, a Cayley graph with minimal $ACPL$ has to be considered optimal, since the routing algorithm cannot contribute to any deviation from S_{min}. The problem here is the CPU intensive path finding process to be executed for each transfer packet. However, if the application is considered link I/O bound and not CPU bound, this scenario might be useful.
- In Scenario 3, a path finding heuristic (see below) is employed which guarantees successful routing in all cases. However, this heuristic might fail to find the shortest path in several cases and might therefore contribute to a deviation from S_{min}. In this context, the complex optimization problem of minimizing the number of atomic link transfer steps for a *combination* of a particular graph (determining an $ACPL$ value) and a particular routing heuristic has to be tackled. For several CPU intensive cases like for example relational join processing, this scenario might be useful in order to save CPU cycles spent on brute force path finding algorithms as in Scenario 2.

Obviously, the main focus has to be on $ACPL$ and on routing algorithms. Nevertheless, the *diameter*

$$D = \underset{v \in V \setminus \{I\}}{MAX} |spa_{I,v}|$$

cannot be totally ignored. It represents a worst case of all virtual point-to-point communication paths in a graph. In our evaluation framework, it allows the comparison to previously published topologies, for which D but not $ACPL$ have been given. Additionally, D can be used relative to k and $|V|$ to define a notion of "packing density": A graph of degree k and diameter D containing a given number of nodes is more attractive than another graph of degree k and diameter D containing less nodes.

Finally, we can compare different topologies also on the basis of the performance of the routing algorithm. In what follows, we concentrate on the path finding heuristic mentioned above for Scenario 3.

In the current evaluation environment, a standard A-Algorithm (see [Nils82]) is employed. In this search strategy, the decision to choose one of the k neighbouring nodes v_s of the node currently investigated is guided by a distance function $\tilde{d}(v_s)$ which estimates the total length of a shortest path $start \rightarrow v_s \rightarrow goal$ from the starting node to the goal via a particular neighbour v_s. This distance is obviously composed of $|spa_{start,\, v_s}|$ and $|spa_{v_s,\, goal}|$, both of which must be estimated at the time of decision. If we denote the corresponding estimating functions by $l(v_s)$ and $h(v_s)$, respectively, then $\tilde{d}$ has the form

$$\tilde{d}(v) = l(v) + w\ h(v)$$

While $l(v)$ is simply the length of the shortest path found so far, the heart of the A-Algorithm is the heuristic $h(v)$ estimating $|spa_{v,\, goal}|$, the influence of which may be tuned by the weight w.

In the context of our routing problem, we use a simple heuristic h, namely the sum of displacements, to estimate the distance between a given permutation $\pi \in P_n$ and I:

$$h(\pi) = \sum_{j=1}^{n} |\ j - \pi(j)\ |$$

The resulting A-Algorithm is fast and reduces the CPU consumption for path finding drastically (see [HiMu92]) but fails to find the shortest path in some cases, as the respective sufficient condition $h(\pi) \leq |spa_{\pi,\, I}|$ is *not* guaranteed. However, w can be used to minimize the number of failures. If $w=0$, the A-Algorithm reduces to a breadth-first strategy like Dijkstra's single source shortest path algorithm with no failures at all but maximum computation time. To find a reasonable value for w for a given Cayley graph, we define the *routing characteristic* $R_C(w)$ of a Cayley graph C with respect to weight w in $\tilde{d}$. $R_C(w)$ combines the total number of routing steps for all virtual point-to-point communication paths with the number of nodes investigated during the search. More precisely, if $S_C^{v,\, I}(w)$ denotes the number of routing steps yielded by the A-algorithm with weight w for a route from v to I ($S_C^{v,\, I}(w) \geq |spa_{v,\, I}|$) and $N_C^{v,\, I}(w)$ denotes the number of nodes visited during the search, then

$$R_C(w) = \sum_{v \in V} (S_C^{v,\, I}(w) + \tau\ N_C^{v,\, I}(w))$$

where τ represents an application specific parameter reflecting the relation between the costs to compute the shortest route and the costs for a routing step. Now, $R_C(w)$ can be minimized by, say, bisection, varying w in the range $0 < w \leq 1$. The resulting values for w and $R_C(w)$ will be denoted by w_C^{opt} and R_C, respectively. In the sequel, the term *routing characteristic* will refer to R_C.

Consequently, the current evaluation of a family *Cayley*(n, k) for Scenario 3 is based on R_C and consists of the following steps:

1) Choose all Cayley graphs with minimal *ACPL*.
2) Determine w_C^{opt} and R_C for each Cayley graph selected in Step 1.
3) Among those Cayley graphs selected in Step 1, choose one with minimal R_C as final optimum.

At the present moment, we do not know whether or not this procedure finds a global optimum. The question is if the Cayley graph with minimal R_C has also minimal *ACPL*, or if the routing algorithm is able to overcompensate a non-minimum *ACPL*. In the latter case, Step 1 could be replaced by

1') Choose all Cayley graphs with *ACPL* below an appropriate threshold.

4. Evaluation Results and Comparison to Related Work

Table 3 below shows the aggregated results of various generation and evaluation runs. One cell of the table corresponds to a given combination $(|V|, k)$ and contains the best evaluation results with respect to Section 3. For each cell, the results may stem from a complete enumeration run, from the intermediate result of a complete enumeration run or from an approximation as outlined in Subsection 3.1. The corresponding tags (source indicators) in the table are C, I and A, respectively. In the first case, no better generator set can be found, i.e. there is no generator set in $GI(n, k)$ which spans a Cayley graph with smaller *ACPL*. Each cell of the table contains a source indicator followed by the diameter and *ACPL* of the chosen graph:

Table 3: Best results for *Cayley*(n, k)

|V|	k=3	k=4	k=5	k=6	k=7	k=8
6	C 2 / 1.400	C 2 / 1.200	C 1 / 1.000			
8	C 2 / 1.571	C 2 / 1.429	C 2 / 1.286	C 2 / 1.143	C 1 / 1.000	
10	C 3 / 1.889	C 2 / 1.556	C 2 / 1.444	A 2 / 1.333	A 2 / 1.222	A 2 / 1.111
12	C 3 / 2.000	C 2 / 1.636	C 2 / 1.545	C 2 / 1.455	C 2 / 1.364	C 2 / 1.273
16	C 4 / 2.400	I 3 / 1.933	A 2 / 1.667	A 2 / 1.600	A 2 / 1.533	A 2 / 1.467
18	C 4 / 2.412	I 3 / 2.059	I 2 / 1.706	A 2 / 1.647	A 2 / 1.588	
20	C 4 / 2.579	C 3 / 2.000	C 3 / 1.789	A 2 / 1.684	A 2 / 1.632	A 2 / 1.579
24	C 4 / 2.609	C 3 / 2.174	C 3 / 1.913	C 2 / 1.739	C 2 / 1.696	C 2 / 1.652
36	C 5 / 3.200	I 4 / 2.571	I 3 / 2.229	A 3 / 2.057	A 3 / 1.943	A 3 / 1.857
48	C 6 / 3.511	I 4 / 2.723	I 3 / 2.408	A 3 / 2.234	A 3 / 2.106	A 3 / 2.021
60	C 5 / 3.678	C 4 / 2.881	C 3 / 2.492	A 3 / 2.356	A 3 / 2.203	A 3 / 2.034
72	C 6 / 4.042	I 5 / 3.070	I 4 / 2.704	A 4 / 2.465	A 3 / 2.296	A 3 / 2.183
120	C 7 / 4.748	C 5 / 3.529	C 4 / 2.983	C 4 / 2.697	I 3 / 2.529	I 3 / 2.403
144	I 8 / 5.077	A 6 / 3.776	A 5 / 3.196	A 4 / 2.846	A 4 / 2.685	A 3 / 2.524
240	I 8 / 5.615	A 6 / 4.255	A 6 / 3.523	A 4 / 3.184	A 4 / 2.895	A 4 / 2.732
360	C 9 / 6.499	A 6 / 4.557	A 5 / 3.866	A 5 / 3.435	A 4 / 3.156	A 4 / 2.936
720	C 12 / 7.580	I 7 / 5.220	I 6 / 4.367	A 5 / 3.894	A 5 / 3.559	A 5 / 3.370
5040	I 15 / 10.539	A 10 / 7.076	A 8 / 5.868	A 7 / 5.149	A 6 / 4.709	A 6 / 4.406

The generators of the best graphs found so far are listed in the Appendix and may be used for practical applications.

Of course, the most interesting point is the *relative* performance of the best Cayley graphs found so far (i.e. the graphs referenced in the Appendix). In other words, we have to compare our results to well-established topologies like binary n-cube graphs as well as to recently proposed alternatives like deBruijn graphs (see [BeDQ86]) or n-star graphs (see [AkKr86]). We choose those three topologies out of a large number of competing topologies for the following reasons. Binary n-cubes belong to the most popular and widely used topologies. Additionally, they are Cayley graphs belonging to the family $Cayley(2n, n)$. For example, the binary 3-cube (a 3-dimensional cube in the usual geometric interpretation) corresponds to the Cayley graph yielded by $Generate(\{213456, 124356, 123465\})$. All n-star graphs are also Cayley graphs belonging to $Cayley(n, n-1)$. They are produced by generator sets in which a particular position is interchanged with each possible other position. For example, the 4-star graph is yielded by $Generate(\{2134, 3214, 4231\})$, i.e. by the generator set in which position 1 is interchanged with each possible other position.

Quite on the contrary, deBruijn graphs have been chosen to include a completely different graph generation model, namely so called ***graphs on alphabets***. In particular, an undirected deBruijn graph of diameter $D=B$ and node degree $k=2b$ for integer B, b has $|V| = b^B$ nodes. Each node is represented by a string of B symbols out of an alphabet of b symbols. Two nodes v_i, v_j are adjacent, iff

the first $B-1$ digits of v_i equal the last $B-1$ digits of v_j or
the first $B-1$ digits of v_j equal the last $B-1$ digits of v_i

In a next step we have to evaluate binary n-cubes, star graphs and deBruijn graphs and compare the resulting data to the best Cayley graph data in Table 3. Regarding binary n-cube graphs and n-star graphs, the graph specifications given above yield results only for a small number of (n, k) combinations, in particular for $k=n$ in case of binary n-cubes and for $k=n+1$ in case of n-stars. As a result, we get a sparse result matrix in both cases. Even worse, the number of nodes in n-cubes does not generally correspond to the number of nodes in best Cayley graphs. Consequently, both evaluation tables (Table 4 for n-cubes and Table 5 for n-stars) contain entries for $ACPL$ and D as well as entries for both values yielded by the closest best Cayley graph. In Table 4, the values for the best Cayley graph with the smallest number of nodes larger than or equal to the n-cube number of nodes have been entered. In Table 5, there are additional entries for the relative improvement in $ACPL$ yielded by the best Cayley graphs. Two conclusions can be drawn with regard to Table 4 and Table 5. On the one hand, n-cubes are not very attractive for communication load balanced applications, since each n-cube is dominated by a best Cayley graph with larger $|V|$. On the other hand, n-stars are more serious contenders but are also outperformed by best Cayley graphs with increasing $|V|$.

Table 4: Diameter and *ACPL* of n-cubes compared to best Cayley graphs

Graph	|V|	k=3	k=4	k=5	k=6	k=7	k=8
8-cube	8	3 / 1.714					
Cayley(4,k)	8	3 / 1.571					
16-cube	16		4 / 2.133				
Cayley(6,k)	16		3 / 1.933				
32-cube	32			5 / 2.581			
Cayley(6,k)	36			3 / 2.229			
64-cube	64				6 / 3.048		
Cayley(6,k)	72				4 / 2.465		
128-cube	128					7 / 3.528	
Cayley(7,k)	144					4 / 2.685	
256-cube	256						8 / 4.016
Cayley(6,k)	360						4 / 2.936

Table 5: Diameter and *ACPL* of n-stars compared to best Cayley graphs

Graph	|V|	k=3	k=4	k=5	k=6
(k+1)-star	24	4 / 2.696			
Cayley(4,k)	24	4 / 2.609			
		3%			
(k+1)-star	120		6 / 3.714		
Cayley(5,k)	120		5 / 3.529		
			5%		
(k+1)-star	720			7 / 4.790	
Cayley(6,k)	720			6 / 4.367	
				9%	
(k+1)-star	5040				9 / 5.880
Cayley(7,k)	5040				7 / 5.149
					12%

Comparing best Cayley graphs to deBruijn graphs is somewhat harder. DeBruijn graphs are not Cayley graphs, they are not even regular and therefore also asymmetric. To our present knowledge, neither a closed form nor a tabular representation for the *ACPL* of deBruijn graphs has been published. Consequently, we compare the number of nodes for a given diameter and a given degree to the maximum number of nodes found for best Cayley graphs. Table 6 below contains the resulting data. Each cell contains the number of nodes in a deBruijn graph and the number of nodes in a best Cayley graph.

Table 6: Number of nodes in deBruijn graphs and best Cayley graphs

D	k=4		k=6		k=8	
	deBruijn	Cayley(n, k)	deBruijn	Cayley(n, k)	deBruijn	Cayley(n, k)
2	4	12	9	24	16	24
3	8	24	27	60	64	144
4	16	60	81	120	256	360
5	32	120	243	720	1024	720
6	64	360	729	720	4048	≥5040
7	128	720	2187	≥5040	16192	

Since the number of nodes in a deBruijn graph grows exponentially with D, the number of nodes in a best Cayley graph cannot dominate the number of nodes in a deBruijn graph with the same diameter and node degree. However, whether or not this property yields advantages with regard to an approximation towards $S_{\min}$ remains an open question at the moment.

5. Conclusions

A systematic generation and evaluation framework for large families of node symmetric graphs is defined and used to compute best Cayley graphs. These graphs are selected with respect to minimal average communication path length and the presence of efficient routing heuristics. Consequently, best Cayley graphs are of particular interest for shared nothing DBMS, since they allow a good approximation to the minimal number of physical routing step needed to simulate $p(p-1)$ virtual point-to-point communication paths used by an DBMS which is running on a shared nothing platform with p processing elements. Best Cayley graphs are compared to popular interconnection structures and shown to dominate n-cubes and n-stars with respect to diameter and average communication path length. A family of asymmetric graphs, namely deBruijn graphs, can not be generally dominated by best Cayley graphs. However, the question if there is a family of asymmetric graphs which yields a better approximation towards the minimal number of physical routing steps in a large number of cases cannot be answered so far.

The near future research agenda contains several points which have been left open in this paper. In particular, we have to compare the current best Cayley graphs to a larger number of node symmetric graphs to check whether or not any other node symmetric graphs structure is superior to all or to some of the current best Cayley graphs. Additionally, the approximative generation schema has to be improved in order to come closer to or even reach optimal results. At the moment, the influence of different routing heuristics on the total number of physical routing steps in a Cayley graph is not fully understood. Appropriate information depends on large-scale practical studies which are currently performed.

Acknowledgements

The authors would like to thank Gabi Kotsis for several pointers to relevant literature.

Appendix: Generator Sets for Best Cayley Graphs

|V|	k	n	G
4	3	4	1243 2134 2143
5	4	5	23451 34512 45123 51234
6	3	4	1243 1324 1432
6	4	4	1243 1324 1342 1423
6	5	5	12354 12435 12453 12534 12543
8	3	4	1243 2143 3412
8	4	4	1243 2134 2143 3412
8	5	4	1243 2134 2143 3412 4321
8	6	4	1243 2134 2143 3412 3421 4312
8	7	4	1243 2134 2143 3412 3421 4312 4321
10	3	5	13254 21435 35142
10	4	5	13254 21435 45231 53412
10	5	5	13254 21435 24153 31524 35142
10	6	5	13254 21435 24153 31524 35142 42513
10	7	5	13254 21435 24153 31524 35142 42513 54321
10	8	5	13254 21435 24153 31524 35142 42513 45231 53412
12	3	5	12354 12435 21354
12	4	4	1342 1423 2143 3412
12	5	4	1342 1423 2143 3241 4213
12	6	4	1342 1423 2143 2314 3124 3412
12	7	4	1342 1423 2143 2314 2431 3124 4132
12	8	4	1342 1423 2143 2314 2431 3124 3412 4132
16	3	6	123465 124365 563412
16	4	6	123465 124356 213465 341256
16	5	6	123465 124356 125634 213456 216543
16	6	6	123465 124356 124365 125634 213456 216543
16	7	6	123465 124356 124365 125634 126543 213456 214356
16	8	6	123465 124356 124365 125634 126543 213456 214356 213465
18	3	6	123465 231546 312546
18	4	6	123465 123546 231465 312465
18	5	6	123465 123564 123645 231546 312546
18	6	6	123465 123546 123564 123645 231546 312546
18	7	6	123465 123546 123564 123645 123654 231546 312546
20	3	5	13254 23415 41235
20	4	5	13254 21435 25314 41352
20	5	5	13254 21435 23541 42513 51243
20	6	5	13254 14532 15423 34125 43521 54213
20	7	5	13254 14532 15423 21435 35142 42513 54321
24	3	4	1243 1324 3412
24	4	4	1243 1324 2143 3214
24	5	4	1243 1324 2143 3214 3412
24	6	4	1243 1324 2143 2341 4123 4321
24	7	4	1243 1324 1342 1423 2134 3241 4213
24	8	4	1243 1324 1342 1423 1432 2134 3214 4231

|V|	k	n	G
36	3	6	123465 132546 213654
36	4	6	123465 132546 213546 321654
36	5	6	123465 123546 132465 213465 321546
36	6	6	123465 123546 132465 213546 321456 321465
36	7	6	123465 123546 132465 132654 213546 321456 321465
36	8	6	123465 123546 123654 132465 132654 213546 321456 321465
48	3	6	123465 125634 564312
48	4	6	123465 123546 125634 214356
48	5	6	123465 123546 125634 213465 216453
48	6	6	123465 123546 124356 125634 213465 216453
48	7	6	123465 123546 124356 125634 213465 214356 216453
48	8	6	123465 123546 124356 125634 126543 213465 214356 216453
60	3	5	13254 21435 45312
60	4	5	13254 21354 21435 52431
60	5	5	13254 21354 23451 42513 51234
60	6	5	13254 21354 21435 23451 42513 51234
60	7	5	13254 14523 21354 21543 23514 41253 52431
60	8	5	13254 14523 21435 21543 24531 51423 52431 54321
72	3	6	123465 132546 456123
72	4	6	123465 132546 213546 465132
72	5	6	123465 123546 132465 456231 645123
72	6	6	123465 123546 132465 456231 645123 654321
72	7	6	123465 123546 132465 213465 456312 546213 564123
72	8	6	123465 123546 132456 213546 321546 456312 564123 654321
120	3	5	12354 14523 45312
120	4	5	12354 14523 43512 45213
120	5	5	12354 12435 14523 35142 42513
120	6	5	12354 12435 14523 34512 45123 53241
120	7	5	12354 12543 15432 25134 31452 35142 43215
120	8	5	12354 12435 23415 24531 34251 41235 51423 53124
144	3	7	1234576 1243657 3714562
144	4	7	1234576 1243657 3714562 4731652
144	5	7	1234576 1243657 3714562 4231765 4731652
144	6	7	1234576 1243657 1643527 3714562 4231765 4731652
144	7	7	1234576 1234765 1243657 1643527 3714562 4231765 4731652
144	8	7	1234576 1243657 1634725 1643527 3714562 4231765 4731652 1243576
240	3	7	1234576 1243657 2137564
240	4	7	1234576 1536247 1567234 7243561
240	5	7	1234576 1536247 1567234 6537214 7243561
240	6	7	1234576 1536247 1567234 4261537 6537214 7243561
240	7	7	1234576 1536247 1567234 4261537 6537214 6574213 7243561
240	8	7	1234576 1236547 1536247 1567234 4261537 6537214 6574213 7243561
360	3	6	124365 132546 215436
360	4	6	124365 132546 215436 523614
360	5	6	124365 132546 156423 213546 425136
360	6	6	124365 132546 156423 213546 425136 43215
360	7	6	124365 132465 132546 156423 215436 523614 643251
360	8	6	124365 132465 132546 156423 215436 321654 523614 643251
720	3	6	123465 132546 425136
720	4	6	123465 132546 215436 54321
720	5	6	123465 123546 145236 463152 564312
720	6	6	123465 123546 125634 146253 456123 524316
720	7	6	123465 123546 125634 146253 456123 524316 532416
720	8	6	123465 123546 125634 146253 341265 456123 524316 532416
5040	3	7	1234576 1243657 3517264
5040	4	7	1234576 1243657 1472563 3517264
5040	5	7	1234576 1243657 1472563 2137654 3517264
5040	6	7	1234576 1243657 1472563 2137654 3517264 5764132
5040	7	7	1234576 1243657 1472563 2137654 3517264 5764132 6452317
5040	8	7	1234576 1243657 1472563 2137654 3517264 5764132 6237514 6452317

References

[AkKr86] S.B. Akers and B. Krishnamurthy, "A Group Theoretic Model for Symmetric Interconnection Networks," in *Proc. of the 1986 Int. Conf. on Parallel Processing*, IEEE Computer Socienty Press (1986).

[BeDQ86] N. Biggs, J.-C. Bermond, C. Delorme, and J.-J. Quisquater, "Strategies for Interconnecrtion Networks: Some Methods From Graph Theory," *Journal of Parallel and Distributed Computing*, vol. 3, no. 4, Academic Press (1986).

[CABT88] G. Copeland, W. Alexander, E. Boughter, and T. Keller, "Data Placement in Bubba," in *Proc. ACM SIGMOD Conf. on Mangement of Data*, ACM Press, Chicago (1988).

[DeWi86] D.J. DeWitt and others, "GAMMA - A High Performance Dataflow Database Machine," in *Proc. of the 12th VLDB Conf.*, ACM Press (1986).

[DeGr92] D.J. DeWitt and J. Gray, "Parallel Database Systems: The Future of High Performance Database Systems," *CACM*, vol. 35, no. 6, ACM (1992).

[Frie90] O. Frieder, "Parallelism - Using the Right Tool for the Right Job," in *Proc. of PARBASE-90*, IEEE Computer Society Press (1990).

[GhDe90] S. Ghandeharizadeh and D.J. DeWitt, "Hybrid Range Partitioning Strategy: A New Declustering Strategy for Multiprocessor Database Machines," in *Proc. of the 16th VLDB Conf.*, Melbourne (1990).

[Grae90] G. Graefe, "Encapsulation of parallelism in the Volcano query processing system," in *Proc. ACM SIGMOD Conf. on Mangement of Data*, ACM Press, Atlantic City (1990).

[Hill87] W.D. Hillis, "The Connection Machine," PhD Thesis, MIT Press, Cambridge Ma. (1987).

[HiMu92] M. Hitz and T.A. Mueck, "Generating Interconnection Topologies Using Cayley Graphs," TR-IFS-127, Dept. of Information Systems, University of Vienna (1992).

[HoSt90] W. Hong and M. Stonebraker, "Parallel Query Processing in XPRS," Tech.Rep. UCB/ERL M90/47, Electronics Research Laboratory, University of California at Berkeley (1990).

[KoMV92] M. Kollingbaum, T.A. Mueck, and G. Vinek, "PARABASE - A federated DBMS architecture supported by a shared nothing database server," in *Proc. of the OpenForum92 Technical Conference*, EurOpen, Utrecht (1992). (to appear)

[LiKB87] M. Livny, S. Khoshafian, and H. Boral, "Multi-Disk Management Algorithms," in *Proc. ACM SIGMETRICS Conf.*, ACM Press, Banff (1987).

[Nils82] N.J. Nilsson, *Principles of Artificial Intelligence*, Springer Verlag, Berlin, Heidelberg, New York (1982).

[PaGK88] D.A. Patterson, G. Gibson, and R.H. Katz, "A Case for Redundant Arrays of Inexpensive Disks (RAID)," in *Proc. ACM SIGMOD Conf. on Mangement of Data*, ACM Press, Chicago (1988).

[ScDe89] D. Schneider and D.J. DeWitt, "A performance evaluation of four parallel join algorithms in a shared-nothing multiprocessor environment," in *Proc. ACM SIGMOD Conf. on Mangement of Data*, ACM Press, Portland (1989).

[ScDe90] D.A. Schneider and D.J. DeWitt, "Tradeoffs in processing complex join queries via hashing in multiprocessor database machines," in *Proc. of the 16th VLDB Conf.*, Melbourne (1990).

[Ston86] M. Stonebraker, "The case for shared nothing," *Database Engineering*, vol. 9, no. 1 (1986).

[WoDY90] J.L. Wolf, D.M. Dias, and P.S. Yu, "An Effective Algorithm for Parallelizing Sort-Merge Joins in the Presence of Data Skew," in *Proc. 2nd Int'l Symposium on Databases in Parallel and Distributed Systems*, Dublin (1990).

On Optimizing Uniformly Bounded Datalog Programs

Jia Liang Han
School of Information Technology
University of Southern Queensland, Toowoomba, Queensland Australia 4350
E-mail: han@zeus.usq.edu.au

ABSTRACT

A recursive rule is uniformly bounded if it is equivalent to a finite number of non-recursive rules regardless of the extensional database. Query optimization for datalog programs composed of two subclasses of uniformly bounded function-free linear recursive rules, Ioannidis' subclass[9] and isolated degenerate cycles[4] is studied. Termination is based on the uniform bound so that the cost for termination is negligible at run-time. Query processing is performed in the predicate-goal graph[3] and constants (or other constraints) in the query are used to instantiate top nodes. This generates only answers during query processing and gives an efficient algorithm. Factorization, differentiation and other optimization techniques are also addressed.

1. Introduction

A linear recursive rule is *uniformly bounded* if it is equivalent to a finite number of non-recursive rules regardless of the extensional database. A recursive program is *uniformly bounded* if all of its recursive rules are uniformly bounded. Although uniform boundedness of function-free linear recursive rules has been studied in the past[12,9,13,14], it has not been used for query optimization. Query optimization is the topic of this paper.

We use the expansion approach[9,13]. A linear recursive rule is equivalent to an infinite number of expansions. For a uniformly bounded linear recursive rule, only a finite number of expansions are necessary to determine the recursive relation. The highest order of these expansions is the *uniform bound*. Of various tests, uniform bounds are known for two subclasses of function-free linear recursive rules: Ioannidis' subclass[9] and isolated degenerate cycles in the variable-predicate (VP) graph[4]. Recursive rules are limited to these subclasses in this paper.

Costs of recursive query evaluation are dominated by access to the stored relations, operations on generated tuples and values, and termination tests. Query optimizations are studied along the following line: (a) termination based on uniform bounds, (b) elimination of irrelevant tuples, (c) set-of-values approach, (d) factorization, which reduces the memory space for generated tuples, (e) differentiation (evaluation based on results from earlier iteration steps) and other fine tunings.

In basic bottom-up evaluations (such as semi-naive evaluation[16]), each iteration produces a fraction of the recursive relation. At the end of each iteration, the newly generated fraction is compared with the current value of the recursive relation. If the increment is fully contained in the current recursive relation, then query evaluation stops. Otherwise, the union of the increment and the current recursive relation becomes the new value of the recursive relation and another iteration begins. Termination tests are often expensive. For a uniformly bounded recursive rule, termination may be achieved by limiting iteration steps, which reduces significantly the cost of termination tests.

Consider a query with constants. A basic bottom-up evaluation often generates many tuples not suitable to the query. This is because a basic bottom-up evaluation does not use constants in the query until all tuples in the recursive relation are generated. The well known magic sets method[1,16] first rewrites the recursive program using the binding information. Then, semi-naive evaluation is used. Magic sets method manifests the idea of *sideways information passing strategies (SIPS)*. The word sideways means a restriction on the recursive relation before its generation. SIPS focus on only "relevant" tuples. We do SIP and other optimization in the *predicate-goal (PG) graph*[3]. We first use constants in the query to instantiate the corresponding top nodes. Then, we satisfy the remaining graph. This method generates only answers no irrelevant tuples. For applicable programs, it is at least as efficient as (usually more efficient than) magic sets method.

The PG graph is also useful for factorization. It is possible that a recursive relation or some other relation can be decomposed into several subrelations of smaller arity. This reduces the memory space required for transient results, thus, improves the space complexity. Another optimization is differentiation. The idea of differentiation is to use results in earlier steps for further derivations. Semi-naive evaluation is differentiation applied to naive evaluation. Fine tunings are based on some properties of PG graphs.

This paper is organized as follows. Section 2 gives the background (expansions and variable-predicate graphs). Section 3 is on uniform boundedness. In section 4, we explain recursive query evaluation in the predicate-goal graph. Recursive query optimization is studied in section 5. Section 6 is discussion and conclusion.

2. Background

We use Prolog notations and definitions in logic programming[11] and deductive databases[16]. All rules here are function-free Horn clauses, i.e., *datalog* rules.

Each deductive database in this paper has one function-free linear recursive rule in addition to some non-recursive rules and facts. We partition such a deductive database into four parts: (1) the recursive rule (RR), (2) the initialization condition (IC), (3) the extensional database (EDB), and (4) rules which define non-recursive relations (NR). The IC consists of *exit rules* and those facts which match the recursive predicate. An exit rule is a non-recursive rule whose rule head matches the recursive predicate. All other facts are in the EDB. The NR is not essential to recursion and is assumed empty in this paper. The IC defines a fraction of recursive relation called the *IC relation*.

Example 2.1: Consider the following program (facts concerning r0, p, q are not shown):

$$\texttt{r(X1,X2,X3,X4) :- r0(X1,X2,X3,X4).} \tag{1}$$

$$\texttt{r(X1,X2,Y1a,Y2a) :- r(X2,X1,Y1b,Y2b),p(Y1b,Y2a),q(Y0b,Y1a).} \tag{2}$$

Rule (2) is linear recursive while rule (1) is an exit rule. The recursive predicate is r. All other predicates are *non-recursive*. □

Definitions: Variables in the rule head — such as X1,X2 in rule (1) or (2) — are called *distinguished variables*. Variables in the recursive predicate in the rule body — such as X1,X2,Y1b,Y2b in rule (2) — are called *recursive variables*. Note that variables can be both distinguished and recursive.

Expansions are obtained by resolutions[11]. Given a linear recursive rule R, we keep a duplicate R'. Without loss of generality, we rename variables in R' such that they are different from R (standardizing apart). Since the recursive rule does not have repeated variables and/or constants (see section 6), the head of R' may be unified with the recursive predicate in the body of R using an mgu. This is a recursive call and the resolvent is the *first expansion*. The recursive predicate in the rule body of the first expansion can be resolved with the duplicate again and the resolvent is the *second expansion*. Higher-order expansions are obtained iteratively. The original recursive rule is the *0th expansion*. (Unfolding[2] obtains same rules as expansions but the interpretation is different.)

Example 2.2: The first and second expansions, respectively, for rule (2) are:

```
r(X1,X2,Y1a,Y2a) :- r(X1,X2,Y1c,Y2c),p(Y1b,Y2a),q(Y0b,Y1a),
        p(Y1c,Y2b),q(Y0c,Y1b).                                   (3)
r(X1,X2,Y1a,Y2a) :- r(X2,X1,Y1d,Y2d),p(Y1b,Y2a),q(Y0b,Y1a),
        p(Y1c,Y2b),q(Y0c,Y1b),p(Y1d,Y2c),q(Y0d,Y1c).             (4)
```

The third, fourth, ... expansions are obtained iteratively. □

We rewrite expansions by replacing recursive predicates in rule bodies by a new predicate `r0` and do likewise for head predicates in the IC. In other words, we interpret the recursive predicate in all expansion bodies as the IC relation. This makes expansions *non-recursive*. We have the following theorem[7].

Theorem 2.1. *For a datalog program of only one linear recursive rule, the recursive relation can be obtained by interpreting the recursive predicate in all expansion bodies as the IC relation.*

Tests of uniform boundedness are stated in the *variable-predicate (VP) graph*[8], a variation of the α-graph[9]. The VP graph is a hybrid graph (with two different types of edges) for a linear recursive rule. Each VP graph is infinite and has an infinite number of subgraphs, one VP subgraph for each expansion. Each VP subgraph is a quintuple (N, R, E, L, W). N is a set of nodes. Each node in a subgraph represents one variable in the expansion. R is a set of *R-edges*, which are for the recursive predicate. E is a set of *E-edges*, which are for the non-recursive predicates. (R-edges and E-edges were called D-edges and U-edges in[8], respectively.) Arrows in the VP graph indicates orientation of arguments in predicates and does not imply directions as in a digraph. For each expansion, a distinguished variable and a recursive variable in the same argument position form an ordered pair, e.g., (`X1`,`X1`), (`Y1a`,`Y1c`), or (`Y2a`,`Y2c`) in rule (3). For each such pair, we draw an R-edge (a broken line with the tail at the distinguished variable). The number of R-edges is equal to the arity of the recursive predicate. For two variables in a non-recursive binary predicate, we draw an E-edge (from the first variable to the second one). A unary non-recursive predicate is represented by a label (predicate symbol) attached to the corresponding node. If the arity of an EDB predicate is greater than 2, then a previous method[9] may be used; a slightly different way is to use hypergraphs. L is a set of labels. The E-edges are labeled according to their predicates. W is a set of weights. Every edge is assigned a *weight*. The weight of an E-edge is zero. Unlike in a digraph, a path is allowed to travel against the arrow of an edge. The weight of an R-edge is +1 if the R-edge is in the same direction of a path and −1 if opposite. The weight of a walk (path, cycle) is

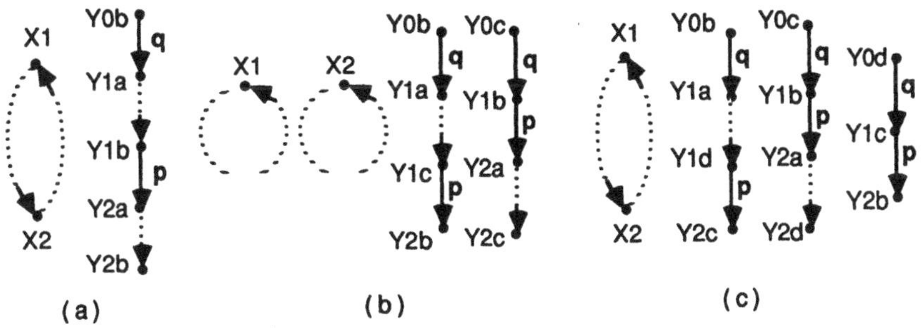

Figure 1. The 0th (a), 1st (b), and 2nd (c) VP subgraphs for rule (2).

the algebraic sum of the weights of all edges of this walk (path, cycle). The first few VP subgraphs for rule (2) are shown in Figure 1.

Nodes of a VP subgraph are partitioned into equivalent classes. Two nodes belong to the same equivalent class if they are connected by a path of edges (regardless of E-edges, R-edges or their directions). Nodes of the same equivalent class form a *component*. A component of a 0th VP subgraph is *degenerate* if it consists of only R-edges. If a degenerate component has only one cycle, then it is an *isolated degenerate cycle*. For example, Figure 1a has two components: one is an isolated degenerate cycle of weight two and the other is a path of E-edges and R-edges.

3. Uniform Boundedness

For tests on uniform boundedness, the containment mapping[9,13] is important.

Definition: Consider two rules $R_1 = r_1 \leftarrow a_1, \ldots, a_n$. and $R_2 = r_2 \leftarrow b_1, \ldots, b_m$. A *containment mapping* m is a variable-to-variable mapping such that

(1) it maps a variable in r_1 to the variable at the corresponding argument position in r_2;

(2) for every predicate $a_i(x_1, \ldots, x_l)$ in the body of R_1 there is some predicate $a_i(m(x_1), \ldots, m(x_l))$ in the body of R_2.

If there is a containment mapping from rule R_1 to R_2, then R_2 is more *restrictive* than R_1 and all tuples derived by R_2 can also be derived by R_1.

The two rules in containment mapping can be two different expansions of the same rule. The following lemmas are given or easily inferred from[9,13]:

Lemma 3.1. *A linear recursive rule is uniformly bounded if there is a containment mapping from the ith expansion to the jth expansion for some $i, j (i < j)$. The bound is no greater than $j - 1$.*

Lemma 3.2. *If there is a containment mapping from rule R_1 to R_2, then the relation defined by R_2 is contained by the relation defined by R_1.*

Ioannidis[9] established a test† on uniform boundedness for a subclass of linear recursive rules. The restrictions are: (1) linear recursive, (2) function-free, (3) no constants in the rule, (4) no repeated distinguished variables, and (5) no degenerate cycles.

Theorem 3.3. *A recursive rule subject to the restrictions above is uniformly bounded iff the weight of every cycle in the corresponding α-graph (or equivalently the 0th VP subgraph) is zero. If it is uniformly bounded then the bound is equal to the maximum weight of any partial path minus one.*

By examining its proof we have the following corollaries:

Corollary 3.3.1. *If a linear recursive rule is uniformly bounded with bound I according to Theorem 3.3, then there is a containment mapping from the Ith expansion to any ith ($i > I$) expansion of this rule.*

Corollary 3.3.2. *For a uniformly bounded linear recursive rule with bound I, the recursive relation is fully specified by the 0th, 1st, ..., Ith expansions.*

Example 3.1: Consider the following linear recursive rule.

```
r(X1a,X1b,X2a,X3a) :- r(X1b,X1c,X2b,X3b),p1(X1c,X2b),p2(X2a,X3b),
        p3(X3a,X1a),q(X2a).                                        (5)
```

Its 0th VP subgraph is shown in Figure 2. It has only one cycle whose weight is zero and the maximum weight of any path is 2. Thus, it is uniformly bounded with bound 1. □

The following theorem[4] is for rules corresponding to isolated degenerate cycles.

Theorem 3.4. *A rule corresponding to an isolated degenerate cycle is uniformly bounded. If the cycle's weight is w, then the $(w-1)$th expansion is redundant and the bound is $w-2$. Its expansions are periodic with period w.*

Example 3.2: The following linear recursive rule (Figure 3)

```
r(X1,X2,X3) :- r(X2,X3,X1).                                        (6)
```

is uniformly bounded with bound 1. □

A 0th VP subgraph may have several components, e.g., Figure 1a or the following example.

Example 3.3: The 0th VP subgraph for the following rule (Figure 4)

```
r(X1,X2,Y1,Y2,Y3) :- r(X2,X1,Y2,Y3,Y1).                            (7)
```

has two isolated degenerate cycles of weight 2 and 3, respectively. □

If a 0th VP subgraph has several components, then the recursive relation may be regarded as the Cartesian product of several subrelations. Using Theorem 3.4 and Corollary 3.3.1, we can prove the following theorem:

† The bound given in[9] is in fact one higher than the bound used here. This is because the value of the bound there is defined as the order of the first redundant expansion.

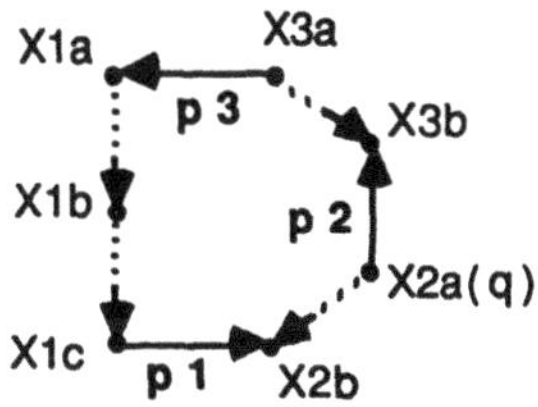

Figure 2. The 0th VP subgraph for rule (5).

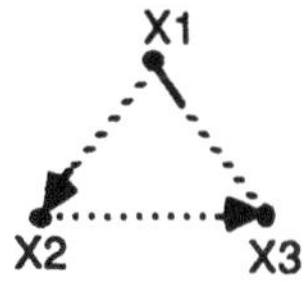

Figure 3. The 0th VP subgraph for rule (6).

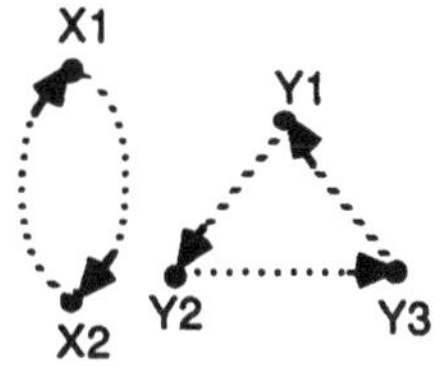

Figure 4. The 0th VP subgraph for rule (7).

Theorem 3.5. *If the 0th VP subgraph of a linear recursive rule consists of isolated degenerate cycles with weights* $w_1, w_2, \ldots$ *and components which satisfy the premises of Theorem 3.3 and they are bounded with bounds* $b_1, b_2, \ldots$, *then the uniform bound is* $lcm(\bigcup_i w_i) - 1 + \max_i(\bigcup_i b_i)$, *where lcm means the least common multiplier.*

For example, rule (2) is bounded with bound 2. Rule (7) of Example 3.3 is bounded with bound 5.

4. The Predicate-Goal Graph and Recursive Query Processing

The *predicate-goal (PG) graph*[3] is derived from the VP graph. One VP subgraph is converted to a PG subgraph of the corresponding order. For convenience, we put nodes corresponding to distinguished variables on the top of a subgraph and call them *top nodes* and arrange them from left to right corresponding to their sequential order in the head predicate. We put nodes corresponding to recursive variables on the bottom of a subgraph and call them *bottom nodes* and arrange them accordingly. We then draw I-edges (for initialization conditions) by connecting adjacent bottom nodes using broken lines and A-edges (for answers) by connecting adjacent top nodes using broken lines. Finally, we delete all R-edges. Figures 5 & 6 are the first few PG subgraphs for rules (2) & (5), respectively.

Definitions: A walk of purely E-edges forms an *E-chain*. A single E-edge is *satisfied* if a fact from the EDB matches this E-edge and instantiates (or agrees with) its two end nodes. An E-chain is *satisfied* if a set of tuples from the EDB satisfies consistently all its E-edges. In a PG subgraph, instantiated top nodes form a *top tuple* and instantiated bottom nodes form a *bottom tuple*.

If all nodes of a subgraph have been instantiated, then these values constitute a *subgraph instance*. A PG subgraph is *satisfiable* if (1) the bottom tuple is in the IC relation, (2) the top tuple agrees with constraints, if any, in the query, and (3) there exists at least one subgraph instance such that all E-edges can be consistently satisfied by the EDB.

The PG graph is related to recursive query processing by the following interpretation: *If there exists an answer to a recursive query, then there is a PG subgraph which can produce this answer. If a PG subgraph is satisfiable, then the obtained top tuples are answers to the recursive query.* Thus, recursive query processing can be accomplished by matching PG subgraphs.

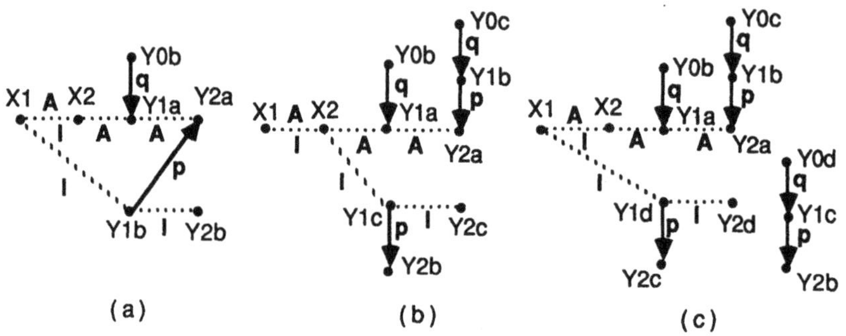

Figure 5. The 0th (a), 1st (b) and 2nd (c) PG subgraphs for rule (2).

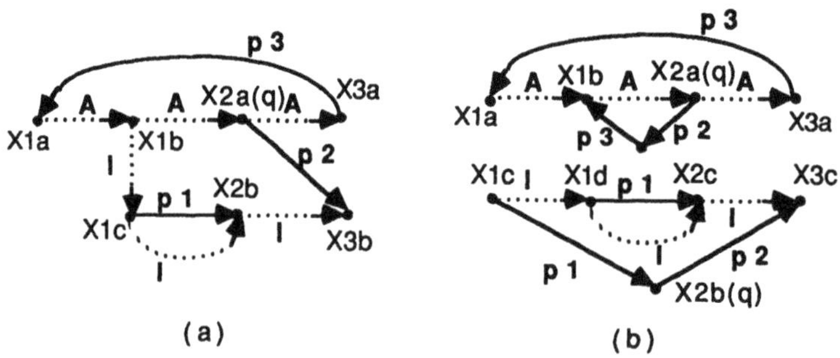

Figure 6. The 0th (a) and 1st (b) PG subgraphs for rule (5).

The recursive relation can be obtained by a simple bottom-up evaluation based on expansions or PG subgraphs. First, the recursive relation is initialized by the IC relation. Iteration is carried out in ascending order of expansions. We evaluate a relation for the expansion body by Algorithm 3.1[16] using the IC relation for the recursive predicate. The obtained relation is projected onto the distinguished variables. This gives a set of (top) tuples, which forms a fraction of recursive relation. The newly obtained fraction is then compared with the current value of the recursive relation. If this fraction is fully contained by the current recursive relation, then query evaluation stops. Otherwise, the union of the fraction and the current recursive relation becomes the new recursive relation. Iteration continues until a fixed point is reached. Finally, constraints (such as constants) in queries are used to restrict the recursive relation to obtain answers. Note that the evaluation order of Algorithm 3.1 is from left to right as in Prolog. The use of PG graphs allows us to satisfy edges in arbitrary order. This will be used in the next section for query optimization.

This bottom-up evaluation is slightly different from naive evaluation or semi-naive evaluation[16]. We refer to all these as basic bottom-up evaluations.

5. Query Optimization

In this section, the following topics are addressed in order: (a) termination, (b) isolated degenerate cycles, (c) sideways information passing, (d) set-of-values approach, (e) factorization, (f) differentiation and other fine tunings.

The cost of a query evaluation consists mainly of five parts:

(C1) the cost of rewriting the program, if any,

(C2) the access cost to the EDB,

(C3) the cost of operations performed in main memory, such as selection, etc.,

(C4) the cost of operations on generated tuples and values,

(C5) the cost of termination tests.

As in relational databases[16], the computational cost is assumed to be dominated by the block access time to secondary memory. Normally, (C2), (C4), and (C5) dominate. The size of generated tuples is often large and stored in secondary memory. This size is critical to the total cost. The smaller this size, the less (C4) and (C5). Reduction of this size also reduces (C2) and (C3) in future iteration steps. Thus, the size of generated tuples is often used as the metric of costs.

In basic bottom-up evaluations, (C5) is often significant because we need to compare the newly obtained fraction with the current value of recursive relation. For a program composed of a recursive rule of bound I, we can use a counter to limit iteration steps or, equivalently, consider only the first $(I+1)$ subgraphs. Thus, (C5) becomes negligible. This optimization is applicable to any bottom-up evaluation or top-down evaluation. Termination based on uniform bounds also saves us from evaluating the $(I+1)$th expansion, thus, reducing (C2), (C3) and (C4) as well.

To use uniform bounds for termination, we have to test uniform boundedness and determine uniform bounds. This requires additional computation. For Theorem 3.3, an algorithm linear in the size of the rule is known[9]. Theorem 3.4 is simple and linear algorithms are available. We should note that the size of a rule is normally very small in comparison with the whole program. Moreover, these calculations can be done in compilation so that (C1) does not contribute to the run-time cost.

A 0th VP subgraph may be an isolated degenerate cycle. The corresponding recursive relation is easy to obtain. It is the closure under cyclic permutation and consists of the IC relation and its cyclic permutations. The number of cyclic permutations required to obtain all independent tuples of the recursive relation is equal to the uniform bound of the recursive rule (given by Theorem 3.4).

Consider a query with some constants. Because of the bindings a tuple of the recursive relation is not necessarily an answer. A basic bottom-up evaluation still derives all tuples regardless whether they are relevant to the query. An argument in the query corresponds to a top node. It seems that we can first instantiate the corresponding top nodes by constants in the query so that only answers are generated. But termination tests require the whole recursive relation not just the fraction restricted by the query. Because here we consider only uniformly bounded recursive programs, termination is not a problem. We can instantiate the corresponding top nodes before satisfy the remaining subgraph. This may be regarded as a type of SIPS. Algorithm 1 below outlines a query evaluation.

Algorithm 1.

(1) determine the uniform bound I;
(2) obtain the 0, 1, ..., Ith PG subgraphs;
(3) **for** $i = 0$ to I **do begin**
(4) instantiate the top nodes corresponding to constants in query;
(5) satisfy E-edges and I-edges;
(6) project the obtained top tuples (extract answers);
(7) **end**

Tuples in the recursive relation generated by Algorithm 1 are answers. Answers must be relevant. In the first approximation of cost analysis (the size of generated tuples as the metric), Algorithm 1 is the most efficient method for applicable programs. In particular, it is more efficient than magic sets method.

Proposition 5.1. *For uniformly bounded recursive programs considered, Algorithm 1 is the most efficient algorithm if the size of generated tuples is used as the metric.*

If generated tuples are to be processed further in query evaluation, for example, in query ?- r(a,X,Y,b),s(X,c), where s is some EDB predicate, then it is advantageous to factor the generated relation into subrelations. Ignoring A-edges and I-edges, E-edges partition nodes of a PG subgraph into components so that nodes in the same component are connected by a path of E-edges (disregard the arrows as in section 2 for VP subgraphs). These components in turn may partition the top nodes into groups. Each group forms a subrelation of the recursive relation. Given an IC tuple and a PG subgraph, we can obtain these subrelations. From the meaning of PG subgraphs, the fraction of the recursive relation due to this IC tuple and PG subgraph is the Cartesian product of the above obtained subrelations. This *factors* a relation into subrelations. For example, in Figure 6b the recursive relation (X1a,X1b,X2a,X3a) may be factored into (X1b,X2a) and (X1a,X3a) two subrelations. Factorization may reduce the size of a relation drastically. Factorization may be also applied to transient non-recursive relations.

Further reduction of costs in (C2) and (C4) is possible. Note that the details of step 5 in Algorithm 1 are not specified. For example, we consider Figure 6(b) for an adorned query r^{bbff}. First, X1a and X1b are instantiated by constants in the query. Suppose we now satisfy the E-chain p1(X1c,X2b),q(X2b),p2(X2b,X3c) and the EDB is p1(a1,b1), p1(a1,b2), p1(a2,b2), q(b1), q(b2), p2(b1,c1), p2(b1,c2), p2(b2,c3), p2(b2,c2). We may satisfy p1(X1c,X2b) by the first tuple followed by satisfying q(X2b) and p2(X2b,X3c) with X2b=b1. Then, we backtrack and satisfy p1(X1c,X2b) by the second tuple and so on. Alternatively, we may obtain all tuples which satisfy p1(X1c,X2b), which results in a set of values for X2b with respect to each instantiation of X1c. Then, we satisfy q(X2b), p2(X2b,X3c). The first method considers one tuple at a time and is similar to Prolog while the second method uses sets of values and is related to joins in relational operations. The set-of-values approach minimizes (C2) and is more efficient.

There is another question on the evaluation order. For example, suppose we have an E-chain of edge p1, p2, p3, p4. Should we satisfy the edges in the order of p2, p4, p3, p1 or in some other order? We suggest the following heuristic. Choose the node which has the fewest possible values. Starting from this node, we satisfy E-edges in their natural sequential order in the E-chain. It is not trivial to compare different evaluation orders and this topic is left to future studies.

Results obtained for the ith subgraph may be used for evaluation of the $(i+1)$th subgraph. We call such a technique *differentiation*. For example, suppose we first satisfy the E-edge `p1(X1c,X2b)` in Figure 6a. We can use the obtained values for the first E-edge of the E-chain `p1(X1c,X2b),p2(X2b,X3c)` in Figure 6b. Differentiation is based on the relationship among E-chains of different subgraphs. Such relationships are studied by the *recursive (rule) structure*[8]. Another interesting related topic is on bindings of one variable to a set of constants such as in[10]. We can instantiate the corresponding top node by sets of values rather than a single constant. The detailed optimization techniques are related to the above, the order of evaluation of E-edges. These techniques are better studied in the context of unbounded programs and are left for the future. Note that in Figure 6a & 6b the two top nodes `X1a,X3a` are connected to nothing except for an E-chain `p3(X3a,X1a)` and this is the same for all higher-order subgraphs. These E-chains form a sequence called a *bounded E-chain sequence*. This is a special case of recursive structure. Once such an E-chain of the ith subgraph is satisfied, no more evaluation is required for E-chains in the bounded E-chain sequence in the jth $(j > i)$ subgraph.

In Figure 6b none of the top nodes is connected to a bottom node by an E-chain. This means that the particular values of the bottom nodes are irrelevant to the top tuples. Thus, there is no point to obtain various instantiations for the bottom nodes. As soon as we find that the bottom part of this PG subgraph can be satisfied for an IC tuple, we can stop processing the bottom part and concentrate on the top part of the PG subgraph. This is similar to the existential queries[15]. This can save the cost considerably if there are many potential ways to satisfy the bottom part.

6. Discussion and Conclusion

Since magic sets method[1,16] is applicable to general recursive programs, it is useful to compare it with the method proposed here in more detail. First, semi-naive evaluation normally is used to evaluate the rewritten program by magic sets method. We can replace termination tests in semi-naive evaluation by a simple counter. For a uniformly bounded recursive program with only one recursive rule, the rewritten program by magic sets often has more than one recursive relation. The new recursive relation is the magic relation. The magic relation is contained by the recursive relation. We can use the bound of the original recursive relation for the magic relation.

The advantage of magic sets is that it evaluates only "relevant" tuples. If the query has no bindings, then all tuples are answers. In the presence of bindings, tuples of the recursive relation may be divided into three categories: (1) answers, (2) relevant tuples which are not answers but must be used in order to derive some answers in future deductions, and (3) irrelevant tuples. The rewritten program by magic sets does not generate irrelevant tuples when evaluated by a basic bottom-up evaluation. But relevant tuples are not necessarily answers. Thus, if measured by the size of generated tuples, Algorithm 1 is at least as efficient as magic sets method because only tuples generated are answers. Algorithm 1 also saves termination costs. Detailed comparisons require more studies on factorization, differentiation and other techniques. The proposed method offers other advantages. Note that magic sets method requires one rewritten program for each different adornment format. The proposed method is applicable to arbitrary adorned queries.

Query optimization in this paper shows the close relationship of relational databases and deductive databases. Satisfying E-chains is equivalent to multiple joins in relational databases. Techniques used in relational databases, such as sorting, indexing, may be used for fine tunings. On the other hand, some techniques in deductive databases may be applied to relational databases. The idea is that query evaluation for relational database may be represented by a graph similar to a PG graph. Constants in a query may be used to facilitate query processing.

Let us consider now further research topics. Uniform boundedness has been studied in[12,9,13,14] and references therein. Generalization to arbitrary recursive rules is difficult. But some generalizations are known. The two subclasses considered in this paper do not allow constants and repeated variables in recursive rules. *A repeated variable* is a variable which appears in more than one argument position in the same predicate occurrence. Constants and repeated variables in a linear recursive rule may be removed from these rules[6].

We so far have considered only programs each having one single linear recursive rule. A program may have more than one recursive rule. Suppose all recursive rules, when considered independently, are uniformly bounded. The dependency graph[16] may be used to analyze such a program. If a self-loop of a dependency graph represents one and only one linear recursive rule, then the program is stratified and termination proposed in this paper and other optimization techniques are still applicable. A self-loop may represent several recursive rules, for example, a program may have rules (1), (2), and (5). We may still treat each recursive rule rather independently. However, it is not easy to prove this and we leave it to the future.

Many unbounded linear recursive rules have some bounded components in 0th VP subgraphs.

Example 6.1: Consider the following recursive rule:

$$\texttt{r(X1,X2,Y1a,Y2a)} :- \texttt{r(X2,X1,Y1b,Y2b),p1(Y1b,Y1a),p2(Y2b,Y2a).} \qquad (8)$$

Its 0th VP subgraph has one component of isolated degenerate cycle of weight two and two cycles each of weight one. Therefore, this rule is unbounded. We know how to handle the uniformly bounded component now. The recursive relation may be regarded as Cartesian product of three subrelations: (X1,X2), (Y1a), (Y2a). If we process each these subrelation independently and combine them together to give the recursive relation, we may reduce the overall cost. □

Study in this paper is useful to investigate these programs in the future.

In this paper, we study query optimization for some subclasses of linear recursive programs, Ioannidis' subclass[9] and isolated degenerate cycles[4]. These recursive programs are uniformly bounded, thus, termination of a query evaluation may be achieved by limiting the number of rule applications. (Termination based on uniform bounds has been proposed for Prolog evaluation[5].) SIPS are achieved in PG subgraphs. The PG graph is used also for factorization, differentiation and other query optimization techniques. Query optimization of deductive databases is closely related to query optimization of relational databases.

ACKNOWLEDGEMENT: I am grateful to James Harland for helpful discussions. Comments from anonymous referees motivate improvement on several technical points such as comparison with magic sets.

References:

1. F. Bancilhon, D. Maier, Y. Sagiv, and J.D. Ullman, "Magic sets and other strange ways to implement logic programs," *Proc. of Symp. on Principles of Database System*, pp.1–15, 1986.
2. P.A. Gardner and J.C. Shepherdson, "Unfold/fold transformations of logic programs," in *Computational Logic: Essays in Honor of Alan Robinson*, eds. J-L. Lassez and G.D. Plotkin, MIT Press, 1991.
3. J.L. Han, "Recursive query processing in predicate-goal graph," H. Kirchner and W. Wechler eds. *Lec. Notes in Comp. Sci.*, vol. **463**, Springer-Verlag, pp.247–261, 1990.
4. J.L. Han, "Uniform boundedness of linear recursive rules," in *Databases in the 1990s*, vol.**2**, B. Srinivasan and J. Zeleznikow eds., World Scientific Pub., pp.127–140, 1991.
5. J.L. Han, "Preventing infinite looping in Prolog," *Proc. of IEEE Intl. Conf. on Tools for Artificial Intelligence*, San Jose, CA, pp.524–525, 1991.
6. J.L. Han, "Handling constants and/or repeated variables in linear recursive programs, " in B. Srinivasan and J. Zeleznikow eds. *Research and Practical Issues in Databases*, World Scientific Pub. Singapore, pp.113–123, 1992.
7. J.L. Han, "On termination of single rule recursions in Prolog," *USQ Working Paper Series, IT-CS-9205*, July, 92.
8. J.L. Han and S-s. Chen, "Graphic representation of linear recursive rules, " *Intl. J. of Intelligent Systems*, vol.**7** pp.317-337, 1992.
9. Y. E. Ioannidis, "A time bound on the materialization of some recursively defined views," *Algorithmica* vol. **1**, pp.361–385, 1986. Also: "Bounded recursion in deductive databases," Technical Report UCB/ERL M85/6, UC Berkeley, February, 1985.
10. D. Kemp, K. Ramamohanarao and Z. Somogyi, "Right-, left-, and multi-linear rule transformations which maintain context information," *Proc. of 16th Intl. Conf. on Very Large Databases*, pp.380–391, 1990.
11. J.W. Lloyd, *Foundations of Logic Programming*, 2nd ed. Springer-Verlag, New York, 1987.
12. J. Minker and J. Nicolas, "On recursive axioms in deductive databases," *Information Systems* vol.**8** pp.1–13, 1983.
13. J. F. Naughton, "Data independent recursion in deductive databases," *J. Computer and System Sciences* vol.**38**, pp.259–289, 1989.
14. J.F. Naughton and Y. Sagiv, "A decidable class of bounded recursions," *Proc. of Symp. Principles of Database Systems*, San Diego, CA, pp.227–236, 1987.
15. R. Ramakrishnan, C. Beeri and R. Krishnamurthy, "Optimizing existential Datalog queries," *Proc. of Symp. on Principles of Database Systems*, pp.89–102, 1988.
16. J.D. Ullman, *Principles of Database and Knowledge-base Systems, vol.I & II*, Computer Science Press, Rockville, Md. 1988.

EARLY EXPERIENCE WITH RECURSION OPTIMIZATION IN AN EXTENSIBLE REWRITER*

Jérôme Fessy and Béatrice Finance
University of Paris VI
MASI-CNRS Laboratory
45 Avenue des Etats-Unis
78 000 Versailles FRANCE

fessy@masi.ibp.fr, finance@masi.ibp.fr

ABSTRACT

Query optimizers transform user submitted queries into a canonical form and then translate the canonical form into an efficient access plan. The first step of query optimization is known as query rewriting. To deal with the complexity of query rewriting and/or query planning, extensible optimizers based on a rule approach have been proposed. The diversity of the tasks that should be integrated in a query rewriter makes it one of the most complex components to write in a DBMS. In particular, the integration of recursion optimization techniques has been often presented as an open issue. This paper describes the integration of recursion optimization techniques as rewriting rules. A global strategy shows how specific and traditional optimization rules interact and how recursion optimization can be improved. The efficiency and the termination of the optimization process are shown. A prototype of the rewriter is operational and has been demonstrated in the EDS ESPRIT project.

1. Introduction

Query optimization in relational systems extended with abstract data types, object oriented systems and deductive systems is a key issue in current database research. To deal with the complexity of query rewriting and/or query planning and with the new system requirements, extensible optimizers have been proposed [8,11,13,6]. The key idea is to generate a query optimizer from rules for transforming plans into alternative plans. Traditionally, query optimization translates a high level user query into an efficient plan for accessing the database. Query optimization can be divided in two phases [13]: query rewriting transforms queries into equivalent simpler ones with better expected performance and query planning primarily determines the method for accessing objects.

The diversity of the tasks that should be integrated in a query rewriter makes it one of the most complex components to write in a DBMS. To cope with this complexity, extensible optimizers have been proposed, among them the EXODUS optimizer [11] and the STARBURST rewriter [13]. They have demonstrated that the rule-based approach to query rewriting assures flexibility and extensibility [12].

However, the integration of recursion in an extensible rewriter is yet a problem. Several distinct methods have been proposed [1,3,20,21,22,23]. However, they essentially remain on paper and all their potentialities have not been extensively used in a real

* This research is supported by the EDS ESPRIT project (EP 2025).

optimizer. Indeed, only STARBURST proposes a concrete solution. It integrates an extension of the Magic Sets method [17]. However, it neither uses all the possibilities offered by other recursion optimization methods, nor proposed to solve the problem of the interaction between recursion optimization rules and traditional ones.

In this paper, we focus on recursive query optimizations in a query rewriting phase. We propose to integrate the Agrawal and Devanbu method [1] and the Magic Sets method [3]. They are chosen for their capacity to cover a wide applicability domain and for their well-known properties. We show that they can be integrated in an extensible rewriter as rewriting rules. A global strategy is introduced to show how specific and traditional optimization rules interact and how recursion optimization can be improved. The efficiency and the termination of the optimization process are demonstrated. A first version of the query rewriter for the EDS parallel database server [16] is operational and has been demonstrated in the EDS ESPRIT project. It has been written in C^{++}.

The organization of this paper is as follows. In Section 2, an overview of the EDS extensible rewriter (also called the logical optimizer) is presented. The Section 3 describes the integration of recursive queries optimization in the extensible optimizer. The Section 4 points out the problem of the optimization strategy whereas the Section 5 focus on the recursion optimization strategy. Finally, we conclude.

2. Context

The EDS server is an extended relational parallel database server developed as part of the EDS ESPRIT project. The server manages relations with simple or complex objects or values. The server query language integrates the essential concepts of relational, object-oriented and deductive databases. Therefore, the optimizer has to deal with complex queries composed of a large number of sub-queries derived from rules.

In this section, we briefly describe the source and target languages of the extensible rewriter. Next, we define the architecture and the main functionalities supported by the EDS query rewriter.

2.1. The source language

The EDS database server uses an extended SQL (ESQL [10]) as a query language, which is the source language of the query rewriter. The main advantages provided by ESQL over SQL are strong support for abstract data types, complex objects with object sharing, and a deductive capability to infer new data from stored data [10]. The deductive capability is provided through an extension of the SQL view mechanism. Hence, ESQL equals the power of the DATALOG logic-based language using statements already available in SQL.

The view in Figure 1 is recursive. It defines the rapidly reachable french town (RRFT). The query in Figure 1 gives the list of towns connected to Lyon by a motorway.

```
CREATE VIEW RRFT (from, to) A S
      ( SELECT *
        FROM Motorway
        WHERE country= "France"
      UNION
        SELECT Motorway.from, RRFT.to
        FROM RRFT, Motorway
        WHERE Motorway.to = RRFT.from
        AND country = "France"

      SELECT *
      FROM RRFT
      WHERE RRFT.to = "Lyon"
```

Figure 1 : A recursive view and an associated query.

2.2. The target language

The target language of the query optimizer is an extended form of relational algebra, called LERA. This language has been chosen for its power of abstraction from the physical implementation and from the query. LERA operators can easily represent ESQL queries.

The basic operations of our algebra are slight extensions of Codd's algebra, as defined for example in [9]. Complex objects support is provided in LERA by the generalization of the relational operators (restriction, projection, and join). Mainly, built-in and user defined function symbols can now appear in the criterion of a restriction, of a join and in the attribute list of a projection.

Recursive views are expressed by a fixpoint operator as shown in [25,4,14]. This operator simply produces the saturation of a relation computed recursively by an algebra expression. For example, we give in the Figure 2 the internal representation of the query given in the Figure 1.

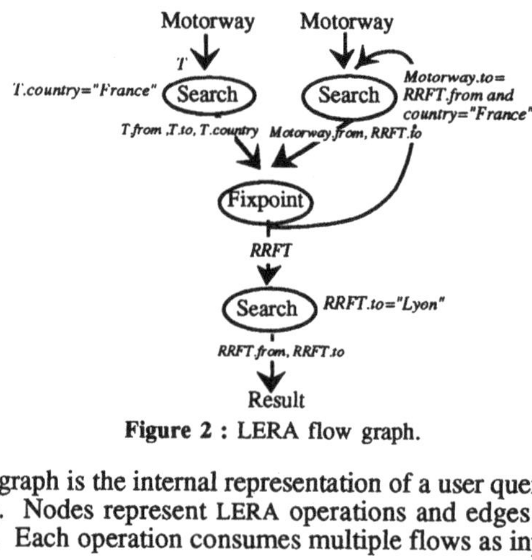

Figure 2 : LERA flow graph.

A LERA flow graph is the internal representation of a user query for query rewriting and query planning. Nodes represent LERA operations and edges represent data flows between operations. Each operation consumes multiple flows as input and produces one flow as output. Each data flow can be consumed by one or more operations. In the later case, data flows are duplicated.

Sometimes, sequences of basic operators can be implemented more efficiently as higher-level compound operators (e.g., filter followed by project). We define the following compound operations : n-ary union (denoted **union**, which performs the union of N relations), n-ary join (denoted **join***, which performs the cartesian product of N relations followed by a filtering), and a compound operation of both projection, restriction and n-ary join (denoted **search**).

These compound operators are closed to tuple calculus expressions and provide the system with the necessary degrees of freedom to logically, and later physically, optimize queries. Tuple calculus is a good starting point for query optimization since it provides an optimizer with the basic properties of queries only. In particular, it avoids that optimization opportunities may become hidden in a particular sequence of algebra operators like projection, restriction, join [15].

2.3. The Extensible Rewriter

In [6], we have proposed an extensible query rewriter based on rule approach. The rewriter takes as input a LERA flow graph generated by the ESQL parser and transforms it into a logically optimized one. The control and the knowledge of the rewriter are separated in order to offer the needed extensibility.

A rule language based on term rewriting has been used to unify the various aspects of query rewrite [7]. Rules are independent and consistent, i.e. they do not produce an incoherent LERA flow graph. A control language has been used to define the strategy that specifies in which order optimization rules must be applied.

As an ESQL query may contain recursive and non-recursive parts, traditional optimizations and recursion optimization techniques should be integrated in the rewriter. In a previous paper [6], SQL optimization rules have been defined. These rules perform aggregate and sub-query transformation, useless operator elimination, merging and permutation of operations (including pushing selection before recursion).

In this paper, we focus on the integration of recursion optimization techniques as rewriting rules on the one hand, and on the control of the optimization process on the other hand.

3. Recursion Optimization Rules

Recursive query support is a new database system functionality. To be able to efficiently answer to these queries, optimizers have to take into account the recursion optimization. In the literature, different methods are proposed. Their integration in an extensible optimizer is a delicate problem. In this section, we show how this problem has been solved in the EDS logical optimizer.

3.1. Recursion Optimization Methods as Graph Rewriting Techniques

The rewriter simplifies the query form by applying transformations. These transformations are LERA graph rewritings. Hence, in order to be integrated in the rewriter, recursion optimization methods must be shown as graph rewriting methods.

Among the set of recursion optimization methods proposed in the literature, two of them have been chosen and integrated in the rewriter : the Magic Set and Agrawal&Devanbu methods. In the following, we describe the two techniques as query graph rewritings.

• Agrawal&Devanbu Rewriting

The Agrawal&Devanbu method [1] is very simple and well adapted to a rewrite process since the transformation process is simply based on algebraic permutations of operators. It is an extension of the method of the pioneers Aho and Ullman [23]. Indeed, the Agrawal&Devanbu method is not only applied on strongly linear recursions but also on linear ones. It aims at pushing query constraints through the recursion.

On a query graph flow, it first consists in isolating a sub-set of query qualification which can be propagated. This sub-set is then moved to the recursion initialization predicates. The figure 3 illustrates this rewriting mechanism on the Motorway example of the Figure 2. On this example, the whole "Search" qualification (RRFT.to='Lyon') is pushed on the graph flow corresponding to the recursion initialization.

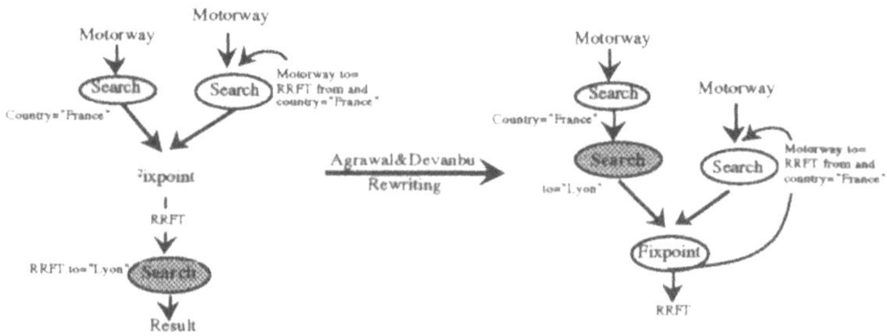

Figure 3 : Agrawal&Devanbu graph rewriting

• Magic Set Rewriting

Magic Set is a well-known and robuste technique [2,3,17]. It is always defined on DATALOG programs. It is a rewriting method that simulates backward chaining. The rewrite can be very complex. It can be applied to any kind of recursion and it is able to propagate complex criteria through the recursion [18].

Two solutions are available to implement Magic Set transformation. The first one is indirect. The query graph is first transformed into its associated Datalog program. Then, the Datalog program is optimized by Magic Set, and finally transformed again into the equivalent LERA flow graph. The second solution is to directly transform the original graph but this is no easy process. However, it should be done for efficiency reasons. For convenience reason and without loss of generality, the basic Magic Set transformation [2] is applied rather than Supplementary Magic Set [3] or Magic Set specialization [19] ones.

In order to facilitate the comprehension of the query graph transformation, we remind in the Figure 4 the optimized DATALOG program. In the Figure 5, we give the LERA flow graph corresponding to the DATALOG program of the Figure 4.

```
RRFT(x, y)    <- Motorway(x, y, 'France')
RRFT(x,y)     <- Motorway(x,z,'France'), RRFT(z,y)
query : ?RRFT(x, 'Lyon')
                              ⇓
Magic_fb(Lyon)
Magic_fb(y), Motorway(x, y,'France' )      -> Magic_bb(z,y)
Magic_bb(x,y), Motorway(x, z,'France' )    -> Magic_bb(z,y)
Magic_bb(x,y), Motorway(x, y,'France' )    -> RRFT_bb(x,y)
Magic_fb(y), Motorway(x, y,'France' )      -> RRFT_fb(x,y)
Magic_fb(y), Motorway(x, y,'France' ), RRFT_bb(z,y)     -> RRFT_fb(x,y)
Magic_bb(x,y), Motorway(x, z,'France' ), RRFT_bb(z,y)   -> RRFT_bb(x,y)
```

Figure 4 : Magic Set Optimization on Datalog

The graph rewriting is based on three steps : (1) the Magic Set initialization, (2) the Magic Set generation and (3) the solution generation. Each step is separately performed and produces its own sub-graph corresponding to the shaded boxes in the Figure 5. These three sub-graphs are merged together to build the optimized result graph. The details of this automatic rewriting mechanism are given in [5].

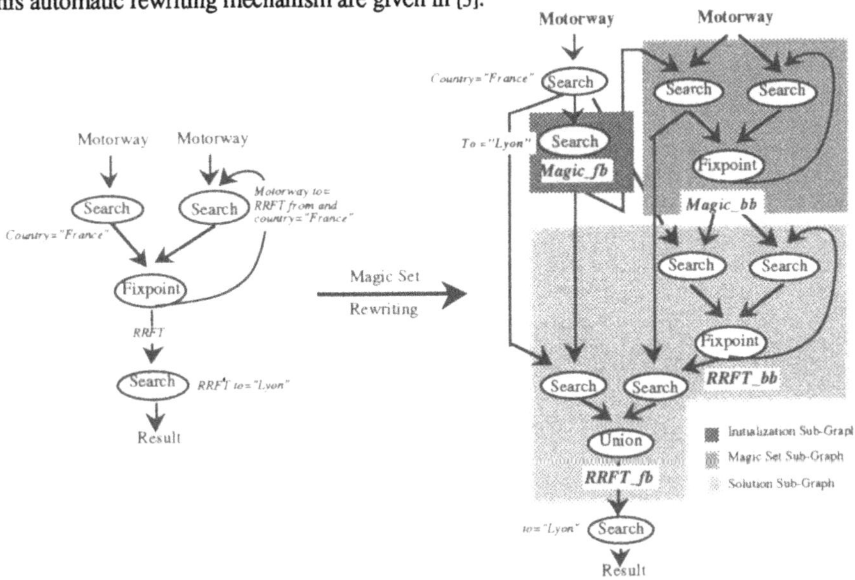

Figure 5 : Direct graph Rewriting of Magic Set

3.2. Recursion Optimization Improvements

For specifying a rewriter, a rule-based approach is powerful because it provides a global view of the recursion optimization process. A global view permits two main improvements of the recursion optimization process.

First, the recursion optimization of Magic Set depends on the ordering of the query definition because the rewriting technique is based on the notion of Sideway Information Pasing (SIP) [24]. If a bad SIP is chosen, the transformed query may be worse than the original onc. Our improvement is to define a canonical form of a cycle that gives a global view of all possible SIPs. For example, the Figure 6 defines the canonical form of the cycle. It mainly consists in deleting the order of operations introduced by the user.

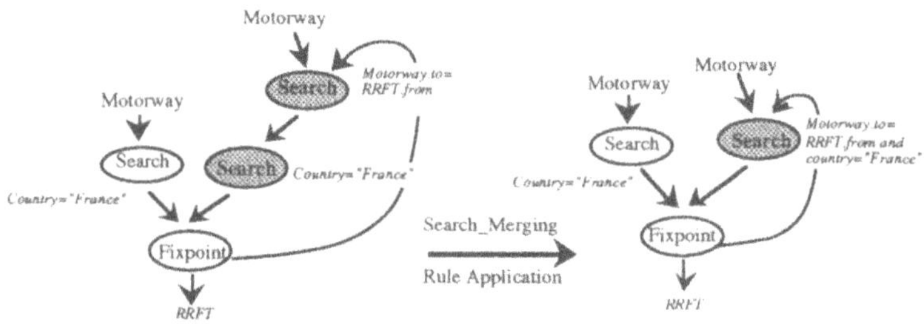

Figure 6 : Cycle Canonical Form

In this example, Search merging rule is applied before the Magic Set one. This transformation is interesting since it offers a higher number of sideway information passing strategies as many constraints are merged together in order to induce the best assignment.

Second, most existing techniques try to propagate constraints through a cycle, but they never take into account redundant calculus in a cycle. For example in the previous figure, the french motorways are evaluated at each step. However, this intermediate result is invariant in the cycle and therefore should be computed only once. To achieve this improvement, we have introduced in our rewriter a rule for extracting invariants. The effect of this rule upon the graph of Figure 6 is depicted in the Figure 7.

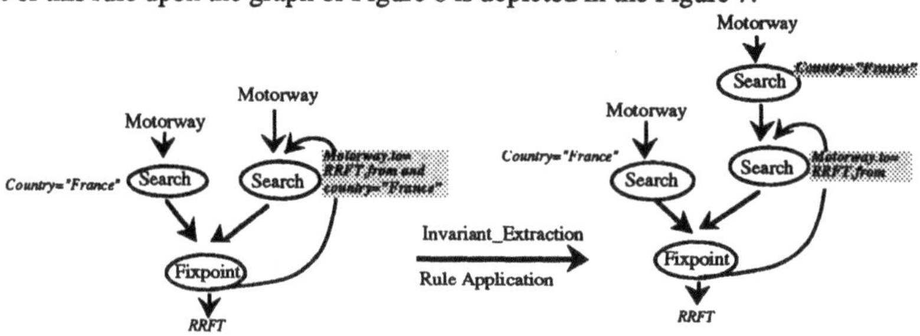

Figure 7 : Invariant Extraction Rule

4. Optimization Strategy

Traditionally in the literature, rewriter designers focus on rule definition and very little on the strategy. Rules concern local optimizations whereas the strategy concerns the global optimization. Rewrite rules perform complex transformations on the query graph. The importance of the strategy is to ensure the efficiency and the termination of the rewrite process. The strategy determines what rule to apply and when, since at any point of the rewrite process, several rules may be eligible to fire. To define a strategy supposes to follow an adequate methodology and to have a language to control the ordering of rules. Our methodology and control language are introduced hereafter.

4.1. Rule Control Language

A strategy consists in three steps : match, select and apply. The first one determines the conflict set. The conflict set defines all firable rules on the query. Then, the second one chooses one rule in the conflict set. Finally, the selected rule is applied. There are mainly two strategies to select a rule in a conflict set: based on priorities or randomly. Therefore, we define two basic constructors that allow the database implementor to define blocks of rules which are run up to a certain limit.

The **Block** constructor corresponds to a random strategy. The syntax to define a Block is :

Block({rules}, credit)

The set of rules specifies the rules which are in the block. The credit is a maximum number of rule application trials. Each time a rule of the conflict set is randomly chosen and evaluated, the credit of the block is decreased by one. Infinite credit means application up to saturation. A block is totally evaluated when the credit reaches zero or if there are no more rules in the conflict set.

The **Seq** constructor corresponds to the rule priority strategy. The syntax to define a Seq is :

Seq((rule), credit)

The list of rules specifies the rule ordering of the sequence according to the rule priority. This strategy can be executed more efficiently than the previous one. Indeed, as each rule is evaluated according to its list ordering, it is not necessary to compute the whole conflict set. It simply contains the first firable rule. Each time a rule is applied, the credit of the sequence is decreased by one. A Seq is totally evaluated when the credit reaches zero or if no more rules in the list are firable.

These two basic strategies can be combined in order to produce more complex strategies. Another constructor has been introduced to allow the database implementor to chain multiple strategies. The Prog constructor corresponds to a serie of basic or complex strategies. The syntax to define a **Prog** is :

Prog ((Prog / Block / Seq), credit)

The list of strategies are evaluated in sequence. When a strategy has been totally evaluated, then the next one is performed. The credit is decreased by one when the last strategy is achieved. A program is totally evaluated when the credit reaches zero or if all strategies of the list are totally evaluated.

4.2. Strategy Definition Methodology

To define a strategy is difficult because of the many parameters that should be taken into consideration. To solve that complexity, we propose a three-step methodology.

First, it is important to identify what is the best output plan for the rewriter. As many solutions exist, heuristics are used to reduce the search space. Generally, they lead to isolate an appropriate subset of rules of the library. For example, the most widely-used heuristic is to push projection and restriction as much as possible on base relations and to produce a canonical form which is a good starting point for physical optimization.

Second, it is important that the transformation process reaches the best solution in regards of heuristics. To ensure this is difficult because the database implementor should take into account all possible interactions between rules. He or she should state the importance of the order of rule firing upon the produced solution and accordingly organize rules using constructors of the control language. It is interesting to note that if the rule system is noetherian, controlling the firing of rules is unnecessary because it leads to a unique canonical form.

Third, among all strategies that satisfy the previous points, the database implementor must choose the most efficient one, i.e. the one which minimizes the number of rules that are to be fired. For example, if two operations are mergeable, then the pushdown of the predicate from one to the other is wasteful since operations will be merged anyway. Rule priority is introduced to solve this problem: search merging rules are given higher priority than pushdown rules.

5. Recursion Optimization Strategy

Following the methodology introduced above, to define a strategy for cyclic queries introduces delicate problems of its own. In the following, we first review these problems that affect both correctness and performance. Then, we propose a global strategy that works and makes the optimization process efficient even in presence of recursion.

5.1. Recursion Complexity

The specific characteristics of recursion optimization rules and their interaction with existing rules in a rewriter raise several problems.

First, the termination guarantee is compromised since the Magic Set rule is always applicable. As it is shown in the Figure 5, although the constraints are propagated through the cycle, it is necessary to keep the initial constraints after the fixpoint. Moreover, several applications of Magic Set on the same cycle does not produce much more optimization than only one [5].

This leads to a paradox in a rule-based rewriter. The Magic Set transformation has to be applied only once per cycle of the query. However, such an application means that the Magic_Set rule should be applied up to saturation on each cycle. The two ways to solve this paradox are to define a context associated with each Fixpoint on the one hand, or on the other hand to use a synonym of the Fixpoint. We advocate the last one since it is more appropriate for a rewriter. It is by definition a rewrite process since a fixpoint operator can be rewrite by a semantically equivalent Syn_fixpoint operator. Doing this rewriting, the rule can only be applied once since unification is based on syntactic recognition.

Another aspect that compromises the termination guarantee is the existence of idempotent rules. For example, the invariant extraction rule breaks Search operators and the Search merging rules does the opposite. The only way to solve this problem is through an adequate strategy. The database implementor must guarantee the termination process by using separated blocks or fixing an execution limit.

Second, if for non-recursive queries, the set of rewrite rules produces a unique canonical form, this is not the case in presence of the Magic Set rule. Indeed, as it should be applied only once on a cycle, all the constraints that should be propagated through the cycle must be known before that rule is applied. Therefore, it is important to control the way rules are applied on each part of the graph.

The control depends on data flows and should be applied from the query root to base relations. There is a simple way to express a LERA operator ordering in the rewriter. It consists in ordering the database facts. This ordering is transparently achieved by the rewriter run-time that manages the fact database, therefore the database implementor only adds or deletes facts regardless of ordering constraints.

Third, recursion optimization is a recent research topic that lacks maturity. For example, there is no result concerning the quality of optimization based Agrawal&Devanbu

method or the Magic Set one. This is a real problem since the optimizer must choose only one alternative. However, in the current state of the art, neither a logical nor a physical optimizer can make this choice because both methods cover different applicability domain.

One way to solve the problem is to define some heuristics that lead to contextually privilege one method over the other. We hope that further researches will conduct to improve them.

5.2. The Global Strategy

The global strategy of our rewriter must satisfy the basic heuristic that aims at pushing as much as possible constraints on base relations and must guarantee the termination of the rewrite process.

In order to propagate as much as possible constraints through a fixpoint operator, it is necessary to group the set of constraints before the cycle. This is efficiently done by first using simplification and merging rules, then traditional permutation rules.

Moreover, as recursion optimization rules are applied on each part of the graph in a controlled way, constraints are correctly propagated on each fixpoint operator since once the constraints are pushed through a fixpoint operator, then simplication and merging rules are applied again.

The process terminates since there is no more fixpoint operator to optimize, and simplification, merging and permutation rules are no more firable. Once all constraints have been propagated, invariant extraction can be achieved. The Figure 8 presents a possible global strategy which subsumes the previous explanations[1] .

```
STRATEGY =
    Prog ((   Prog  ((
                        Seq ((    Simplification_rules, Merging_rules,
                                  Traditionnal_permutation_rules), ∞ ),
                        Seq  ((    Agrawal&Devanbu_rule, Magic_Set_rule), 1)),
                        ∞ ),
              Seq  (( Invariant_extraction_rule), ∞ )),
         1).
```

Figure 8 : EDS Rewriter Global Strategy

As simplification, merging and traditional permutation rules have a "noetherian" property, they can be grouped in a block. Furthermore, for efficiency reasons it is better to define priority ordering. Identically, we define a priority between Agrawal&Devanbu and Magic Set rules. The Agrawal&Devanbu rule is favorized as it is more closer to a rewrite process. Priorities between these rules are defined owing to the Seq constructor.

This global strategy shows that the rule control language is powerful enough to support complex optimization strategies.

[1] For convenience reasons, the terms 'Simplification_rules', 'Merging_rules' and 'Traditional_permutation_rules' are used in the strategy to explain the set of associated rules.

6. Conclusion

One key aspect of query optimization is the control strategy which determines what rule to apply and when. If a rule-based rewriter simplifies the integration of new rules, their integration in the control strategy is not done so easily. So the extensibility of a rewriter should not only consist in easily adding new rules. They should be easily integrated into the control strategy which must control all their interactions.

This paper presented the integration of recursion optimization techniques in the extensible EDS query rewriter. It is (to our knowledge) the first paper that gives a global view of this problem. The integration of the Agrawal&Devanbu and Magic Set methods as independent optimization rules has been presented. A rule control language has been introduced to support complex optimization strategies. It garantees the extensibility of the control strategy. An example of a global strategy has been presented. It shows how the interaction of specific and traditional optimization rules can be controled and how recursion optimization can be improved. The efficiency and the termination of the optimization process are demonstrated. An operational rewriter prototype has been developped in the EDS ESPRIT project. More work is needed to improve recursion optimization heuristics.

7. References

[1] Agrawal.R, Devanbu.P :*"Moving Selections into Linear Least Fixpoint Queries"*, In the Proc. of the 4th Int. Conf. on Data Engineering, Los Angeles, 1988.

[2] Bancilhon F., Maier D., Sagiv Y., Ullman J.D.:*"Magic Sets and other strange ways to implement logic programs"*, In the proc. of the 5th ACM Symp. on Principles of Database Systems, Cambridge, 1986.

[3] Beeri C., Ramakrishnan R.: *"On the Power of Magic"*, In the Proc.of the 6th ACM SIGACT-SIGMOD-SIGART Symp. on Principles of Database Systems (PODS), San Diego, 1987.

[4] Ceri S., Gottlob G., Lavazza L.:*"Translation and Optimization of Logic Queries : the Algebraic Approach"*, In the proc. of the int. Conf. on Very Large Database (VLDB), Kyoto, 1986.

[5] Fessy J., Cartaux X.:"Optimisations de Requêtes Récursives par le Méthode Magic Set", Internal Rapport, University of Paris6, 1990.

[6] Finance B., Gardarin G.:*"A rule-Based Query Rewriter in an Extensible DBMS"*, In Proc. of the 17th Int. Conf. on Data Engineering, Kobe, Japan, 1991.

[7] Finance.B:*"Une PLate-forme pour la Génération d'Optimiseurs Extensibles"*, PD Thesis MASI Lobaratory, University of Paris 6, 1992.

[8] Freytag J.C.:*"A Rule-Based View of Query Optimization"*, In the proc. of the ACM SIGMOD, San-Fransisco, 1987.

[9] Gardarin G, Valduriez P:*"Relational Databases and Knowledge Bases"*, Book, Add-Wesley, 1989.

[10] Gardarin G., Valduriez P.:*"ESQL : An Extended SQL with Object and Deductive Capabilities"*, In the Proc. of the Int. Conf. on Database and Expert System Applications, Vienna, Austria, 1990.

[11] Graefe G., Dewitt D.:*"The EXODUS Optimizer Generator"*, In the ACM-SIGMOD. Proc. USA, 1987.

[12] Haas L.M., Chang W., Lohman G.M., McPherson J., Wilms P.F., Lapis G., Lindsay B., Pirahesh H., Carey M.J., E. Shekita E.:*"Starburst Mid-Flight: As the Dust Clears"*, IEEE Transactions on Knowledge and Data Engineering, 1990, Vol.2.

[13] Hasan W., Pirahesh H.:*"Query Rewrite Optimization in Starburst"*, IBM Research Report RJ 6367 (62349).

[14] Ioannidis Y., Wong E.:*"An Algebraic approach to Recursive Inference"*, Expert Database Systems, Larry Kerschberg Editor, 1987.

[15] Jarke M., Koch J.:*"Query optimization in Database Systems"*. ACM 1984, VOL 16.

[16] Lopez M. et. al.:*"The EDS Parallel Database Server"*, Esprit Report. Esprit II EP 2025. European Declarative System Project, 1990.

[17] Mumick.I.S, Pirahesh.H, Finkelstein.S.J , Ramakrishnan.R:*"Magic is Relevant"*, In the Proc. of SIGMOD, 1990.

[18] Mumick.I.S, Finkelstein.S.J, Pirahesh.H.:*"Magic Condition"*, In the Proc. of the 9th ACM SIGACT-SIGMOD-SIGART symp. on Princ. of Database System. Tennessee. 1990.

[19] Naughton. JF, Ramakrishnan R, Sagiv Y, Ullman JD: *"Efficient Evaluation of Right-, Left-, and Multi-Linear Rules"*, in the Proc. of PODS, 1989.

[20] Rohmer J., Lescoeur R. et Kerisit J.M.:*"The Alexander Method, a Technique for Processing of Recursive Axioms in Deductive Databases"*, New Generation Computing, Springer-Verlag Ed. 1986.

[21] Sacca.D, Zianolo.C:*"The Generalized Counting Method for Recursive Logic Queries"*, In the Proc. of the 1th Int. Conf. on Database Therory, 1986.

[22] Sacca.D, Zianolo.C :*"Magic Counting Methods"*, In the proc of ACM, 1987.

[23] Ullman J.D., Aho A.V.:*"Universality of Data Retrievial Languages"*, In the Proc. of the 6th POPL, ACM, 1979.

[24] Ullman J.D.:*"Principle of Database and Knowledge-Base Systems"*, Book. Computer Science Press, Rockville, MD, 1988.

Finiteness Properties of Database Queries

(Extended Abstract)

Inderpal Singh Mumick
AT&T Bell Laboratories
600 Mountain Avenue
Murray Hill, NJ 07974, USA
mumick@research.att.com

Oded Shmueli*
AT&T Bell Laboratories
600 Mountain Avenue
Murray Hill, NJ 07974, USA
oshmu@cs.Technion.AC.IL

Abstract

We investigate the problem of checking whether the number of derivation trees of a Datalog program with duplicate semantics is finite or not. We show that given a safe stratified query and an edb, it is possible to check, in polynomial time, whether the query has a finite number of derivation trees. However, it is undecidable to check whether a safe stratified query has a finite number of derivation trees for every possible edb. We identify two classes of queries for which checking finiteness over all edbs is decidable. We also define duplicate semantics for Datalog (and thereby for the newly proposed variants of recursive SQL) queries with stratified negation. Since evaluation involving counting of duplicates may not terminate in recursive SQL, this problem is of significant practical importance.

1 Introduction

A *relation* is a set of tuples, where each tuple occurs exactly once. A *table* is a multiset of tuples, where each tuple can occur multiple times. The multiple copies of a tuple in a table are called *duplicates*. A database system that supports tables is said to support duplicates.

The relational and deductive database models are built on relations and do not support duplicates[3, 14, 2]. The semantics of a query in such relational and deductive

*Current address: Computer Science Department, Technion, Haifa, Israel 32000.

databases can be defined in terms of derivations — a fact is in the answer to a query if it can be *derived* from the given database relations. The idea has been formalized through derivation trees[8] (a fact is in the answer if there exists one or more derivation tree for it).

Many commercially available relational database systems support duplicates, and need a duplicate semantics for recursive queries. There is also a need for duplicates in many database applications, and the question of duplicate semantics in the presence of recursion is an important one.

The semantics for recursive and nonrecursive queries with duplicates has also been defined in terms of derivation trees[11, 9]. Given a query, a fact is defined to be in the answer with multiplicity m if there are m derivation trees for the fact. A definition and enumeration of derivation trees for *Datalog with tables*, a language similar to SQL without the difference and aggregation operators, was given by Mumick[9]. A duplicate semi-naive evaluation algorithm to evaluate duplicate semantics was also given.

It is possible for a fact to have an infinite number of derivations. Consider the following example:

EXAMPLE 1.1 (Path Query:) We are given an edge(X, Y) relation, and need to find the number of paths between every pair of nodes X and Y. A path(X, Y) table can be defined in Starburst SQL[10] as follows:

```
(N):  CREATE VIEW path(X,Y) AS
          ((SELECT X,Y FROM edge)
           UNION ALL
           (SELECT e.X, p.Y FROM edge e, path p
            WHERE e.Y = p.X)).

(Q):  SELECT X, Y, COUNT (*) FROM path GROUPBY X,Y.
```

The path view in Starburst SQL is equivalent to the following definition in Datalog if we interpret path as a multiset predicate.

```
(N1):  path(X,Y) :- edge(X,Y).
(N2):  path(X,Y) :- edge(X,Z) & path(Z,Y).
```

If the edge relation has a cycle then the number of derivation trees for a fact can be infinite. For instance, given edge $= \{(1,2), (2,3), (3,2)\}$, the fact path$(1,3)$ has an infinite number of derivation trees. Duplicate semantics requires that the fact path$(1,3)$ be derived with a multiplicity of *infinity*, so that the query Q derives the fact $(1, 3, \infty)$. □

Note that if the given **edge** relation is acyclic, both the duplicate semi-naive and the not-so-naive evaluation methods would terminate and correctly compute the answer. It can be shown that the duplicate semi-naive and the not-so-naive evaluation methods work as long as the number of derivation trees is finite. However, there is no known algorithm that would recognize that a fact would be derived infinitely many times. The duplicate semi-naive evaluation[9] would not terminate on the above program given a cyclic **edge** relation. An evaluation under ordinary set semantics without eliminating duplicates, such as the not-so-naive evaluation[8], would also not terminate. Due to the cost of duplicate elimination, such evaluation techniques are very common for nonrecursive queries in commercial databases, and could be useful for certain recursive queries.

A solution to the problem of determining tuple multiplicity would enable the following:

1. We can determine whether a given query has a finite answer under multiset semantics used in many commercial database systems, such as those based on SQL (DB2, SQL/DS, Nonstop SQL). The results are also important in defining a meaningful duplicate semantics for SQL extended with recursion.

2. We can determine whether an evaluation method that does not eliminate duplicates will terminate. Duplicate elimination is an expensive operation, so that even when multiset semantics is not required, relational database systems often evaluate queries without eliminating duplicates.

3. Incremental view maintenance algorithms[4] can rely on the number of derivations. The applicability of such algorithms can be determined by our techniques. Gupta, Katiyar, and Mumick[4] have proposed an algorithm for incremental view maintenance by keeping track of the number of derivation trees for each fact. The method is applicable to SQL queries, as well as to deductive databases that do not use duplicate semantics. However, their algorithm works only if the number of derivation trees is finite.

Thus, for all of the above applications, we need to detect for a given program whether or not it has an infinite number of derivations. If it has an infinite number of derivations, then the duplicate semi-naive evaluation, the not-so-naive evaluation, and the incremental evaluation methods cannot be used.

We define two problems relating to checking finiteness of number of derivation trees. The first problem asks for finiteness under one given edb instance. This problem is shown to be decidable in polynomial time for Datalog extended with safe stratified negation. The second problem asks for finiteness under all possible values for the edb. This problem is shown to be undecidable for Datalog extended with safe stratified negation, and decidable for Datalog extended with constants, disequalities ($\neq$), and negation on unary edb's.

To work with programs with negation, we need to define derivation trees and duplicate semantics for programs with safe stratified negation. We extend the definition of Mumick[9] (for positive programs) to safe stratified programs.

The paper is organized as follows. Section 2 outlines some of the notation and definitions used in the rest of the paper. Section 3 presents duplicate semantics for programs with safe stratified negation. In Section 4 we discuss the finiteness problem under one given edb. We give a polynomial time algorithm for deciding finiteness. The universal finiteness problem is introduced in Section 5, and we present various decidability and undecidability results in the subsections. Conclusions are presented in Section 6.

2 Notation

We use Datalog, mostly as defined in Ullman[14]. A mapping between a class of SQL queries and Datalog with extensions for negation and aggregation is given in Mumick[9]. We do not consider aggregation in this paper. Predicates in a Datalog program are of two types: An **edb** predicate is one for which a relation is stored in the database. An edb predicate does not appear in the head of any rule. An **idb** predicate is defined by rules in the program, and no relation is stored in the database for an idb predicate.

The results in this paper are applicable to SQL extended with recursion and to Datalog. We could choose to use either Datalog syntax or SQL syntax. We have chosen to use Datalog syntax since many concepts are easier to explain in Datalog syntax. However, all definitions and results extend to SQL with recursion.

Definition 2.1 Range Restricted Datalog: Range restricted Datalog is Datalog in which for every rule, every head variable appears in a positive body literal. We consider only range restricted Datalog and extensions thereof. □

Definition 2.2 DDatalog: Duplicate Datalog, or DDdatalog, is Datalog with all idb predicates interpreted as multisets, and all edb predicates interpreted as sets. The multiplicity of each tuple derived in DDatalog is important. The semantics for

DDatalog is as defined by Mumick[9]. Briefly, each distinct derivation tree for a fact adds one to its multiplicity in the derived set. □

Definition 2.3 Safe Negation: Given a rule r with negated subgoals, the negation is defined to be safe if every variable in the negated subgoals also appears in a positive subgoal of rule r. □

Definition 2.4 Stratum Numbers: Assume an assignment of stratum numbers as follows. Let the *dependency graph* of the program have predicate names as nodes; a directed edge (p, q) is in the edge set if there is a rule headed by a q atom and having in its body a p literal. Construct a *reduced dependency graph* of the given program by collapsing every strongly connected component of the dependency graph to a single node. A reduced graph is guaranteed to be acyclic. A topological sort[1] of the reduced dependency graph assigns a stratum number to each node. If a node represents a strongly connected component, all predicates in the strongly connected component are assigned the stratum number of the node. By convention, the base predicates are assigned stratum number = 0. □

Definition 2.5 Stratified Negation: Given a rule r with negated subgoals, the negation is defined to be stratified if every negated subgoal belongs to a lower stratum. □

3 Duplicate Semantics for safe stratified programs

We first define derivation trees for a DDatalog program P extended with safe stratified negation. The following definition captures all derivations for each fact derived by program P, so that duplicate semantics of program P is obtained by counting the number of derivation trees.

Definition 3.1 Derivation trees for safe stratified DDatalog programs: Derivation trees for predicates of stratum i are defined inductively over i.

For $i = 0$, that is, for edb predicates, each atom in the given edb relations forms one derivation tree for itself.

Inductively, assume that it is known which atoms of predicates of stratum i or less have a derivation tree, and all the derivation trees of atoms of predicates of stratum i or less have been defined.

For each rule r for a predicate of stratum $i + 1$ of the form

(r): $(h \text{ :- } b_1, b_2, \ldots, b_k, \neg c_1, \neg c_2, \ldots, \neg c_j)$.

with $k > 0$, and for each k-tuple

$$(t_1, t_2, \ldots, t_k)$$

of derivation trees for ground atoms

$$(d_1, d_2, \ldots, d_k)$$

that unify with subgoals

$$(b_1, b_2, \ldots, b_k)$$

with θ as the (necessarily, most general) unifier, such that the ground atoms

$$c_1\theta, c_2\theta, \ldots, c_j\theta$$

do not have any derivation tree, there is a derivation tree for $h\theta$, with $h\theta$ as the root label, and

$$(t_1, t_2, \ldots, t_k, \neg c_1\theta, \neg c_2\theta, \ldots, \neg c_j\theta)$$

as the children, in that order, and r as the edge label from the root to the children. □

Duplicate Semantics The duplicate semantics of a program is given by prescribing multisets to the derived relations. Given a DDatalog program P with safe stratified negation and an edb E, let a be a fact for predicate p and let there be m_a distinct derivation trees for a in E. Then, the multiset extension of p has m_a copies of fact a.

4 Finiteness

Definition 4.1 Finiteness Problem for a Language L: Given a program P in language L, a distinguished predicate q, and an instance E of the extensional database, does every derivable tuple of q have a finite number of derivation trees? □

In this section we show that the finiteness problem is decidable for DDatalog with safe stratified negation. We then give a polynomial time (in the size of the database) algorithm to check finiteness.

4.1 *Decidability of the Finiteness Property*

Given a safe stratified program P and an instance E of the extensional database, one can use several evaluation methods, amongst them the semi-naive bottom-up method[14], to compute the set of derivable atoms. For finiteness to be decidable for safe stratified programs, we need to show that it is possible to mark each derivable atom to indicate whether it has a finite or infinite number of derivation trees. An atom is marked f if it has a finite number of derivation trees, and is marked ∞ if it has an infinite number of derivation trees.

We give an inductive description of a semi-naive marking algorithm (Algorithm 4.1) for marking derivable atoms of a safe stratified program P using edb E. We use the following notation: An atom a is said to be of stratum i if it is an atom of a predicate of stratum i. We first state two lemmas.

Lemma 4.1 *Given a safe stratified program P and an edb E with k constants, there exists a constant G such that the number of derivable atoms is less than G. Further, G is a polynomial in k.* □

Proof: Let A be the maximum arity of any predicate in program P, let there be m predicates in program P, and let there be k constants in edb E. Then, the number of possible atoms is $G = mk^A$. Thus the number of derivable atoms is less than G, a polynomial in k. □

Lemma 4.2 *Given a program P, an edb E, and an integer constant $h \geq 0$, the number of derivation trees of height $h+1$ or less is, at most*

$$(r^{(n^h-1)/(n-1)})(mk^A)^{n^h}$$

where $r, n.m, k$, and A depend on program P. □

The *semi-naive marking algorithm* proceeds stratum by stratum. At each stratum we compute all derivable facts, along with a marking for finiteness or infiniteness. Computation within a stratum is done in a manner similar to the semi-naive bottom-up evaluation method[14]. The semi-naive marking algorithm is polynomial in the size of the database. Further optimizations to the semi-naive marking algorithm are possible, but we have not considered them since our intention is to show polynomial complexity.

For each atom a computed by the semi-naive algorithm, the semi-naive marking algorithm computes a triple

$$(a, \mathsf{mark}(a), \mathsf{deriving}(a))$$

where $\mathsf{mark}(a)$ is the finiteness/infiniteness marking of atom a, and $\mathsf{deriving}(a)$ is the set of all atoms of the same stratum as atom a used to derive atom a. The deriving set is maintained only if $\mathsf{mark}(a)$ is finite.

Algorithm 4.1 Semi-Naive Marking Algorithm: The algorithm works stratum by stratum, starting from stratum 0 and going up one stratum at a time.
Stratum 0: All edb atoms are marked f.
Stratum $i+1$: Inductively assume that all derivable atoms of stratum i or less have been derived and marked. We derive and mark the atoms of stratum $i+1$.

We do a semi-naive evaluation, modified to keep track of the mark field and the deriving sets. The mark of an atom can change from finite to infinite during the evaluation, but it cannot change from infinite to finite. For each derived atom a of stratum $i+1$ with a finite mark, the set $\mathsf{deriving}(a)$ consists of all atoms of stratum $i+1$ used to derive atom a.

In the first iteration of the semi-naive evaluation all derived atoms of stratum $i+1$ are derived using only facts of stratum i or less. If all positive atoms (of stratum i or less) used to derive fact a are marked finite, mark atom a as finite, else mark atom a as infinite. The deriving sets are all empty.

During a subsequent iteration of the semi-naive evaluation, consider, in some arbitrary order, each atom a derived in the iteration. Let the atom a be derived using some rule r and the previously derived atoms $g_1, \ldots, g_k$ of stratum $i+1$ and lower. Further processing is driven by the following conditions:

1. If atom a had been derived earlier, and has an infinite marking, do nothing. Specifically, the atom a is not included in the new δ relations of the semi-naive evaluation.

2. If atom a had not been derived earlier, or if atom a had been derived earlier but had a finite marking, define a new deriving set, $\mathsf{deriving}^{\nu}(a)$, for atom a that includes the old $\mathsf{deriving}(a)$, the atoms $g_1, \ldots, g_k$, and the deriving sets of atoms $g_1, \ldots, g_k$:

$$\mathsf{deriving}^{\nu}(a) = \mathsf{deriving}(a) \cup \{g_1\} \cup \ldots \cup \{g_k\} \cup \mathsf{deriving}(g_1) \cup \ldots \cup \mathsf{deriving}(g_k)$$

Note that the old deriving(a) is empty if atom a had not been derived earlier. Further processing depends on deriving$^\nu(a)$:

(a) If any atom in deriving$^\nu(a)$ is marked infinite, or if $a \in$ deriving$^\nu(a)$, change mark(a) to infinite, and consider atom a to be a new fact (include it in the δ relations of the semi-naive evaluation).

(b) If Case 2a does not apply, and deriving$^\nu(a) \neq$ deriving(a), change deriving(a) to deriving$^\nu(a)$, and consider atom a to be a new fact (include it in the δ relations of the semi-naive evaluation).

(c) If Cases 2a and 2b do not apply, do nothing. Specifically, the atom a is not included in the new δ relations of the semi-naive evaluation.

EXAMPLE 4.1 Consider the path program N of Example 1.1. Let the edb be $E_2 = \{(1,1)\}$.

In the first iteration of the semi-naive marking algorithm, we derive the atom $p(1,1)$ using rule $N1$. The mark is finite and the deriving set is empty. In the second iteration, the algorithm derives $p(1,1)$ again, using rule $N2$ and atoms $e(1,1)$ and $p(1,1)$. The new deriving$^\nu$ set for $p(1,1)$ now includes the atom $p(1,1)$. By Case 2a, the atom $p(1,1)$ is given an infinite mark. □

Theorem 4.1 *The semi-naive marking algorithm marks an atom a as infinite iff there are infinitely many distinct derivations of a in E.* □

Theorem 4.2 *The semi-naive marking algorithm terminates in time polynomial in the size of the database.* □

Theorem 4.3 *The finiteness problem for safe stratified DDatalog is decidable in polynomial time.* □

5 Universal Finiteness

Definition 5.1 Universal Finiteness Problem for a Language L: Given a program P in language L, with a distinguished predicate q, does every derivable tuple of q have a finite number of derivation trees for every extensional database E ? □

EXAMPLE 5.1 The path program N of Example 1.1 does not have a finite number of derivation trees for the edb $E = \{(1,2),(2,1)\}$. Program N is written in language DDatalog (or recursive SQL).

If there were an algorithm to check whether any given DDatalog program has a finite number of derivation trees, the universal finiteness property would be decidable for DDatalog. □

In this section we prove that

1. The universal finiteness problem is *undecidable* for Duplicate Datalog with stratified negation (Section 5.1).
2. The universal finiteness problem is *decidable* for Duplicate Datalog with constants and disequalities ($\neq$) (Section 5.2).
3. The universal finiteness problem is *decidable* for Duplicate Datalog with base negation on unary edbs (Section 5.3).

5.1 *Duplicate Datalog with Safe Stratified Negation*

Definition 5.2 Languages $DD^{\neg}$ and $D^{\neg}$: Consider range-restricted DDatalog with safe stratified negation. All idb predicates are interpreted as multisets. Call the above language $DD^{\neg}$.

Consider range-restricted Datalog with safe stratified negation. All idb predicates are interpreted as sets. Call the above language $D^{\neg}$. □

Theorem 5.1 *The universal finiteness problem for language $DD^{\neg}$ is undecidable.* □

Proof: The equivalence problem for language $D^{\neg}$ can be reduced to the universal finiteness problem for language $DD^{\neg}$. The equivalence problem for language $D^{\neg}$ is known to be undecidable[13], so the undecidability for the universal finiteness problem follows.

Given the equivalence problem T: Is $(P_1, q_1) \equiv (P_2, q_2)$, derive program P by taking a union of programs P_1 and P_2 (assume all idb's are distinct) and adding the following three rules:

$$q(X,Y) :- q_1(X,Y) \ \&\ \neg q_2(X,Y).$$
$$q(X,Y) :- q_2(X,Y) \ \&\ \neg q_1(X,Y).$$
$$q(X,Y) :- q(X,Y).$$

It is easy to see that predicate q evaluates to an empty set iff $(P_1, q_1) \equiv (P_2, q_2)$. Further, if q_1 and q_2 differ in tuple (a,b), then $q(a,b)$ has an infinite number of derivations.

Thus (P, q) has a finite number of derivation trees iff $(P_1, q_1) \equiv (P_2, q_2)$. □

5.2 *Duplicate Datalog with Constants and Disequalities*

Definition 5.3 Language $DD^{c\neq}$: Consider range-restricted Duplicate Datalog with constants and disequalities. A disequality is of the form $X \neq Y$ or $X \neq c$, where X and Y are variables that must also appear in a positive body literal of the rule, and c is a constant. Call the above language $DD^{c\neq}$. □

Theorem 5.2 *The universal finiteness problem for language $DD^{c\neq}$ is decidable.* □

Proof: Given a program P with distinguished predicate q, with k_1 constants $(b_1, \ldots, b_{k_1})$, and with k_2 being the maximum number of variables in a rule, let $E_{k_1+k_2}$ be a database consisting of all edb atoms that can be constructed from the $k_1 + k_2$ distinct symbols $\{b_1, \ldots, b_{k_1}\} \cup \{f_1, \ldots, f_{k_2}\}$.

We will prove that if there exists a database E for which some atom a of predicate q has a derivation tree of height h, then in the particular database $E_{k_1+k_2}$ also there is a derivation tree of height h for a related (in a way to be explained) atom a' of predicate q. Then, if atom a has an infinite number of derivations in database E, it must have derivation trees of an infinite number of heights in database E, and a related atom a' must also have derivation trees of an infinite number of heights in database $E_{k_1+k_2}$. We can then check finiteness of program P on the database $E_{k_1+k_2}$ using the techniques of Section 4 and obtain an answer to the universal finiteness problem.

Inductive Hypothesis We prove, by induction, that if there exists a database E, say with the n constants $(a_1, \ldots, a_n)$, that derives a derivation tree of height h for an atom $p(d_1, \ldots, d_m)$, where $d_i \in (\{a_1, \ldots, a_n\} \cup \{b_1, \ldots, b_{k_1}\})$, and $[d_{i_1} = d_{j_1}, \ldots, d_{i_q} = d_{j_q}]$ are the only q equality relationships amongst the arguments, and $[d_{u_1} = b_{v_1}, \ldots, d_{u_g} = b_{v_g}]$ are the only g instances of the constants from $\{b_1, \ldots, b_{k_1}\}$ in $(d_1, \ldots, d_m)$, then

1. Every atom $p(e_1, \ldots, e_m)$ of predicate p that can be constructed from the $k_1 + k_2$ constants $\{f_1, \ldots, f_{k_1}\} \cup \{b_1, \ldots, b_{k_2}\}$ under the following constraints:

   (a) $[e_{i_1} = e_{j_1}, \ldots, e_{i_q} = e_{j_q}]$ are the only q equality relationships amongst the arguments.

   (b) $[e_{u_1} = b_{v_1}, \ldots, e_{u_g} = b_{v_g}]$ are the only g instances of the constants from $\{b_1, \ldots, b_{k_1}\}$ in $(e_1, \ldots, e_m)$.

   has a derivation tree of height h from database $E_{k_1+k_2}$.

2. There is at least one p atom that satisfies the constraints of Case 1, and therefore has a derivation tree of height h from database $E_{k_1+k_2}$.

The induction is over the height h of the derivation tree for an atom of predicate p in program P.

Details of the inductive proof are omitted. □

EXAMPLE 5.2 We again consider the transitive closure **path** program of Example 1.1. There are no constants or disequalities in program N. The maximum number of variables in a rule = $k_2 = 3$. Thus we can check universal finiteness by checking finiteness against a complete database E_3 of 3 constants 1, 2, and 3. (In this case, since there are no disequalities, only one constant suffices). The atom **edge**(1, 1) is in the edb E_3, and the semi-naive marking algorithm will mark atom **path**(1, 1) as having an infinite number of derivations. □

5.3 *Duplicate Datalog with Restricted Forms of Negation*

In this section we consider two types of negation for which universal finiteness is decidable. First we allow negation on unary edb predicates, and second we allow stratified negation in programs where all edb predicates are unary.

Definition 5.4 Language $DD^{\neg(edb,1)\neq}$: Consider range-restricted Duplicate Datalog with safe negation on unary edb predicates, and with disequalities ($\neq$). A disequality is of the form $X \neq Y$, where X and Y are variables that must also appear in a positive body literal of the rule. Call the above language $DD^{\neg(edb,1)\neq}$. □

Theorem 5.3 *The universal finiteness problem for language* $DD^{\neg(edb,1)\neq}$ *is decidable.* □

Proof: The proof for Theorem 5.3 uses the idea that unary edb's basically define sets, and a collection of unary edb's identify constants to be of certain *types*, depending on which sets they are a member of. The proof is very similar to the proof for Theorem 5.2. A particular database E_k is constructed with the property that the finiteness test using edb E_k gives the answer to the universal finiteness question for a given program P. The database E_k is populated so as to have sufficiently many constants of enough types that all derivation trees on an arbitrary database E can be mapped onto derivations in database E_k. □

If constants are added to the above languages $DD^{\neg(edb,1)\neq}$ and $D^{edb(1)\neg\neq}$, the universal finiteness problem is still decidable.

6 Conclusions

We defined two properties related to checking finiteness of derivation trees.

The first property is *finiteness*. A query and an edb are finite if the query has a finite number of derivation trees. We have shown that it is possible to determine, in polynomial time, whether a recursive SQL query without aggregation, or alternatively a Datalog program with safe stratified negation, has a finite number of derivation trees. The decidability results would extend, in a straightforward manner, if stratified aggregation were included.

It would be ideal to be able to determine for a query whether it has a finite number of derivation trees for all edbs. This is captured by the concept of *universal finiteness*. We show that universal finiteness is undecidable for Datalog (or recursive SQL) extended with safe stratified negation. However, for queries that do not use negation, or where negation is limited to unary edbs, universal finiteness can be checked.

The results are encouraging, and should lead to work in developing more efficient algorithms to test infinities while evaluating queries. Applications are available in evaluating recursive SQL queries, influencing the ISO definition of recursion in SQL, determining whether the optimization of delaying duplicate elimination during query evaluation is applicable, and checking if incremental view maintenance through counts can be used. It should also be possible to evaluate queries that have infinite answers and give a finite representation of the infinite answers.

Mumick[9] considers a language *Datalog with tables* that permits edbs and idbs to be sets or multisets. The results presented in this paper extend to such a generalization.

There are several related issues that need more work. Can we check for universal finiteness for a language that allows base negation on all edb's? It is of interest to determine if a query has a finite number of derivation trees when all (or a few) edb relations are restricted to be acyclic. We define an edb relation $R(\bar{X}, \bar{Y})$ of even arity to be acyclic if the transitive closure of the relation does not have a path from $\bar{X}$ to $\bar{X}$. Is the universal finiteness problem for DDatalog decidable under the acyclicity constraint? Is the universal finiteness problem for DDatalog extended with safe negation on edb predicates decidable under the acyclicity constraint? For example, the transitive closure program has the universal finiteness property under an acyclicity constraint on the edge relation.

The universal finiteness problem is related to satisfiability, and we believe that some of the techniques used to check satisfiability[7, 6] may be useful in solving the above finiteness problems. We need more efficient algorithms for checking finiteness and universal finiteness. This paper presents initial work showing the problems to be decidable, and should lead to more efficient algorithms. An interesting related problem is to assign meaningful counts to the number of derivations when there are an infinite number of derivations. There is potential application for this in incremental view maintenance.

References

[1] A. V. Aho, J. E. Hopcroft, and J. D. Ullman. *Data Structures and Algorithms.* Addison-Wesley, 1983.

[2] S. Ceri, G. Gottlob, and L. Tanca. *Logic Programming and Databases.* Springer-Verlag, 1990.

[3] E. F. Codd. A relational model of data for large shared data banks. *Communications of the ACM*, 13(6):377–387, 1970.

[4] A. Gupta, D. Katiyar, and I. S. Mumick. Counting solutions to the view maintenance problem. In *Workshop on Deductive Databases*, Washington, D. C., November 14 1992.

[5] ISO_ANSI. Iso-ansi working draft: Database language sql2 and sql3; x3h2; iso/iec jtc1/sc21/wg3, 1990.

[6] A. Levy, I. S. Mumick, Y. Sagiv, and O. Shmueli. Equivalence, query-reachability, and satisfiability in datalog. In *Workshop on Deductive Databases*, Washington, D. C., November 14 1992.

[7] A. Levy and Y. Sagiv. Constraints and redundancy in datalog. In *Proceedings of the Eleventh Symposium on Principles of Database Systems (PODS)*, pages 67–80, San Diego, CA, June 2-4 1992. ACM SIGACT-SIGMOD-SIGART.

[8] M. Maher and R. Ramakrishnan. Déjàvu in fixpoints of logic programs. In *North American Conference on Logic Programming (NACLP)*, October 16-20 1989.

[9] I. S. Mumick. *Query Optimization in Deductive and Relational Databases.* PhD thesis, Stanford University, Stanford, CA 94305, USA, Dec. 1991. Technical Report No. STAN-CS-91-1400. Also available from University Microfilms International, 300 N. Zeeb Road, Ann Arbor, MI 48106. (313)761-4700.

[10] I. S. Mumick, S. J. Finkelstein, H. Pirahesh, and R. Ramakrishnan. Magic is relevant. In *Proceedings of ACM SIGMOD 1990 International Conference on Management of Data*, pages 247–258, Atlantic City, NJ, May 23-25 1990.

[11] I. S. Mumick, H. Pirahesh, and R. Ramakrishnan. The magic of duplicates and aggregates. In *Proceedings of the Sixteenth International Conference on Very Large Databases (VLDB)*, pages 264–277, Brisbane, Australia, August 13-16 1990.

[12] I. S. Mumick and O. Shmueli. Aggregation, computability, and complete query languages. In *Workshop on Structural Complexity and Recursion-theoretic Methods in Logic Programming*, Washington, D. C., November 13

1992. Also Available as AT&T Technical Memorandum 11256-090820-14TMS, AT&T Bell Labs, September 1992.

[13] O. Shmueli. Decidability and expressiveness aspects of logic queries. In *Proceedings of the Sixth Symposium on Principles of Database Systems (PODS)*, pages 237–249, San Diego, CA, Mar. 1987. ACM SIGACT-SIGMOD-SIGART.

[14] J. D. Ullman. *Principles of Database and Knowledge-Base Systems, Volumes 1 and 2.* Computer Science Press, 1989.

Verification of a Two Pass Restart Algorithm for ARIES

Dean Kuo

S.S.R.C., Basser Department of Computer Science, F09,
University of Sydney, NSW, 2006, Australia.
email : dean@cs.su.oz.au

Abstract

In this paper, we show how to verify a two pass recovery algorithm for ARIES. The work uses the I/O automata model as its formal model and the definition of correctness is one that is based on the user's view of the database.

1 Introduction

Correctness is vital in many database systems. To show correctness of a system, we must model and verify it. Testing is not sufficient to show correctness as it only shows the presence of errors. There are two major sources of problems in a database system. One is due to the concurrent activities. The other is due to the system using memory to cache data. When a crash occurs, the data in memory is lost. The database must then recover by reconstructing the database by using information on stable storage (disk).

ARIES [10], is an important recovery method that has been implemented in varying degrees in many systems. ARIES uses three passes of the log to recover from a crash. The first pass is the analysis pass where the dirty pages table and transaction table are reconstructed. The second pass is the redo pass where history is repeated. The final pass is the undo pass where the actions from loser transactions are undone. In [6], we showed an alternative restart algorithm for ARIES using only two passes of the log. The key idea of this restart algorithm is for the analysis pass to scan the log backwards and write compensation log records. The final pass is the redo pass where history is repeated. The redo pass is identical to ARIES' redo pass. In this algorithm, actions from loser transactions are undone as follows: the analysis pass writes compensation log records and then the redo pass (thinking it is redoing the compensation) undoes the effects of the original transaction. Unlike other two pass algorithms, the algorithm of [6] does not require the data manager to enforce a no steal policy.

Verification of concurrency control algorithms have been done extensively, [1, 2]. For recovery algorithms, [5] modeled and verified a data manager based on ARIES. In this paper, we modify the model presented in [5] to model the algorithm presented in [6]. Thus, our model includes the same features as in [5]. That is, the model includes asynchronous checkpointing, write-ahead logging and fine granularity locking. Also, the model allows crashes to occur during recovery. However, the model does not include logical logging or partial rollbacks. In this paper, we are able to use some of the lemmas (invariants) in [5], for two reasons. First, the redo pass and normal processing of both algorithms are identical. Second, the proof in [5] is structured. For example, to show the correctness of the redo pass in the two pass algorithm, we only require to show that the post conditions of the analysis pass of both algorithms are the same. Similarly, to show the correctness of the two pass algorithm, we must show that the post conditions of the two restart algorithms are the same.

Other related work in understanding recovery algorithms includes [1, 3, 4, 8]. In [8], a simple unrealistic data manager was modeled and verified. Checkpoints were not modeled, thus recovery had to scan the whole log. In [1] and [4], algorithms are presented and classified but not verified. In [3], general conditions are proved on log maintenance, without which the information needed for recovery might not be available after a crash. However, that work does not show that specific recovery mechanisms use the information correctly.

2 Background

This section gives a brief overview of ARIES [10], the two pass restart algorithm for ARIES [6] and the I/O automata [9]. Also, we give an overview of the model used to verify the correctness of a data manager based on ARIES [5].

2.1 ARIES

Overview ARIES is a new recovery algorithm by Mohan *et al* [10]. The recovery algorithm requires three passes of the log. An analysis pass where the dirty pages table and transaction table are reconstructed. This pass is followed by the redo pass where history is repeated. The final pass is the undo pass where the effects of non-committed transactions are undone.

Data Structures The important data structures in ARIES are the log, dirty pages table, transaction table and the database.

The log consists of seven fields but not all of them are always used. Each log record has a log sequence number (LSN). This value is monotonic increasing. Each log record also records the transaction identifier (TransID) of the transaction that wrote the log record. Log records from the same transaction are linked backwards via a previous LSN (PrevLSN) pointer. Also, each log record contains a field *Data* where the operation is logged. In the case of our model, where we assume that there is a finite set of data items and physical logging, the field consists of three subfields. They are: before image (Bf), after image (Af) and the name of the data item (Di) of the operation affected.

The transaction table and dirty pages table are used to keep track of the state of active transactions and dirty pages respectively. Each entry, for a transaction, in the transaction table shows the current state of the transaction, the last log record written by the transaction (LastLSN) and the next log record to be undone, for the transaction, in a rollback (UndoNxtLSN). Each dirty page in the database has an entry in the dirty pages table. The entry contains a field RecLSN. This is the LSN of the logged operation that caused the page to become dirty.

The database consists of many pages. All pages are allocated a location in stable storage (disk) and some may also be cached in memory.

The algorithm The role of the analysis pass is to reconstruct the dirty pages table and the transaction table. Also, the pass returns the *RedoLSN*. This value is then passed onto the redo pass so that it knows where to start processing.

Reconstruction of the dirty pages table is straightforward. For each page, the pass finds the log record that may have caused the page to become dirty. At the end of the analysis pass, the *RedoLSN* returned by the pass is the minimum *RecLSN* in the table.

For the transaction table the pass finds, for each non-terminated transaction, the last log record written by the transaction (LastLSN) as well as the next log record to be undone for the transaction (UndoNxtLSN).

The redo pass repeats history. It starts processing from the *RedoLSN* that was returned by the analysis pass. The pass terminates when it processes past the end of the log. When the pass processes a log record it determines, via the dirty pages table and the database, if the effects of the logged operation is missing. If it is, then the operation is redone. Otherwise, the log record is ignored. The pass then processes the next log record in the log. At the end of the redo pass, all logged operations are thus in the database.

The final pass is the undo pass. It undoes the effects of non-terminated transactions. The undo pass continuously undo the effects of the log record pointed to by the maximum *UndoNxtLSN* entry in the transaction table and updates the transaction table. The pass terminates when the transaction table is empty[1]. An entry

[1]In a distributed database the pass terminates when all transactions in the table are in the prepared state.

in the table is removed when all updates from the non-terminated transaction have been undone. Thus, at the end of the undo pass, the effects of all non-terminated transaction have been undone. After the undo pass has terminated, the system is back to normal processing.

2.2 The Two Pass Restart Algorithm

There are three crucial differences between the two pass algorithm and the ARIES restart algorithm. First, the analysis pass scans the log backwards (in reverse chronological order) rather than forwards as in ARIES. Second, compensation log records are written during the analysis pass but no *undos* occur. Finally, the undo pass is not present. The algorithm for the redo pass and normal processing remain unchanged. The pseudo code (taken from [6]) is shown in the appendix.

Comparing the analysis pass from the ARIES algorithm with the analysis pass of the two pass algorithm, the latter has an additional responsibility. It must write compensation log records for each update from a non-terminated transaction, that does not already have one. The compensation log records that are written are identical to those written during the undo pass of ARIES.

Reconstruction of the dirty pages table is straightforward. The analysis pass scans the log backwards and finds, for each page, the log record that may have caused the page to become dirty.

The transaction table is constructed and consulted during the analysis pass. The table is used to determine exactly which updates are from non-terminated transactions that have not been compensated. This is similar to the way ARIES' undo pass uses the reconstructed transaction table. Only active transactions can have entries in the transaction table. That is, transactions that have not committed or rolled back completely. The most important entry in the table is the *UndoNxtLSN*. This shows exactly, for each non-terminated transaction, which updates have already been compensated.

2.3 Basic Definitions of the I/O Automata Model

This section gives a brief summary of [9]. An execution β of an I/O automaton is an alternating sequence of states and actions. For example $\beta = s_0\pi_1 s_1\pi_2 s_2\pi_3 s_3...$ where s_i is the state of the automaton after the action π_i and s_0 is the start state. There are three types of actions, *input, output* and *internal. Input* actions are generated by the environment, *output* and *internal* actions are generated autonomously, and *output* actions have the added property that they transmit output actions to the environment. The internal and output actions are expressed by *preconditions* and *effects*. The *preconditions* describe the state the I/O automaton must be in for the action to be possible (enabled) while the *effects* show the transition from the old state to the new state. Input actions are always enabled so only the *effects* are given. The actions of the I/O automaton are atomic, that is there are no intermediate states showing only part of the effects of the action.

2.4 Model of a Data Manager Based on ARIES

In [6], we modeled a data manager based on ARIES. The model included the following features: 1) asynchronous checkpointing, 2) write-ahead logging, 3) fine granularity locking. However, it did not model logical logging or partial rollbacks. The paper also made the following assumptions: 1) execution is strict [1], that is each read and write by a transaction is delayed until the last writer transaction has terminated; 2) there is a finite set of data items in the database; 3) the data items never move from one page in the database to another.

We now give a brief description of the model in [6].

Data Structures There is a one to one correspondence from the data structures for the ARIES algorithm to the model. For example: the transaction table is modeled as an array *TT*, indexed by transaction identifiers. The dirty pages table is modeled as an array *DP* indexed by page identifiers. The log is modeled as an array indexed by *LSN*. Stable storage and cache are modeled as arrays *Stable* and *Cache* respectively. Both are indexed by page identifiers. We use *SystemState* to reflect the state of the system. The possible values are: *down, restart* and *normal*.

We also have some additional data structures in the model. These are used to control the I/O automata. For example, in a state, we use the set *ActiveSet* and other conditions to determine the actions that are enabled. Also, we use the variables *AnaLSN* and *RedoLSN* as the loop counters for the analysis pass and the redo pass respectively.

The Model The model uses all three types of actions of the I/O automata. The input and output actions are used to model respectively the requests from the scheduler to the data manager and the acknowledgment from the data manager to the scheduler. The internal actions model the internal steps of the data manager.

In the model, each action contains as many steps of the system subject to the constraint that either 1) there are no write accesses to stable storage but any number of reads. Also, there may be only one access to each shared data structure and all accesses to them are properly latched. One may first argue that the model, and therefore the verification, is not complete due to the concurrent activities of transaction and crashes may occur at any time. We claim that the model and verification does not omit anything significant for the following reasons. Firstly, the effects of a crash occurring during the sequence of steps that are modeled in one atomic action is equivalent to the effects of a crash occurring at the beginning or at the end of the sequence. Secondly, each value that is written to a shared data structure (dirty pages table, transaction table, and the page) may be flushed out to stable storage. Finally, latches are held on shared data structures. Thus, no other concurrent activities in the real system can effect the steps modeled in the action.

For example, the write procedure is modeled by three actions: an input action *WriteReq(T,x,v)*, an internal action *Write(T,x,v)* and an output action *Ack-Write(T,x,v)*. The input action enables the internal action. The internal action models all of the following: fetching the page, updating the database, updating the transaction table and dirty pages table and enabling the output action. The output action then acknowledges the completion of the write.

The analysis and redo pass are each modeled using two actions and the undo pass is modeled with three actions. For the analysis and redo pass, one action models the pass processing a log record and the other terminates the pass. For the undo pass, one action models the processing of a log record, the second writes an *end rollback* log record when a transaction has been rolled back completely. The final action terminates the pass.

3 Model of the Two Pass Algorithm

We modify the model presented in [5] for our model. The data structures are identical to the model presented in [5]. We use all the actions from the model in [5] except the actions for the analysis pass and undo pass. The analysis pass is modeled using three actions. The first action, *Ana*, models the analysis pass processing a log record. The second action, *Anab*, models the writing of an *end rollback* log record when all updates from a transaction have been compensated. The final action, *AnaTerm*, terminates the analysis pass. These actions may be found in [7]. There are no actions for the undo pass as the undo pass is not required in the two pass algorithm.

4 Verification

4.1 Definitions

Our definition of correctness is the same as in [5]. Before we can define correctness, we must make some preliminary definitions. We shall only describe these definitions informally. The formal definitions may be found in [5]

We first define the possible states of a transaction. They are: ***active transactions***, ***requested to terminate transactions*** and ***terminated transactions***. A transaction is active if it has requested a read or write but has not requested to terminate (commit or rollback). In addition, a crash has not occurred. (A crash can be viewed as a request by active transactions to be rolled back.) *Requested to Terminate* transactions are defined as those that have already requested to terminate but the data manager has not yet acknowledged the completion of the request. Terminated transactions is defined as those that have requested to terminate and the data manager has acknowledged the completion of the request.

Our definition of a transaction corresponds to the definition given in [1]. That is, the possible requests from a transaction are *write, read, commit* and *rollback.* Once a transaction has requested to commit or rollback, the transaction can no longer make anymore requests. Reads and writes, by a transaction to a data item, must be ordered. Also, transactions can write to a data item at most once.

Definition 1 $S_k.Lwr_{log[a..b]}(x)$
Define $S_k.Lwr_{log[a..b]}(x)$ *as the last log record whose LSN lies between a and b and with the following properties: it is of type* update *or* compensate *and it logged an operation on the data item* x.

Definition 2 $S_k.Lcw_{log[a..b]}(x)$
Define $S_k.Lcw_{log[a..b]}(x)$ *as the last log record, in state* S_k*, whose* LSN *lies between a and b, of type* update *or* compensate *and affected the data item* x*, and where the transaction that wrote the log record has committed* [2].

Definition 3 $S_k.DB[PID]$
The data manager maintains a buffer in memory in which some pages are cached. Thus, we define the state of a page in the database as the page in cache, if the page is in cache. Otherwise, the state of the page in the database is the state of the page in stable storage.

Definition 4 $Update(T, x)$
Define the value $Update(T, x)$ *as the* LSN *of the log record of transaction* T *that logged an update to the data item* x*. If no such log record exists, then it is defined as* -1*. As each transaction can update a data item once, the value of* $Update(T, x)$ *is therefore unique.*

Definition 5 $S_k.Unflsh(PID, a, b)$.
The set $S_k.Unflsh(PID, a, b)$ *is defined to indicate the log records, whose* LSN *lies between a and b that may have dirtied the page* PID.

Definition 6 $S_k.Runflsh(PID)$
The set $S_k.Runflsh(PID)$ *is then defined to indicate which log records are missing from the page* PID *in stable storage. In addition, we add an extraneous element,* $S_k.LgLSN$ *into this set. Thus, this set is never empty. (This is required in some of our lemmas.)*

---

[2] A transaction is defined as committed if an *end commit* log record, for the transaction, has been flushed to stable storage.

The formal definition of correctness is given below. This is identical to the correctness definition in [5].

Definition 7 *Correctness.*
If $\pi_j = AckRead(T, x, v)$ *then*

$$v = \begin{cases} v^* & \text{if } \exists w, w < j, \pi_w = WriteReq(T, x, v^*) \\ S_j.Lcw_{log[1..S_j.LgLSN-1]}(x).Data.Af & \text{otherwise} \end{cases}$$

That is, if a transaction reads a data item which it has not written to, then it should return the last committed value. Otherwise, it should return the value it wrote.

4.2 Lemmas

We state and describe, in this section, the crucial lemmas in the verification. The full proofs may be found in [7]. Due to the similarities between the two pass algorithm in [6] and the ARIES algorithm, we were able to use some of the lemmas of [5].

The first two lemmas show the correctness of the analysis pass and the checkpointing procedure. Lemma 8 shows, for each state, the correct state of the transaction table and the dirty pages tables. Lemma 9 then shows that the compensation log records that are written contain, in their after image, the last committed value.

Lemma 8 *Let*

$$S_k.Alsn' = \begin{cases} S_k.AnaLSN + 1 & \text{if } Ana \in S_k.ActiveSet \\ 1 & \text{otherwise} \end{cases}$$

$$S_k.UpdateBy'(T) = \left\{ lsn : \begin{array}{l} S_k.log[lsn].TransID = T, \\ S_k.log[lsn].Type = \text{`update'}|\text{`comp'} \\ S_k.Alsn' \le lsn < S_k.LgLSN. \end{array} \right\}$$

$$S_k.m'_T = max(S_k.UpdateBy'(T)).$$

Suppose $S_k.SystemState \neq$ *'down'.*

1. *If* $S_k.Unflsh(PID, S_k.Alsn', S_k.LgLSN - 1) = \emptyset$ *then* $S_k.DP[PID] = \emptyset$.

2. *If* $S_k.Unflsh(PID, S_k.Alsn', S_k.LgLSN - 1) \neq \emptyset$ *then*

   if $Ana \in S_k.ActiveSet$ *and* $S_k.ReadBgnChkpt = FALSE$ *then*

   $S_k.DP[PID].RecLSN \le min(S_k.Unflsh(PID, S_k.Alsn', S_k.LgLSN-1))$

else $S_k.DP[PID].RecLSN \leq min(S_k.Runflsh(PID))$.

3. *If* $\nexists e$ *such that* $S_k.Alsn' \leq e < S_k.LgLSN$, $S_k.log[e] = [\text{'end'}, T, \cdots]$ *and* $S_k.UpdateBy'(T) \neq \emptyset$ *then* $S_k.TT[T].LastLSN = S_k.m'_T$
   If $S_k.log[S_k.m'_T].Type = \text{'comp'}$ *then*

$$S_k.TT[T].UndoNxtLSN = S_k.log[S_k.m'_T].UndoNxtLSN$$

   else $S_k.TT[T].UndoNxtLSN = S_k.m'_T$.

4. *If* $\exists e$ *such that* $S_k.Alsn' \leq e < S_k.LgLSN$, $S_k.log[e] = [\text{'end'}, T, \cdots]$ *or* $S_k.UpdateBy'(T) = \emptyset$ *then* $S_k.TT[T] = \emptyset$.

Lemma 9 *If* $S_k.SystemState \neq \text{'down'}$, $S_k.TT[T] \neq \emptyset$ *and* $\exists wr$ *such that* $wr < k$, $\pi_{wr} = WriteReq(T, x, v)$, $\forall wr', T', wr < wr' < j$, $\pi_{wr'} \neq WriteReq(T', x, v')$ *and* $S_k.Update(T, x) > S_k.TT[T].UndoNxtLSN$ *then*

$$S_k.Lwr_{log[1..S_k.LgLSN-1]}(x).Data.Af = S_k.Lcw_{log[1..S_k.LgLSN-1]}(x).Data.Af.$$

At the end of the analysis pass, lemma 8 shows, for each dirty page PID,

$$S_k.DP[PID].RecLSN \leq min(S_k.Runflsh(PID)) \quad (1)$$

and for each non-dirty page PID

$$S_k.DP[PID] = \emptyset. \quad (2)$$

The proof of lemmas 8 and 9 are by induction. Thus, their statements shows us the loop invariants of the analysis pass. The most interesting case in the proof of lemma 8 is when the analysis pass processes the last successful checkpoint's begin log record. After the pass processes it, the contents of both tables reflect the state of the whole log. This shows the correctness of the checkpointing procedure. The proof of lemma 9 is similar to the correctness proof of the undo pass in [5]. It uses the assumption that the execution is strict to show that when a compensation log record is written, the last committed value is written into the log record's after image.

Lemmas 8 and 9 show, as in [5], that the reconstructed dirty pages table contains the correct values. The correctness of the redo pass is only dependent on the analysis pass being able to reconstruct the dirty pages table. As the algorithm for the redo pass of both algorithms are identical, we can thus use the lemmas in [5] that showed the correctness of the redo pass to show the correctness of the redo pass in the two pass restart algorithm. That is, at the end of the redo pass, for each data item x,

$$S_k.DB[page(x)].x = S_k.Lwr_{log[1..S_k.LgLSN]}.Data.Af. \quad (3)$$

We also show that each active transaction at the time of the crash will have an entry in the transaction table sometime during the analysis pass. Now, as an entry is only removed from the transaction table when the *UNL* entry is 0, thus each update by these transactions will be compensated.

The correctness of the recovery method then follows from lemma 9 and (3). We say that the recovery method is correct if each data item, that was updated by an active transaction, has its last committed value restored. Formally, if T was active when the crash occurred and updated the data item x, then at the end of recovery

$$S_k.DB[Page(x)].x = S_k.Lcw_{log[1..S_k.LgLSN-1]}(x).Data.Af. \tag{4}$$

Normal processing of both ARIES and the algorithm presented in [6] are identical. Also the post conditions of both recovery algorithms are the same. It follows from the work in [5] that the two pass restart algorithm is correct.

5 Conclusion and Future Work

This paper showed how to verify the correctness of a two pass restart algorithm for ARIES using the work in [5]. The full proofs of the new lemmas can be found in [7].

In our future work, we would like to extend the two pass algorithm to the more general case of logical logging. Also, we would like to extend our proof to include logical logging and partial rollbacks.

Acknowledgment The author wishes to thank Alan Fekete for his encouragement and criticism of this work.

References

[1] P. Bernstein, V. Hadzilacos, and N. Goodman. *Concurrency Control and Recovery in Database Systems.* Addison-Wesley, 1987.

[2] A. Fekete, N. Lynch, M. Merritt, and W. Weihl. Commutativity-based locking for nested transactions. *Journal of Computer and System Science*, 41(1):65–156, August 1990.

[3] V. Hadzilacos. A theory of reliability in database systems. *JACM*, 35:121–145, 1988.

[4] T Harder and A Reuter. Principles of transaction-oriented database recovery. *ACM Computing Surveys*, 15:287–317, 1983.

[5] D Kuo. Model and verification of a data manager based on ARIES. In *Proceeding of the 4th International Conference on Database Theory*, pages 231–245, October 1992. Full version available as SSRC Technical Report 22.1, Basser Department of Computer Science, University of Sydney, Sydney, NSW, 2006, Australia.

[6] D Kuo. A two pass restart recovery algorithm for ARIES. Technical Report SSRC 23.1, Basser Department of Computer Science, University of Sydney, Sydney, NSW, 2006, Australia, February 1992. Submitted for publication.

[7] D Kuo. Verification of a two pass restart recovery algorithm for ARIES. Technical Report SSRC 26.1, Basser Department of Computer Science, University of Sydney, Sydney, NSW, 2006, Australia, August 1992.

[8] D Kuo and A Fekete. Model and verification of a data manager. In *Proceedings of the 15th Australian Computer Science Conference*, January 1992. Full version available as SSRC Technical Report 15.1, Basser Department of Computer Science, University of Sydney, Sydney, NSW, 2006, Australia.

[9] N. Lynch and M. Tuttle. An introduction to input/output automata. *CWI-Quarterly*, 2(3):219–246, 1989.

[10] C Mohan, D Haderle, B Lindsay, H Pirahesh, and P Schwarz. ARIES: a transaction recovery method supporting fine-granularity locking and partial rollbacks using write-ahead-logging. *ACM Transactions on Database Systems*, 17(1):94–162, March 1992.

6 Appendix: The Analysis Pass Pseudo Code

```
TransTable = ∅; DirtyPages = ∅; ReadEndChkpt = FALSE; ReadBgnChkpt = FALSE;
Term = ∅; Flushed = ∅;
LogRec = LogRead(EndOfLog);
while (((not ReadBgnChkpt) or (TransTable ≠ ∅)) and (LogRec ≠ NULL))
/*logRec = NULL when the analysis pass has processed past the start of the log.*/
    if ((not ReadBgnChkpt) and (LogRec.Type == 'update'|'comp'))
        if ((LogRec.PageID ∉ Flushed) and (LogRec.PageID ∉ DirtyPages))
            Insert(LogRec.PageID, LogRec.LSN) into DirtyPages
        if ((LogRec.TransID ∉ Term) and (LogRec.TransID ∉ TransTable))
            Insert(T, LogRec.LSN, LogRec.LSN) in TransTable;
    endif;
    case (LogRec.Type)
        'update' | 'comp' :
            T = LogRec.TransID;
            if LogRec.Type = 'update'
                if ((T ∉ Term) and (LogRec.LSN ≤ TransTable[T].UndoNxtLSN))
                    LogWrite('comp', T, ···);
                    if (LogRec.PageID ∉ DirtyPages)
                        /* LgLSN is the LSN of the log record just written. */
```

```
                    Insert(LogRec.PageID, LgLSN) into DirtyPages table;
                TransTable[T].LastLSN = LgLSN;
                TransTable[T].UndoNxtLSN = LogRec.PrevLSN;
            endif;
        else
            if ((T ∉ Term) and (LogRec.LSN ≤ TransTable[T].UndoNxtLSN))
                TransTable[T].UndoNxtLSN = LogRec.UndoNxtLSN;
        endif;
        if (TransTable[T].UndoNxtLSN == 0)
            LogWrite('end', T, ···, ['rollback']);
            delete T from the TransTable;
            Term = Term ∪ {T};
        endif;
    'osfile_return':
        for each PID ∈ LogRec
            Flushed = Flushed ∪ PageID;
    'end': Term = Term ∪ LogRec.TransID;
        delete T from the transaction table;
    'endchkpt':
        ReadEndChkpt = TRUE;
        Chkpt.TransTable = LogRec.TransTable;
        Chkpt.DirtyPages = logRec.DirtyPages;
    'bgnchkpt':
        if (ReadEndChkpt = TRUE); /*this is the last successful checkpoint's begin log record*/
            ReadBgnChkpt = TRUE;
            for each entry PID ∈ Chkpt.DirtyPages
                if (PID ∉ Flushed)
                    if (PID ∉ DirtyPages)
                        Insert(PID, Chkpt.DirtyPages[PID].RecLSN) into dirty pages table;
                    else
                        DP[PID].RecLSN = Chkpt.DP[PID].RecLSN;
                    endif;
            for each entry T ∈ Chkpt.TransTable;
                if((T ∉ TransTable) and (T ∉ Term))
                    Insert(Chkpt.TransTable[T]) into the transaction table;
            endif;endcase;
if (not ReadBgnChkpt)
    LogRec = PrevLog();
else
    UndoNxt = max(UndoNxtLSN) from the transaction table;
    LogRec = LogRead(UndoNxt);
endif;
ndwhile;
RedoLSN = min(RedoLSN) from the dirty pages table;
```

A TEMPORAL ALGEBRA BASED ON AN ABSTRACT MODEL

MEHMET A. ORGUN
School of Mathematics, Physics, Computing and Electronics
Macquarie University, North Ryde, NSW 2109, Australia

and

HAUSI A. MÜLLER
Department of Computer Science, University of Victoria
P.O.Box 3055, Victoria, B.C. V8W 3P6, Canada

ABSTRACT

This paper introduces a temporal relational algebra (TRA) for querying temporal databases. TRA is based on an abstract model, in which a temporal database is regarded as a collection of time-varying relations. However, the model does not lend itself to any particular representation of time-varying data, and in the algebra there is no explicit manipulation of time. This abstraction level is achieved by extending the relational algebra point-wise upon the set of natural numbers. Therefore TRA naturally inherits all properties of and methodologies available for the relational algebra. During the evaluation of TRA expressions, portions of (potentially infinite) time-varying relations are retrieved from a given temporal database when needed. The paper also gives examples of time-specific and time-relative queries, and of combining time-varying data by temporal join and splicing. The formal properties of TRA, which can be used for query optimization, are also outlined.

1. Introduction

The relational algebra[3] operates on a model in which each relation reflects the current reality as it is best known of the enterprise being modeled. The model cannot deal with the notion of a history, or how each relation has evolved into what it is now. Having recognized the need to incorporate the time dimension into the relational model, a significant number of research efforts have been directed towards studying various aspects of this problem and providing models and query languages for the specification and querying of time-varying data; Snodgrass[13] provides a recent summary of the status of research on temporal databases. In one of the earlier studies, Clifford and Warren[2] proposed a state-oriented model, in which each tuple in a given time-varying relation is time-stamped. More recently, interval-based approaches have been proposed to model the time dimension at both the tuple level and the attribute level.[1, 4, 5, 12] In these approaches, the underlying time dimension over which intervals are defined is a collection of moments in time linearly ordered by an *earlier-than* relation.

Most of the temporal algebras reported in the literature rely heavily on the underlying models and the way the time dimension is represented. For instance, the algebras proposed by Tansel,[1] Gadia[5] and Sarda[12] are not algebras in the mathematical sense (i.e., they are not closed since expressions do not always evaluate to time-varying relations of the underlying models). This is mainly because the operators provided in these algebras are in fact designed to exploit actual representations of time-varying data and to manipulate complex time-varying attributes and temporal elements such as intervals. Tansel's and Sarda's algebras also include an operator to drop the time components of a given time-varying relation to obtain *snapshot* relations (i.e., slices of time-varying relations at particular moments in time.) Clifford[1] argues that a temporal algebra should be an algebra in the mathematical sense, and should have the familiar relational algebra as a special case. We agree with Clifford; when these conditions are satisfied, it becomes possible to transfer smoothly all the tools and methodologies available for the relational algebra to temporal algebras.

In this paper, we propose a temporal (relational) algebra which we call TRA, as a *point-wise* extension of the relational algebra. In other words, TRA by design has the relational algebra as a special case for each moment in time. Time-varying data from different moments in time are joined through the use of temporal operators, not by the use of explicit references to time. In the underlying abstract model for temporal databases, time-varying relations are an (infinite) collection of finite relations indexed by moments in time (i.e., natural numbers). Intuitively, this corresponds to a representation in which time-varying data is modeled at the tuple level by time-stamping. Therefore the model may introduce a fair amount of redundancies, but the representation of time-varying data at the implementation level need not be based on this abstract model. If the representation is *homogeneous*,[5, 6] that is, attribute values coexist in any given tuple, we can switch from interval representation at tuple or attribute level to time-stamping of tuples and vice versa. Therefore we can study the formal properties of TRA without any concern over how time-varying data is actually represented. We believe that freedom from representation is an important aspect of a temporal algebra. It is unlikely that an algebra based on a specific representation can be used for another representation easily.

In the following, we first outline the underlying abstract model for temporal databases. In section 3, we describe the operations of TRA, and provide the meaning (denotation) of TRA expressions based on temporal semantics. The meaning of any expression is always a time-varying relation, which can be used in other expressions subject to arity restrictions. In section 4, we demonstrate how time-varying queries may be formulated in TRA. We give examples of time-specific and time-relative queries, and of combining time-varying data by temporal join and splicing. In section 5, we study the formal properties of TRA which can be used for query optimization, and in particular show that TRA inherits all properties of the relational algebra, which is one of our main objectives. In section 6, we relate our work to other approaches to temporal databases and point out further research directions.

2. The Underlying Model

In the underlying model, a temporal database is a collection of time-varying relations where a time-varying relation is a collection of finite relations indexed by moments in time. The collection of moments in time is the set of natural numbers, denoted as ω. As complex time-varying attributes or intervals are not employed in the abstract model, time-varying relations are in First Normal Form.[7, 15] The elements of ω are uninterpreted, and can be in terms of hours, days, weeks and so on, depending on the intended application domain; the model need not know, and does not tell, which one. However, we assume that the interpretation is uniform with respect to the granularity of time; in other words, time-varying relations with different interpretations of time within the same temporal database are not supported.

An n-ary relation over a given domain U is an element of $\mathcal{P}(U^n)$ where $\mathcal{P}(S)$ denotes the power set of a given set S. An n-ary time-varying relation tr over the domain U is a mapping from the collection of moments in time to n-ary relations over U. In other words, tr is an element of $[\omega \rightarrow \mathcal{P}(U^n)]$ (i.e., an element of the set of functions from ω to $\mathcal{P}(U^n)$). We write $< tr(0), tr(1), tr(2), \ldots >$ for tr where for all $t \in \omega$, $tr(t) \in \mathcal{P}(U^n)$. We also have an ordering relation between time-varying relations defined as follows. Let r and s be time-varying relations with the same arity. We say that $r \sqsubseteq s$ if and only if for all $t \in \omega$, $r(t) \subseteq s(t)$. In other words, $\sqsubseteq$ is the point-wise extension of the subset relation upon ω.

In the abstract model, a temporal database is a mapping from a given set of relation symbols to time-varying relations over U. Let *Rel* be a countable set of relation symbols and U a given domain over which relations are defined. We require that U have at least one element and be countable. In practice, we require that U be finite. For any given temporal database db and an element p of *Rel* with arity n, the meaning of p in db is given as

$$db(p) \in [\omega \rightarrow \mathcal{P}(U^n)].$$

The set of temporal databases over U, denoted as $\mathcal{DB}$, is defined as follows:

$$\mathcal{DB} = [Rel \rightarrow \bigcup_{n \in \omega} [\omega \rightarrow \mathcal{P}(U^n)]].$$

Here we have that $db \in \mathcal{DB}$. It is also the case that $\mathcal{DB}$ is a complete lattice induced by the ordering relation $\sqsubseteq$.

In short, the model provides an abstract formalism for temporal databases, based on temporal semantics.[11] We just fix a set of relation symbols and a domain, and pick a certain member of $\mathcal{DB}$ modeling the current status of the temporal database. In more technical terms, members of $\mathcal{DB}$ are called "temporal interpretations."

We now give a concrete example of a temporal database.

Example 1 Let `emp(Name,Dept,Salary)` be an employee relation where `emp` $\in$ *Rel*, `Name` is the name of an employee, `Dept` the name of the department the employee works in, and `Salary` the salary of the employee. The `Name` attribute is the key for the `emp` relation. Suppose that we are interested in the employee relation from time 0 to time 3. We assume that the employee relation came into existence at time 0 (at the initial moment in time). Given any $db \in \mathcal{DB}$, the employee relation symbol `emp` is assigned in *db* to a (ternary) finite relation at each moment in time. For instance, it is possible that *db*(`emp`) is the time-varying relation from time 0 to time 3 depicted as follows.

$0 \longmapsto$	Bob	Shoes	2400
$1 \longmapsto$	Bob	Toys	2500
	Joy	Shoes	2250
$2 \longmapsto$	Bob	Toys	2500
	Joy	Shoes	2350
$3 \longmapsto$	Bob	Shoes	2600
	Joy	Toys	2450
	Kim	Toys	2000

In this example the logical time is interpreted as months. In the employee relation, Bob starts working in the Shoes department, moves to the Toys department with a raise in his salary, works there for two months, and then moves back to the Shoes department with another raise and so on. ∎

Since the abstract model does not preclude (or assume) any form of representation of time-varying data, we can use time-stamped tuples, intervals, time-varying attributes and so on (or even a non-uniform representation within the same model). The choice for the representation does not affect TRA or its properties, because the temporal operators of TRA are not designed to exploit actual representations of time-varying data (see below). The representation only affects how TRA is going to be implemented.

In order to drop the homogeneity restriction, we could add a special value into the domain of $\mathcal{DB}$ representing the null value $\perp$,[7] and impose a partial order in which the null value is below every other element, but no two other elements in the domain are comparable. (This means that the domain is *flat*.) This partial order induces another one among tuples, and then among relations and so on, all the way to the elements of $\mathcal{DB}$. However, to simplify the following presentation, we only consider non-null values.

In the abstract model, a provision is made for specifying infinite relations (i.e., an infinite collection of finite relations). In practice, we are interested in finite portions of infinite relations at moments in time or over intervals. Since the portions of infinite relations can be computed when needed, there is no need to restrict the model, or the algebra for that matter.

3. Temporal Relational Algebra

In this section, we first introduce the temporal relational algebra TRA, and then provide the denotational semantics of its expressions. TRA is a point-wise extension of the relational algebra upon ω defined as follows: The signature of TRA includes all operators of the relational algebra, and the universe of TRA is the set of time-varying relations $\bigcup_{n \in \omega}[\omega \rightarrow \mathcal{P}(U^n)]$. Let ∇ be a unary operator of the relational algebra, and ∇_T the corresponding operator of TRA. For any given time-varying relation r, the following holds. For all $t \in \omega$, we have that

$$\nabla_T(r)(t) = \nabla(r(t)).$$

Similarly for the binary operators. Here the operator ∇_T denotes the point-wise operation on the universe of TRA corresponding to the operator ∇. In short, when restricted to moments in time, TRA by design has the relational algebra as a special case. Yaghi[16] studied a similar notion in another context. Example uses of the operators of TRA are given in the following section.

3.1. *Operations*

An expression of TRA consists of compositions of algebraic operators and relation symbols. There are three kinds of algebraic operators: (1) point-wise operators, or operators of the relational algebra,[3] (2) temporal operators, and (3) aggregation operators. These operators are applied to time-varying relations and yield time-varying relations as a result which can then be used as operands in other operations. The signature of TRA is extended with temporal and aggregation operators summarized below. We assume the reader is familiar with the notions of a comparator and comparator formula; Ullman[15] discusses these concepts in detail. Throughout, we use infix notation for binary operators.

Point-wise Operators Point-wise operators are $\cap, \cup, \times, -, \pi_X$, and σ_F. Here X is a finite sequence of comparator values, and F is a comparator formula. All of $\cap$, $\cup$ and $(-)$ take two arguments (time-varying relations) with the same arity. At any given time t, the outcome of a point-wise operation depends *only* on the values of its arguments at time t. For instance, given the expression $r \cap s$ where r and s are time-varying relations, the resulting time-varying relation is the point-wise intersection of r and s (i.e., $r \cap s =< r(0) \cap s(0), r(1) \cap s(1), r(2) \cap s(2), \ldots >$ or, equivalently, $(r \cap s)(t) = r(t) \cap s(t)$ for all $t \in \omega$).

Temporal Operators The temporal operators `first`, `next` and `prev` take one argument; `fby[.]` is a binary operator (in fact, a family of binary operators). The temporal operator `first` freezes a time-varying relation at its initial value; `next` and `prev` shift a given time-varying relation in the corresponding direction; and `fby[.]`

does temporal splicing (i.e., cutting and pasting of time-varying relations). Read r `fby[t]` s as "r up to time t, followed by s after t." We call t as the *cut point* for `fby[t]`. In general, at any given time t, the outcome of a temporal operation may depend on the values of its arguments possibly at time t and at other moments in time. For instance, given a time-varying relation r, we have that **first** $r =< r(0), r(0), r(0), \ldots >$ (i.e., the value of **first** r at time t depends on the value of r at time 0); and **next** $r =< r(1), r(2), r(3), \ldots >$ (i.e., the value of **next** r at time t depends on the value of r at time $t+1$). From here on, we use the notation $\texttt{next}^n$ and $\texttt{prev}^n$ as syntactic sugar for n-folded applications of **next** and **prev**. For practical purposes, both operators can be parameterized to provide a more succint syntax.

Aggregation Operators Let $x \in \omega$. Aggregation operators are $\texttt{sum}_x$, $\texttt{avg}_x$, **count**, $\texttt{max}_x$ and $\texttt{min}_x$ with their obvious interpretations. These point-wise operators are applied to time-varying relations with arbitrary arities, and produce unary time-varying relations as a result.

3.2. Denotational Semantics

Given a temporal database db, an expression E over db contains only those relation symbols defined in db, and values from the domain of db. The meaning of an expression of TRA is a time-varying relation, just like the meaning of a relation symbol. Let $[\![E]\!](db)$ denote the meaning (denotation) of E with respect to db. We assume that all expressions are legal, i.e., arities of arguments given in an expression match with respect to the operations involved, and so do the types of attributes over which aggregation operations are performed.

In particular, for a relation symbol $p \in Rel$ with arity n, we are given that $db(p) \in [\omega \rightarrow \mathcal{P}(U^n)]$ where U is the domain of db. Thus $[\![E]\!](db)$ is also an element of $[\omega \rightarrow \mathcal{P}(U^k)]$ for some $k \in \omega$. In general, given an expression E, we have that

$$[\![E]\!] \in [\mathcal{DB} \rightarrow \bigcup_{n\in\omega} [\omega \rightarrow P(U^n)]].$$

The following is the formal definition of the denotation function $[\![.]\!]$.

Definition 1 *Let $db \in \mathcal{DB}$, $s, x \in \omega$, and A and B be* TRA *expressions. The denotations of each kind of expressions of* TRA *are defined as follows.*

1. $[\![p]\!](db) = db(p)$ *where* $p \in Rel$.
2. $[\![A \bigtriangledown B]\!](db) = [\![A]\!](db) \bigtriangledown [\![B]\!](db)$ *where* $\bigtriangledown$ *is any of* $\cap, \cup, \times$ *and* $-$.
3. $[\![\bigtriangledown A]\!](db) = \bigtriangledown[\![A]\!](db)$ *where* $\bigtriangledown$ *is any of* π_X, σ_F, $\texttt{sum}_x$, $\texttt{avg}_x$, $\texttt{max}_x$ $\texttt{min}_x$ *and* `count`.
4. $[\![\texttt{first}\ A]\!](db) = \lambda t.[\![A]\!](db)(0)$.

5. $[\![\texttt{next}\ A]\!](db) = \lambda t.[\![A]\!](db)(t+1)$.

6. $[\![\texttt{prev}\ A]\!](db) = \lambda t.\begin{cases} [\![A]\!](db)(t-1), & t > 0 \\ \emptyset, & t = 0 \end{cases}$

7. $[\![A\ \texttt{fby[}s\texttt{]}\ B]\!](db) = \lambda t.\begin{cases} [\![A]\!](db)(t), & t \leq s \\ [\![B]\!](db)(t), & t > s \end{cases}$

Item 1 is the basis case of the definition, which also establishes the connection to a given temporal database. Item 6 implies that the value of any expression of the form **prev** A at time 0 is the empty set, because we cannot go into the past beyond time 0.

For TRA to be an algebra in the mathematical sense, we need to show that all operations of TRA are closed; in other words, the denotation function $[\![.]\!]$ assigns a time-varying relation to each (legal) expression. This can be done by case analysis on the denotations of TRA expressions. We state the following theorem without proof.

Theorem 1 *The denotation function $[\![.]\!]$ is well-defined, i.e., for any legal expression E over a temporal database db, $[\![E]\!](db) \in \bigcup_{n\in\omega}[\omega \to \mathcal{P}(U^n)]$.*

We have the following lemma which states that the meaning of point-wise operators is the same at all moments in time. Therefore we can tell what a point-wise operator does to its argument by looking at the results from each moment in time. The lemma can be naturally extended to include binary point-wise operators.

Lemma 2 *Let ∇ be a unary point-wise operator of* TRA *and db a temporal database. For all time-varying relations r and s with the same arity, and for all $t, u \in \omega$, if $r(t) = s(u)$, then $\nabla(r)(t) = \nabla(s)(u)$.*

It is also natural to talk about the denotation of temporal operators. For instance, given the expression **next** E, we have that both $[\![E]\!](db)$ and $[\![\texttt{next}\ E]\!](db)$ are time-varying relations. So we may regard the temporal operator **next** as a mapping from time-varying relations to time-varying relations. More formally, we have that

$$\texttt{next} \in [\bigcup_{n\in\omega}[\omega \to \mathcal{P}(U^n)] \to \bigcup_{n\in\omega}[\omega \to \mathcal{P}(U^n)]].$$

In fact, we can obtain the definition of **next** from the definition of the denotation function $[\![.]\!]$ by λ-abstraction as $\texttt{next} = \lambda r.\lambda t.r(t+1)$. All of the operators of TRA (point-wise or not) enjoy a similar formulation of their denotations. We study the formal properties of the operators of TRA later in the paper.

4. Querying Time-Varying Data

This section gives some examples of querying time-varying data. Since there is no explicit manipulation of time in expressions of TRA, queries to find times of when things happen cannot be formulated. This is a tradeoff for the level of abstraction that we seek. For instance, given an employee relation we cannot answer the query "When did the employee X get promoted to the manager?" However, we can ask the query "Did the employee X get promoted to the manager at a particular time t or within the period of time from s to t?" As TRA is an algebra in the mathematical sense, the outcome of any expression is a time-varying relation, and thus can be used in other expressions only subject to arity restrictions. This is not possible in many other proposed temporal algebras.

In the following, we stipulate that all queries be evaluated at a given moment t in time (say, "now", "today", "this month" and so on) or over an interval identified by its starting and ending times. The evaluation of a query over an interval is performed by evaluating the query at all moments over the interval. We regard an interval as a window through which time-varying data may be queried. This is simply a computability requirement; time-varying relations are finite at particular moments in time or over intervals, but infinite in the aggregate.

4.1. Time-Specific Queries

In many applications, a snapshot of time-varying data at a particular moment in time is of interest. Queries of this kind are time-specific. Suppose we are given a temporal database *db* including the employee relation from example 1 and a department relation `dept(Dept,Manager)`. The `Dept` attribute is the key for the department relation. From here on, we refer to the attributes in a given relation by their positions. For instance, `Name` in `emp` is the 1st attribute. In the following examples, the logical time is interpreted as "months".

Example 2 Consider the query "How much did Bob earn in month 3?" It does not matter when this time-specific query is asked (two months ago, this month or several years later); the answer is always the same. The following is the query as a TRA expression:

$$\pi_3(\sigma_{1=\text{“}bob\text{”}}(\texttt{first next}^3\,\texttt{emp})).$$

The temporal operator(s) `first` $\texttt{next}^3$ move the context to month 3. Therefore a temporal selection can be achieved through temporal operators. Since Bob made \$2600 in month 3, the answer is the relation $\{< 2600 >\}$ whenever the query is evaluated. Let E be the expression given above. Then we have that $[\![E]\!](db) = \lambda t.\{< 2600 >\}$. ∎

4.2. *Time-Relative Queries*

Sometimes we are interested in what happens relative to a reference point in time, say "now", "today" and so on. For instance, we may pose queries like "Who was the manager of the Toys department two months ago?", or "Is Bob going to get a raise next month?". In such a query, there is no explicit reference to time, thus the outcome of the query depends on *when* it is evaluated. Queries about the future are not problematic, because it is assumed that the temporal database completely models the reality about the employee and department relations. If future data is not available yet, the answer would be the empty set in the model.

Example 3 Consider the query "How much did Bob earn last month?" The following is the query as a TRA expression:

$$\pi_3(\sigma_{1=\text{``}bob\text{''}}(\texttt{prev emp})).$$

The temporal operator **prev** moves the context to the last month relative to the reference point. Therefore the answer to this query may vary depending on when it is evaluated. At time 0, the answer is the empty set (implied by the semantics of **prev**); at time 1, $\{< 2400 >\}$; at times 2 and 3, $\{< 2500 >\}$ and so on. ∎

4.3. *Temporal Join*

Temporal operators also allow us to combine time-varying data from different moments in time. For instance, we may be interested in what happened over a period of time in a given department. The period of interest may be time-specific or time-relative. In the following, we first introduce a notation for representing intervals. Let $x, y \in \omega$.

- Time-specific intervals are denoted as $[x, y]$ where $x \leq y$.
- Time-relative intervals are denoted as $[(+/-)x, (+/-)y]$ where $(+/-)x \leq (+/-)y$. The following are time-relative intervals: $[-3, +5]$, $[-6, -1]$ and $[+2, +4]$, the first of which overlaps with "now".

The expression $[x, y]E$ is interpreted as finding all those tuples in E that are common at every moment in time over the interval $[x, y]$. With this interpretation, interval operators become a syntactic sugar for expressions involving temporal selections and intersections. For instance, the expression $[-1, +1]E$ is a shorthand notation for

$$\texttt{prev}\, E \cap E \cap \texttt{next}\, E.$$

Such expressions in fact do "temporal join", i.e., combine time-varying data from different moments in time. But this is not to be confused with the join operation $\bowtie_F$ from the relational algebra.

Example 4 Consider the (time-relative) query "Find all those employees in the Toys department who did not get a raise in the last two months". The following is the query:

$$\pi_1([-2,-1](\sigma_{2=\text{"toys"}}\mathtt{emp})).$$

If any employee in the Toys department did not get a raise over the interval $[-2,-1]$, the corresponding employee tuples would be the same. That is why we can formulate the query by temporal intersection. ∎

Suppose we are interested in the total salary of an employee in the Toys department over a period of time. We can answer such a query by aggregation operations over time-varying data joined by temporal selections and unions. We use a different notation for intervals over which time-varying data are joined by unions. Let $< x, y >$ denote an interval defined just like $[x, y]$. Then the expression $< 1, 3 > E$ is a syntactic sugar for

$$\mathtt{first\ next}\, E \cup \mathtt{first\ next}^2\, E \cup \mathtt{first\ next}^3\, E.$$

Example 5 Consider the query "Did Bob earn more than his manager from the month 1 to 3?" This is a time-specific *yes/no* query; therefore we just provide as answer a binary tuple with Bob's and his manager's total salaries for the period. The query in TRA may be formed in two parts: an expression to find the total salary Bob earned, and an expression to find the total salary Bob's manager earned. Here is the first part, call it A:

$$\mathtt{sum}_3(< 1,3 > (\sigma_{1=\text{"bob"}}\mathtt{emp})).$$

Here is the second part, call it B:

$$\mathtt{sum}_3(< 1,3 > (\pi_2((\pi_2(\sigma_{1=\text{"bob"}}\mathtt{emp})) \underset{1=1}{\bowtie} \mathtt{dept}) \underset{1=1}{\bowtie} \mathtt{emp})).$$

We assume that $\bowtie_F$ is the point-wise θ-join operator, defined in terms of other point-wise operators of TRA. The final expression is obtained by selection from the Cartesian product of A and B, i.e., $\sigma_{1>2}(A \times B)$. If Bob worked under different managers over the interval $< 1,3 >$, the salaries of all those managers would be lumped together. ∎

Example 6 Consider the query "Find all those employees who worked in the Toys department at one time or another." The answer to the query involves temporal selections from all moments in time, and therefore it is, in general, not computable. However, in practice, the range of the query should be restricted to the interval from the beginning up to "now", or up to the time of utterance of the query. Therefore the query is expressed as follows:

$$\pi_1(< 0, now > (\sigma_{2=\text{"toys"}}\mathtt{emp})).$$

Here *now* refers to the moment in time at which the query is being evaluated. It is the responsibility of the implementation to supply the time of evaluation in place of *now*. ∎

4.4. Temporal Splicing

In some cases, we are interested in a different form of temporal join, i.e., that of cutting out a portion of a time-varying relation, and pasting a portion of another one in its place. This is achieved by the binary temporal operator `fby[.]`.

Example 7 Suppose that a 10% overall salary increase is planned as from month t and the management wants to study its long term effects on the company. The temporal database is now extended with a new employee relation, say `projected-emp`, modeling the salary increase starting at month t. For analysis, all references to the employee relation before month t should be regarded as references to the original `emp` relation, and at and after month t as references to the `projected-emp` relation. In time-relative queries, it is impossible to determine which relation should be used since there are no explicit references to time. Therefore we provide a solution by "temporal splicing". The following TRA expression

$$\texttt{emp fby}[t-1]\ \texttt{projected-emp}$$

should be used whenever the employee relation is required. The operator `fby`$[t-1]$ guarantees that `emp` is used up to and including the cut point at $t-1$. Note that `fby[.]` cannot be defined in terms of other operators of TRA, thus it is employed as a primitive operator. ∎

5. Properties of TRA

In this section, we study the formal properties of TRA. Since TRA (without any temporal or aggregation operators) is a point-wise extension of the relational algebra, a "point-wise completeness[7] " result immediately follows. However, this is not quite satisfactory, because such a result does not tell us anything about the properties of temporal operations such as temporal selection, temporal join, and temporal splicing. Furthermore, "temporal completeness" is not a well established notion, as there are many approaches to temporal algebras, based on a variety of interpretations of time, and it is not clear what set of temporal operators are necessary in a temporal relational algebra. We may attempt to define "temporal completeness" as the ability of a temporal algebra to join temporal data over any finite set of intervals. (We can easily demonstrate that TRA has this property.) However, this is a crude definition, which needs to be based on formal grounds. Thus we defer the discussion of this issue until more research is done.

It is known that the operators of the relational algebra except the set difference are monotonic. Since TRA is a point-wise extension of the relational algebra, the monotonicity result immediately extends to the point-wise operators. In fact, TRA inherits all properties of the relational algebra, because the meaning (properties) of point-wise operators can be reduced to the meaning (properties) of the corresponding operators in the relational algebra. Thus, we have the following theorem.

Theorem 3 *The properties of monotonicity, commutativity, distributivity and associativity are preserved under point-wise extensions.*

We also have that all temporal operators of TRA are monotonic. For instance, consider the temporal operator **next**. Given time-varying relations r and s where $r \sqsubseteq s$, we have that $\mathtt{next}(r) \sqsubseteq \mathtt{next}(s)$ (i.e., **next** is monotonic) if and only if for all $t \in \omega$, $\mathtt{next}(r)(t) \subseteq \mathtt{next}(s)(t)$ if and only if for all $t \in \omega$, $r(t+1) \subseteq s(t+1)$. Since $r \sqsubseteq s$ holds, we conclude that **next** is monotonic. In TRA, it can also be shown that monotonicity is closed under composition. Therefore we have the following results.

Theorem 4 *All temporal operators of* TRA *are monotonic.*

Theorem 5 *In* TRA, *monotonicity is closed under composition.*

We also have that temporal operators commute with the point-wise operators. For instance, consider the selection operator π_X and temporal operators. Then the following algebraic properties are theorems of TRA:

$$\pi_X(\nabla(r)) = \nabla(\pi_X r),$$

$$\pi_X(r\ \mathtt{fby}\,[t]\ s) = (\pi_X r)\ \mathtt{fby}\,[t](\pi_X s)$$

where ∇ is any of **first**, **next** and **prev**. It can be shown that aggregation operators do not commute with either point-wise operators or temporal operators.

We can also formalize the interaction between the temporal operators of TRA. The following lemma states *some* important properties of the temporal operators.

Lemma 6 *Let* $r, s, v \in \bigcup_{n \in \omega}[\omega \rightarrow \mathcal{P}(U^n)]$ *and* $t, x \in \omega$. *The following are theorems of* TRA.

1. $\mathtt{next}(\mathtt{first}(r)) = \mathtt{first}(r)$.
2. $\mathtt{next}(\mathtt{prev}(r)) = r$.
3. $\mathtt{first}(r\ \mathtt{fby}\,[t]\ s) = \mathtt{first}(r)$, *regardless of* t.
4. $r\ \mathtt{fby}\,[t](s\ \mathtt{fby}\,[x]\ v) = r\ \mathtt{fby}\,[t]\ v$, *when* $t \geq x$.
5. $r\ \mathtt{fby}\,[t](s\ \mathtt{fby}\,[x]\ v) = (r\ \mathtt{fby}\,[t]\ s)\mathtt{fby}\,[x]\ v$, *when* $t \leq x$.

The proofs of these properties are straightforward. For instance, item 1 can be proved as follows: Let $r = < r(0), r(1), r(2), \ldots >$ be a time-varying relation. Given the definition of **first** as $\lambda r.\lambda t.r(0)$, we have that $\mathtt{first}(r) = < r(0), r(0), r(0), \ldots >$. Then, as **next** shifts a given time-varying relation to the left (and drops its first element), we have that $\mathtt{next}(\mathtt{first}(r)) = < r(0), r(0), r(0), \ldots >$.

The intuitive understanding of these properties is given as follows: Item 1 implies that **first** freezes a given time-varying relation at its value at time 0 (i.e., **first**(r) is an invariant of time). Item 2 is the cancellation axiom of **prev** followed by **next** (i.e., shifting a time-varying relation to the right and then immediately to the left has no effect). Item 3 is a consequence of the semantics of **first** and fby[.]. Item 4 asserts that only the first cut point matters in nested applications of fby[.]'s with non-increasing cut points. Item 5 states the condition under which fby[.] is associative.

The properties given above (along with some others that have not been mentioned here) can be used to manipulate TRA expressions for query optimization, which is an important aspect in implementations of query languages based on the relational algebra. There are many other properties of TRA which tell us when we cannot simplify an expression any further. For instance, it can be shown that **first**, **next** and **prev** do not commute with fby[.]; and that **next** and **prev** are not complete inverses (i.e., **prev**(**next**(r)) $\neq$ **next**(**prev**(r))).

We now introduce another useful property of operators. Let ∇ be an operator of TRA. We say that ∇ is "conjunctive" if and only if

$$\nabla(r \sqcap s) = \nabla(r) \sqcap \nabla(s).$$

In other words, a conjunctive operator commutes with $\sqcap$, which also reasserts that $\sqcap$ is a point-wise operator. It can be shown that all the temporal operators of TRA (as well as $\sqcap$, π_X and σ_F) have the conjunctivity property. Moreover, when $r \sqsubseteq s$, conjunctivity implies monotonicity.

Theorem 7 *The following operators of* TRA *have the conjunctivity property:* $\sqcap$, π_X, σ_F, **first**, **next**, **prev** *and* fby[.].

In a given expression, we can use the conjunctivity property to push temporal operators inside, and then use the properties given in lemma 6 (and others) to simplify the expression further.

6. Discussion

There are many other reported approaches to specifying and querying of time-varying data, most of which extend relational model with extra time attributes, and introduce (temporal) algebras and query languages. In the following, we relate our work to some other approaches, and point out the similarities and differences between our approach and others. Note that we use the term "temporal databases" to refer to those databases that model only "valid time[14]".

Clifford[1] proposed a model and a relational algebra for modeling and querying temporal databases. The model is based on an extension of the relational model with complex attributes, some of which are functions from moments in time or intervals to attribute values. In the algebra, this representation of time-varying data is exploited, and the temporal operators are specifically designed to manipulate these complex attributes. No formal semantics is offered for the algebra. Tansel[1] described another model and a temporal algebra to handle the time dimension. Just as in Clifford's approach, Tansel's model strives to minimize data redundancies using intervals and complex time-varying attributes, while at the same time providing a number of algebraic operators to manipulate various representations of time-varying data. The temporal algebra also includes an operator to drop the time components of a given time-varying relation to obtain snapshot relations. As a consequence, it does not satisfy the closure property and thus it is not an algebra in the mathematical sense.

Sarda[12] proposed another temporal algebra, with similar features as Tansel's. The outcome of expressions in Sarda's algebra may be time-varying relations, intervals and snapshot relations. Sarda also outlined a query language based on an extension of SQL with temporal operators. Gadia's approach[5] is similar to Sarda's; temporal elements (intervals) are explicitly manipulated in the temporal algebra, as well as time-varying relations. Gadia also considered a calculus-based query language along with the temporal algebra and showed their equivalence. We have not yet considered a calculus-based temporal query language.

McKenzie and Snodgrass[9] introduced an extension of the relational algebra with two *rollback* operators that can support both the valid time and transaction time, i.e., times of updates to the database. [14] Rollback operators are used to fetch snapshots of time-varying relations in a given temporal database, which are then manipulated by the operators of the relational algebra. The use of rollback operators is in a way similar to the use of the temporal operator `first` followed by a number of `next`'s. Moreover, expressions in the algebra always evaluate to snapshot states given time-varying relations. Therefore operators of the algebra may be regarded, with a very loose interpretation of the term, as *point-wise* extensions of those of the relational algebra. The denotational semantics of operators of the algebra are also given. However, the underlying model can only support a finite collection of snapshot states. The query language also provides an update operation.

In contrast with the approaches discussed above, TRA is based on a point-wise extension of the relational algebra, and hence it inherits all the properties of and methodologies already available for the relational algebra. [15] The importance of having the familiar relational algebra as a special case of a temporal algebra has been recognized by several researchers[1, 9, 12] (but, in our opinion, not exactly fulfilled.) Moreover, as far as TRA is concerned, it does not matter how time-varying data is represented (let it be in terms of tuples extended with time-stamps, intervals or complex attributes) as long as time-varying relations can be extracted from the representation. Freedom from representation ensures portability. For instance, Orgun and Wadge proposed TRA as a query language for a modular, temporal extension of DATALOG.[10] Temporal DATALOG provides a succint formalism for modeling temporal databases based on the logic programming paradigm.

As future work, we are considering extending TRA to support "transaction time[14]". The necessary formalism in the abstract model is already there induced by the complete lattice of temporal databases. For instance, the least element in the lattice would model the initial database in which all time-varying relations represent empty relations at all moments in time. In such a model, update operations can be formalized as mappings between temporal databases. Another tact for future work is to extend the model to allow for time-varying relations with a non-uniform interpretation of time in the same temporal database.

As iteration through moments in time is implicitly available in the temporal semantics of TRA, we are considering an equational extension in which recursive queries can be formulated. For instance, the following equation

$$tc = r \; \mathtt{fby[0]} \; (\mathtt{prev} \; tc \cup \pi_{1,3}(\mathtt{first} \; r \underset{2=1}{\bowtie} \mathtt{prev} \; tc))$$

defines an iterative solution, with recursion into the past, to find the transitive closure of a given binary relation represented by the time-varying relation r at time 0. From the equation, we have that $tc(0) = r(0)$. As time progresses, tc step-by-step approximates to the transitive closure of $r(0)$. We can extract the transitive closure of $r(0)$ as soon as $tc = \mathtt{prev}\; tc$ at some $t \in \omega$. However, we need to use the fix-point techniques[8] to explain the meaning of the equation, or a given set of (mutually recursive) equations.

7. Concluding Remarks

The major difference between our approach to temporal algebras and many others reported in the literature is that TRA is a "temporal algebra" in the mathematical sense, and that it is based on temporal semantics. TRA is *not* a specialized algebra to manipulate explicit representations of time-varying data or temporal elements such as intervals. Consequently, it has a much smoother semantics than many other proposed temporal algebras. We can easily introduce extra temporal operators into TRA and try out new ideas owing to the level of abstraction offered by it. We believe that representation is an implementation issue, and should not influence the design of temporal algebras and the choice of temporal operators thereof. Query optimization strategies can be directly based on the formal properties of TRA, and should be considered in conjunction with actual representations and storage structures. A prototype implementation based on time-stamped tuples, which also supports recursive equations, is under way.

8. Acknowledgements

We would like to thank Scott R. Tilley and Jimmy H. M. Lee for their helpful comments on an earlier draft of this paper.

9. References

1. J. Clifford and A. U. Tansel. On an algebra for historical relational databases: Two views. In *Proceedings of the 1985 ACM SIGMOD International Conference on Management of Data*, pages 247–265. Association for Computing Machinery, 1985.
2. J. Clifford and D. S. Warren. Formal semantics for time in databases. *ACM Transactions on Database Systems*, **8**(2):214–254, June 1983.
3. E. F. Codd. A relational model of data for large shared data banks. *Communications of the Association for Computing Machinery*, **13**(6):377–387, 1970.
4. S. Dutta. Generalized events in temporal databases. In *Proceedings of the Fifth International Conference on Data Engineering*, pages 118–125. IEEE Computer Society Press, 1989.
5. S. K. Gadia. A homogeneous relational model and query languages for temporal databases. *ACM Transactions on Database Systems*, **13**(4):418–448, December 1988.
6. S. K. Gadia and C. S. Yuen. Inadequacy of interval timestamps in temporal databases. *Information Sciences*, **54**:1–22, 1991.
7. D. Maier. *The Theory of Relational Databases*. Computer Science Press, 1983.
8. Z. Manna. *Mathematical Theory of Computation*, chapter 5. McGraw-Hill, 1974.
9. E. McKenzie and R. Snodgrass. Extending the relational algebra to support transaction time. In *Proceedings of the 1987 ACM SIGMOD International Conference on Management of Data*, pages 467–478. Association for Computing Machinery, 1987.
10. M. A. Orgun and W. W. Wadge. A relational algebra as a query language for Temporal DATALOG. In *Proceedings of DEXA '92, The Third Conference on Database and Expert Systems Applications*, Springer-Verlag, 1992.
11. N. Rescher and A. Urquhart. *Temporal Logic*. Springer-Verlag, 1971.
12. N. L. Sarda. Algebra and query language for a historical data model. *The Computer Journal*, **33**(1):11–18, 1990.
13. R. Snodgrass. Temporal databases: Status and research directions. *SIGMOD RECORD*, **19**:83–89, December 1990.
14. R. Snodgrass and I. Ahn. A taxonomy of time in databases. In *Proceedings of the 1985 ACM SIGMOD International Conference on Management of Data*, pages 236–246. Association for Computing Machinery, 1985.
15. J. D. Ullman. *Principles of Database and Knowledge-Base Systems*, volume 1. Computer Science Press, 1988.
16. A. A. Yaghi. *An Intensional Implementation Technique for Functional Languages*. PhD thesis, Dept. of Computer Science, University of Warwick, Coventry, England, 1984.

ARMSTRONG RELATIONS FOR FUNCTIONAL AND MULTIVALUED DEPENDENCIES IN RELATIONAL DATABASES

MILLIST. W. VINCENT
School of Computer and Information Science, University of South Australia, Adelaide 5095
(Email: m.vincent@unisa.edu.au)

B. SRINIVASAN
Department of Computer Science, Monash University Melbourne 3168
(Email: srini@bruce.cs.monash.edu.au)

ABSTRACT

An Armstrong relation for a set of constraints Σ is a relation which satisfies those constraints implied by Σ and violates every other constraint not implied by Σ. A new method for constructing an Armstrong relation is presented for the case when Σ consists of functional dependencies and multivalued dependencies with non-empty left hand sides. The technique results in a relation with significantly fewer tuples than the only other known method. The new technique is based on the construction of a two tuple relation which satisfies Σ but violates a specific dependency not implied by Σ.

1. Introduction

The concept of an Armstrong relation has been found to be useful in several theoretical and practical aspects of relational databases [1-12]. We will begin by a brief survey of Armstrong relations and their uses.

One starts with a set of constraints, denoted by Σ, that limits the number of legal states that a relation can have. The most widely used types of constraints used in relational databases are *functional dependencies* (FD's) [13] and *multivalued dependencies* (MVD's) [14], but for the moment we will generalize these and allow a constraint to be any sentence in first order logic [6, 15]. Let Σ then be a set of such sentences and let σ be any single sentence. We say that Σ *logically implies* σ, which we will denote by $\Sigma \Rightarrow \sigma$, if every relation that satisfies Σ also satisfies σ. For example, if Σ is the set of FD's $\{A \rightarrow B, B \rightarrow C\}$ then $\Sigma \Rightarrow A \rightarrow C$.

Let Σ be a set of sentences and let Σ^+ be the set of all the sentences that are logically implied by Σ. Then an *Armstrong relation* for Σ is a relation which satisfies Σ^+ and *no other sentences*, i.e. the relation violates every sentence σ which is not in Σ^+.

For instance, let Σ be the set of FD's $\{EMP \rightarrow DEPT, DEPT \rightarrow MNGR\}$. Then the example [9] shown in Figure 1 is an Armstrong relation for Σ.

EMP	DEPT	MNGR
Hilbert	Maths	Gauss
Pythagoras	Maths	Gauss
Turing	Computing	Von Neumann
Einstein	Physics	Gauss

Figure 1. An Armstrong relation for the FD's {EMP→DEPT, DEPT→MNGR}

It can be seen that this relation satisfies all the FD's in Σ but violates every FD not in Σ^+. For example, the FD *MNGR→DEPT* is not Σ^+ and the relation violates this FD because *Gauss* is the manager of two different *DEPT*s.

A practical application of Armstrong databases is in the area of database design tools [11, 12]. The essential idea in some of these tools is that after the database designer specifies a set of FD constraints to the tool, the tool then displays to the designer an Armstrong relation for the set of FD's. The intention is that this can assist the designer to notice any FD's which may have been inadvertently omitted from the set of FD's because the displayed Armstrong relation will violate every such FD. For instance, in the example shown in Figure 1 the designer would observe that *Gauss* manages two departments and, if this is not appropriate, then the original set of FD's can be modified. Obviously, for such an approach to be useful the Armstrong relation should be as small as possible and, as will be discussed later, although in the worst case the number of tuples in an Armstrong relation can be exponentially proportional to both the number of FD's and the number of attributes[4], in many practical examples the size can be significantly smaller [11].

The question of when an arbitrary set of constraints has an Armstrong relation has been well researched. Armstrong and Fagin [1, 2] answered the question affirmatively for the case of FD constraints and later Beeri *et. al.* [3] showed the same for combined FD and MVD constraints. The existence of Armstrong relations for more general classes of constraints has also been investigated [5-10]. However, the problem of actually generating Armstrong relations has only been investigated for the FD case. For this case, Beeri *et. al.* [4] derived upper and lower bounds for the size of Armstrong relations and gave an algorithm for generating an Armstrong relation for a given set of FD's. They also showed that in the worst case the number of tuples in an Armstrong relation is exponentially proportional both to the number of attributes in the relation and the number of FD's. Later, Mannila and Raiha [11] gave a more efficient algorithm for generating an Armstrong relation and proved a result that demonstrated that if a relation is in *Boyce-Codd Normal Form* [16] and has a small number of candidate keys, then the size of an Armstrong relation can be much smaller than in the worst case.

In this paper we examine the problem of generating an Armstrong relation when the constraints contain both FD and MVD's. As mentioned previously, for Armstrong relations to be useful in areas such as database design tools, it is important that an Armstrong relation be as small as possible in order to facilitate its examination. The contribution of this paper is to give a method for constructing an Armstrong relation which results in a significant smaller relation than the only other known method for the case of infinite attribute domains - that given by Beeri *et. al.* [3] in their proof of the 'strong' completeness property of the inference rules for FD's and MVD's. Silva and Melankoff [12] also gave a method for constructing an Armstrong relation from a set of FD's and MVD's, but their technique is only applicable for the case where the size of attribute domains are finite since number of tuples in the relation they generate is proportional to the size of the attribute domains, whereas the method of Beeri *et. al.* and ourselves covers the case of infinite attribute domains.

We now briefly compare the method of construction of Beeri *et. al.* and the one presented here. In their construction, they first created a relation for each dependency not in Σ^+ such that the relation satisfied Σ but violated the chosen dependency in Σ^+. The size of each of these relations is exponentially proportional to the number of sets in the dependency base (see later). They then formed a union of all these relations to create a single Armstrong for Σ.

In our construction, we also create the final Armstrong relation by combing relations generated for each dependency not in Σ^+, but these initial relations are much smaller than the ones constructed by Beeri *et. al.* since each contains exactly two tuples. The existence of such relations can be deduced from the construction used in Beeri's paper and another result due to Sagiv *et. al.* [17]. This result states that if a relation *r* satisfies a set Σ of FD's and MVD's but violates some other MVD or FD σ, then there exists a two tuple sub relation of *r* which satisfies Σ but violates σ. Since Beeri *et. al.* showed how to construct such a relation *r*, the theorem of Sagiv *et. al.* implies that there exists a two tuple relation with the required property. However, the result of Sagiv *et. al.* is an existence proof and doesn't provide a method for the construction of such a relation. We provide an explicit construction of this two tuple relation. Moreover, we show that our construction is necessary in that any other two tuple relation with the same property must have a similar structure.

2. Definitions and Notation

The notation used in this paper is the standard notation used in the database literature [18, 19]. A universe *U* is a finite set of attributes, each attribute having an associated domain of values. The *domain* of an attribute $A \in U$ is denoted by DOM(*A*) and in this paper is assumed to be infinite. As usual, the symbols *A*, *B*, *C*, . . and their subscripts represent single attributes and *V*, *W*, *X*, . . and their subscripts denote sets of attributes. The union of attribute sets *X* and *Y* is denoted by *XY* rather than $X \cup Y$. *X* - *Y* denotes set difference.

A *relation scheme* *R* is a subset of *U*. Let the elements of a relation scheme be denoted by $R = \{A_1, . . A_n\}$. A *tuple* over *R* is an element of $DOM(A_1) \times . \times .$

DOM(A_n) where × denotes the cartesian product. A *relation instance* (or simply a *relation*) r over R, denoted by $r(R)$, is a *finite* set of tuples defined over R. In this paper, all relations are defined over a single relation scheme R and so $r(R)$ will often be denoted simply by r.

If t is a tuple over R and X is a subset of R, then $t[X]$ is the *restriction* of t to the attributes in X.

2.1. Functional and Multivalued Dependencies

A *functional dependency* (FD) is a constraint denoted by $X \rightarrow Y$ where X and Y are sets of attributes. A relation r *satisfies* the FD $X \rightarrow Y$, if for all $t_1, t_2 \in r$, if $t_1[X] = t_2[X]$ then $t_1[Y] = t_2[Y]$, otherwise it *violates* the FD. A *multivalued dependency* (MVD) is a constraint denoted by $X \rightarrow\rightarrow Y$. A relation r satisfies the MVD $X \rightarrow\rightarrow Y$ if for all t_1, $t_2 \in r$ with $t_1[X] = t_2[X]$, there exists a tuple t_3 in r such that $t_3[X] = t_1[X]$, $t_3[Y] = t_1[Y]$ and $t_3[R - XY] = t_2[R - XY]$. A relation r *satisfies* a set Σ of FD's and MVD 's if it satisfies every dependency in Σ, otherwise it *violates* Σ. We shall assume that X and Y in any MVD $X \rightarrow\rightarrow Y$ are disjoint because of the result [14] that $X \rightarrow\rightarrow Y$ is satisfied if and only if $X \rightarrow\rightarrow Y - X$ is satisfied.

As mentioned in an earlier section, it is much easier to establish logical implication using a set of inference rules rather than using the definition of logical implication. Following is a set of inference rules for FD's and MVD's that has been shown to be complete [3].

FD rules:

A1: If $Y \subseteq X$, then $X \rightarrow Y$ (reflexivity)
A2: If $X \rightarrow Z$ and $Y \subseteq U$, then $XY \rightarrow ZY$ (augmentation)
A3: If $X \rightarrow Y$ and $Y \rightarrow Z$, then $X \rightarrow Z$ (transitivity)

MVD rules:

A4: If $X \rightarrow\rightarrow Y$ then $X \rightarrow\rightarrow (R - X - Y)$
A5: If $X \rightarrow\rightarrow Y$ and $V \subseteq W$, then $WX \rightarrow\rightarrow VY$
A6: If $X \rightarrow\rightarrow Y$ and $Y \rightarrow\rightarrow Z$ then $X \rightarrow\rightarrow (Z - Y)$
A7: If $Y \subseteq X$, then $X \rightarrow\rightarrow Y$

Combined FD and MVD rules:

A8: If $X \rightarrow Y$ then $X \rightarrow\rightarrow Y$
A9: If $X \rightarrow\rightarrow Y$, $Z \subseteq Y$, $W \cap Y = \emptyset$ and $W \rightarrow Z$, then $X \rightarrow Z$

The following rules, although derivable from those above, are useful and will be needed in the next section.

A10: If $X \rightarrow YZ$ then $X \rightarrow Y$
A11: If $X \rightarrow\rightarrow Y$ and $X \rightarrow\rightarrow Z$ then $X \rightarrow\rightarrow YZ$

The *closure* of a set of attributes X with respect to a set Σ of MVD's and FD's, denoted by X^+, is the set of attributes such that an attribute $A \in X^+$ if $X \rightarrow A$ can be derived from Σ and the inference rules. The dependency basis for a set of attributes X, denoted by DEP(X), is a set of attribute sets such that a set Y is in DEP(X) if $X \rightarrow\rightarrow Y$ can be derived from a finite application of the inference rules. We note that since rules A1 - A9 have been shown to be complete, then both X^+ and DEP(X) are exactly those dependencies which are logically implied by Σ. In practice, rather than using DEP(X) it is easier to work with a slightly different set, called MDEP(X), which converts DEP(X) to a set of minimal disjoint sets. Writing the elements in MDEP(X) as $\{X_1, .. X_p, X^+_1, .. X^+_j, W_1, .. W_n\}$ it can be shown [20] that MDEP(X) has the following properties:

(i) MDEP(X) covers R, i.e. $R = \cup Z_i$ where $Z_i \in$ MDEP(X);
(ii) The sets in MDEP(X) are disjoint;
(iii) $Y \in$ DEP(X) if and only if $Y = \cup Z_i$ where $Z_i \in$ MDEP(X);
(iv) $X_1, .. X_p$ are single attribute sets such that $X = \cup X_i$;
(v) $X^+_1, .. X^+_j$ are single attribute sets such that $X^+ - X = \cup X^+_i$.

3. Constructing an Armstrong Relation

We will now describe a method for constructing an Armstrong relation for a set of FD's and MVD's. First, we present a preliminary lemma needed in the main proof.

Lemma 1. *Let R be a relation scheme and let Σ be a set of MVD's and FD's. Then for any MVD $X \rightarrow\rightarrow Y$ which is not logically implied by Σ, there exists $V \in$ MDEP(X) such that $V \cap Y \neq \emptyset$, $V \cap (R - XY) \neq \emptyset$ and $V \cap X^+ = \emptyset$.*

Proof. As outlined earlier, the sets in MDEP(X) are disjoint and can be written as $\{X_1, .. X_p, X^+_1, .. X^+_j, W_1, .. W_n\}$ where $X_1, .. X_p$ are the single attributes of X; $X^+_1, .. X^+_j$ are the single attributes in $X^+ - X$ and $W_1, .. W_k$ are sets of attributes that are disjoint from X^+. Since XY and $R - XY$ cover R, then for every set $V \in$ MDEP(X) either $V \subseteq XY$ or $V \subseteq R - XY$ or ($V \cap XY \neq \emptyset$ and $V \cap R - XY \neq \emptyset$). Suppose that there is no V in MDEP(X) which has a non-empty intersection with both XY and $R - XY$. Then partition MDEP(X) into $V_1, .. V_j$ which are subsets of XY and $V_{j+1}, .. V_n$ which are subsets of $R - XY$. Since Y is not in DEP(X) by assumption, it follows that $Y' = Y - V_1 .. V_n \neq \emptyset$ or else inference rule A11 would imply the contradiction that Y is in DEP(X). But since MDEP(X) covers R, it follows that $Y' \subseteq V_{j+1}, \ldots V_n$ which contradicts the assumption that $V_{j+1}, \ldots V_n$ has an empty intersection with XY. So there has to be a V in MDEP(X) such that $V \cap XY \neq \emptyset$ and $V \cap R - XY \neq \emptyset$. However V cannot be any of the sets $X_1, \ldots X_p, X^+_1, \ldots X^+_j$ since each of these sets contains a single attribute and so cannot have a non-empty intersection with the disjoint sets XY and $R - XY$. Hence V must be one of the sets $W_1, \ldots W_n$ and the result is established. □

We now use the lemma two create a two tuple relation which satisfies every dependency in Σ but violates a specific dependency not in Σ. The construction is quite simple. If the dependency to be violated is an MVD $X \rightarrow\rightarrow Y$, then by the previous Lemma we can choose an element W_i from MDEP(X) such that W_i has non-empty intersection with Y and $R - XY$. If instead the dependency to be violated is an FD $X \rightarrow Y$, then we show in the following theorem that in this case there must also exist a W_i with a non-empty intersection with Y. The relation required is then one whose tuples are equal on every attribute except those in W_i. This method is now specified more precisely.

Algorithm: Construction of a two tuple relation for a set of FD's and MVD's.
Input: A set Σ of FD's and MVD's and an MVD $X \rightarrow\rightarrow Y$ or an FD $X \rightarrow Y$ not logically implied by Σ.
Output: A two tuple relation which violates $X \rightarrow\rightarrow Y$ (or $X \rightarrow Y$) but satisfies Σ.
Method:
1. If the dependency to be violated is an MVD $X \rightarrow\rightarrow Y$ choose a W_i from MDEP(X) such that $W_i \cap Y \neq \emptyset$ and $W_i \cap (R - XY) \neq \emptyset$.
2. If the dependency is an FD $X \rightarrow Y$ then choose a W_i from MDEP(X) such that $Y \cap W_i \neq \emptyset$.
3. Construct a relation of two tuples t_1 and t_2 as follows. If $A \in W_i$, choose values from DOM(A) such that $t_1[A] \neq t_2[A]$ otherwise let $t_1[A] = t_2[A]$.

The structure of the constructed relation is shown in Figure 2.

X_1	.	X_p	X^+_1	.	X^+_j	W_1	.	W_i	.	W_n
1	1	1	1	1	1	1	1	0	1	1
1	1	1	1	1	1	1	1	1	1	1

Figure 2.

We now verify that a relation constructed by Algorithm 1 has the stated properties.

Theorem 2. *The relation constructed in Algorithm 1 satisfies Σ but violates the MVD $X \to\to Y$ (or $X \to Y$).*

Proof. As before, let the sets in MDEP(X) be denoted by $\{X_1, .. X_p, X_1^+, .. X_j^+, W_1, .. W_n\}$. Firstly, if the dependency to be violated is an MVD $X \to\to Y$, then by Lemma 1 the set W_i in Step 1 of the algorithm always exists. If instead the dependency to be violated is an FD $X \to Y$, then by assumption $Y \not\subseteq X_1 .. X_p X_1^+ .. X_j^+$ and so $Y \cap W_1 .. W_n \neq \emptyset$ since MDEP(X) covers R and thus there exists W_i such that $Y \cap W_i \neq \emptyset$ and so the set required in Step 2 always exists. We now show that the relation created in Step 3 satisfies the requirements of the theorem. For convenience, relabel the elements of MDEP(X) so that W_i is relabelled as W_1.

Firstly, if the dependency to be violated is an MVD $X \to\to Y$ then by the definitions of W_1, t_1 and t_2, it follows that $t_1[X] = t_2[X]$, $t_1[Y] \neq t_2[Y]$ and $t_1[R - XY] \neq t_2[R\text{-}XY]$, from which it follows that r violates $X \to\to Y$. If the dependency is an FD $X \to Y$ then it is violated since $t_1[X] = t_2[X]$ and $t_1[Y] \neq t_2[Y]$.

Consider now the satisfaction of the dependencies in Σ. Firstly, let $V \to Z$ be any FD in Σ and suppose to the contrary that it is violated in r. Let $W = X_1 .. X_p X_1^+ .. X_j^+ W_2 .. W_n$. By the construction of r, for $V \to Z$ to be violated one must have that $V \subseteq W$ and $Z \cap W_1 \neq \emptyset$. From $V \to Z$ and inference rules A5 and A8, it follows that $W \to\to Z$ and combining with the fact that $X \to\to W$ from rule A11 and using the transitivity rule A6 gives $X \to\to Z - W$ which is the same as $X \to\to Z \cap W_1$ since MDEP(X) covers R. From rule A10 it also follows that $V \to Z \cap W_1$. Then, since $V \subseteq W$ and the fact that W and W_1 are disjoint, it follows that V and $Z \cap W_1$ are disjoint and so by rule A9 $X \to Z \cap W_1$ and thus $Z \cap W_1 \subseteq X_1 .. X_p X_1^+ .. X_j^+$. This is a contradiction since $Z \cap W_1$ is a non-empty subset of W_1 but by property (ii) of MDEP(X), W_1 is disjoint from $X_1 .. X_p X_1^+ .. X_j^+$.

The next part of the proof is based on the method used by Beeri *et al.* [3]. Consider now the case of any MVD $V \to\to Z$ in Σ and suppose to the contrary that it is violated. From the definitions of t_1 and t_2, the only way for this to happen is for $V \subseteq W$, $Z \cap W_1 \neq \emptyset$ and $(R - VZ) \cap W_1 \neq \emptyset$. We can note that these conditions imply that $Z \cap W_1$ is a proper subset of W_1. Since $V \subseteq W$ it follows by rule A5 that $W \to\to Z$ is in DEP(X). Also, by rule A11 $X \to\to W$ is in DEP(X) and so using the transitive rule $X \to\to Z - W$, that is $X \to\to Z \cap W_1$, is in DEP(X). This is a contradiction since by property (iii) of MDEP(X), $Z \cap W_1$ must be a union of elements in MDEP(X) but this cannot occur since by property (ii) the sets in MDEP(X) are disjoint and $Z \cap W_1$ is a non-empty proper subset of W_1. Hence r satisfies $V \to\to Z$ and the result is established. □

The construction method used in the theorem is illustrated in the following example [20].

Example 1. Let $R = \{A, B, C, D, E, F, G\}$ and $\Sigma = \{AB \rightarrow\rightarrow DE, E \rightarrow\rightarrow F, E \rightarrow C\}$. Standard algorithms [21] can be used to show that if we let $X = AB$, then $X^+ = \{A, B, C\}$ and DEP(X) = $\{A, B, C, DE, F, G\}$. Also, the MVD $AB \rightarrow\rightarrow CE$ is not in DEP(X) and the set DE in MDEP(X) has non-empty intersection with CE and $R - ABCE = DFG$. The relation in Figure 3 satisfies Σ but violates $AB \rightarrow\rightarrow CE$. In contrast, if the construction in [3] is used then the number of tuples in the relation would be $2^{(|MDEP(X)| - |X^+|)} = 2^{6-3} = 8$. The relation that would be constructed by this alternative technique is illustrated in Figure 4.

A	B	C	D	E	F	G
1	1	1	1	1	1	1
1	1	1	0	0	1	1

Figure 3.

A	B	C	D	E	F	G
1	1	1	0	0	0	0
1	1	1	0	0	0	1
1	1	1	0	0	1	0
1	1	1	0	0	1	1
1	1	1	1	1	0	0
1	1	1	1	1	0	1
1	1	1	1	1	1	0
1	1	1	1	1	1	1

Figure 4.

The following result shows that any two tuple relation which satisfies a set of FD's and MVD's but violates some other MVD or FD must have a similar structure to the one created by the theorem.

Lemma 3. *Let R be a relation scheme, Σ a set of FD's and MVD's and let $X \rightarrow\rightarrow Y$ (or $X \rightarrow Y$) be a dependency which is not logically implied by Σ. As before, denote the elements in MDEP(X) by $\{X_1, \ldots X_p, X^+_1, \ldots X^+_j, W_1, \ldots W_n\}$. Then for any two tuple relation which satisfies Σ but violates $X \rightarrow\rightarrow Y$ (or $X \rightarrow Y$), both tuples are identical on every set in MDEP(X) except for one W_i.*

Proof. Firstly, since r violates $X \to\to Y$ (or $X \to Y$) then both tuples must be identical on the sets $X_1, \ldots X_p$. They must also be identical on $X_1^+, \ldots X_j^+$ or else r would violate some FD in Σ. Obviously the two tuples must then differ on some W_i since MDEP(X) covers R and the two tuples cannot be identical. Suppose they differ on two sets W_i and W_j. Then since the sets in MDEP(X) are disjoint, it follows that $t_1[W_i] \neq t_2[W_j]$ and $t_1[R - XW_i] \neq t_2[R - XW_i]$ and so r violates $X \to\to W_i$ since the tuples are identical on X. This contradicts the assumption that r satisfies Σ and so the two tuples can only differ on one W_i. □

Lastly, we use Theorem 2 to create an Armstrong relation for Σ.

Theorem 4. *Let R be a relation scheme and Σ a set of MVD's and FD's with non-empty left hand sides. Then there exists an Armstrong relation for Σ consisting of 2k tuples where k is the number of dependencies not in Σ^+.*

Proof. For each dependency not in Σ^+, construct a two tuple relation according to Theorem 2 but use distinct attribute values in each relation so that none of the relations have a common attribute value. This can be done since we are assuming infinite domains for attributes. Then create a relation r by forming a union of all these two tuple relations. It then follows directly by Theorem 2 and the fact that all the two tuple sub-relations contain distinct values that r is an Armstrong relation for Σ. □

A few comments on the restriction to non-empty left hand sides in this last theorem are appropriate. Even though Theorem 2 is still valid if either the dependencies in Σ or the dependency to be violated has an empty left hand side, the method in Theorem 4 does not produce an Armstrong relation if there are dependencies in Σ with empty left hand sides. For example, suppose that $R = \{A, B, C\}$ and $\Sigma = \{\emptyset \to\to C\}$. Then the construction of the two tuple relation for the FD $A \to B$ yields the relation {<*1, 1, 1*>, <*1, 0, 1*>} and the construction for $B \to C$ yields {<2, 2, 2>, <2, 2, *3*>} both of which satisfy $\emptyset \to\to C$. Yet when the relations are combined together according to Theorem 4, as shown in the following figure, then the resulting relation doesn't satisfy $\emptyset \to\to C$ since it is not the product of its projections on AB and C.

A	B	C
1	1	1
1	0	1
2	2	2
2	2	3

We note that the original method of Beeri *et al.*[3] is also only valid for the case when the dependencies in Σ have non-empty left hand sides. They showed later [4] that their construction can be modified to work for the case of FD constraints by setting the values for any attribute A such that $\emptyset \rightarrow A \in \Sigma^+$ to be the same in every tuple. However this technique doesn't work for MVD constraints and so it remains an open question of how to modify either our or Beeri's method to handle this case.

4. Conclusions

In this paper we have investigated the problem of constructing an Armstrong relation for a set of FD and MVD constraints. We have shown a method which results in a relation with significantly fewer tuples than the only other known construction method. We now briefly discuss some other aspects of generating Armstrong relations which need to be investigated.

The construction method that we have proposed in this paper, while being an improvement over the other method, is by no means optimal since we create a two tuple relation for every dependency not in Σ^+ and this is more than is necessary. For instance, if one has constructed a relation which violates an FD $X \rightarrow Y$, then the relation must also violate any FD not in Σ^+ of the form $X' \rightarrow YZ$ where $X' \subseteq X$ and so it is not necessary to create a separate relation for these FD's. In fact, what one needs to do is to select the smallest set of dependencies from those not in Σ^+ such that if those dependencies are violated then every other dependency not in Σ^+ is also violated. This is similar to what one does in creating a minimal cover for a set of FD's [22], except that in this case the constraints are FD violations rather than FD satisfaction. The problem of developing sets of inference rules for FD violations has also arisen in other contexts [20, 23, 24].

5. Acknowledgments

Thanks to the helpful comments from an anonymous referee in pointing out the need to consider dependencies with empty left hand sides.

6. References

1. R. Fagin, Functional Dependencies in a Relational Database and Propositional Logic, *IBM Journal of Research and Development* **21**(6), (1977), 534-544.
2. W.W. Armstrong, Dependency Structures of Data Base Relationships, *IFIP Conference*, (1974), 580-583.
3. C. Beeri, R. Fagin & J. Howard, A Complete Axiomatization for Functional and Multivalued Dependencies in Database Relations, *ACM SIGMOD International Conference on Management of Data*, (1977), 47-61.

4. C. Beeri, M. Dowd, R. Fagin & R. Statman, On the Structure of Armstrong Relations for Functional Dependencies, *Journal of the Association for Computing Machinery* **31**(1), (1984), 30-46.

5. J. Demetrovics, J. Ronyai & L.H.n. Son, On the Representation of Dependencies by Propositional Logic, *3rd Symposium on Mathematical Fundamentals of Database and Knowledge Base Systems*, (1991), 230-241.

6. R. Fagin, Horn Clauses and Database dependencies, *Journal of the Association for Computing Machinery* **29**(4), (1982), 952-985.

7. R. Fagin, Armstrong databases, *7th IBM Symp. on Mathematical Foundations of Computer Science*, (1982),

8. R. Fagin, D. Maier, J. Ullman & M. Yannakakis, Tools for Template Dependencies, *SIAM Journal of Computing* **12**(1), (1983), 36-59.

9. R. Fagin, Armstrong databases for Functional and Inclusion Dependencies, *Information Processing Letters* **16**((1983), 13-19.

10. J. Grant & H.E. Jacobs, On a Family of Generalized Dependency Constraints, *Journal of the Association for Computing Machinery* **29**(4), (1982), 986-987.

11. H. Mannila & K. Räihä, Design by Example: An Application of Armstrong Relations, *Journal of Computer and System Sciences* **33**, (1986), 126-141.

12. A.M. Silva & M.A. Melankoff, A method for helping discover the dependencies of a relation, in *Advances in Data Base Theory* , ed. Gallaire, H., Minker, J. & Nicolas, J.M. (Plenum Press, New York, 1981).

13. E.F. Codd, Further Normalization of the Database Relational Model, in *Data Base Systems* , (Prentice-Hall, 1972) 34-64.

14. R. Fagin, Multivalued Dependencies and a New Normal Form for Relational Databases, *ACM Transactions on Database Systems* **2**(3), (1977), 262-278.

15. R. Fagin & M. Vardi, The Theory of Data Dependencies - A survey, in *Mathematics of Information Processing* , ed. Anshell, M. & Gewritz, W. (American Mathematical Society, Providence, 1986) 17-91.

16. E.F. Codd, Recent Investigations in Relational Database Systems, *I.F.I.P. Conference*, (1974), 1017-1021.

17. Y. Sagiv, C. Delobel, D.S. Parker & R. Fagin, An Equivalence Between Relational Databases and a Fragment of Propositional Logic, *Journal of the Association for Computing Machinery* **28**(3), (1981), 435-453.

18. D. Maier, *The Theory of Relational Databases* (Computer Science Press, 1983).

19. J.D. Ullman, *Theory of Database and Knowledge-Base Systems* (Computer Science Press, 1988).

20. J. Paredaens, P. DeBra, M. Gyssens & D.V. Gucht, *The Structure of the The Relational Database Model* (Springer-Verlag, Berlin, 1989).

21. C. Beeri, On the Membership Problem for Functional and Multivalued Dependencies in Relational Databases, *ACM Transactions on Database Systems* **5**(3), (1980), 241-259.

22. R.C. Shock, Computing the minimal cover of functional dependencies, *Information Processing Letters* **22**((1986), 157-159.

23. B. Thalheim et. al., Open problems in database theory, in *Proc. 1st Symposium on Mathematical Fundamentals of Database Systems, Lecture Notes in Computer Science no. 305* , (Springer Verlag, 1988) 241-247.

24. J.M. Janas, On Functional Independencies, *Foundations of Software Technology and Theoretical Computer Science, 8th Conference*, (1988), 487-508.

The Intelligent Developer — Towards the automated implementation of information systems

Anthony Berglas
University of Queensland*

Abstract

While there has been considerable research into formal methods for the analysis and design of information systems, techniques for implementation remain relatively primitive. By building a knowledge base of commonly used programming techniques it has been possible to automatically program substantial applications from succinct definitions. Further, a novel two pass mechanism has enabled complex programs to be implemented without altering the generated code while still making full use of a conceptual schema. The technique has been validated in a new tool, the *Intelligent Developer* (ID) which has been found to facilitate a substantial improvement in productivity over traditional CASE/fourth generation techniques. This paper discusses both the underlying structure of the knowledge base and practical experience gained by introducing the tool into a production environment.

Keywords: Information Systems, Automatic Programming, CASE, Implementation Knowledge.

1 Introduction

The *Intelligent Developer* (ID) provides a mechanism to represent and utilize the *detailed* knowledge programmers use to realize information system designs. This enables most implementation logic to be automatically inferred directly from an extended conceptual schema. The knowledge base comprises a series of *building blocks*, each of which may be considered to be a mini expert in a multi agent system.

*E-Mail berglas@cs.uq.oz.au.

These building blocks may interrogate conceptual schemas and interact with each other in a well defined manner, and more sophisticated application programmers may develop new ones.

Zoom is a typical building block that generates code to "pop up" a sub-window showing more details about a record whose key is displayed on a screen. It can also create help messages to indicate to the end user that this is possible, and include documentation fragments in the user manual.

Most of an information system's definition is entered into a NIAM [14] conceptual schema using a GUI[1] layout tool, the *Conceptual Designer* (CD). This model provides all the information necessary to produce a relational table design, as well as many sophisticated integrity constraints.

The model has been extended to allow implementation hints to be integrated with the schema. For example, a predicate (eg. "Customer Has a Name") may be flagged as *keyworded selective*, which means that, by default, the ID will use this column to select Customer rows via an automatically created keyword table. Simple business rules could also be included in the schema to indicate how derived values should be calculated, and what processing should be done when an entity is retrieved or updated.

The ID can create many programs directly from information in the schema. However, real applications involve complexities that need more specific definition at the program level. The ID uses a two pass mechanism that allows implementors to selectively override and augment generated programs as is inevitably required when dealing with the complexities of real applications, *without* altering the generated 4GL code.

Building blocks enrich the vocabulary with which applications are described as well as being tools for their implementation. For example, once a *thesaurus* block has been developed that can classify entities into specialization hierarchies, one can simply say "Products have a multi-parent thesaurus" without having to specify the data and rules required to implement it. These references to a library of common techniques provides another paradigm for the specification of information systems that complements established schema, data flow and rule based ones.

The ID has been used in production for eighteen months and it has been possible to code about three programs per programmer day for medium sized (100 program) applications, which is a 300% improvement over results obtained using conventional CASE/4GL technology. These applications have been easier to design because fewer cost/benefit trade-offs needed to be made. More importantly the resultant systems have been much easier to maintain because of the greatly reduced quantity of code that needs to be considered.

[1]Graphical User Interface, ie. mice and windows.

This paper will now review related work before describing the overall structure of the ID in more detail. The ability of application programmers to write additional building blocks will then be demonstrated followed by a brief catalog of some actual building blocks. Finally, experience of using the tool in production and some suggestions for further research will be discussed.

2 Related Work

Conventional techniques for the description of information systems such as entity relationship diagrams[4], NIAM[14] and data flow analysis[22], provide languages which can specify their overall structure but are insufficiently detailed to enable automatic implementation. Functional decomposition may be used to capture considerable detail about how programs are to be coded, but it is the specification of this detail that the ID makes redundant. Systems such as Rubis[18], Tempora[10] and CSP[2] [7] introduce triggers, temporal business rules and state transitions to static schemas, which are important contributions but they say little about how they should actually be implemented.

On the other hand, GUI tool kits (eg. Athena and Motif[11]) simplify implementation by providing a library of detailed user interaction techniques (widgits) with good ones such as Garnet[12] making it easy to define new widgits by separating their input techniques from their graphical representations. User interface management systems (UIMs) such as the UofA UIMs[21] and Serpent[20] work at a higher level by separating dialog details from style considerations such as how to lay out different types of menus. ITS[23] allows the style rules themselves to be specified in a non-procedural manner. However, as these systems are designed to implement any GUI application they do not utilize the application semantics captured by information systems techniques.

The Programmer's Apprentice[17] is designed to assist software engineers by understanding a program's semantic structure. Program fragments are modeled in the *plan calculus* which describes their data and control flow, with common fragments being recorded in a library of *clichés*. Thus, as syntax editors enable programs to be manipulated in terms of their syntactic structure, the Programmer's Apprentice can manipulate programs in terms of their underlying algorithms.

The Requirements Apprentice[16] utilizes more abstract clichés to transform informal descriptions into accurate specifications. The clichés are organised into specialization hierarchy and a complex reasoning system (Cake) is used to match clichés with descriptions and to infer omissions and inconsistencies.

[2]Communicating Sequential Processes

Clichés are similar to the ID's building blocks, but the ID utilizes the constraints inherit in its more specialized domain of information systems. In particular, the ID assumes the broad design has been captured in a conceptual schema which provides a powerful description of an *information* system that is not explicit in the Apprentices. Further, the plan calculus would be less useful in the ID because most building blocks are constrained by the fairly well defined control flows imposed by a user interface methodology.

Telos[13] provides an interesting mechanism to represent knowledge about all aspects of the software process in temporal classes, KIWI[1] is an experiment on the use of knowledge representation techniques as the primary application data store, and KBMS[2] is a production oriented expert system that can seamlessly access external relational data bases. Although these applications of artificial intelligence techniques to information systems are interesting, they do not address the problems of efficiently implementing ordinary applications.

4GLs such as DBQ/AG[6] do contain *some* implementation knowledge which is why they have been able to produce substantial increases in productivity compared with 3GLs. However, this knowledge is limited to moving the cursor around the screen and relating screen fields to columns in tables so *production quality* programs typically entail several hundred lines of code. Most commercial CASE tools[3] such as IEW[9] and RIDL[5] concentrate on high level system and data modeling, with construction layers providing little more than screen painters and functional decomposition editors. Advanced tools such as Oracle's CASE*Generator[15] do know how to create basic maintenance screens with referential integrity automatically included, but again there is no explicit concept of the knowledge and certainly no way for application programmers to extend it. Further, when the tool proves insufficient to produce a complete program, Oracle recommends editing the generated 4GL code directly which prevents the tool being used for the maintenance of this now large body of generated code.

3 The Intelligent Developer

As illustrated in figure 1, the ID produces 4GL applications and documentation using a two stage process. The programmer enters most of an application's definition into a conceptual schema using the Conceptual Designer, but may also edit the intermediate code produced by the meta generator before the main generator is invoked.

The conceptual schema contains a pure NIAM model that has been extended to capture information that is useful during implementation. These include:-

- Whether a subtype is collapsible, eg. if People may be Students or Lecturers, should one, two or three tables be created.

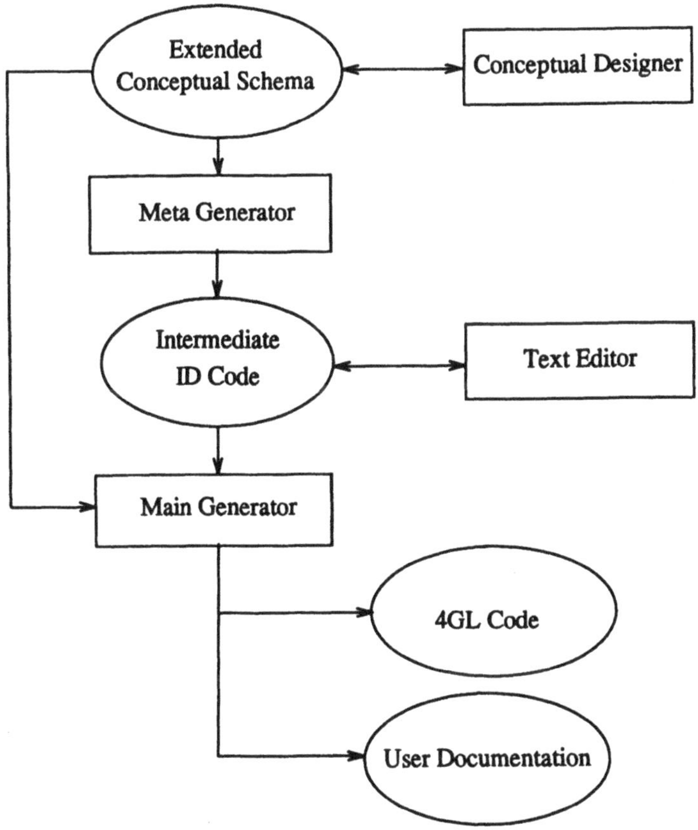

Figure 1: Data flow within the intelligent developer.

- Whether a column is useful to *describe* an entity, eg. when a Student Number is entered into a Class List screen, their Name should normally be displayed as confirmation, rather than their Grade Point Average, say.
- Arbitrary code to be executed whenever the value of a virtual column is required (derived facts).

It is convenient to be able to view and manipulate both the logical and implementation models on the one diagram, although the user may elect to only view the logical aspects. Using an integrated approach also avoids the problem of matching a separate physical model back to a changed logical model to preserve implementation details during regeneration. Further, where de-normalization is necessary it is explicitly identified as such on the main diagram, rather than than being implicit in changes made to a generated physical model. The Conceptual Designer also enables large schemas to be split into several scopes.

The Meta Generator automatically creates complete programs that have a standard structure directly from the conceptual schema. It does this by applying a global layout algorithm to design user interfaces, and by recognizing implementation parameters in the conceptual schema such as which columns are *descriptive* (eg. the Student Name). The meta generator may also accept additional parameters that explicitly override any of its decisions concerning a particular program.

About two thirds of all application programs may be created in this manner, which is desirable because these programs may be automatically regenerated in response to changes in the schema. However, real applications contain a significant number of programs that involve structural complexities that cannot be *conveniently* specified as overrides to a one pass generator. Unfortunately, it is precisely these complex programs that are difficult to write.

One solution to this problem is to encourage programmers to directly edit the hundreds of lines of generated 4GL code. However, once this is done the programs may *never* be regenerated and so are completely divorced from the conceptual schema. Even if the modifications are minor and were quick to make, entire programs will have to be maintained. However, the modifications are not normally minor because if they were they could have been specified as overrides to the meta generator, so the resultant programs usually contain a large amount of manual code interspersed amongst unsuitable generated code. As the cost of maintaining an application usually far exceeds that of its implementation this technique is clearly unacceptable.

To minimize these problems, the ID employs an intermediate language in which most substantial programming is performed. This language is flexible enough to enable any 4GL program that may be written to be conveniently developed, but can express complex programs in a few dozen lines. A typical statement in the language[3] is:-

```
FFIELD Staff@ID, LOOKUPS Staff@Surname, TAG "Supervisor".
```

This places a field containing the Identification of a Staff member in the next position on the screen, interrogates the schema to determine its data type, help prompt, selection pop-up program etc. and looks up the Employee's Surname while performing the referential integrity test. However, the tag displayed to the left of the field on the screen is "Supervisor" rather than "Staff Member" as specified in the schema. All these features are then automatically documented in the user manual.

[3]The actual syntax is slightly different.

Thus for most programs the main generator is invoked immediately after the meta one. However, the intermediate code may be directly edited for non-standard programs without throwing the baby out with the bath water because most of the inferencing and schema interactions are performed by the *main*, not *meta* generator.

4 The Inspection Example

Motor vehicles are regularly inspected so that they can be rejected for registration if any defects are suspected. The following ID generated screen maintains information about these inspections[4]:-

```
--- [......] --- [......] ----------- Inspections --------- [......] ---

Inspect Nr        : ..........

Registration Nr : ______  [.          ............................]
Staff Id          : .....               [.................]
Insp Date         : ........
Location          : .  [........]
Failed            : .
Comments          : ....................................................

Defect Type          Description          Severity      Comment        ([.])

----------   [.........................     ]       ....................
----------   [.........................     ]       ....................
----------   [.........................     ]       ....................
----------   [.........................     ]       ....................
----------   [.........................     ]       ....................
----------   [.........................     ]       ....................
----------   [.........................     ]       ....................
----------   [.........................     ]       ....................
```

Although this screen is fairly simple it involves detailed logic that would require many hours to implement manually using a good 4GL, and even small applications contain dozens of these programs. The processing that is involved to implement this program includes the following:-

1. Display an existing Inspection once its Nr has been entered, or generate a

[4]The 4GL does not provide GUI capabilities yet. This problem is being addressed separately.

new Nr being careful about multi-user locking problems. Alternatively the Nr may have been passed to this program as a parameter.

2. Pop up the Inspection Selection program upon user command if the Nr is not known.

3. Check the user's access rights to update Inspections.

4. Allow the Registration Nr of the vehicle being inspected to be entered, perform referential integrity checks, lookup its *owner's* name (indirectly) and enable the Vehicle Selection and Maintenance programs to be popped up.

5. Likewise for the Staff, Location and Defect Type Fields.

6. Maintain the list of Defect Subforms in a scrolling region, with the total number of rows selected displayed in the "`([.])`" field.

7. Check that *obsolete* defects types are not used.

8. Should a defect be considered Severe the entire inspection fails, but this may be overridden by the user. Unlike all the previous processing this is a business rule that is specific to this application.

9. Allow the user to Commit or Roll Back the transaction, possibly invoking a different program by entering its name in the Lazy Menu field.

This program was produced automatically by the Meta Generator. The resultant intermediate code is displayed in figure 2.

`Header` (1 → in figure) provides the first line on the screen which includes a "lazy menu" option and displays the current user, program name and system date. The Header building block is only responsible for the relative position of these components — it invokes other building blocks to instantiate each component on the screen. If the programmer had wanted a different layout, they would have explicitly invoked these sub-blocks instead of Header.

`FField` (2 →) statements creates other fields based on schema definitions. `Lookups` defines fields that are to be retrieved from related tables while the `Lookup-Col+` and `Tab` parameters control a simple secondary layout algorithm (most layout decisions are made by the meta generator).

`Do-Field` (3 →) adds explicit, ad hoc 4GL code to the program. When procedural code is necessary, the 4GL is an appropriate language, and the ability to use it ensures that the ID does not restrict what a programmer may do. The `Insp@Failed` field has an explicit documentation fragment that corresponds to

```
   PROGRAM-BODY Inm.

1→HEADER.

   FFIELD Insp@Nr.

   PSEUDO-FASSIGN Insp. ; Retrieve/Insert/Update the row.

   FFIELD Insp@Vecl-Nr, LOOKUPS Vecl@Type Vecl@Owner-Nr.
   FFIELD Vecl@Type, LOOKUP-COL+: 2.
   FFIELD Vecl@Owner-Nr, HIDDEN,
          CHANGED-BY Insp@Vecl-Nr, LOOKUPS Org@Name.
   FFIELD Org@Name, TAB rd, READ-ONLY.

2→FFIELD Insp@Stf-Id, LOOKUPS Stf@Surname.
   FFIELD Stf@Surname, TAB rd, READ-ONLY.

   FFIELD Insp@Insp-Date.
   FFIELD Insp@Location, ENUM-LOOKUP Insp@Location-E.
   FFIELD Insp@Location-E, LOOKUP-COL+ 2.
   FFIELD Insp@Failed, DOC
4→    "The user may explicitly override the failure status
       which is normally inferred from the Defect Severity.".
   FFIELD Insp@Comments.

   TABLE-SUBFORM Adfc. ; A line in the scrolling region.

   FFIELD Adfc@Dfct@Id, LOOKUPS Dfct@Description Dfct@Severity.
   FFIELD Dfct@Description, READ-ONLY, SIZE 30.

   FFIELD Dfct@Severity, READ-ONLY.
3→DO-EXIT, ; 4GL code invoked when the subform exits.
     "!If Dfct@Severity = 'R' And Insp@Failed Is Null
        Fset Insp@Failed = 'Y'
      Endif".

   FFIELD Adfc@Comment.

   END-SUBFORM. SUBFORM-FIELDS. ; Place the eight scrolling lines.

   CHECK-REF-INTEG. ; Mainly deletions.
   END-PROGRAM-BODY.
```

Figure 2: Intermediate code for the Inspection Maintenance

this explicit code (4 →). These fragments may be associated with with all ID objects such as Forms, Fields and Pages, and augment or override the automatically produced documentation.

The important point is that the intermediate language is sufficiently flexible to make editing the final 4GL code unnecessary while being powerful enough to enable programs to be defined succinctly. Many parameters are provided to modify or suppress all automatic deductions allowing application programmers to create unconventional programs. However, most of the ID's inferencing may be used most of the time, so that even the most unusual programs may be implemented much more effectively than with any 4GL. Indeed, the natural language specification for the Inspection program is four times bigger than the *intermediate* code.

5 User Written Building Blocks

Even simple programs like Inspection Maintenance involve the use of dozens of building blocks. Although the Intelligent Developer contains a large library of generic building blocks, application programmers' appetite for new ones seems insatiable. Because building blocks have a well defined structure, it is possible for them to develop new ones that can become indistinguishable from those in the standard library.

Most user written building blocks are very application dependent, such as one to create File Number fields (eg. `1992-QA-1234`) and perform special validation on them. These are like simple macros except that they may interrogate their environment to determine, for example, the data type of a previously declared field.

More sophisticated programmers may develop generic building blocks. C or Cobol say nothing about the nature of finished applications, while 4GLs dictate basic parameters. However, tools like the ID control most aspects of an application's behavior, so it is important that these tools may be controlled and extended. The example in figure 3 was written to implement a new user interface standard that states that end users should be able to default the value of date fields to the current system date if they press the '`#`' key.

Building blocks are described in Common Lisp which provides powerful control and data structures. `Def-FField-Block` tells the ID that `My-Date` is a new building block and that it has a special parameter `No-Auto-Date`. The block describes itself by incorporating this information and the following string into the programmer's manual and on line help. It will be automatically invoked for all fields created by `FField`.

Having determined that the current field is an appropriate `Date` field and that the block has not been suppressed, `My-Date` appends code to the current field to

```
(Def-FField-Block (MY-DATE :FField) ; Name of the new FField block.
          (Name Frame Field Doable &Key No-Auto-Date) ; Parameters
  "Looks for fields of type Date and creates code to make them
   default to the system date if '#' is pressed, otherwise they are
   incremented by one day."

  (When (And (Eq (fd:qField-Type Field) ':Date) ; This field is a Date
             Doable                              ; It is not Display Only
             (Not No-Auto-Date))                 ; Not suppressed

     (fs:Do-Key (:Key #\# :Prompt "Default Date")
        "!IF" Name "IS NULL
            FSET" Name "= Q-SYSTEM-DATE
         ELSE
            FSET" Name "=" Name "+ 1 DAY
         ENDIF")

     (fi:Doc-Field Field
        "Pressing '#' defaults this field to today's date
         if it was null, otherwise it is incremented by one day.") ))
```

Figure 3: Application programmer written building block.

test for and process '#' requests. Finally a documentation fragment is appended to the appropriate part of the end user's manual. Tightly integrating the production of documentation and code works well in practice because the decisions that need to be made about what code should be generated are similar to those regarding the documentation to be created. The resulting manuals have a repetitive style, but users like reference manuals to be consistent.

The ability for application programmers to write new building blocks is perhaps the most powerful feature of the ID. Most programming teams will have one or two more technical members that maintain a local ID library that, in effect, embodies the team's implementation expertise. Naturally this power needs to be managed so each application is not written in its own ID sublanguage.

6 A Selective Catalog

The ID contains many dozens of building blocks, but the following selection provides an overview of the sort of things that they do.

- The Meta Generator

  Maintenance-Program Constructs a complete maintenance program out of a header, a main table (eg. Inspections), and scrolling regions of sub-tables (eg. Inspection-Defects).

  Keyworder Builds programs that will produce a secondary table of keywords from columns in a primary table.

- Referential Integrity

  Check-FDelete Checks that records are not deleted while others are referencing them. Alternatively the referencing records may also be deleted or nulled.

  Zoom Knows that if a field is a foreign key to a separate table, the user may wish to pop up a maintenance screen that displays more detail about the other table.

- Style

  VField Places fields on a screen in *vertical* mode, lined up in columns with a '`:`' after the tag.

  Result-Size Places a field to the right of the scrolling region headings (by default) that displays the number of rows selected, ie. the '`([.])`' field.

- Structural

  Pseudo-FAssign Inserts, updates or deletes rows from the primary table in a maintenance program.

  Printer-Selection Allows users to select a printer and run a report.

- Non-Functional

  Lazy-Menu Allows users to directly enter the name of the next program that they wish to run in the top left field in the screen.

  Check-Right Tests users access rights.

- Coding Aids

  Shadow Maintains shadow fields that contain previous values of displayed fields.

  FError Formats error messages of various severity, possibly retrieving the text from an end user maintained table.

7 Experience in Production

The ID has been used by application programmers since early 1991 to develop significant applications including Property Management, Payroll, Personal and Records Management systems. During this time the following observations have been made:-

- Programming productivity was substantially improved, from about 200 function points per man month[19] using conventional CASE/4GL technology to about 600 points per month using the ID.
- The most important factor to the ID's effectiveness was the details of just what the various building blocks did. Application programmers wrote several new building blocks and appreciated the ability to control their environment.
- User documentation of an application would traditionally take almost as long to develop as the code, so the ID's ability to automate most of its production was considered to be very important.
- The *quality* of the finished applications was improved in the following ways:-
  - There were fewer programmer errors found during systems integration, because there was less programming.
  - The user interfaces were highly consistent — a problem with earlier projects. Programmers have to do extra work to override the ID's standard methods.
  - Being automatically produced, the documentation is more accurate.
  - The applications had enhanced functionality because fewer cost/benefit trade-offs needed to be made.
- Most importantly, the applications are easier to maintain. Previously, programs had been developed by copying templates and modifying them, but while this technique improved productivity initially, the resultant programs were large and so difficult to review.

This radical change to productivity enables projects to be managed using a prototyping methodology in which the broad systems analysis is performed as normal but the fine details are determined during implementation. This approach has several advantages namely:-

- Users find it easier to review working applications than static documents.
- The prototypes are delivered with automatically produced documentation.

- Draft applications gives users confidence that real progress is being made.
- Users can usually start using parts of an imperfect application immediately to enter reference data.
- Projects may be commenced sooner so as to ensure that they remain relevant to an organisation's current needs because unlike conventional prototypes, these draft applications are not discarded but can be refined into the finished application.

8 Further Work

Future development of the ID could investigate the following issues:-

- While manually editing the intermediate code minimizes the problems of regeneration, the problem still remains so a method of relating explicited modifications back to the meta level would be useful.
- The ID generates 4GL code statically to provide efficient solutions with current technology. As computers become faster, it becomes feasible to design user interfaces dynamically. Thus end users could interactively describe the view of the data that they want at a particular time and less structured data bases could be supported.
- Much of the effectiveness of the ID's building blocks is derived from the ability of conceptual schemas to describe information systems. However, schemas make no comment about the dynamic aspects of an application which could be described by additional models such as those illustrated by Rubis or Tempora.
- The meta generator makes it feasible for sophisticated end users to build simple applications themselves. However, this will require additional attention to ease of use and error detection issues. If the building blocks were organised more formally, they might be able to report errors sooner and to help the user decide where they are relevant. As the ID becomes more intelligent end users will be able specify more powerful systems.
- Create abstract building blocks that understand more about the real world, eg. the sorts of ways documents are stored in a Records Management System. It will certainly be possible to build very generic packages, but to what extent these application blocks may be used and combined in unforeseen ways presents an unresolved question. Experience with the Requirements Apprentice suggests that a sophisticated reasoning engine is required to do this effectively.

- As the building blocks generate code and documentation, they could also generate formal proofs of correctness in a language like VDM[8]. These could then be given to an independent tool to verify that the programs match a specification. Much of the VDM specification could be derived automatically from the conceptual schema.

9 Conclusion

The Intelligent Developer addresses the problem of implementing and maintaining information systems once the systems analysis has been completed. Its primary contributions are:-

- recognizing that application programmers use a large number of specific techniques to implement a design,
- representing this knowledge as an extendible library of *building blocks*,
- utilizing the fact that conceptual schemas are good descriptions of information systems, and
- using a two pass mechanism to resolve the conflicting goals of being able to create programs directly from a conceptual schema while also enabling complex, non-standard applications to be produced.

By greatly reducing the time required to implement applications, the ID has changed the way projects may be managed. The ID works effectively with well established relational technology, and has been used to successfully develop substantial applications by non-technical programmers.

10 Acknowledgement

Assistance in preparing this paper was gratefully received from Bob Colomb of the University of Queensland. The Intelligent Developer was written for and is marketed by BHA Computer of 1/303 Corrination Drive, Milton, Brisbane.

References

1. M. Ahlsen, A. D'Atri, P. Johannesson, E. Laenens, N. Leone, P. Rullo, P. Rossi, F. Staes, L. Tarantino, L. Von Beirendonck, van F. Cadsand, Van W.

Santvliet, J. Vanslembrouck, B. Verdonk, and D. Vermeir The KIWIS Knowledge Base Management System. In *Advanced Information Systems Engineering, Third International Conference, CAiSE 1991*, Springer-Verlag Lecture Notes in Computer Science vol. **498**, pp. 79–95.

2. AICorp *KBMS Tutorial and Presentation Manager Guide,* Waltham MA USA, 1991.

3. G. Buckworth Detailed Review of CASE Tools. Tech. Rep., Dept. of Computing and Mathematics, Deakin University, 1991.

4. P. Chen The Entity Relationship Model: Towards a unified view of data. *ACM Trans. Database Systems* vol. **1**, Num. 1, 1976, pp 9–36.

5. O. De Troyer *RIDL-*: A tool for the computer aided engineering of large data bases in the presence of integrity constraints,* Tech. Rep. INFOLAB, Tilburg University, 1989.

6. Information Technology International. *The DBQ/Form Reference Manual,* Brisbane Australia, 1990.

7. M. Jackson *System Development,* Prentice-Hall, 1984.

8. C. Jones *Systematic software development using VDM* Prentice Hall, 1990.

9. Knowledgeware Inc. *The IEW Reference Manual,* 1990.

10. P. McBrien, M. Niézette, D. Pantazis, A. Seltveit, U. Sundin, B. Theodoulidis, G. Tziallas, and R. Wohed A Rule Language to Capture and Model Business Policy Specifications (Tempora). In *Advanced Information Systems Engineering, Third International Conference, CAiSE 1991*, Springer-Verlag Lecture Notes in Computer Science vol. **498**, pp. 307–318.

11. Mips Computer Systems. *RISCwindows Motif Reference Manual,* Sunnyvale CA USA, 1989.

12. B. Myers, D. Giuse, B. Dannenberg, B. Zanden, D. Kosbie, P. Marchal, E. Pervin, A. Mickish, and J. Kolojejchick *The Garnet Toolkit Reference Manuals: Support for Highly-Interactive, Graphical User Interfaces in Lisp.* Carnegie Mellon University, CMU-CS-90-117, 1990.

13. J. Mylopoulos, A. Borgida, J. Matthias, and Mq Koubarakis Telos: Representing Knowledge About Information Systems. In *ACM Trans. Information Systems* Vol **8** Num 4, 1990 pp 325–362.

14. G. M. Nijssen and T. A. Halpin *Conceptual Schema and Relational Database Design.* Prentice Hall, 1989.

15. Oracle Corporation. *The CASE*Generator Reference Manual,* 1991.

16. H. Reubenstein The Requirements Apprentice: Automated Assistance for Requirements Acquisition. In *IEEE Trans. Software Engineering* Vol **13** Num 3, 1991 pp 226–240.

17. C. Rich and R. Waters *The programmer's Apprentice*, ACM Press (Addison-Wesley), 1990.

18. C. Rolland, C. Cauvet, P. Nobecourt, C. Proix, Pq Collignon, J. Lingat, and C. Souveyet The Rubis System. In *IFIP Working Conference on Computerized Assistance During the Information Systems Life Cycle, CRIS 88,* North-Holland, pp 193–235.

19. E. Rudolph *Accounting for Software Development.* Charismatic Management Software, Melbourne Australia, April 1989.

20. SEI Joint Program Office. Serpent Overview. Carnegie Mellon University, 1989.

21. G. Singh and M. Green Automating the Lexical and Syntactic Design of Graphical User Interfaces: The UofA UIMS. In *ACM Trans. Graphics,* vol. **10** Num 3, 1991, pp. 213–254.

22. E. N. Yordon and C. C. Constantine *Structured Design.* Yordon Press and Prentice Hall, 1975.

23. C. Wiecha, W. Bennett, S. Boies, J. Gould, and S. Greene ITS: A Tool for Rapidly Developing Interactive Applications. In *ACM Trans. Information Systems,* vol **8** Num 3, 1990, pp. 204–236.

TOWARDS A GENERAL THEORY FOR THE EVOLUTION OF APPLICATION DOMAINS

H.A. PROPER

AND

TH.P. VAN DER WEIDE

Department of Information Systems, University of Nijmegen,
Toernooiveld, NL-6525 ED Nijmegen, The Netherlands,
{erikp,tvdw}@cs.kun.nl

ABSTRACT

In this article we focus on evolving information systems. First a delimitation of the concept of evolution is discussed. The main result is a first attempt to a general theory for such evolution. In this theory, the underlying data model is a parameter, making the theory applicable for a wide range of modelling techniques.

1. Introduction

As has been argued in [17] and [6], there is a growing demand for information systems, not only allowing for changes of their information base, but also for modifications in their underlying structure (conceptual schema and specification of dynamic aspects). In case of snapshot databases structure modifications lead to costly data conversions and reprogramming.

The intention of an evolving information system ([5]) is to be able to handle updates of all components of the so-called *application model*, containing the information structure, the constraints on this structure, the population conforming to this structure and the possible operations. The theory of such systems should, however, be independent of whatever modelling technique is used to describe the application model. In this paper, we discuss a general theory for the evolution of application models. The central part of this theory will make weak assumptions on the underlying modelling technique, making it therefore applicable for data modelling techniques such as ER ([3]), NIAM ([15]) and PSM ([9]), and action modelling techniques such as Task Structures ([21]), DFD ([2]) and ExSpect ([8]).

Version modelling in engineering databases can be seen as a restricted form of evolving information systems ([13], [12]). An important requirement for evolving information systems, not covered by version modelling systems, is that changes to the structure can be made on-line. In version modelling, a structural change requires the replacement of the old system by a new system. Other research regarding evolving information systems can be found in [14], in which an algebra is presented that allows relational tables to evolve by changing their arity.

The structure of the paper is as follows. In section 2 we describe the approach that has been taken to the concept of evolution. We will not focus on a particular modelling technique. In section 3 we describe what the minimal requirements of a modelling technique. By considering all elements that may be subject to evolution, we then introduce in section 4 the application model universe, and describe what constitutes a application model version. Finally, in section 5 the evolution of an application model is formally introduced, and some properties of wellformedness are presented.

2. An Approach to Evolving Information Systems

In this section we discuss our approach to evolving information systems. We start with the identification of that part of an information system that may be subject to evolution. From this identification, the difference between a traditional information system, and its evolving counterpart, will become clear. This is followed by a discussion on how the evolution of an information system is modelled.

2.1. A hierarchy of models

According to [7], a conceptual (i.e. complete and minimal) specification of a universe of discourse consists of the following components:

1. an *information structure*, a set of *constraints* and a *population* conforming to these requirements.
2. a set of *action specifications* describing the transitions that can be performed by the system.

The set of action specifications is referred to as the *action model.* The *world model* encompasses the combination of information structure, constraints and the population. A conceptual specification of a universe of discourse, containing both the action and world model, is called an *application model* ([5], [6]). The resulting hierarchy of models is depicted in figure 1.

2.2. An example of evolution

Traditionally, a *world model* consists of a fixed data model according to some data modelling technique, and a population conforming to this data model. The *action*

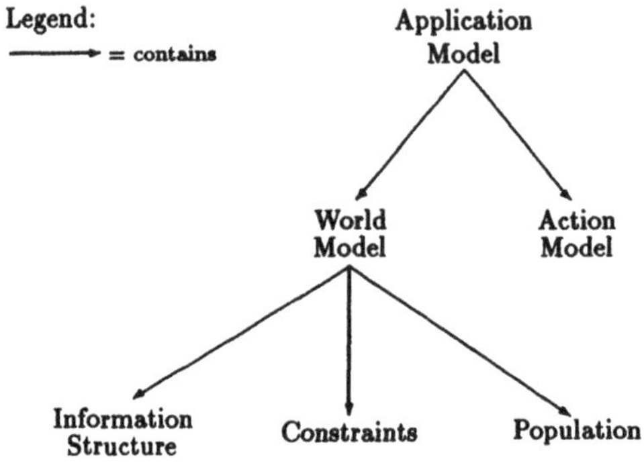

Figure 1: A hierarchy of models

model describes all possible transitions on populations, and is usually modelled by means of Petri-net like specifications (such as ExSpect or Task Structures), or languages such as SQL. The evolvable part of the application model in these cases is restricted to the population.

Some traditional information systems do allow however, to a limited extend, modifications of other components from the application model. For example, adding a new table in an SQL system is easily done. However, changing the arity of a table, or some of its attributes, will result in a time consuming table conversion, which also leads to loss of the old table! In an evolving information system, the entire application model is allowed to evolve on-line, without loss of any information.

As an illustration of an evolving universe of discourse, consider a rental store, for audio records (LP's). In this store a registration is maintained of the songs that are recorded on the available LP's. In order to keep track of the wear and tear of LP's, the number of times an LP has been lent is registered. The information structure and constraints of this universe of discourse are modelled in figure 2 in the style of ER, according to the conventions of [23]. Note the special notation of attributes (Title) using a mark symbol (#) followed by the attribute (# Title).

An action specification in this example is the rule Init-freq, stating that whenever a new LP is added to the assortment of the store, it's lending frequency must be set to 0:

```
ACTION Init-freq =
   WHEN ADD Lp: x DO
      ADD Lp: x has Lending-frequency of Frequency: 0
```

This action specification is in the style of Lisa-D ([10]). Note that the keyword 'has' connects object types to relation types, and the keyword 'of' just the other way

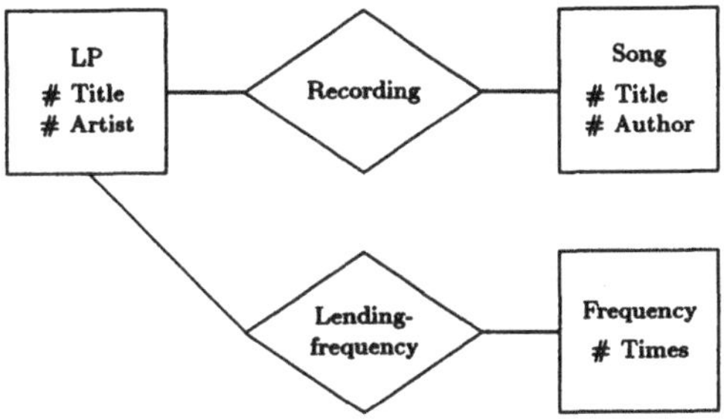

Figure 2: The Data Model of an LP rental store

around.

After the introduction of the compact disc, and its conquest of a sizeable piece of the market, the rental store has transformed into an 'LP and CD rental store'. This leads to the introduction of object type Medium as a generic term for LP's and CD's. The relation type Medium-type effectuates the subtyping of Medium into LP and CD. In the new situation, the registration of songs on LP's is extended to cover CD's as well. The frequency of lending, however, is not kept for CD's, as CD's are hardly subject to any wear and tear. As a consequence, the application model has evolved to figure 3.

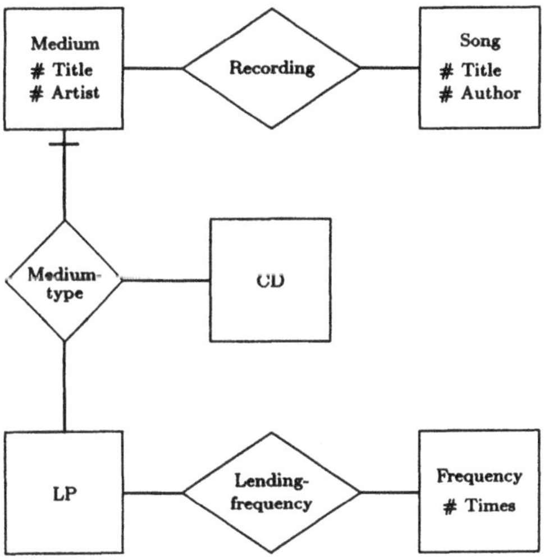

Figure 3: The Data Model of a LP and CD rental store

The action specification **Init-freq** evolves accordingly, now stating that whenever a medium is added to the assortment of the rental store, it's lending frequency is set to 0 provided the medium is an LP:

```
ACTION Init-freq =
  WHEN ADD Medium: x DO
    IF Lp: x THEN
      ADD Lp: x has Lending-frequency of Frequency: 0
```

2.3. The approach

The two ER schemata, and the two action specifications, as discussed above, correspond to two distinct snapshots of an evolving universe of discourse. Several approaches can be taken to the modelling of this evolution. A first approach is to model the history of application model elements by adding birth-death relations to all object types in the information structure ([18]). This approach, however, is very limited, as it only enables the modelling of evolution of the population of an information system. For example, the evolution of the Recording relation type can not be modelled in this approach. Evolution of other application model elements than population, can then be descibed by a meta model approach.

This paper takes another approach, and treats evolution of an application model as a separate concept. There still are two alternatives to deal with the history of application models. The first one is to maintain a version history of application models in their entirety, leading to a sequence of snapshots of application models. The second one is to keep a version history per element, so keeping track of the evolution of object types, instances, methods, etc.

An advantage of this second alternative is that it enables one to state rules about, and query the evolution of distinct objects. This alternative also allows for the formulation of rules concerning the well formedness of the evolution of application model elements ([16]). The first alternative clearly does not offer this oppertunity, as it does not provide relations between successive versions of the application model.

Furthermore, the snapshot view from the first alternative can be derived by constituting the application model version of any point of time from the current versions of its components. In the theory of evolving application models we will therefore adapt the second alternative.

An *application model element history* describes the history of an application model element, and is seen as a partial function assigning to points of time the actual occurrence (version) of the element. For example, when CD's are added to the assortment of the rental store, the version of the application model element **Recording** changes from a relation type that registrates songs on LP's to a relation type that registrates songs on Media. An *application model history* is a set of application model element histories. The current version of an application model then is constituted by the current versions of all application model elements.

3. A World Model for Application Models

In this section we take a closer look at application models, and define what constitutes an application model version. An application model version is formulated conforming to some modelling technique. The only assumption on this modelling technique is, that it delimits an *application model universe*, i.e., the space for the evolution of application models.

3.1. The Information Structure Universe

The kernel of the application model universe is formed by the *information structure universe* $\mathcal{U}_{\mathcal{I}} = \langle \mathcal{L}, \mathcal{N}, \sim, \rightsquigarrow \rangle$, fixing the evolution space for information structures. Further refinements of the information structure universe depend on the chosen data modelling technique (such as NIAM, ER, PSM and Object Oriented data models), and are beyond the scope of the theory in this paper. For our purposes, an information structure universe is assumed to provide (at least) the above components, which are available in all conventional high level data modelling techniques.

3.1.1. Object Types

The central part of an information structure is formed by its object types (referred to as object classes in object oriented approaches). Two major classes of object types are distinguished. Object types who's instances can be represented directly (denoted) on a medium (strings, natural numbers, etc) form the class of label types $\mathcal{L}$. The other object types, for instance entity types or fact (relation) types, form the class $\mathcal{N}$. The example of figure 2 contains nine object types: three entity types **Record**, **Song** and **Frequency**, two relation types **Recording** and **Lending-frequency**, and four label types **Title**, **Artist**, **Author** and **Times**.

3.1.2. Type Relatedness

For object types, the (reflexive and symmetrical) relation $\sim$ expresses *type relatedness* between object types (see [11]). Object types x and y are termed type related ($x \sim y$) iff populations of object types x and y *may* have values in common. Type relatedness corresponds to mode equivalence in programming languages ([22]). The relation of type relatedness can be recognised in conventional modelling techniques like ER, NIAM, or PSM, as well as object oriented data modelling techniques. Typically, subtyping and generalisation lead to type related object types. For the data model depicted in figure 2, the type relatedness relation is the identity relation: $x \sim x$ for all object types x.

3.1.3. The Identification Hierarchy

In data modelling, a crucial role is played by the notion of object identification: each object type of an information structure should be identifiable. In a subtype hierarchy however, a subtype inherits its identification from its super type, whereas in a generalisation hierarchy the identification of a generalised object type is inherited from its specifiers. For the data model depicted in figure 3 this means that instances of LP and CD are identified in the same way as instances of Medium. An object type from which the identification is inherited, is termed a *parent* of that object type. The inheritance hierarchy (identification hierarchy) is provided by the relation $x \rightsquigarrow y$, meaning that x is the parent of y. For figure 3 this leads to: $\mathsf{Medium} \rightsquigarrow \mathsf{LP}$ and $\mathsf{Medium} \rightsquigarrow \mathsf{CD}$.

Object types in an information structure that have no parent are called *roots* as they form the roots of the inheritance hierarchy (a directed acyclic graph). The roots of an object type y are found by: $x \,\mathsf{RootOf}\, y \equiv (x = y \vee x \rightsquigarrow y) \wedge \neg\exists_x [z \rightsquigarrow x]$.

For every data model from conventional data modelling techniques, a parent ($\rightsquigarrow$) and root (RootOf) relation can be derived. If no specialisations or generalisations are present in that data model, the parent relation will be empty. As a result, the root relation will be the identity relation. For instance the root relation for figure 2 is: $x \,\mathsf{RootOf}\, x$ for every object type x.

3.2. Properties of Information Structure Universes

Two interesting properties on the root and parent relation are:

Lemma 3.1 (*common roots*)

$$x \sim y \iff \exists_z [z \,\mathsf{RootOf}\, x \wedge z \sim y]$$

The intuition behind this property is that type relatedness must be based on the type relatedness of some root. Furthermore, type relatedness of roots implies type relatedness of object types:

Theorem 3.1 (*type relatedness propagation*)

$$\exists_{z_1,z_2} [z_1 \sim z_2 \wedge z_1 \,\mathsf{RootOf}\, x \wedge z_2 \,\mathsf{RootOf}\, y] \iff x \sim y$$

These properties have been proven in [16].

4. Secondary elements of Application Models

The hierarchy of models (see figure 1) describes how an application model is constructed from other (sub)models. However, this hierarchy disregards relations that must hold between these submodels, for example, the relation between a population and the information structure. These relations are crucial elements of an application model, as they form the fabric of the application model.

4.1. *Application Model Universe*

An application model version is bound to the *application model universe* $\mathcal{U}_\Sigma$, which is captured in the tuple: $\langle \mathcal{U}_\mathcal{I}, \gamma, \mu, \mathcal{D}, \Omega,$ Depends$\rangle$. The information structure universe $\mathcal{U}_\mathcal{I}$ was introduced in the previous section.

4.1.1. *Constraints*

Most data modelling techniques have a language in which constraints can be expressed, resulting in the set γ of all possible constraint definitions. Constraints are treated as application model elements, that assign to (some) object types a particular constraint definition. A constraint is said to be *owned* by an object type, if the object type has assigned a constraint definition by the constraint. Constraints are inherited via the identification hierarchy. However, as in object oriented data modelling techniques, overriding of constraint definition in identification hierarchies is possible (see for instance [19]).

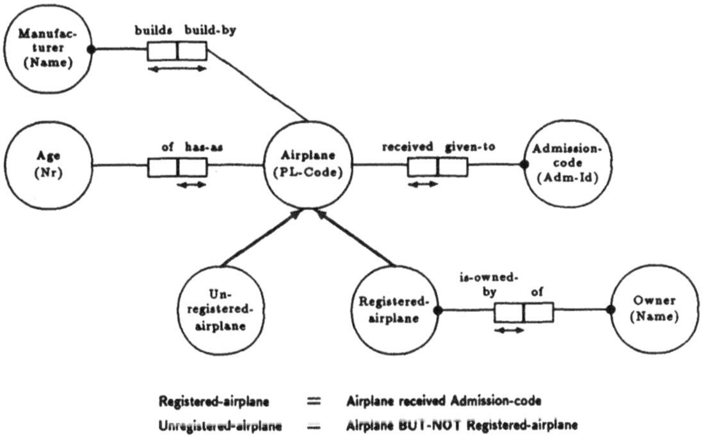

Figure 4: Constraint assignment

As an illustration of the assignment of constraints to object types, consider figure 4. The depicted data model is conforming to NIAM, while the subtype defining rules have been formulated in LISA-D. The modelled universe of discourse is concerned with the administration of airplanes. As airplanes should be replaced in time, the age of an airplane is an important attribute. Furthermore, an airplane may be registered by an aviation association, in which case it has associated an admission code. The owner of registered planes is maintained by the administration.

The graphical constraints contained in this data model, are assigned to object types in the following way:

C_1 : Manufacturer
↦ TOTAL { Manufacturer.builds }
C_2 : Airplane
↦ UNIQUE { Airplane.has-as }
C_3 : Admission-code
↦ TOTAL { Admission-code.given-to }

All these constraints are owned by a single object type. A more interesting case with respect to inheritance results by adding the following constraint:

All airplanes must have associated a manufacturer or an age. Unregistered airplanes must have both.

The object type assignment for this constraint is:

C_4 : Airplane
↦ TOTAL { Airplane.build-by, Airplaine.has-as }
C_4 : Registered-airplane
↦ TOTAL { Airplane.build-by, Airplaine.has-as }
C_4 : Unregistered-airplane
↦ TOTAL { Airplane.build-by } AND TOTAL { Airplaine.has-as }

The constraint C_4 is considered to be owned by object types Airplane, Registered-airplane and Unregistered-airplane.

A constraint c, in an application model version, will therefore be a (usually very sparse) partial function $c : \mathcal{O} \rightarrowtail \gamma$, providing for every object type a *private* definition of the constraint. Each modelling technique will have its own possibilities to formulate inheritance rules, thus governing the mapping c. The set of constraints in an application model version at time t is denoted as $\mathcal{R}_t$.

4.1.2. Methods

The action model part of an application model version will be provided as a set of action specifications. The set of possible action definitions (μ) depends on the chosen modelling technique for the action model. As for constraints, a modelling technique dependent inheritance hierarchy can be recognized. A method m is regarded as a partial function $m : \mathcal{O} \rightarrowtail \mu$, assigning action specifications to object types. The set of all methods present in an application model version is: $\mathcal{M}_t$.

4.1.3. Domains

The separation between concrete and abstract world is provided by the distinction between the information structure $\mathcal{I}$, and the set of underlying (concrete) domains in $\mathcal{D}$ ([10]). Therefore, label types in an information structure version will have to be related to domains. An application model version contains a mapping Dom_t providing the relation between label types and domains. Some examples of such domain assignments, in the context of the rental store, are: Times ↦ Natno, Title ↦ String , where Natno and String are presumed to be (names of) concrete domains.

4.1.4. Instances

The population of an information structure is not, as usual, a function that maps object types to sets of instances. Rather, an instance is considered to be an independent thing, which can evolve by itself. Therefore, (non empty) sets of object types are associated to instances, specifying the object types having the instance as an instantiation. This association is contained in the relation $\mathsf{HasTypes}_t \subseteq \Omega \times \wp(\mathcal{O})$, where Ω is the set of all possible instantiations of object types. An example of such an association is: $\left\langle l_1, \left\{\mathsf{Medium}, \mathsf{Lp}\right\}\right\rangle$, meaning l_1 is an (abstract) instance of entity types Medium and Lp. The population of an object type, traditionally provided as a function $p : \mathcal{O} \rightarrow \wp(\Omega)$, can be derived from the association between instances and object types: $\mathsf{Pop}_t(x) = \left\{v \in \Omega \;\middle|\; v\ \mathsf{HasTypes}_t\ Y \wedge x \in Y\right\}$.

4.1.5. Evolution dependency

Every method and constraint specification refers to (uses) a set of object types and denotable instances. This relation is provided in the application model universe by means of the dependency relation (Depends). The relation Depends is modelling technique dependent, but is not subject to evolution.

The intuition behind this relation is as follows: $x\ \mathsf{Depends}\ y$ means that if y is not present in an application model version, then x can not be used in that version. A consequence is, that in case of evolution of application models, when y evolves to y', then x must be adapted appropriately.

As an example, consider the second action specification from the rental store example. This action specification depends on object types Medium, Lp and Frequency. It, furthermore, depends on the domain assignment: Frequency $\mapsto$ Natno. If one of the object types, or the domain assignment, is terminated or changed, the action specification has to be terminated or changed accordingly.

4.2. Application Model Versions

An application model version (Σ_t) over information structure universe $\mathcal{U}_\mathcal{I}$ is determined by the following components: $\mathcal{O}_t$, $\mathcal{R}_t$, $\mathcal{M}_t$, $\mathsf{HasTypes}_t$, Dom_t. With a version of the application model, we can associate the following version of the information structure: $\mathcal{I}_t = \langle \mathcal{L}_t, \mathcal{N}_t, \sim_t, \rightsquigarrow_t \rangle$ where:

— $\mathcal{L}_t = \mathcal{O}_t \cap \mathcal{L}$,
— $\mathcal{N}_t = \mathcal{O}_t \cap \mathcal{N}$,
— $x \sim_t y \equiv x \sim y \wedge x, y \in \mathcal{O}_t$, and
— $x \rightsquigarrow_t y \equiv x \rightsquigarrow y \wedge x, y \in \mathcal{O}_t$.

As an overview of the components of an application model version, a meta model is provided in figure 5. This (meta) data model is conforming to the PSM data modelling technique, an extention of the NIAM modelling technique. The object types $\mathcal{R}_t$ and $\mathcal{M}_t$ in figure 5 are power types, the data modelling pendant of power sets in set theory.

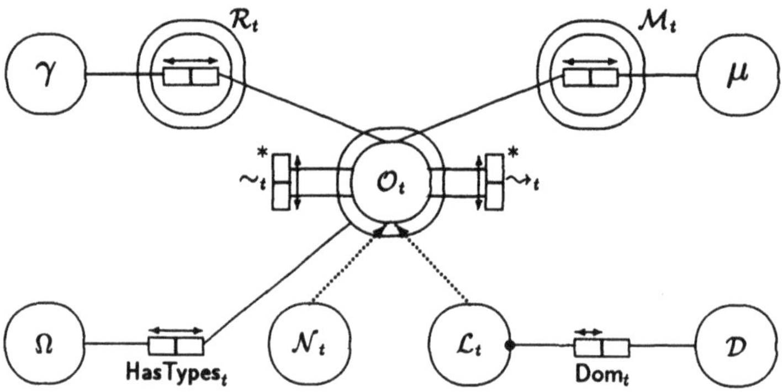

Figure 5: A meta model for information structures

Every application model version must adhere to some rules of wellformedness. Some of these rules are modelling technique dependent. Nonetheless, some general rules about application model versions can be stated. In [16] a formalisation of these rules is provided.

An object type x is called *alive* at a certain point of time t, if it is part of the application model version at that point of time ($x \in \mathcal{O}_t$). Furthermore, an object type x is termed *active* at a certain point of time, if there is an instance with x as one of its associated types (v $\textsf{HasTypes}_t\, X \wedge x \in X$).

A first rule of wellformedness states that every active object type must be alive as well. This rule can be popularised as: 'I am active, therefore I am alive'. Furthermore, the set of object types associated to an instance must be mutually type related, as their populations share at least this value.

From the very nature of the root relation it immediately follows that instances are included upwards, towards the roots. As a result, every instance of an object type is also an instance of its parents (if any). This rule has a structural pendant as well. Every living object type should be accompanied by one of its parents (if any). If all object types in a data model have a non empty instantiation, i.e. every object type is active, the latter (structural) rule immediately follows from the former (population) rule. However, when some non-root (alive) object type is not active, implying that its parent(s) do not have to be active, it does not follow that at least one of its parents must be alive. Therefore, a rule demanding this explicitly is required.

Constraints and methods are defined as mappings from object types to constraint and method definitions respectively. Thus, object types that own a constraint or a method must be alive. Furthermore, object types that own the same constraint or method, have to be type related. Finally, due to inheritance, if a constraint is defined for a parent object type, it must be defined for its children as well.

For populations some interesting properties have been proven [16]. An first example states: every instance of an object type is also an instance of one of its roots.

Lemma 4.1 $\mathsf{Pop}_t(x) \subseteq \bigcup_{y\,\mathsf{RootOf}\,x} \mathsf{Pop}_t(y)$

From the nature of type relatedness it follows that the populations of roots which are not type related are mutually exclusive. This rule can be generalised to all object types, leading to:

Lemma 4.2 $x \not\sim y \Rightarrow \forall_{t,u} [\mathsf{Pop}_t(x) \cap \mathsf{Pop}_u(y) = \varnothing]$

For the proofs of these properties, refer to [16].

5. Evolution of Application Models

The basis of the theory for evolving application models is formed by the concept of *evolution continuum*, capturing both dimensions of evolution of application models, being the universe of application model and time. The evolution continuum serves as a state space for evolutionary navigation: $\mathcal{LS} = \langle \mathcal{T}_s, \mathcal{U}_\Sigma \rangle$

Time, essential to evolution, is incorporated into the evolution continuum through the algebraic structure $\mathcal{T}_s = \langle \mathcal{T}, F \rangle$, where $\mathcal{T}$ is a (discrete) time axis, and F a set of functions over $\mathcal{T}$. In this paper, the time axis is regarded as an abstract data type. Several ways of defining a time axis exist, see e.g. [4], [20] or [1]. The time axis is the axis along which the application model evolves (through the application model universe).

An application model element history is a partial function, that assigns to points of time the actual version of the element, and thus is a partial mapping $\mathcal{T} \rightarrowtail \mathcal{AME}$, where $\mathcal{AME}$ is the set of all evolvable elements of an application model: $\mathcal{O} \cup \mathcal{R} \cup \mathcal{M} \cup \mathsf{HasTypes} \cup \mathsf{Dom}$. An application model history over an information structure universe $\mathcal{U}_\mathcal{I}$ then is defined by:

Definition 5.1

$$\mathcal{AMH} \subseteq \mathcal{T} \rightarrowtail \mathcal{AME} \qquad \square$$

As a first rule of wellformedness, the evolution of application model elements is bound to classes. For example, an object type may not evolve into a method, and a constraint may not evolve into an instance. A consequence of this rule is that an application model history can be partitioned into the history of its object types, its constraints, its methods, its populations, and its concretisations (of label types):

Definition 5.2

object type histories:
$\mathcal{H}_{type} = \left\{ h \in \mathcal{AMH} \;\middle|\; \exists_t[h(t) \in \mathcal{O}] \right\}$,
constraint histories:
$\mathcal{H}_{constr} = \left\{ c \in \mathcal{AMH} \;\middle|\; \exists_t[c(t) \in \mathcal{R}] \right\}$,
method histories:
$\mathcal{H}_{meth} = \left\{ m \in \mathcal{AMH} \;\middle|\; \exists_t[m(t) \in \mathcal{M}] \right\}$,
population histories:
$\mathcal{H}_{pop} = \left\{ g \in \mathcal{AMH} \;\middle|\; \exists_t[g(t) \in \mathsf{HasTypes}] \right\}$,
concretisation histories:
$\mathcal{H}_{dom} = \left\{ d \in \mathcal{AMH} \;\middle|\; \exists_t[d(t) \in \mathsf{Dom}] \right\}$. □

An application model version $\mathcal{I}_t = \langle \mathcal{L}_t, \mathcal{N}_t, \sim_t, \rightsquigarrow_t \rangle$ is easily derived from the application model history:

Definition 5.3

object types:
$\mathcal{O}_t = \left\{ h(t) \;\middle|\; h \in \mathcal{H}_{type} \wedge h{\downarrow}t \right\}$,
constraints:
$\mathcal{R}_t = \left\{ c(t) \;\middle|\; c \in \mathcal{H}_{constr} \wedge c{\downarrow}t \right\}$,
methods:
$\mathcal{M}_t = \left\{ m(t) \;\middle|\; m \in \mathcal{H}_{meth} \wedge m{\downarrow}t \right\}$,
population:
$\mathsf{HasTypes}_t = \left\{ g(t) \;\middle|\; g \in \mathcal{H}_{pop} \wedge g{\downarrow}t \right\}$,
concretisations:
$\mathsf{Dom}_t = \left\{ d(t) \;\middle|\; d \in \mathcal{H}_{dom} \wedge d{\downarrow}t \right\}$. □

In this definition $f{\downarrow}t$ is used as an abbreviation for $\exists_s [\langle t, s \rangle \in f]$, stating that (partial) function f is defined at time t.. As an example of evolution, the following table respresents three object type evolutions ($h_1, h_2, h_3 \in \mathcal{H}_{type}$) from the rental store (see section 2):

$\mathcal{H}_{type}$	h_1	h_2	h_3
t_1	o_1	o_2	–
t_2	o_1	o_2	–
t_3	o_1	o_2	–
t_4	o_1	o_3	o_4
t_5	o_1	o_3	o_4

where $t_1, \ldots, t_5 \in \mathcal{T}$, and $o_1, \ldots, o_4 \in \mathcal{O}$ are object types, such that:

o_1 = 'Entity type: Record'
o_2 = 'Fact type: Recording of Song on Record'
o_3 = 'Fact type: Recording of Song on Medium'
o_4 = Entity type: Medium'

Note that the evolution step (from figure 2 to figure 3) takes place at point of time t_4. Two example instance evolutions ($g_1, g_2 \in \mathcal{H}_{pop}$), obeying the above schema evolution, are:

$\mathcal{H}_{pop}$	g_1	g_2
t_1	$\langle i_1, \{o_1\}\rangle$	$\langle i_2, \{o_2\}\rangle$
t_2	$\langle i_1, \{o_1\}\rangle$	$\langle i_2, \{o_2\}\rangle$
t_3	$\langle i_1, \{o_1\}\rangle$	$\langle i_3, \{o_2\}\rangle$
t_4	$\langle i_1, \{o_1, o_4\}\rangle$	$\langle i_4, \{o_3\}\rangle$
t_5	$\langle i_1, \{o_1, o_4\}\rangle$	$\langle i_4, \{o_3\}\rangle$

where $i_1, \ldots, i_4 \in \Omega_\infty$ are instances such that:

i_1 = 'Brothers in Arms'
i_2 = ⟨'Money for nothing', 'Brothers in Arms'⟩
i_3 = ⟨'Brothers in Arms', 'Brothers in Arms'⟩
i_4 = ⟨'Brothers in Arms', 'Brothers in Arms'⟩

The interpretation of this table leads to:

$g_1(t_4) = \langle i_1, \{o_1, o_4\}\rangle$ means: 'Brothers in Arms' is both a Record and a Lp at t_4,
$g_2(t_3) = \langle i_3, \{o_2\}\rangle$ means: Song 'Brothers in Arms' is Recorded on Record 'Brothers in Arms',
$g_2(t_4) = \langle i_4, \{o_3\}\rangle$ means: Song 'Brothers in Arms' is Recorded on Medium 'Brothers in Arms'.

As an outline of the hitherto defined concepts, a (meta) data model, relating all defined concepts, is provided in figure 6. The data model depicted there is conform the PSM modelling technique, and uses the notion of schema objectifications (object type $\mathcal{AMH}$), and powertyping (object type $\wp(\mathcal{O})$). The population of an objectified schema at hand is to be looked upon as one single abstract object instance of the object type corresponding to the objectified schema. Powertyping is, as stated before, the data modelling pendant of powersets from set theory.

6. Conclusions and Further research

In this paper we presented a first attempt to a general theory for the evolution of application models, supporting evolving information systems. As a next step a set of well formedness rules on evolution steps has to be defined, since not all evolution steps of application models will correspond to sensible/valid evolution steps in an actual universe of discourse.

Furthermore, in order to validate the theory, it must be applied to some modelling techniques. In the near future we will therefore apply this theory to PSM, a data modelling technique serving as a common base for data modelling techniques such as NIAM, ER, and IFO, and to Task Structures, a powerfull action modelling technique. A query and manipulation language must be defined supporting the evolution of information systems. Finally, the consequences of evolution for the internal representation of information structures should be studied.

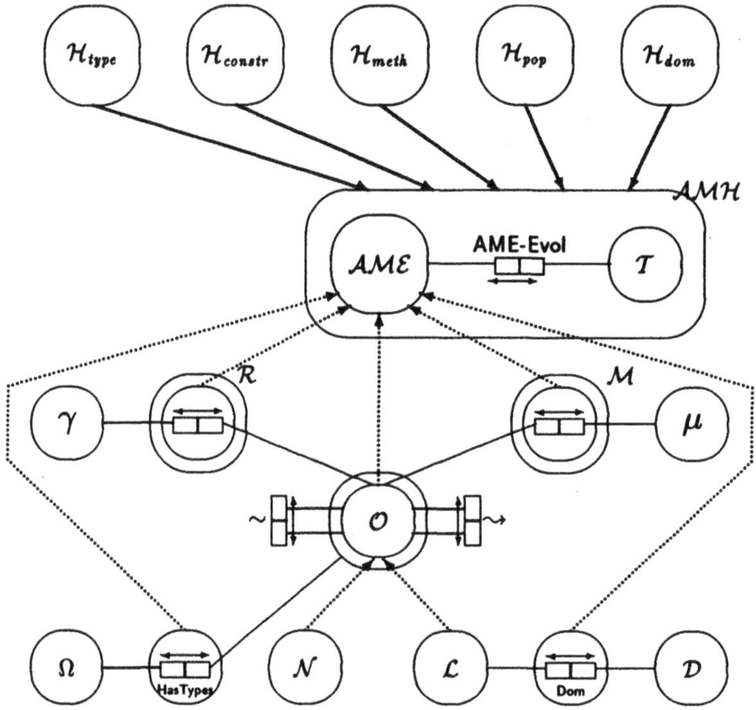

Figure 6: A meta model for the evolution system

Acknowledgements

The investigations were partly supported by the Foundation for Computer Science in the Netherlands (SION) with financial support from the Netherlands Organization for Scientific Research (NWO).

References

1 J.F. Allen. Towards a General Theory of Action and Time. *Artificial Intelligence*, 1984(23):123–154, 1984.

2 P.D. Bruza and Th.P. van der Weide. The Semantics of Data Flow Diagrams. In *Proceedings of the International Conference on Management of Data*, pages 66–78, Hyderabad, India, 1989.

3 P.P. Chen. The entity-relationship model: toward a unified view of data. *ACM Transactions on Database Systems*, 1(1):9–36, 1976.

4 J. Clifford and A. Rao. A simple, general structure for Temporal Domains. In C. Rolland, F. Bodart, and M. Leonard, editors, *Temporal Aspects in Information Systems*, pages 17–28. North-Holland/IFIP, 1987.

5 E.D. Falkenberg, J.L.H. Oei, and H.A. Proper. A Conceptual Framework for Evolving Information Systems. In H.G. Sol and R.L. Crosslin, editors, *Dynamic Modelling of Information Information Systems II*, pages 353–375. North-Holland, 1992.

6 E.D. Falkenberg, J.L.H. Oei, and H.A. Proper. Evolving Information Systems: beyond Temporal Information Systems. In *Proceedings of the Data Base and Expert System Applications Conference (DEXA 92)*, pages 282–287, Valencia, Spain, September 1992.

7 J.J. van Griethuysen, editor. *Concepts and Terminology for the Conceptual Schema and the Information Base.* Publ. nr. ISO/TC97/SC5-N695, 1982.

8 K.M. van Hee, L.J. Somers, and M. Voorhoeve. Executable Specifications for Distributed Information Systems. In E.D. Falkenberg and P. Lindgreen, editors, *Information System Concepts: An In-depth Analysis.* North-Holland/IFIP, 1989.

9 A.H.M. ter Hofstede, H.A. Proper, and Th.P. van der Weide. Data Modelling in Complex Application Domains. In P. Loucopoulos, editor, *Proceedings of the Fourth International Conference on Advanced Information Systems Engineering, CAiSE'92*, pages 364–377, Manchester, United Kingdom, May 1992.

10 A.H.M. ter Hofstede, H.A. Proper, and Th.P. van der Weide. Formal Definition of a Conceptual Language for the Description and Manipulation of Information Models. Technical Report 92/10, SERC, Software Engineering Research Centre, Utrecht, The Netherlands, July 1992.

11 A.H.M. ter Hofstede and Th.P. van der Weide. Expressiveness in Conceptual Data Modelling. Technical Report, Accepted for publication in Data & Knowledge Engineering, Software Engineering Research Centre, Utrecht, The Netherlands, July 1991.

12 M. Jarke, J. Mylopoulos, J.W. Schmidt, and Y. Vassiliou. DAIDA: An Environment for Evolving Information Systems. *ACM Transactions on Information Systems*, 20(1):1–50, January 1992.

13 R.H. Katz. Toward a Unified Framework for Version Modelling in Engineering Databases. *ACM Computing Surveys*, 22(4):375–408, 1990.

14 E. McKenzie and R. Snodgrass. Schema Evolution and the Relational Algebra. *Information Systems*, 15(2):207–232, 1990.

15 G.M. Nijssen and T.A. Halpin. *Conceptual Schema and Relational Database Design: A fact oriented approach.* Prentice Hall of Australia Pty Ltd, 1989.

16 H.A. Proper and Th.P. van der Weide. A General Theory for the Evolution of Application Models. Technical Report (In Preperation), Department of

Information Systems, University of Nijmegen, The Netherlands, 1992.

17 J.F. Roddick. Dynamically changing schemas within database models. *The Australian Computer Journal*, 23(3):105–109, August 1991.

18 R. Snodgrass and I. Ahn. A Taxonomy of Time in Databases. In *Proceedings of the ACM SIGMOD International Conference on the Management of Data*, pages 236–246, Austin, 1985.

19 O. de Troyer. The OO-Binary Relationship Model: A Truly Object Oriented Conceptual Model. In R. Andersen, J.A. Bubenko, and A. Sølvberg, editors, *Proceedings of the Third International Conference CAiSE'91 on Advanced Information Systems Engineering*, pages 561–578, Trondheim, Norway, May 1991. Lecture Notes in Computer Science 498.

20 G. Wiederhold, S. Jajodia, and W. Litwin. Dealing with the Granularity of Time in Temporal Databases. In R. Andersen, J.A. Bubenko, and A. Sølvberg, editors, *Proceedings of the Third International Conference CAiSE'91 on Advanced Information Systems Engineering*, pages 124–140, Trondheim, Norway, May 1991. Lecture Notes in Computer Science 498.

21 G.M. Wijers, A.H.M. ter Hofstede, and N.E. van Oosterom. Representation of Information Modelling Knowledge. In V.-P. Tahvanainen and K. Lyytinen, editors, *Proceedings of the Second Workshop on the Next Generation of CASE Tools*, pages 159 - 217, Trondheim, Norway, May 1991.

22 A. van Wijngaarden, B.J. Mailloux, J.E.L. Peck, C.H.A. Koster, M. Sintzoff, C.H. Lindsey, L.T. Meertens, and R.G. Fisker. *Revised Report on the Algorithmic Language ALGOL 68*. Springer-Verlag, 1976.

23 E. Yourdon. *Modern Structured Analysis*. Prentice Hall, 1989.

Control of a Management Information System by Rules

Eva Gardyn
Consultant, Simsion Bowles and Associates
15 Collins Street, Melbourne, Victoria 3000, Australia

Keith G Jeffery
Head, Systems Engineering Division
Informatics Department, Rutherford Appleton Laboratory
Chilton, Didcot, Oxfordshire OX11 0QX UK

ABSTRACT

Total data processing systems based on logic programming or rule-based technology have not always been successful. A strategy for using rule-based technology embedded within a conventional management information system framework allows the appropriate, flexible and optimal use of rule-based technology while sacrificing little or none of the efficiency and familiarity of conventional commercial data processing. The approach raises some interesting issues.

1.0.0 Introduction

1.1.0 Background

This paper describes a design for a management information system based on the use of rules. Although the work was done in connection with a project at a major bank[3] , there is no implied commitment that this system will be implemented in full or in part. Nonetheless, the design work has raised some interesting and illuminating issues: these are addressed in the paper.

1.2.0 TPS

In most commercial organisations, TPSs (transaction processing system) have been developed to handle the main 'line-of-business' applications, and specifically to handle known, stable requirements which include standard data processing activities on predefined data structures where the data content is known. The transaction is typically of a duration less than one second, affects only a small part of the database, has relatively trivial processing operations (eg simple update) and is run concurrently with many other transactions using the same (or similar) program code and affecting the same database. TPSs are application specific.
The supporting software systems have evolved from specificity to generality. In the IBM domain, for example, the use of CICS (Customer Information

Control System) and IMS (Information Management System) is common in many different applications in banking, insurance and manufacturing. Such systems are usually capable of supporting only a hierarchic or network data structure and are characterised by the use of pointers to link groups of data items (usually called physical records, segments or records). The programming technology ranges from assembler code through 3GLs (third generation languages) to the use of 4GLs (fourth generation languages). The increased levels tend to reduce development time at the expense of runtime efficiency.

1.3.0 MIS

It was realised early in most DP (Data Processing) Departments that the database of a TPS could be used for MIS (management information system) purposes. Standard reports (produced by extraction and summary through the TP environment) were soon replaced by enquiry systems, where the user 'filled in a request form' on screen and the TPS delivered a pre-formatted extract/summary report.

However, the need for ad-hoc reports to meet new information requirements showed up some problems; the time taken for programmers to code the new process was unacceptable, the data structure was commonly non-optimal for the required search (degradations to serial searching were not uncommon) and inappropriate for the required summaries, and there was no flexibility to add additional data (a database unload/schema change/reload sequence was necessary).

The solution was to copy the TPS database, restructuring it into an optimal canonical form for MIS purposes. Essentially, this meant restructuring it into a normalised relational database with data summary of certain numeric attributes grouped by certain other attribute(s) at an appropriate level. The availability of an easy-to-use query language (this was the claim!) - SQL (Structured Query Language) - and suitable reporting tools ensured end-user acceptance.

The MIS database was thus not the up-to-date data, but a copy as of a given date/time. This caused some problems for requirements of current data, but for most MI purposes was adequate. Indeed, there is some advantage if all participants at a meeting have reports deived from a database with a single date-stamped image of the enterprise. More sophisticated systems allowed incremental update of the MIS database from the TPS database.

With the addition of a layer on top for OSS (office support system), this three-layer model consisting of TPS, MIS (and/or DSS (Decision Support System)) and OSS is becoming well-established [5].

1.4.0 Reality

In the environment where the work described in this paper was done, the problem was that there were multiple TPSs with different (but overlapping) schemas. The differences and overlaps confused both syntactic and semantic issues.

Multiple MISs had been produced, each related (usually) to one TPS. The end-user (an executive requiring information) had to access many different systems to obtain that required, and the outputs were inconsistent because they were based on inconsistent standards for data collection, validation, meaning (semantics), representation (syntactics), constraints (both related to data type and to banking practice) and summary processing performed to date. Worse, standard outputs required for reporting, input to other (commonly external) systems and other purposes were also full of inconsistent data.

The General Ledger(GL) was also used to source MIS, as it is a central repository of an organisation's operational data. The GL is sourced from multiple TPSs but is limited to a single way of classifying the operational data (through the Chart of Accounts) and can only provide data classified this way to MISs. Other MI databases were therefore proposed and built to meet reporting needs that required different ways of classifying the same operational data.

1.5.0 Need for change

Thus, change was required. A new environment was needed to allow:
(a) consistent report and output production;
(b) consistent management information;
(c) new requirements to be handled as the business changed.

The new environment had some constraints:
(1) existing TPSs should not be disturbed (business must continue);
(2) existing MISs should be replaced progressively.

2.0.0 The Requirement

The essentials of the requirement are:

(a) Fast access to information for defined outputs: the outputs can be required for the following purposes:(1) statutory (2) regulatory (3) management. The definition of the output required can change both with the requirements of different countries (based on different legislation) and with time.
(b) The system must be suitable for use by executive end-users.
(c) The system must deliver consistent and correct summary information.

(d) The data structures must be such that the requirements can be accommodated flexibly and efficiently, and the output information must be structured to meet the particular defined need - which may change with country and time.
(e) The system must provide 'Standard Reports' on all the organisation's data based on multiple classification sets - which change i.e. the predefined summarised accounts of the General Ledger (as defined in the Chart of Accounts and derived from the multiple TPS DBs) are no longer appropriate.

3.0.0 The Architecture

3.1.0 Description

The major decision was to go back to base transaction data. All summaries of the base data into the General Ledger or into the multiple MISs had, associated with them, some implicit (occasionally explicit) constraints, processing and assumptions. The base transactions recorded the essential business of the bank. However, the attributes recorded with each transaction were not necessarily sufficient to allow the record to 'stand alone' and be interpreted correctly by processing software. The additional necessary explicit attributes were usually hidden implicitly in the TPS systems.

The non-financial attributes associated with each transaction were separated from the financial data - but linked by the unique primary key. This allowed flexibility in handling the use of the attributes as the financial data was used in different roles; i.e. the functional dependency between the financial and non-financial attributes was conditional and partial. (For an interesting discussion of this problem in a non-application way see [4]).

The next major decision was to place some intelligence at the TPS/MIS interface to:

(a) perform schema reconciliation;
(b) interpret the requested data in terms of the available TPS data;
(c) apply any conversions or transformations required for consistency;
(d) apply any summary processing on numeric attributes grouped by other attribute(s);
(e) deliver the requested data.

It is at this point that the potential use of rules became apparent; there is a need to express:

(a) the conditional functional dependencies in the data;
(b) the conditional output of attributes from the TPSs to the MIS;
(c) the additional attributes needed explicitly in the MIS and existing only implicitly in the TPSs;

(d) the conditional transformations of the attribute values on output;
(e) the required summaries by attribute;
(f) the set of attributes required for any particular output report, based on the requirement in 2(a)

Further, another use of rule-based technology (linked with semantically defined data structures) forseen was the handling of semantic relationships between attributes in some sort of class hierarchy - using the 'isa' and 'ako' relationships. This avenue has, as yet, only been explored partially, but is expected to solve many of the problems associated with schema reconciliation - especially attribute-name matching.

This led naturally to consideration of rule-based systems for knowledge elicitation from the domain (banking) experts. Given the semantic model, and the domain knowledge, then automated reclassification of transactions (based on non-financial attribute values) from all the different TPSs should be possible and achievable on entry into the MIS. The natural way of achieving this is by the use of 'production' or 'control' rules; essentially a kind of non-procedural programming based on constraints.

3.2.0 Advantages

The major advantage of this approach to the TPS ==> MIS data copying problem is flexibility; the MIS database is controlled by rules which in turn encapsulate both the data processing constraints (eg type or domain constraints) and the processing constraints (banking procedures and associated legislation) - either or both of which sets of constraints can change with time and location (country).

The other advantage is of a modelling nature; the building of the rule-sets ensures that the data processing and business aspects of the system are encapsulated in a formal way which allows reasoning, prediction and manipulation at the level of intensional rather than extensional data.

In short; the advantage is that a change in the environment requires only a change of rules in a well-understood and formal structure to reconfigure the data processing system to meet the new requirements of the business.

3.3.0 Disadvantages

The major disadvantage is cost - seen as performance problems which require hardware investment to overcome. The major component of this cost is the need always to extract the MIS DB from TPS base transaction data - and hence handle billions of records rather than the few hundreds of records in summary datasets.

This problem is overcome by the storage (for MIS predefined and ad-hoc reporting and output requirements) of not only the required schema and rules but also summary data in the required canonical form - extracted, summarised and pre-stored each time the MIS database is refreshed. The argument is that this is done once, for many subsequent requests, rather than performing this operation for each separate request.

There is a potential problem of replicated data - summaries of the values of the same attributes stored several times as a result of different extraction and summary processes based on differing requirements expressed as rules. This problem (taken to an extreme) would recreate the very problem that the new system is trying to solve. However, it is predicted that the number of summary datasets in the MIS DB will be very small (ideally one) and carefully controlled - and at least the method of extraction from the TPS database will be documented formally.

4.0.0 The Design

4.1.0 Overview

There are essentially two different subsystems or aspects of the design:

(a) an 'extraction subsystem' to extract data from the TPS databases and create the canonical MIS database;
(b) a 'user subsystem' to accept user requests and process them using the MIS database.

Both share the concept of output requirements specification (including constraint enforcement and transformation) by the use of rules. Both could benefit from the semantic net/class hierarchy defined by rules, and by the use of knowledge elicitation techniques to define the rule-sets (see section 3.1.0). The relationship is indicated in Fig.1.

4.2.0 Extraction subsystem

The main task of the extraction subsystem is:

(a) to take the defined output schema (i.e. the schema of the MIS database);
(b) to take the defined input schema (i.e. the integrated schema from all the TPS database schemas);
(c) to extract data through (b) to be stored in the MIS database through (a).

The lack of standard nomenclature, and worse, of standard meanings of attribute names, means that a set of rule-based information is required attached to each attribute to describe the semantic equivalences or partial equivalences (synonyms) and semantic differences (homonyms). This is achieved by a mapping of a class hierarchy of the intensional data with 'isa' and 'ako' relationships.The interesting issue is schema reconciliation.

Additional rules attached to each attribute describe not only the constraints (integrity constraints and referential constraints) but also the equivalent of O-O (object-oriented) methods - a set of rule-based procedures (functions) to handle transformation (including translation) and summary by defined attribute(s), of attribute values when participating in a reconciled schema.

```
-------------------------------------------------------------
     End-user1                                    End-user2

+----------------+ +----------------+ +----------------+
|     Defined    | |    Rule-Set    | |   Create new   |
|    Task        | |    Defining    | |   Task         |
+----------------+ |     Output     | +----------------+
                   |    Reports     |
                   |                |
                   +----------------+


------------------ ------------------ ------------------
                         MIS Database
------------------ ------------------ ------------------


                      +--------------+
                      | Rule-Set     |
                      | Defining     |
                      | Extraction   |
                      | To MIS DB    |
                      | From TPS DBs |
                      +--------------+

+-------+  +-------+   +--------+   +--------+  +-------+
|TPS    |  | TPS   |   |TPS     |   |TPS     |  |TPS    |
|DB     |  |DB     |   | DB     |   |DB      |  |DB     |
|1      |  |2      |   |3       |   |4       |  |5      |
+-------+  +-------+   +--------+   +--------+  +-------+
```

Figure 1: Overall Architecture

The actual extraction process involves the relational operators select, project and join. There are optimal orderings of these operators acting on relations (or equivalent processes acting on non-relational databases) which can be defined formally by the use of a representative hypergraph and associated superkeys. For detail see [9].

4.3.0 User Subsystem

The structure of the user subsystem is best expressed in a high-level metacode:

The requirement statement for any given task (i.e. specification at user level) can be parsed to determine whether it is the name of predefined task (selection, processing and report output) or a request for dialogue to create a new defined task.

```
Check taskname against task index;
    if exists then Proceed                /*to execute predefined task*/
        else Create Dialogue              /*for new task*/

Proceed - extract rule-set for task and apply:
        (a) select/project rules to MIS database
        (b) joins to selected subsets
        (c) any ordering (x within y within z)
        (d) any 'group by' needs
        (e) any calculation eg totalling
EndProceed
```

It should be noted that there are possible optimisations here, especially with the ordering of (a) and (b) for particular relations. The formally correct sequence can be obtained [9].

Create Dialogue - elicit user requirements step
(a) which data sources (relations in the MIS database)
(b) which data fields (attributes)

This elicits the output schema required for the report or standard output. If all attributes are unique (which they could be if the extraction from the TPS databases to the MIS database has ensured this) then there are no reconciliation problems requiring user-decision. However, there may be reconciliation problems between the user's semantic interpretation of the attribute name and that stored in the system. This will require additional dialogue to resolve.

(c) processing required.
Create task - checking step
(a) check data fields chosen against schema for

(1) existence
(2) type
(3) usage (eg primary key, foreign key)
if mismatch, resolve with user through dialogue

(b) check processing required
(1) any violation of business rules?
(2) any violation of schema constraints?
if violation, resolve with user through dialogue
(3) same as some other task? (potential re-use of code)
(4) available processing modules? (re-use of code)
if not, pass to DP Department to create low-level processing modules

Create task - create & store step
(a) store specified task (as rules)
(b) optimise
(c) select pre-built code modules for sub-tasks
(d) store code

End Create Dialogue

4.4.0 Advantages

The requirement specifications for both data and processing are held as rules, and are thus easily understood (or interpreted) by both end-users and data processing staff. The specifications can be checked formally for consistency. Finally, such a scheme encourages the mapping of functional specifications of the processing required to re-usable and generic code for common data processing operations - expressed mainly through the relational algebra.

4.5.0 Disadvantages

The major disadvantage is that the generally designed code for performing the relational algebra operators (and equivalent arithmetic, statistical etc functions) could be less efficient than specifically designed code to perform an equivalent function on a predefined data schema. However, this disadvantage is shared with all generalised DBMSs.

4.6.0 The Rule-Set Design

4.6.1 Introduction

The potential uses of rules in the system were outlined in 3.1.0. The design problem is to find a suitable representation for storage and manipulation of the rules, as well as their evaluation.

4.6.2 Rule Representation

It has been argued elsewhere, that a suitable form of storage for validation (or, more generally, constraint) rules is a relation representing an ATN (augmented transition network)[6]. Such a representation allows for easy manipulation using relational technology, yet is sufficiently expressive for the domain of interest. The same representation can also be used for business (domain-specific, processing) rules.

The basic tuple is <<Sin>,<Sout>,<opd1>,<opd2>,<opr>>
where:

Sin	is the incoming state
Sout	is the outgoing state
opd1, opd2	are the operands in the goal
opr	is the operator of the goal

Just as in the validation example[6] the successful traversal of the ATN results in a process being fired :
example: <age> <150> <GT> : 'if age > 150 then fire'

However, in the validation context the operator of the goal was restricted to Boolean comparators and the nodes to states. This is sufficient for validation and for constraint enforcement. However, attribute value transformation requires functions which are triggered by the rule evaluating to 'true'; the required process can be represented either:

(a) as a further arc in the graph with input and output states at nodes Sin and Sout, and with the process representing the function being represented by the arc;

(b) or as a node in the graph (which can be thought of as having (a) internally) - this representation is closer to that of Petri Nets as used by Solvberg[10].

There are advantages and disadvantages to each representation; the implications of each were evaluated and it was discovered that both share a lack of expressivity; they do not represent adequately the required constraints, conditions (temporal or atemporal) or units of work (transactions) - all of which are required in the system design process.

More recent work[7,8] has indicated that extending the transition network formalism (below) allows greater expressiveness:

<Sin><Sout><precondition><process><postcondition>

where the first two elements position the tuple describing the transition (last 3 elements) within the network . Any one or two elements of the transition can be null; typically a constraint will have either a precondition, or a postcondition, or both - but not a process. A process without pre- or post-conditions will be triggered under all circumstances if that part of the extended transition net is traversed.

Preconditions and postconditions are stored as first-order logic predicates, and for ease of implementation utilise the technique adopted in [6]:

example : <account-balance> <100000> < LE >
i.e. if account-balance less-than-or-equal-to 100000 then expression evaluates to true and this part of the transition is traversed.

4.6.3 Investigation of this Representation

This representation was considered against the requirements list in 3.1.0.

(a) Conditional Functional Dependencies:
Consider a relation in second normal form, split into two relations because of conditional functional dependencies. The relations might be:
R1 : account-id, account-name, account-type, account-owner, owner-address, credit-limit, credit-rating
R2 : account-id, account-balance
Now consider a query which is analysing accounts in credit against credit-limit. Depending on the intention of the querier, different account-types might be included in the set to be analysed. The use of rules can make the intention explicit: <credit-rating-query?><select account-type-current> <null>
i.e. 'if it is a credit-rating query, select accounts of type current'

Similarly, in a mailing process, the targetted address for an account statement may be a person's home or busines address depending on some combination of values of attributes such as account-type, account-name etc.

(b) Conditonal output:
The intended recipient of an output report may condition the attributes whose values are output. It would not be usual for a customer to receive a report including his confidential credit-rating, for example :
< customer-report?> <report preparation><credit-rating not present?>
i.e. 'if credit-rating is not selected for a customer-report fire'

(c) Additional attributes:
Rather than store additional data, it is common practice to calculate attribute values when the new attribute value (ephemeral and not stored) can be computed from other (existing and stored) attribute values and/or constants:
<percentage-change?><(new-account-balance/old-account-balance)*100>
<null>

i.e. 'percentage change is new / old balance multiplied by 100'

(d) Conditional Transformation:
For certain output reports, it is necessary to transform all values of certain attributes :
<balance-in-Yen?> <balance-in-A-dollars * exchange-rate> <null>
i.e. 'convert balance in Yen to Australian dollars'

(e) Required Summaries:
Certain reports will be expected to include summaries, such as subtotal by type of expenditure within a cost-centre code. These can also be represented by rules: <grand-total-balance?> <SUM(account-balance)> <null>

(f) Required Set of Attributes:
Different types of output report contain different attributes. Rules can be a simple way of expressing this :
<monthly-account-statement?> <monthly-run> <null>
<credit-transaction?> <monthly-run> <null>
i.e. 'include credit transactions in monthly statements'

Note the use of two rules together in this, slightly contrived, example. This leads to another interesting characteristic of the network; a transition representing a state change at, say, the enterprise modelling level (eg a major account moves from being in credit to being in loss) can be expanded into more detailed sub-networks , until a detailed specification of data and process (such as might be used for programming, or for code-generation) is reached. However, this is related more to the systems development method than to the representation of rules for this application.

4.7.0 The Rule-Set - Constraint Enforcement

The changing requirements of the business domain will cause changes in the rules. These changes have to be consistent, in order to maintain a consistent (at any one time) MIS database and reports and outputs based upon it. The state of the MIS database will obviously evolve with time, both as new values for attributes occur and as the database schema evolves to meet new requirements for management information.

There are two main strategies that could be used: to validate each new or amended rule for consistency at the intensional data level upon update, or to defer consistency checking until a given checkpoint when the complete rule-set is revalidated.

The advantage of the former is that it ensures consistency, and leaves the potential for inconsistency only a very small window of time. However, the validation (consistency checking) process is computationally expensive, although various limiting strategies have been described[2] . The advantage of the latter is the converse; the aggregated computation is less, but at the cost of a potentially inconsistent rule-set.

For any application the relative costs and benefits must be assessed; for this application the requirement for a consistent intensional database is overriding and so consistency checking on update is chosen.

4.8.0 The Rule-Set - Interaction with Processing

The main interaction is directed; that is rules trigger processes. In fact, completed traversal of the ATN causes a trigger to fire the process.

The other interaction is feedback; that is processes affect rules. The outputs from certain processes could change the constraints or even the data content and structure described in the schema - with associated descriptive rules. In the current design this feedback is disabled.

5.0.0 Discussion

The system design outlined here has as an essential notion the concept of pre-stored, pre-compiled generic codes which handle the relational (algebra) operators and other commonly required functions (such as those for aggregation, simple statistics etc).

Some modern rule-based systems are starting to demonstrate adequate performance even for non-toy applications eg MegaLog[1]. This raises the possibility of avoiding the need for precompiled procedural code - with runtime binding of the data schema controlled by rule-based constraints - and having a conformant system using rules at all levels from specification to runtime support. Such a possibility raises interesting questions of performance, concurrency, security and issues concerning functionality and expressive power. There are plans to explore these possibilities.

6.0.0 References

1. Bocca,J;'Megalog:A Platform for developing Knowledge Base Management Systems' *ECRC Internal KB Report* . No. 75 1990.

2. Das,S.K;Williams,M.H;'Integrity Checking Methods in Deductive Databases: A Comparative Evaluation' *Proceedings BNCOD7* pp 85-116 1989. Cambridge University Press.

3. Gardyn,E.;'Strategic Information Systems Planning at the National Australia Bank' *MBA Thesis, Royal Melbourne Institute of Technology,* 1990.

4. Halassy,B;'Application of Relational Normalforms in CASE-Tools' *Proceedings CAiSE90 Conference*, Stockholm. Lecture Notes in Computer Science No.436 1990. Springer-Verlag.

5. Jeffery,K.G.;'Databases and Office Automation' *Proceedings BNCOD4* pp 215-229 1985. Cambridge University Press.

6. Jeffery,K.G;Lay,J;Curtis,T.;'Logic Programming and Database Technology Used for Validation within Transactions' *Proceedings BNCOD7* pp 71-84 1989. Cambridge University Press

7. Jeffery,K.G: 'Intelligent Systems Development Using Extended Transition Networks' *Journal of Intelligent Information Systems* 1(2) : Kluwer : to appear October 1992

8. Jeffery,K.G;Kalmus,J.R;Asirelli,P;Aquilino,D: 'Representation of Constraints in an Extended Transition Network' *Proceedings ERCIM Database Workshop* 3, Pisa, September 1992

9. Orlowska,M.E.;Jeffery,K.G.; 'A Functional method of Data Processing Based on Relational Algebra' *Proceedings CAiSE91 Conference*, Trondheim, May 1991. Lecture Notes in Computer Science 498 Springer-Verlag

10. Solvberg,A: 'Behaviour-Specification in an Information Systems Analysis Context' *Proceedings BNCOD5* pp 71-86 1986. Cambridge University Press.

Author Index

www.ingramcontent.com/pod-product-compliance
Lightning Source LLC
LaVergne TN
LVHW060543180926
848329LV00007B/41
9789810213312